Insurance Administration

Second Edition

LOMA (Life Office Management Association, Inc.) is an international association founded in 1924. LOMA is committed to a business partnership with its worldwide members in the insurance and financial services industry to improve their management and operations through quality employee development, research, information sharing, and related products and services. Among LOMA's activities is the sponsorship of the FLMI Education Program—an educational program intended primarily for home office and branch office employees.

The ***FLMI Education Program*** consists of two levels—Level I, *Fundamentals of Life and Health Insurance*, and Level II, *Functional Aspects of Life and Health Insurance*. Level I is designed to help students achieve a working knowledge of the life and health insurance business. Level II is designed to provide a more detailed understanding of life and health insurance and related business and management subjects. Students who complete Level I receive a certificate. Students who complete both levels earn the designation Fellow, Life Management Institute (FLMI) and receive a diploma.

Statement of Purpose:
LOMA Educational Programs Testing and Designations

Examinations described in the *LOMA Education and Training Catalog* are designed solely to measure whether students have successfully completed the relevant assigned curriculum, and the attainment of the FLMI and other LOMA designations indicates only that all examinations in the given curriculum have been successfully completed. In no way shall a student's completion of a given LOMA course or attainment of the FLMI or other LOMA designation be construed to mean that LOMA in any way certifies that student's competence, training, or ability to perform any given task. LOMA's examinations are to be used solely for general educational purposes, and no other use of the examinations or programs is authorized or intended by LOMA. Furthermore, it is in no way the intention of the LOMA Curriculum and Examinations staff to describe the standard of appropriate conduct in any field of the insurance and financial services industry, and LOMA expressly repudiates any attempt to so use the curriculum and examinations. Any such assessment of student competence or industry standards of conduct should instead be based on independent professional inquiry and the advice of competent professional counsel.

Insurance Administration

Second Edition

Jane Lightcap Brown, Ph.D., FLMI, ACS, ALHC
Kristen L. Falk, FLMI, ACS, AIAA, AIRC, ARA

LOMA®
Information That Works
FLMI Education Program
Life Management Institute LOMA
Atlanta, Georgia
www.loma.org

Information in this text may have been changed or updated since its publication date. For current updates, visit www.loma.org.

FLMI 301 Text

Authors:	Jane Lightcap Brown, Ph.D., FLMI, ALHC, ACS Kristen L. Falk, FLMI, ACS, AIAA, AIRC, ARA
Manuscript Editor:	Barbara Foxenberger Brown, FLMI, ACS, AIAA
Exam Editor:	Donna Dorris, FLMI, ACS, AIAA, ALHC
Project Managers:	Joyce Abrams Fleming, J.D., FLMI, ACS, AIRC, AIAA, ALHC, PAHM, HIA, MHP Julia K. Wooley, FLMI, ALHC, ACS, HIA, MHP
Production/Editorial Manager:	Michelle Stone Weathers, ACS
Copyeditor:	Sally M. Farnham
Indexer:	Robert D. Land, FLMI, ACS
Permissions Coordinator:	Iris F. Hartley, FLMI, ALHC
Production/Print Coordinator:	Amy Souwan
Print Buyer:	Audrey M. Hiers
Cover Design:	Kathleen Ryan, FLMI, PAHM, ACS, AIAA, AIRC, ARA
Administrative Support:	Aurelia Kennedy-Hemphill Natalie Cape Sanders Marion Markus
Typography:	Fishergate, Inc.
Cover Photography:	Images © 1996 PhotoDisc, Inc.

10 09 08 07 06 05 04 03 02 10 9 8 7 6 5 4 3 2 1

Library of Congress Cataloging-in-Publication Data

Brown, Jane Lightcap.
Insurance administration / Jane Lightcap Brown, Kristen L. Falk. — 2nd ed.
p. cm.
Includes index.
ISBN 1-57974-145-2
1. Insurance companies—United States—Management. 2. Insurance, Life—United States—Management. 3. Insurance, Health—United States—Management. 4. Reinsurance—United States—Management. I. Falk, Kristen L. II. Life Office Management Association. Life Management Institute. III. Title.

HG8531 .B76 2002
368′.0068—dc21

2001038685

ISBN 1-57474-145-2

Printed in the United States of America

Contents

Chapter 6: Underwriting Specialized Policies and Supplemental Coverages . . . 120

Chapter 7: Underwriting Individual Health Insurance . . . 146

Chapter 15: Administering Disability Income and Critical Illness Insurance Claims . . . 326

Chapter 16: Scope and Organization of Customer Service . . . 358

Preface

Without the enthusiasm and willingness of many highly qualified industry experts to work with the authors to revise and thoroughly update the first edition of this text, *Insurance Administration,* Second Edition, would not have been possible. In addition, industry volunteers who serve on LOMA's Education Council, acting on behalf of LOMA's members, identify the association's most urgent educational needs and guide LOMA staff activities to meet those needs. On behalf of LOMA and its membership, we would like to express our gratitude to the Education Council, to those who worked on the textbook development panel of the first edition, and to the reviewers of the second edition. They all willingly expended enormous amounts of time and energy to contribute their considerable expertise to the development of this textbook.

First Edition Acknowledgments

Text Materials

Materials from the first edition of *Insurance Administration* provided a firm foundation upon which the authors of the second edition were able to build. Figures and other materials from the first edition that are used in the second edition are done so with permission from the publisher.

Textbook Development Panel

Because *Insurance Administration,* Second Edition, draws heavily upon research originally conducted for the first edition of the textbook, we first thank the industry experts who served on the review panel for and made enormous contributions to *Insurance Administration*, Jane Lightcap Brown, (Atlanta: LOMA, 1997).

Textbook Review Panel

On behalf of LOMA, we especially wish to extend our heartfelt thanks to the members of the textbook review panel for *Insurance Administration,* Second Edition. Always a delight to work with, these individuals provided essential research materials, read and commented on the manuscript, answered numerous questions from the authors, and provided ideas for ensuring that the book is accurate, complete, and relevant to today's insurance companies. With unfailing good humor and graciousness, the textbook review panel gave of their personal time, provided an invaluable perspective gained from their many years of professional experience and education, and guided the authors through the development of the book:

- James Belknap, FLMI, ALHC, ACS, Claim Manager, Pacific Life Insurance Company
- Richard Catozzi, Underwriting Director, MetLife
- C. Joseph Dahl, FALU, CLU, FLMI, Vice President, Underwriting, Sun Life Financial
- Patricia A. Deike, ACS, Manager—Service Processing, CUNA Mutual Life Insurance Company
- Shaun Downey, FLMI, Assistant Vice President, Client Services, Manulife Reinsurance
- Philip E. Glassley, FLMI, Vice President, Individual Underwriting, American United Life Insurance Company
- Philip R. Harbottle, ALHC, Assistant Vice President, Accident & Health Claims, AIG Claims Services, Inc.
- Sue A. Jacobson, FLMI, ACS, Manager: Contact Center, CUNA Mutual Life Insurance Company
- John Harold Jones, Jr., FLMI, AALU, CLU, ChFC, Senior Underwriter, CNA Life Insurance
- Sherry Myers, FLMI, CLU, RHU, Investigations Auditor, Lutheran Brotherhood
- Lon D. Oakley, Jr., FLMI, ACS, Membership Acquisition and Relationship Management Projects Team, USAA Life Insurance Company
- Josephine Pagnozzi, FLMI, ACS, ARA, Vice President, Reinsurance Services, AXA Corporate Solutions Life Reinsurance Company
- Lawrence B. Ruark, Ph.D., CLU, FLMI, ACS, AIAA, AIRC, Compliance Consultant, Sun Life Assurance Company of Canada
- Maureen T. Shippy, FLMI, ACS, ARA, Assistant Vice President and Director of Client Services, Lincoln Re

LOMA Staff and Consultants

At LOMA we are fortunate to have an able team consisting of many members of LOMA's Education Division staff and other LOMA staff to help create this textbook. The following individuals deserve special mention for the work they performed on this text. Joyce Abrams Fleming, J.D., FLMI, ACS, AIRC, AIAA, ALHC, PAHM, HIA, MHP, Director, Education & Training, served as project manager, providing much-welcomed support and guidance. Barbara Foxenberger Brown, FLMI, ACS, AIAA, Senior Associate, Education & Training, served as manuscript editor and made many invaluable suggestions for improving the text. Donna Dorris, FLMI, ACS, AIAA, ALHC, Senior Associate, Examinations Department, served as examinations editor, reviewed the manuscript, and made many helpful suggestions. Barbara Foxenberger Brown, FLMI, ACS, AIAA, Senior Associate, Education & Training; Jane Lightcap Brown, Ph.D., FLMI, ALHC, ACS, Senior Associate, Education & Training; and Jennifer W. Herrod, FLMI, ACS, AIAA, PAHM, ARA, Senior Associate, Education & Training, performed research for other projects that established a valuable foundation for several chapters of this textbook. Mary C. Bickley, J.D., FLMI, AIRC, ACS, AIAA, PAHM, Associate, Education & Training; Monica R. Maxwell, J.D. FLMI, Associate, Education & Training; and Miriam Orsina, FLMI, ACS, PAHM, Senior Associate, Education & Training, generously provided the authors with source material. Mark Adel, FLMI, ACS, PAHM, Senior Associate, Education & Training; and Patsy L. Heil, Ph.D., FLMI, ALHC, ACS, AIAA, ARA, PAHM, Senior Associate, Education & Training, kindly reviewed portions of the manuscript. JoAnn Stone Appleton, FLMI; Donna Dorris, FLMI, Senior Associate, Examinations Department; and Robert Hartley, FLMI, ACS, ALHC, CLU, ChFC, RHU, PAHM, Senior Associate, Examinations Department, developed the *Prep Pak for FLMI 301,* reviewed the manuscript of *Insurance Administration,* Second Edition, and made many helpful suggestions. Jennifer W. Herrod, FLMI, ACS, AIAA, PAHM, ARA, Senior Associate, Education & Training, also reviewed portions of the manuscript and made valuable suggestions. Aurelia K. Hemphill, Administrative Assistant III, Education & Training; Natalie Cape Sanders, Administrative Assistant II, Editorial/Production Department; and Marion Markus, Administrative Specialist, Examinations, cheerfully provided administrative support. JoAnn Stone Appleton, FLMI, prepared the *Instructor's Kit for FLMI 301,* reviewed the entire manuscript, and made many helpful suggestions.

Audrey M. Hiers, Inventory and Product Sourcing Administrator, Education and Training, provided business support for production of the project. In LOMA's Production Department, Kathleen Ryan, FLMI,

ACS, AIRC, AIAA, ARA, PAHM, Production Coordinator I, Production Department, designed the cover; Amy Souwan, Production Coordinator II/Scheduling Coordinator, Production Department, coordinated the typesetting and the printing. LOMA consultant Sally M. Farnham copyedited the text. LOMA consultant Iris F. Hartley, FLMI, ALHC, obtained permission for use of copyrighted material, read the manuscript, and made many valuable suggestions. Another LOMA consultant, Robert D. Land, FLMI, ACS, drafted the index. A special word of thanks to Michelle Stone Weathers, ACS, Manager, Editorial/ Production Department, who coordinated the entire production process and was a joy to work with.

From the staff of LOMA's Information Center, Olivia Blakemore, ACS, Technical Administrator, Information Center, along with Mallory Eldridge, Writer/Analyst, Information Center; Janet Smith, Information Center Researcher; and Patricia Touchstone Toups, Librarian, frequently assisted with research for the project.

Also, thanks to William H. Rabel, Ph.D., FLMI, CLU, Senior Vice President, Education Division, and Katherine C. Milligan, FLMI, ACS, ALHC, Second Vice President, Education & Training, for their ongoing encouragement and support.

Jane Lightcap Brown, Ph.D., FLMI, ACS, ALHC
Kristen L. Falk, FLMI, ACS, AIAA, AIRC, ARA
Atlanta, Georgia
2002

Introduction

The purpose of *Insurance Administration*, Second Edition, is to describe the functions of insurance administration, and the practices and procedures insurers use for administering insurance. This book discusses how companies organize their underwriting departments, the legal issues involved with underwriting, the underwriting of individual and group insurance, reinsurance and reinsurance administration, the organization and administration of claims, and customer service activities in insurance companies.

This book has been designed for students who are preparing for the FLMI 301—Insurance Administration examination, which is part of the Fellow, Life Management Institute (FLMI) and other LOMA designation programs. Several features have been included in each chapter to help you organize your studies, reinforce your understanding of the materials, and prepare for the examination. As we describe each of these features, we give you suggestions for studying the material.

- **Learning Objectives.** The first page of each chapter contains a list of learning objectives to help you focus your studies. Before reading each chapter, review these learning objectives. Then, as you read the chapter, look for material that will help you meet the learning objectives.

- **Chapter Outline.** The first page of each chapter contains an outline of the chapter. Review this outline to gain an overview of the material that will be covered; then scan through the chapter to familiarize yourself with the presentation of the information. By looking at the headings and figures, you will get a preview of how the various subjects relate to each other.

- **Key Terms.** The key terms and concepts associated with insurance administration are reviewed and explained in this text. All of the important terminology introduced in this text is defined or explained when it is first used. Important terminology is highlighted with ***bold italic type*** when the term is first defined and is included in a list of key terms at the end of each chapter. All key terms also appear in a comprehensive glossary at the end of the book. As you read each chapter, pay special attention to these key terms.

- **Figures.** Figures appear throughout the text and are designed to illustrate or give examples of the text's discussions of selected important topics. Note that information contained in figures may be tested on the examination for this course and other LOMA courses.

- **Insights.** Insights appear throughout the text and are designed to amplify the text's descriptions of certain topics. These insights should help you get a better feel for the functional areas and activities involved in insurance administration. Information contained in insights may be tested on the examinations for this course and other LOMA courses.

- **Glossary.** A comprehensive glossary containing definitions of all key terms appears at the end of the book. Each glossary entry indicates in which chapter a key term is discussed. The glossary includes references to important equivalent terms, acronyms, and contrasting terms or concepts.

Using LOMA Study Aids

LOMA has prepared study aids designed to help students prepare for the Course FLMI 301 examination. LOMA recommends that you use all of the study aids available for this course. **Studies indicate that students who use LOMA study aids consistently perform significantly better on LOMA examinations than students who do not use these study aids.**

Using the Prep Pak for This Course

In addition to this book, LOMA's *Prep Pak for FLMI 301* is assigned reading for students preparing for the FLMI Program examination. Used along with this textbook, the Prep Pak will help you master the course material. The Prep Pak includes chapter review exercises, practice exam questions, a full-scale sample examination in both paper and electronic format, and answers to every question in the Prep Pak.

The Prep Pak may be revised periodically. To ensure that you are studying from the correct texts, check the current *LOMA Education and Training Catalog* for a description of the texts assigned for the examination for which you are preparing.

Finally, course instructors should know that LOMA has prepared an *Instructor's Kit for FLMI 301*, designed to help company instructors prepare to teach preparatory classes for the FLMI 301 examination.

Suggested Introductory Reading

Some students may find it helpful to undertake a quick review of material related to this course in two LOMA *StepOne Series* publications:

- *Intro to Underwriting* (1999) provides an overview of the underwriting concepts that you might encounter in studying *Insurance Administration*, Second Edition.

- *Intro to Reinsurance* (1999) provides an overview of the reinsurance concepts that you might encounter in studying *Insurance Administration*, Second Edition.

CHAPTER 1

Overview of Insurance Administration

Chapter Outline

The Administration of Insurance

Insurers' Responsibilities to Customers

Insurance Administration Functions
- Underwriting
- Reinsurance
- Claim Administration
- Customer Service

Other Insurance Functions
- Marketing
- Actuarial
- Accounting
- Legal
- Human Resources
- Information Systems

Computer-Based Technology in Insurance Administration
- Personal Computers
- Policy Issue Systems
- Expert Systems
- Remote Computing and Electronic Data Interchange
- Integrated Image Processing
- The Internet

Objectives

After reading this chapter, you should be able to

- List insurers' responsibilities to their customers
- Explain the focus of underwriting, reinsurance, claim administration, and customer service
- Describe the insurance functions of marketing, actuarial, accounting, legal, human resources, and information systems
- List and describe ways that computer-based technology is used in the functions of insurance administration

Like every dynamic industry, the life and health insurance industry has many functions and interrelationships. You're beginning a study of the functions involved in ***insurance administration***, which we define as the activities associated with assessing risk and issuing policies, obtaining reinsurance, handling claims, and providing customer service. In this textbook, you'll learn about insurance administration activities and the important role they play within life and health insurance companies.

This textbook assumes that you have a basic understanding of individual and group life and health insurance products.*

In the following chapters, we'll examine the insurance administration activities performed for these types of products. As you study the material in this textbook, you'll learn more about the ways that insurance administration employees cooperate to fulfill an insurer's responsibilities to its customers. If you work in or with an insurance organization, you'll also gain a greater appreciation of the ways you can enhance the productivity, efficiency, and effectiveness not only of your own area, but also of other areas in your company.

The Administration of Insurance

The activities of insurance administration connect an insurer and its customers from the time a policy is applied for through the time a claim is settled. After a customer applies for insurance coverage or for modifications to existing coverage, insurance administration ensures that every customer receives effective and appropriate policy service.

Administering insurance contracts includes four functions: underwriting (which is typically considered a part of *new business*), reinsurance, claim administration, and customer service. We'll begin this chapter with a discussion of how insurance administration enables an insurer to fulfill its responsibilities to customers. Then we'll give you an overview of the four insurance administration functions and of the areas of an insurance company with which those functions coordinate. Finally, we'll discuss the computer-based technology used in insurance administration.

---

*In this textbook, we'll use the term *health insurance* to refer to both medical expense coverage and disability income coverage. We'll use the term *disability income* to refer only to disability income coverage.

Insurers' Responsibilities to Customers

An insurer has many customers who do not receive insurance coverage from the insurer. These customers include salespeople (such as agents and brokers), service providers (such as doctors, nurses, hospitals, and clinics), reinsurance companies, beneficiaries, and shareholders of stock companies. On the other hand, the ***premium-paying customers*** of an insurance company include its insureds and policyowners. For the sake of simplicity, we will assume that an applicant and a proposed insured are the same person unless otherwise specified. We will, therefore, use the terms *applicant* and *proposed insured* interchangeably.

For practical, ethical, and legal reasons, an insurer has responsibilities to its customers. From a practical perspective, the insurer intends to operate profitably. From an ethical perspective, the insurer conducts its business honestly to protect the interests of all concerned. And from a legal perspective, the insurer must provide the benefits specified in the contracts between the insurer and its customers and must otherwise adhere to requirements imposed by law. To be successful, an insurer needs to manage and administer carefully its responsibilities, many of which relate directly to the functions involved in insurance administration. Figure 1-1 summarizes an insurer's responsibilities to customers.

FAST FACT

In 1999, 69% of families in the United States owned some type of life insurance.[1]

FIGURE 1-1. An Insurer's Responsibilities to Customers.

- To follow consistent, equitable risk selection practices
- To provide prompt and equitable claim handling
- To provide excellent customer service
- To preserve customers' privacy and ensure confidentiality
- To maintain adequate financial resources
- To establish and maintain ethical business practices

In accepting risks, an insurance company has a responsibility to *follow consistent risk selection practices.* The insurer must examine carefully every application for insurance and evaluate each application according to the insurer's established guidelines. These guidelines, based on the insurer's and the industry's experience and actuarial projections, must be the same for every comparable case. Individuals with similar risk profiles should be treated similarly. The underwriting performed as a part of insurance administration helps to ensure fair, consistent risk selection.

FAST FACT

In 1999, over 366 million life insurance policies were in force in the United States.[2]

Insurers also have a responsibility to *provide prompt and equitable claim handling.* Providing equitable claim handling includes assessing every claim in accordance with the terms of the contract. Insurers also have a responsibility to deny any invalid claim.

Another responsibility of insurers to their customers is to *provide excellent customer service* in all aspects of the business. When a customer applies for new coverage, adds a rider to existing coverage, requests a change of beneficiary, or interacts with the insurer in any other way, the customer expects and deserves prompt, correct, empathetic, and tactful responses from the insurer. Similarly, when an agent asks for information or conducts other business with the insurer's employees, the transaction should be conducted in an equally prompt, correct, empathetic, and tactful manner.

Preserving customers' privacy and ensuring confidentiality are also essential responsibilities of insurance companies. Insurers must take care to use only lawful, reasonable, and ethical means of obtaining information. Insurers should use only accurate information, restrict access to personal information to only those people who have a business-specific need for it, and establish written guidelines for information handling so that employees will know exactly how to treat confidential information. Recent federal legislation defines more specifically how insurers must protect all forms of information acquired about their customers.

In creating and fulfilling the provisions of insurance contracts held by customers, insurers have a primary responsibility to *maintain adequate financial resources* to pay the agreed-upon benefits if insured events occur. Insurers must, therefore, conduct business so that they remain financially stable and profitable. To strengthen their financial positions, insurers focus on using resources wisely, reducing waste, managing expenses, and becoming more efficient in serving their clients effectively. Efficiently and effectively administered coverage helps protect an insurer's financial position and enables the organization to provide top-quality insurance protection.

An insurer's responsibility to *establish and maintain ethical business practices* encompasses many activities and behaviors. Every area of an insurance company, including each area involved in insurance administration activities, is responsible for behaving ethically. Nearly every insurer develops a business practice code of ethics. For an example of one insurer's code of ethics, read Insight 1-1.

Insight 1-1. Code of Ethics: USAA's Core Values.

USAA* is committed to the highest standards of ethics and professional conduct in day-to-day business operations as well as in interactions with our members, our fellow employees, our business partners, and our community. USAA corporate business activity and individual employee conduct at all levels will be consistent with our core values.

SERVICE, LOYALTY, HONESTY & INTEGRITY

SERVICE: We will give outstanding, responsive service to our members and fellow employees. Our products and services will be of the highest quality and value at fair prices. We will treat others as we wish to be treated, with courtesy, dignity, and respect. We will provide service to the communities in which we do business—through corporate and individual employee involvement in volunteer service and participation in the political process.

LOYALTY: We will be loyal and respectful toward members and toward each other, putting the association first in the face of conflicting business interests as long as that is consistent with other ethical principles. To this end, we will safeguard confidential and proprietary information.

HONESTY: We will be truthful, sincere, law-abiding, and straightforward in our communications and dealings with members and with each other.

INTEGRITY: We will consistently behave in ways that are ethical, earning the respect of members by being steadfast in our commitment to act in both their best interests and the interests of the association, regardless of any business, social, economic, or personal pressures to the contrary.

*Note: USAA stands for United Services Automobile Association.
Source: Excerpted from "USAA's Core Values," *USAA Code of Business Ethics & Conduct* (September 2001): 3. Used with permission.

Insurance Administration Functions

Now we'll look briefly at the insurance administration functions of underwriting, reinsurance, claim administration, and customer service. We'll examine each of these functions in detail in later chapters. Figure 1-2 illustrates the four primary insurance administration functions.

Underwriting

Underwriting is the process of (1) assessing and classifying the degree of risk represented by a proposed insured or a group of insureds with respect to a specific insurance product and (2) making a decision to

FIGURE 1-2. Insurance Administration Functions.

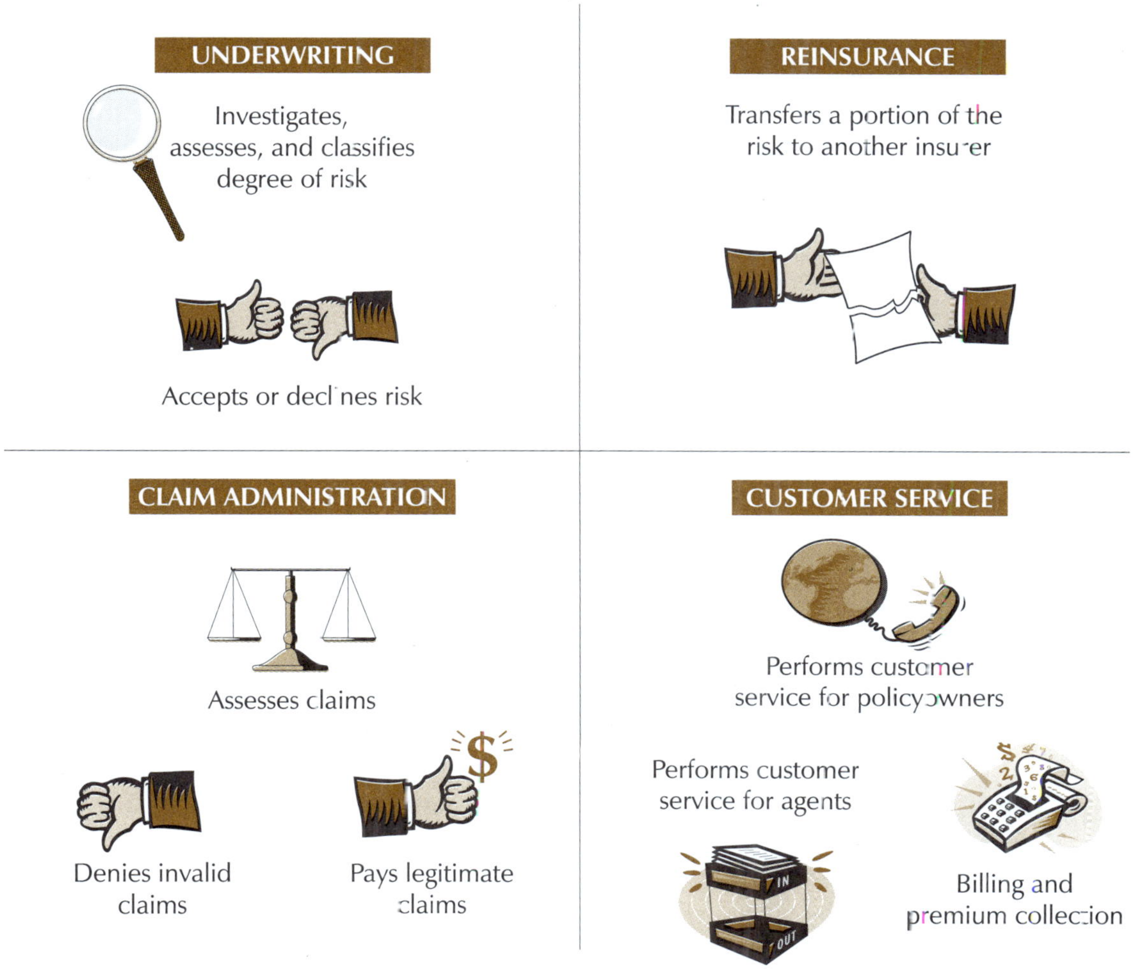

accept or decline the risk. Sensible underwriting decisions are extremely important in ensuring that an insurer will remain financially strong and will be able to fulfill its responsibility to pay legitimate claims. If an insurer accepts too many questionable risks without making appropriate premium adjustments, the insurer will pay more in claims than it can afford. If an insurer fails to accept enough appropriate risks at appropriate rates, the insurer will not prosper.

Underwriting is one of the primary functions that make up the group of activities known as new business. ***New business*** is the general term used to describe all the activities required to market insurance, submit applications for insurance, investigate and evaluate the risks associated with those applications, and issue and deliver insurance policies.

The term *new business* can have a variety of meanings. Salespeople, such as agents and brokers, may think of new business as potential clients, as all the activities they engage in to sell insurance, or as applications submitted. Insurance company home office employees may think of new business as applications received or as the area of the insurer that receives applications, assesses the risks, and issues policies. In this textbook, we use the term *new business* to refer to insurance applications submitted and to the activities of receiving applications, investigating and selecting risks for products that require underwriting, and issuing policies.

After an application for coverage is approved, the underwriter transfers documents and electronically stored information to the policy issue staff. ***Policy issue*** is the insurance company function that involves preparing the insurance contract and facilitating the delivery of the policy to the customer. Although underwriting and policy issue are distinct, they are closely related and are often combined within a single operating unit within an insurance company.

Reinsurance

Reinsurance can be broadly defined as a form of insurance that enables an insurer to be reimbursed for covered losses claimed under insurance policies the insurer has issued. Briefly, reinsurance is insurance for an insurer. In a reinsurance arrangement, one insurer transfers a portion of risk to a second insurer, which agrees to pay part of the claims of the first insurer in exchange for part of the premium.

FAST FACT

In 1999, over two-thirds of life insurers in the United States reinsured at least some of their business.[3]

In our discussion of reinsurance in Chapters 9 through 11, we'll not only examine the ways in which insurers obtain reinsurance to share the risk on a case, but we will also give you a thorough introduction to the subject of reinsurance. We'll explain various types of reinsurance coverage, the relationship between an insurer and a reinsurer, the features of reinsurance treaties, and the administration of reinsurance.

Claim Administration

An insurer has a legal and an ethical obligation to pay all legitimate claims and to deny its liability for all others. As a part of the activities of insurance administration, the ***claim administration*** function assesses each claim made and decides whether or not the claim is legitimate. The insurer pays each legitimate claim according to the terms of the policy.

Customer Service

Maintaining a positive relationship with all its customers is essential for an insurance company. ***Customer service*** refers to the broad range of activities, consistent with contractual provisions, that help keep customers satisfied so that they will continue doing business with an insurer and speak positively about the insurer to other potential customers. ***Policyowner service*** is a specific type of customer service that includes all the service activities performed for people or groups who own or hold insurance policies. Successful insurers provide top-quality service to all their customers.

Other Insurance Functions

Insurance administration staff typically coordinate many aspects of their work with other insurance company functions such as marketing, actuarial, accounting, legal, human resources, and information systems. We'll introduce these functions now, and throughout this book we'll discuss the ways that insurance administration staff interact with these functions.

Marketing

Marketing is the way an insurer identifies its customers, defines and develops the products that its customers want, and sells and distributes products to customers. In addition to these primary activities, marketing seeks to enhance the insurer's competitive position by (1) gathering information about the insurer's business environment, including data on its competitors, and (2) assessing the insurer's sales performance in the marketplace.

Insurers distribute their products in various ways, including by agents, by brokers, by financial institutions, by the Internet, and by direct response methods. In this book, we'll refer to any person or entity that sells insurance as an ***agent.*** The insurer's marketing function typically has a unit devoted to providing marketing support to agents and agencies.

Actuarial

An insurer's ***actuarial*** staff use mathematical principles to predict the rates of illness, injury, disability, and death among insureds. Actuarial staff also calculate legal reserve liabilities and the premium rates for insurance products and conduct research on trends in mortality and morbidity rates, policy lapses, policy loans, company expenses, and interest rates. An insurer uses actuarial information to develop assumptions used in pricing products and in selecting risks.

Accounting

The process of collecting, analyzing, and reporting financial data is known as ***accounting.*** An insurer's accounting staff develop information that is used throughout the company to make decisions and to satisfy financial reporting requirements.

Legal

The ***legal*** staff help an insurer follow the laws and regulations affecting the insurer's relationships with customers, prospective customers, employees, agents, other insurers, vendors, and government agencies. An insurer's legal function protects the insurer's legal rights and reviews company activities to be certain the insurer fulfills its legal responsibilities.

Many insurers have established compliance functions, which may be part of the legal function or may operate independently of it. ***Compliance*** is the function responsible for ensuring that an insurer and its agents follow all applicable state, provincial, and federal insurance requirements and regulations.

Human Resources

The ***human resources*** function monitors the availability of qualified workers; recruits and screens applicants; helps select qualified employees; plans and presents appropriate orientation, training, and development for each employee; and administers employee benefit programs. Human resources staff also guide an insurer's management in conducting performance appraisals of employees and in determining compensation levels for various jobs. Finally, human resources personnel assist with employee separations resulting from resignation, layoff, retirement, or discharge.

Information Systems

The function called ***information systems*** facilitates the collection, manipulation, and distribution of data and information, enabling employees who need the resulting information to get it. Most insurance companies have installed computer networks to enhance the speed, accuracy, and efficiency of work activities. An automated office system enables an insurer to save time and money by performing tasks that otherwise would be done manually or would be performed by outside vendors.

Computer-Based Technology in Insurance Administration

Most insurers use computer-based technology to support the functions of insurance administration. This technology includes personal computers, policy issue systems, expert systems, remote computing and electronic data interchange (EDI), integrated image processing, and the Internet.

Personal Computers

Personal computers (PCs) can enhance accuracy in the functions of insurance administration by guiding users to enter correct, complete information. Users who have access to sophisticated computer systems can also locate information about medical conditions, rating requirements, coverage requirements, guidelines for underwriting, and many other aspects of underwriting, as well as information relating to the reinsurance and claim administration functions. Networking or linking personal computers among functional areas allows many users to access the same information and computer resources at the same time. Networking computers also enables agents to communicate directly with insurers and can speed the handling of all aspects of insurance administration.

Policy Issue Systems

You'll recall that policy issue involves preparing the insurance contract and facilitating the delivery of the policy to the customer, usually by the agent who sold the policy. Insurance companies generally use automated systems to produce the policy documents. ***Policy issue systems*** (1) create a computerized client record that contains the customer's name, contact information, and policy number; (2) verify receipt of the initial premium payment; and (3) verify that all underwriting requirements have been met.

Expert Systems

An ***expert system*** is a sophisticated computer application that manipulates information based on established facts and an insurer's experience data to suggest solutions to problems. Research information and commentary from the insurer's staff and from outside experts can become part of the expert system and can be used for all insurance administration functions, as well as for actuarial studies, auditing, performance appraisal, and strategic planning. An insurer can benefit from an expert system's consistency, quick turnaround time, and speed for many kinds of underwriting and other business decisions.

To give you only a few examples, an underwriting expert system can determine if all the values in a blood test arriving electronically from a lab are within normal limits. An expert system can also itemize regulations in certain states and provinces and otherwise assist the underwriter in identifying and resolving potential underwriting problems and opportunities. When claims are submitted on coverage that has been underwritten, the expert system can match the claims against the original underwriting information to judge the accuracy of underwriting decisions. Insight 1-2 presents additional information about the development of expert systems used in underwriting, the first area of insurance administration that we'll discuss.

Remote Computing and Electronic Data Interchange

Some insurance companies use ***remote computing***, an electronic technology that allows users to (1) input and send information to a computer from a distant site and (2) gain access to the programs and information on a distant computer. In some instances, remote computing links only the computers within one organization; in other instances, an organization links the computers in its main office to computers in its branch offices. An organization also can use remote computing to link its computers with those of vendors and other organizations.

Some remote computing is accomplished through a specialized technology known as ***electronic data interchange (EDI),*** a computer-to-computer information exchange that uses a more uniform format than is used for much remote computing. EDI is neither company-specific nor company-owned, but is a public standard for electronic movement of data. By establishing a uniform, standardized format for information, companies in any industry and in any country can exchange computer-readable data efficiently and cost-effectively. EDI provides companies with a fast, automated, paperless, postage-free information flow.

Insight 1-2. Expert Systems.

The use of expert systems in underwriting has developed through generations of systems that have progressively increased in complexity. These include the following:

FIRST GENERATION:
Screening Systems

Screening systems were developed by the largest companies in the 1970s to decrease general expenses. These systems allowed for the entry of information from the application and screened out or accepted clean nonmedical cases that previously were handled by manual jet screening units. The remainder of the cases was referred to underwriters.

SECOND GENERATION:
Information Display Systems

These systems appeared in the mid-1980s and were designed to save underwriters time and thereby improve productivity. Information display systems provided underwriting manuals in an automated format and allowed users to rapidly search underwriting materials.

THIRD GENERATION:
Initial Underwriting Systems

These systems were developed to improve service to the field by approving some cases automatically and eliminating cases not needing review by an underwriter. Initial underwriting systems extend the capability of the first-generation systems and go beyond screening to identify underwriting problems, automatically underwrite some cases, and order further information on other cases.

FOURTH GENERATION:
Expert Decision Assistance Tools

These decision assistance systems help underwriters both analyze complex impairments and manage their administrative workload. Using fourth-generation systems can reduce claim expenses by enhancing consistency in the underwriting process.

FIFTH GENERATION:
Total Underwriting Systems

A new generation of underwriting systems integrates all the components discussed above into a single information system that handles the entire underwriting process. These systems can provide advantages in general expense reduction, improved service to the field, and claim expense reduction. The system's multiple components include application data entry, screening initial underwriting, process requirements, workflow management, information display, impairment underwriting, and management information.

Source: Adapted from "Expert Systems in Underwriting," *Lincoln National Reinsurance Medical Resource* (March/April 1990): 5. Used with permission of Lincoln National Life Reinsurance Company.

For instance, staff in underwriting and claim administration may use EDI to exchange information quickly with agents, paramedical companies, medical laboratories, inspection agencies, regulatory bodies, banks, and any other entities with which the insurer does business. The types of information exchanged include laboratory test results, medical test billing and payment information, and life insurance applications and the reports on their status.

Integrated Image Processing

Integrated image processing is a computer-based method of capturing, indexing, storing, retrieving, and distributing documents in electronic form. Integrated image processing scans documents with a machine that functions much like a photocopier and that produces digitized copies of the documents for electronic storage. Employees use personal computers to request certain documents, which can be displayed on high-resolution monitors and then printed if necessary. Integrated image processing saves time and enables employees to request information easily, thereby enhancing their ability to make fast, accurate decisions.

The Internet

Insurers increasingly are providing administrative services to customers on the Internet. Although many insurers use the Internet primarily to market their products or to provide information to consumers, some insurers now provide everything from an online application process that includes instant underwriting to allowing customers to make premium payments online.

Key Terms and Concepts

insurance administration
premium-paying customers
underwriting
new business
policy issue
reinsurance
claim administration
customer service
policyowner service
marketing
agent
actuarial
accounting
legal
compliance
human resources
information systems
policy issue systems
expert system
remote computing
electronic data interchange (EDI)
integrated image processing

Endnotes

1. ACLI, *Life Insurers Fact Book 2000* (Washington, D.C.: American Council of Life Insurers, 2000), 1.
2. Ibid., 2.
3. Ibid., 147.

CHAPTER 2 Scope and Organization of Underwriting

Chapter Outline

Risk Assessment

Underwriting Philosophy and Underwriting Guidelines
- Equitable to the Insureds
- Equitable to the Insurer
- Deliverable by the Agent

Overview of Underwriting
- Performing Field Underwriting
- Reviewing the Application for Insurance
- Gathering Additional Information
- Making an Underwriting Decision

Policy Issue
- Individual and Group Policy Issue Procedures

Organization of Underwriting
- Case Assignment System
- Work Division System
- Combination System

Decision Options and Authority Levels
- Decision Options
- Authority Levels

Objectives

After reading this chapter, you should be able to

- Explain the effect of antiselection on risk assessment
- Discuss the characteristics of a risk class, and distinguish among the preferred, standard, substandard, and declined risk classes
- Define the impact of an insurer's underwriting philosophy, underwriting guidelines, and experience in guiding the insurer's underwriting decisions
- List and define four basic underwriting activities
- Explain the procedural differences in policy issue for individual and group coverages
- Explain the job accountabilities of an underwriter, a chief underwriter, and medical and clerical staff
- Summarize two approaches to case assignment in underwriting
- Define independent, team, jet unit, and committee underwriting
- Explain the reasons that underwriters are given various levels of decision authority

Underwriting is an essential insurance administration function. We will devote seven chapters of this textbook to underwriting, beginning in this chapter with a discussion of the scope and organization of underwriting. In Chapters 3 through 8, we'll continue our discussion by considering the legal issues that affect underwriting, the factors involved in underwriting individual life insurance, the factors involved in underwriting specialized policies, the factors involved in underwriting individual health insurance, and the factors involved in underwriting group coverage.

In this chapter, we'll provide an overview of underwriting purposes and procedures. Then you'll be ready to learn how underwriters examine risks and make decisions about them. We will first discuss risk assessment, which is the foundation of underwriting, and explain the importance of an insurer's underwriting philosophy and underwriting guidelines. Next, we will present an overview of underwriting and explain the procedures involved in policy issue. We'll conclude by explaining how the underwriting function is organized and how decision options and authority levels are assigned.

Risk Assessment

An insurer designs its premium structure so that each insured person or group is charged premiums according to the amount of risk that each represents in relation to others insured by the product. A person or group who represents a greater amount of risk is charged a proportionately greater premium for coverage.

Underwriting is responsible for ***risk assessment,*** which is a process that involves determining the degree of risk represented by each proposed insured person or group according to a range of criteria established when the insurance product was designed and priced. Underwriters assess individual applicants and groups for coverage and evaluate the level of risk according to an individual applicant's impairments or a group's characteristics. For purposes of insurance, an ***impairment*** is any aspect of a person's health, family history, occupation, activities, or lifestyle that could increase that person's expected mortality or morbidity risk. Underwriting for life insurance is particularly concerned with ***mortality,*** which is the relative incidence of death occurring among a given group of people. Underwriting for health insurance is particularly concerned with ***morbidity,*** which is the relative incidence of sickness and injury occurring among a given group of people.

In assessing the degree of risk represented by a proposed insured, an underwriter considers the factor of antiselection, which produces a higher degree of risk. ***Antiselection*** is the tendency of people who suspect or know they are more likely than average to experience loss to apply for or renew insurance to a greater extent than do people who lack such knowledge of probable loss. For example, a person who believes he has a serious illness may be more likely to purchase insurance than a person who believes he is in good health.

After evaluating the degree of risk, the underwriter decides whether to (1) issue insurance as applied for, (2) issue insurance with modifications in coverage or premium rate, or (3) decline to issue insurance. The goal of underwriting is to accept the greatest number of qualified proposed insureds while keeping the insurer financially stable and profitable.

During risk assessment for individual life insurance, applicants are assigned to risk classes. A ***risk class*** is a group of insureds who represent a similar level of risk to an insurance company. Although each insurer defines the parameters of its own risk classes, most insurers identify classes as preferred, standard, substandard, and declined.

- The ***preferred class*** generally designates proposed insureds whose anticipated mortality is significantly lower than average and who represent the least degree of risk. Some insurers establish preferred tobacco and preferred nontobacco subclasses. Increasing numbers of insurers underwrite according to use or nonuse of any tobacco product during a specified period. Some insurers also have a preferred class based on driving records. Increasingly, insurers are creating a number of different preferred classes.

- The ***standard class*** includes people whose anticipated mortality is average, that is higher than the mortality predicted for people in the preferred class, but lower than the mortality predicted for people in the substandard class. Traditionally, the standard class has been divided into standard nontobacco and standard tobacco subclasses.

- The ***substandard class,*** also called *special risk,* usually includes people whose anticipated mortality is higher than average, but who are still considered to be insurable. Many insurers establish this class for proposed insureds who are recovering from serious illnesses or accidents, whose occupations or avocations produce a greater risk of illnesses or accidents, or whose medical or physical findings are outside the normal ranges.

- The ***declined class*** is used only for proposed insureds whose impairments and anticipated extra mortality are so great that the insurer cannot provide coverage at an affordable cost for them or who have recent medical events such that mortality cannot be accurately predicted.

During risk assessment for individual health and disability income insurance, applicants are generally evaluated according to their age, impairments, and type of coverage requested, but are not typically assigned to risk classes as are people who apply for life insurance coverage. Risk assessment for group life and health insurance generally does not involve risk classes; instead, risk assessment is based on such factors as the nature of the business or other group, the demographic characteristics of the employees or other persons to be insured, and the type and amount of coverage. We'll discuss risk assessment for group insurance coverage in Chapter 8.

FAST FACT

In 1999, 13% of individual life insurance policies purchased in the United States were issued as "preferred," 81% as "standard," and 6% as "substandard."[1]

Underwriting Philosophy and Underwriting Guidelines

An insurer's ***underwriting philosophy*** (also referred to as the insurer's *underwriting objective*) is a philosophy that guides its risk selection and classification procedures. The underwriting philosophy generally reflects the insurer's strategic business goals and includes its pricing assumptions for products. An insurer's underwriting philosophy strongly shapes its underwriting guidelines.

Underwriting guidelines are general standards that specify the parameters within which an applicant may be assigned to one of the risk classes established for each insurance product. These guidelines for individual coverages typically encompass a number of characteristics including, but not limited to, height and weight, blood pressure, cholesterol levels, presence of specific impairments (such as coronary artery disease, diabetes, and cancer), and indications of specific behaviors (such as substance abuse, driving while intoxicated, tobacco use, and participation in certain avocations). Underwriting guidelines for group coverages typically encompass the different set of factors mentioned earlier, such as the demographic characteristics of the people to be insured and the type and amount of coverage.

In establishing its underwriting philosophy and underwriting guidelines, an insurer considers ***industry experience***, which is collected data about insurance claim experience generated by intercompany and industry-wide studies. These studies generally are conducted by large insurers, reinsurance companies, and industry associations. An insurer also uses the experience data from its own insurance products. Industry experience and an insurer's own experience are useful guides for the insurer's future actions and decisions, especially for establishing underwriting requirements, risk classes, and premiums for new coverages. As an insurer's experience changes over time, the insurer may modify its underwriting philosophy and underwriting guidelines.

However they evolve, an insurer's underwriting philosophy and underwriting guidelines focus on approving and issuing coverage that is

- Equitable to the insureds
- Equitable to the insurer
- Deliverable by the agent

Equitable to the Insureds

Risk classification maintains equity among insureds and groups by ensuring that each insured pays a premium rate that reflects the degree of risk that the insured represents. For example, the insurer assigns a person who represents a standard risk to a standard risk class and charges a standard premium rate for a person of that age. Another person who represents a significantly greater-than-average risk is usually assigned to a substandard risk class and is charged a higher premium rate. A third person who represents an unacceptable level of risk is not issued coverage.

Similarly, two groups of employees proposed for long-term disability income coverage may be accepted for coverage, but may be charged different premium rates because their work represents different levels of risk. By charging higher rates for higher risks and by declining risks it can't afford to cover, an insurer is better able to provide coverage for all the risks it does accept.

In order to maintain equity among insureds, risk assessment and risk classification must be as objective as possible—that is, the risks must be evaluated fairly, without bias or prejudice. Being objective in underwriting is sometimes difficult, however, because an underwriter makes decisions under considerable pressure from agents, actuaries, and insurance company management. Agents want underwriters to issue coverage quickly and to assign proposed insureds to preferred or standard classes. Actuaries want underwriters to use risk classification methods that keep morbidity and mortality rates very close to those on which the pricing assumptions for the insurance product are based. The insurer's management wants underwriters to accomplish both these objectives—fast issue and favorable morbidity and mortality results—while keeping underwriting costs as low as possible.

Equitable to the Insurer

An insurer's underwriting guidelines help to ensure that the underwritten coverage will be equitable to the insurer. Without assigning each person or group equitably to a risk class, an insurer may find that it has approved a block of policies that, on the whole, represent an unacceptably high level of risk. A ***block of policies*** (also known as a *block of business*) is a group of policies issued to insureds who are in the same risk classification. An insurance company that has issued a high-risk block of policies may receive an excessive number of claims and may be less able to pay all legitimate claims. Moreover, without proper risk classification, an insurer may price a product too high to compete favorably in the marketplace. Finally, an approach of "one price fits all" can result in product pricing that is not competitive for preferred and standard cases and so attracts an inordinate number of substandard cases.

Deliverable by the Agent

An applicant for individual insurance makes the final decision whether to accept an insurance policy at the time the policy is delivered. If a buyer chooses not to accept a policy when an agent attempts to deliver it, the policy is said to be ***undeliverable*** or *not taken.* One of many reasons that a policy may be undeliverable is that an underwriting decision to classify a proposed insured as representing a high risk can result in a premium rate that is higher than the buyer anticipated or in coverage that is different from that which the buyer expected.

When an agent presents information about an insurance product to a proposed insured, the agent usually quotes a premium that is based on the insurer's standard premium rates. If the underwriter's assessment results in assigning the proposed insured to a substandard class, the application is said to be *rated.* ***Rating*** an application means approving a higher-than-average risk by charging a higher-than-usual premium rate for the coverage applied for or by limiting the amount or type of coverage to be provided. When an application is rated, the agent may have difficulty delivering the policy to a client. Frequently, people who have been rated apply to other companies for competitive quotes. An agent whose company always assesses a higher premium than the competition may have difficulty finding customers to purchase his company's policies. For group coverage, the same principle applies: a proposed group may refuse to purchase a policy that requires a premium greater than the amount the group expects to pay for a specified amount of coverage or that offers less coverage than the group wishes to obtain at a specified price.

One of the greatest challenges facing the underwriter is explaining tactfully and persuasively to an agent the reasons for rating or declining an application for insurance so that the agent will be satisfied that the underwriting decision was equitable. A successful underwriter not only makes defensible decisions, but also earns the confidence and respect of agents in doing so. Underwriters help form a productive relationship with agents by

- Completing work on each case in a timely manner
- Keeping the agent informed of progress in cases that are delayed because of requirements for additional information
- Communicating with the agent about the rating or declining of an application without violating the confidentiality of information sources
- Making use of opportunities to educate agents and their staffs about the insurer's underwriting philosophy and guidelines

Overview of Underwriting

As you now know, underwriting is the process of (1) assessing and classifying the degree of risk represented by a proposed insured or a group of proposed insureds and (2) making a decision to accept or decline the risk. Whether underwriting an individual or a group, underwriters follow a general rule: approve the coverage as applied for if the proposed insured represents an acceptable risk, and decline the risk or establish other conditions if the proposed insured represents an excessive risk.

In certain situations, such as those concerned with small amounts of life or health coverage for large numbers of proposed insureds, underwriting can be so routine that much of it can be handled automatically, often by specialized computer systems. Underwriting is as much an art as a science, however, and thus may require human interaction, especially for complex or unusual cases. Insight 2-1 explains how technological developments may affect underwriting in the future.

Underwriting consists of four activities:

1. Performing field underwriting
2. Reviewing the application for insurance
3. Gathering additional information to make a sound decision
4. Making an underwriting decision on the case

Performing Field Underwriting

Underwriting a proposed insured often begins well before an application for insurance reaches the insurer's home office underwriters.

Insight 2-1. Underwriting Is Still Needed Online.

No reasonable person could argue that the insurance industry will be exempt from the Internet's dramatic impact. So it becomes not a question of if, but of how. Determining this impact begins with anticipating consumer reaction to insurance in the electronic age.

Internet consumers will expect an almost instantaneous acceptance of their application. They will have little tolerance for medical exams or anything else they perceive as a delay or complication.

Confidentiality is also an issue. Consumers might be reluctant to provide detailed medical and financial information online. Privacy and confidentiality have always been a concern, even with policies sold the "old-fashioned" way. But in the electronic world, these issues are magnified by the threat of hacker interception.

Our analysis of e-commerce must then address how these new behaviors affect the future of underwriting. Will the onset of e-commerce ultimately lead to its demise? I respond with a confident "no." Although the Internet changes how we do business, underwriting will still be an essential function in a system offering voluntary individual life insurance. The key lies in identifying the changes, preparing for them, and then learning to use them to our advantage.

A few changes we expect:

Specialized products. Most likely, the industry will begin to develop products specifically designed for electronic sale. These products will be simple, straightforward, and easy to understand. Underwriting will be necessary, but limited to questions on the application only. To reasonably minimize a company's risk, maximum face amounts could be established. Pricing will reflect lower acquisition costs and higher mortality due to the reduced level of underwriting.

Not all consumers will be satisfied with this product pricing, and there will still be a significant market for products that require more traditional underwriting approaches. Underwriting is often the key to keeping insurance affordable.

Faster underwriting. I believe this will enhance the risk-selection process. First, electronic methods improve communication with customers, reinsurers, paramedical facilities, laboratories, and other vendors, resulting in quicker and better underwriting decisions. For example, information from an electronic application can feed into an expert underwriting system and—if no concerns are identified—a policy can be issued instantly. Policy output can be stored on a compact disk and mailed or downloaded from a secure Web site.

Better information. The Internet will give underwriters access to more detailed and accurate underwriting information. Obtaining an applicant's medical records, traditionally the greatest cause of underwriting delays, could be simplified by scanning the records and sending them as an e-mail attachment or by downloading images of the records from a medical facility's Web site. Another possibility is searching a physician's database for diagnostic codes used for billing purposes and making an underwriting decision based on those codes.

It's true that technology affects every aspect of our business and, therefore, may have a more dramatic impact than other changes faced by our industry. We might have to change our methods, but the need for appropriate risk selection and premium classification will remain.

Source: Excerpted from Greg Linde, "Underwriting Is Still Needed Online," *Best's Review* (June 2000): 131. © A.M. Best Company, Inc.; used with permission of the publisher.

Field underwriting is the process of screening applicants who have requested coverage and gathering initial information about a proposed insured. Consider the following two typical situations:

> An insurance agent learns of a prospective purchaser of life insurance and arranges a meeting. At the meeting, the agent and the prospect determine a need for life insurance and choose an appropriate plan. The agent completes an application for coverage and submits the application to the insurer.

By assessing the proposed insured's qualifications for coverage, the agent has performed field underwriting.

A 60-year-old woman receives a direct mail solicitation for an insurance policy. She reads the promotional materials that say, "If you are between the ages of 25 and 65, you may be eligible for..." The woman calls the toll-free telephone number listed in the mailing and asks the insurer's representative some questions. Satisfied that she wants the coverage, she answers the application questions asked by the insurer's telephone representative and applies for a policy by telephone. In this situation, the insurer has performed field underwriting by using informational materials that enabled the woman to pre-screen herself.

Field underwriting refers to information-gathering activities used by an agent or a telephone representative to determine an applicant's suitability for insurance coverage. If field underwriting indicates that a person or group represents an inappropriate risk, the agent may discourage the prospect from applying for the coverage, thus saving the insurer the expense of evaluating that risk.

Agents also contribute to effective underwriting by reporting complete information. If a proposed insured for individual coverage describes having health problems, the agent can facilitate underwriting by recording clearly, accurately, and completely such information as the precise name of each medical problem; dates and types of treatment, medication, and surgery; and the names and addresses of the proposed insured's physicians and other health care providers, and dates of visits to them. Most insurance applications include an ***agent's statement,*** reserved for the agent's comments about the applicant or the proposed insured. Some agents provide such information in a letter addressed to the insurer. We'll discuss the agent's statement in connection with health insurance applications in Chapter 7.

Reviewing the Application for Insurance

After field underwriting is complete and the agent sends the application to the insurer, the underwriting staff assigns the case a number or code for identification and tracking purposes. The application goes through a manual or an automated checking process to verify that the application form is the proper one for the state in which the policyowner resides; the amount and type of coverage applied for is appropriate, considering the age and circumstances of the proposed insured; and the agent and the insurer are licensed to sell the type of coverage requested in the policyowner's state of residence.

Next, the staff search the insurer's records for information, such as previous health insurance claims or life insurance applications submitted by the proposed insured. Most insurers perform the search by using computers. After the information, if any, is attached to the application, the case is assigned to an underwriter or to a special team of underwriters.

In reviewing an insurance application, the underwriter assesses the information it contains according to the underwriting guidelines established by the insurer for the applied-for coverage. The underwriter also looks at other documents submitted with the application. These documents may include the results of medical examinations and tests performed on the applicant and questionnaires answered by the applicant.

Gathering Additional Information

To assess some cases, the underwriter needs additional information. The amount of additional information can be as small as the response to a single question that was left blank on an application or as extensive as the results of a complete medical examination. As the amount of requested information increases, so do the cost and the time required to obtain and assess the information.

For each insurance product, most insurers develop a ***table of underwriting requirements*** to specify the kinds of information the underwriter considers in assessing the insurability of a proposed insured. Generally, applications that represent a greater degree of risk —for example, large amounts of coverage or insurance for older people—require greater amounts of information for underwriting.

Figure 2-1 shows a portion of a table of underwriting requirements for various ages and amounts of individual life insurance coverage. As the amount of insurance applied for increases within each age grouping, the amount of underwriting information also increases. For example, a person between the ages of 31 and 40 can apply for up to $99,999 of life insurance on a ***nonmedical basis***—that is, without being required to undergo a medical examination. To apply for up to $300,000 of life insurance, that person would need a blood profile, and to apply for up to $1,000,000 of coverage, that person would need a paramedical report, a blood profile, and a urine sample. An underwriter might request even more information if the applicant had certain impairments.

> **FAST FACT**
>
> In 1999, group life insurance purchases made up 39% of the total life insurance purchases in Canada.[2]

Note also that as the age of an applicant increases, the evidence of insurability required for underwriting also increases, and the amount of insurance that may be applied for without medical evidence of insurability decreases. On the chart in Figure 2-1, ages above 46 require at least a paramedical report as evidence of insurability for coverage

FIGURE 2-1. Portion of a Table of Underwriting Requirements for Individual Life Insurance.

Age at Last Birthday	Total of All Coverage	Underwriting Requirements
16–30	Up to $99,999	Nonmedical
	$100,000 to $400,000	Nonmedical, blood profile, urine
	$400,001 to $1,500,000	Paramedical report, blood profile, urine
	$1,500,001 to $3,000,000	Paramedical report, blood profile, urine, ECG, inspection report
	$3,000,001 and up	Medical exam, blood profile, urine, ECG, inspection report
31–40	Up to $99,999	Nonmedical
	$100,000 to $300,000	Nonmedical, blood profile
	$300,001 to $1,000,000	Paramedical report, blood profile, urine
	$1,000,001 to $2,000,000	Paramedical report, blood profile, urine, ECG, inspection report
	$2,000,001 and up	Medical exam, blood profile, urine, ECG, inspection report, Attending Physician's Statement (APS)
41–45	Up to $99,999	Nonmedical
	$100,000 to $500,000	Paramedical report, blood profile, urine
	$500,001 to $1,500,000	Paramedical report, blood profile, urine, ECG
	$1,500,001 to $3,000,000	Medical exam, blood profile, urine, ECG, inspection report
	$3,000,001 and up	Medical exam, blood profile, urine, ECG, inspection report, APS
46–50	Up to $50,000	Nonmedical
	$50,001 to $99,999	Paramedical report
	$100,000 to $200,000	Paramedical report, blood profile
	$200,001 to $1,000,000	Paramedical report, blood profile, urine, ECG
	$1,000,001 to $3,000,000	Medical exam, blood profile, urine, ECG, inspection report
	$3,000,001 and up	Medical exam, blood profile, urine, ECG, inspection report, APS

greater than $50,000. We will define and discuss the underwriting sources mentioned in the chart—for instance, APSs, medical examinations, paramedical reports, and inspection reports—in Chapter 4.

A typical table of underwriting requirements for group life and health insurance contains similar specifications. Unless a group is very small, the requirements are usually figured according to the demographics of the whole group. For example, a group's characteristics may permit an insurer to underwrite monthly short-term disability income coverage up to $2,000 as guaranteed issue requiring no other underwriting information. A group member who is eligible for a monthly benefit greater than $2,000, however, is usually required to supply evidence of insurability.

Sometimes an underwriter speaks directly with an attending physician's staff to gather information—for instance, to learn more about a specific disorder, to verify dates and details of treatment, and to clarify the reasons for certain diagnoses and medications. Personal contact allows an underwriter to obtain precise information and increases the underwriter's knowledge about medical matters.

Consumer reporting agencies or the insurer's underwriters can conduct a ***personal history interview (PHI),*** a conversation with the proposed insured during which an underwriter clarifies information and gathers additional information needed for underwriting. The personal history interview is conducted by telephone or in person. The interviewer usually calls the interviewee to schedule a convenient time for the interview, allowing the proposed insured to choose whether the interview should take place during the daytime or the evening.

One advantage of a personal history interview is that an underwriter can find out more about an applicant's health history than is contained in a medical report. The underwriter can ask the proposed insured to comment on that information and can check the accuracy of the statements contained in the medical report. Furthermore, the personal history interview serves as a means of verifying the accuracy and thoroughness of the agent who submitted the application. If an underwriter knows that a certain agent has occasionally erred in filling out applications in the past, the underwriter can use the personal history interview to ensure that all the information is correct and complete.

Making an Underwriting Decision

After considering all the relevant data, the underwriter makes a decision on the case. Depending on the type and amount of coverage and the underwriter's experience, the underwriter's decision may be subject to review by a more experienced underwriter, an underwriting manager, or, in some cases, the insurer's medical director.

If the underwriter decides to issue coverage as applied for, she releases the file to the policy issue unit or department, which produces a policy and delivers it to the agent or to the proposed insured. The underwriter or a member of the underwriting staff communicates the underwriting decision to the agent. If the decision is either to issue coverage with modifications or to decline coverage, the underwriter usually tells the agent the reason for the decision, without violating the insurer's and the jurisdiction's rules about confidentiality. Some jurisdictions also require that the insurer tell the applicant the reason the coverage was modified or declined.

Policy Issue

After underwriting is complete and coverage has been approved, an insurer issues a policy for delivery (usually by an agent) to the insured person or group. As we mentioned in Chapter 1, most insurers use automated systems to produce policy documents promptly and accurately. An insurer's information system typically creates a client record and verifies that the initial premium payment has been received and that all policy requirements have been met.

Individual and Group Policy Issue Procedures

The procedures for policy issue differ slightly for individual and group coverage. Individual coverage requires only that a document be produced and delivered, usually by the agent, to the insured person. Group coverage, by contrast, requires an installation process.

Installing a group contract includes enrolling each employee or other covered person. The insurer's information system produces not only a contract for the group policyholder, but also a certificate and an enrollment card for each covered person. During installation, the agent or group representative presents information about the insurance plan to the insureds and distributes a certificate to each person. Each covered person completes an enrollment card. We'll discuss the group enrollment process in more detail in Chapter 8.

Organization of Underwriting

The chief underwriter oversees an insurer's underwriting activities. Not only is the chief underwriter an expert in risk selection, but she also is quite knowledgeable about claim handling and customer service. The chief underwriter is responsible for monitoring the cost and quality of underwriting, including making decisions on vendors and services the insurer uses to obtain medical information and inspection reports. In addition to handling personnel matters and underwriter training, the chief underwriter serves as a liaison with the insurer's reinsurance and claims functions. In most insurance companies, the chief underwriter suggests age and amount requirements to the actuaries, who use those requirements in establishing prices for products. In some insurance companies, the chief underwriter works with the insurer's legal staff on contract wording.

Under the leadership of the chief underwriter, the underwriters are accountable for assessing risks according to relevant information and making appropriate decisions. To work effectively, each underwriter must develop detailed, wide-ranging knowledge that takes years to master. An underwriter gradually gains an understanding of the insurer's products and marketing distribution system, underwriting philosophy and guidelines, and customer service. In assessing risks, the underwriter becomes familiar with business-related information, special risk evaluation, and medical information.

Figure 2-2 lists more specifically the types of information that underwriters are generally required to know to perform their jobs successfully.

FAST FACT

Of the individual life insurance policies purchased by Canadians during 1999, about 4% were extra risk.[3]

FIGURE 2-2. Information Underwriters Need to Know.

BUSINESS-RELATED INFORMATION

- The insurer's products and pricing assumptions
- The insurer's marketing distribution systems and the ways the underwriter may communicate with agents
- The insurer's underwriting philosophy, guidelines, and requirements
- Legal issues related to underwriting
- Sources of underwriting information
- The insurer's computer-based system
- Customer service principles applied to internal and external customers, including written and telephone communication skills

SPECIAL RISK EVALUATION

- Underwriting for occupation, motor vehicle violations, avocation and hazardous activities civilian and military aviation, alcoholism, drug abuse, criminal activity, foreign residence, and recent immigration

MEDICAL INFORMATION

- The circulatory system, blood pressure, coronary artery disease, congenital heart disease, heart arrhythmia and murmurs, cerebral vascular disease, and peripheral vascular disease
- Neurology
- Endocrine and metabolic disorders
- Respiratory disorders
- Urinary and reproductive system disorders
- Musculoskeletal disorders
- Digestive system disorders
- Eye, ear, nose, and throat disorders
- Blood disorders
- Psychiatric disorders

Most insurers also employ physicians as medical experts for underwriting. Large insurers usually appoint a medical director to lead a medical underwriting staff composed of physicians and other medical personnel. The responsibilities of the medical staff include developing and updating the insurer's medical underwriting guidelines, as well as consulting with underwriters on cases with unusual or difficult medical histories.

Some insurers establish separate underwriting units to handle various types of applications—for life, disability, health, and other types of coverage. Generally, insurers organize the work of underwriting according to a case assignment system, a work division system, or a combination of the two systems. Figure 2-3 outlines these systems for organizing underwriting.

FIGURE 2-3. Systems for Organizing Underwriting.

CASE ASSIGNMENT SYSTEM

- Age and face amount requested
- Type of application or policy change
- Geographic origin or agent

WORK DIVISION SYSTEM

- Independent underwriting
- Team underwriting
- Jet unit underwriting
- Committee underwriting

Case Assignment System

A ***case assignment system*** establishes a basis for giving a case to an appropriate person or group for underwriting. The case assignment system enables an underwriter to specialize in certain types of cases. The basis used to assign case files to underwriting varies depending on the size of the insurer, the number of applications usually received, and the difficulty of the cases to be underwritten. Most common case assignment systems distribute cases according to one of the following characteristics:

1. Age of the proposed insured and face amount requested
2. Type of application or policy change
3. Geographic origin of the application or the location of the agent submitting the application

A drawback of the case assignment system is that underwriters can become well informed only about their own areas of specialization. As a result, employees' vacations and absences may cause an underwriter to work temporarily—and probably less productively—with "unfamiliar" cases. This problem can be reduced, however, by periodic rotation of assignments and cross-training so that several underwriters become familiar with the characteristics of other types of cases.

Age of the Proposed Insured and Face Amount Requested

Some insurers assign life insurance cases to underwriters according to the age of the proposed insured and the face amount of the coverage requested. Disability cases may be assigned according to the monthly benefit amount applied for, and health insurance cases may be assigned according to the policy limit. In this type of case assignment system, each underwriter is assigned only cases for amounts that the underwriter is authorized to approve.

Type of Application or Policy Change

If cases are based on the type of application or on a type of change requested—usually an increase in the coverage amount or the addition of a rider—certain underwriters may be assigned only nonmedical applications, only applications requiring a medical examination report, only combination business (that is, applications for life and health coverage on the same person), or only requests for accidental death benefit (ADB) coverage. In some insurance companies, underwriters specialize in life, medical expense, or disability coverage.

Geographic Origin or Location of Agent

If the geographic origin of the application is the basis of an insurer's case assignment system, underwriting is divided into regional sections, with each section handling all business submitted by agents within a specific geographic area. Alternatively, some insurers assign specific agents to certain underwriters, regardless of the geographic location. Either of these case assignment methods enables an underwriter to become familiar with the quality of agents' business and to develop effective working relationships with the agents.

Case assignment on the basis of geographic origin also enables underwriters to become more knowledgeable about legislative and regulatory differences among various jurisdictions, as well as to learn more about specific impairments or occupations that may be peculiar to a certain geographic region. For example, black lung disease is more likely to occur in areas where coal is mined than in other areas.

Work Division System

A ***work division system*** divides cases according to the person or group that underwrites them. Types of work division include

- Independent underwriting
- Team underwriting
- Jet unit underwriting
- Committee underwriting

Independent Underwriting

In many insurance companies, applications are assigned to underwriters who work alone to assess each risk. Some insurers assign to independent underwriters only large-amount cases or those requiring extensive research.

Team Underwriting

Team underwriting is a risk selection approach in which underwriters are divided into small groups. The team usually includes one or more senior underwriters who handle large-amount or complex cases, and one or more lower-level underwriters who handle simpler cases. Clerical staff assist the team by performing preliminary application processing and ordering additional information.

Team underwriting usually enables team members to exercise considerable autonomy in making underwriting decisions. Members of the team are responsible for setting work assignments and establishing priorities for them. Team members make recommendations to the chief underwriter on such issues as team training and development, schedules of work and vacations, solutions to production problems, and conflict resolution. Compared to other underwriting methods, team underwriting can be more cost-effective and can provide the agents with faster service.

Jet Unit Underwriting

Designed to underwrite simple cases quickly, ***jet unit underwriting*** is a risk selection approach that establishes a group of two to four employees who screen applications that meet specific criteria and who approve certain types of applications for immediate policy issue. For example, life insurance applications that are eligible for consideration by a jet unit have specific characteristics, such as the following:

- Proposed insured's age, height, and weight are within specified ranges.
- Proposed insured has no significant health problems and has an acceptable occupation.
- Application is being made for an amount of insurance below a specified limit, usually $50,000 to $100,000, depending on the proposed insured's age and the insurer's requirements.
- Applicant has not made an unusual beneficiary designation.
- Applicant has answered all questions on the application.
- Insurer's records contain no adverse underwriting information on the proposed insured.

A jet unit usually is not authorized to request further information or to rate or decline an application except for certain specified impairments. All applications that are not issued immediate coverage are sent from the jet unit to other underwriting staff, who gather additional information and decide on the cases. Some jet units are equipped with electronic systems that further speed underwriting by scanning and checking applications.

Committee Underwriting

Cases involving large coverage amounts or special problems, such as combinations of impairments or unusual occupations, may require committee evaluation. ***Committee underwriting*** is a risk selection approach in which a committee of highly qualified people from inside and outside the underwriting function is called together for case assessment.

Usually the committee is composed of the chief underwriter, the medical director, and representatives from the legal, actuarial, and agency functions. By pooling their technical expertise, the committee members can reach an appropriate decision on cases that otherwise might have to be passed from person to person in a less efficient manner.

Combination System

Some insurers combine a case assignment system with a work division system. For example, a jet unit may handle only applications for health coverage under one type of policy, or an underwriting team may handle only term life insurance applications from a specific geographic area or from a certain agent.

Insight 2-2 discusses ideas for building an effective underwriting team. (In this Insight, "team" does not necessarily refer to "team underwriting" as discussed earlier in this section.)

Decision Options and Authority Levels

Underwriters have varying levels of authority to make decisions. In this section, we'll discuss decision options and levels of decision-making authority in underwriting.

Decision Options

After examining the information in a case file, an underwriter typically makes one of the following decisions:

1. Accept the risk and issue the coverage as requested.
2. Accept the risk, but add a substandard rating or limit the coverage by attaching an exclusion rider to the policy contract. An ***exclusion rider*** is an amendment that limits a policy's benefits by excluding from coverage certain types of risk, such as death benefits for a death resulting from an aviation accident or disability income benefits for a specified, usually preexisting, impairment.
3. Decline the risk.

Rather than make a decision immediately, the underwriter may decide to gather more information. If the underwriter requests or waits for information before making a decision, the case will be held in a pending or suspense file. Eventually, the case will be accepted or declined. If the case is accepted, the insurer will issue a policy to the proposed insured. If the case is declined, the underwriting decision will be communicated to the agent and to the applicant.

Authority Levels

Underwriting is not a rigid or scientific discipline with absolute rules governing every decision. Therefore, an underwriter needs the ability to make well-reasoned judgments and the authority to act on those judgments.

In general, an underwriter's authority to rate or decline an application increases with the underwriter's level of experience. Underwriters

Insight 2-2. Build a Strong Underwriting Team.

Effective risk selection begins with effective candidate selection for your underwriting team. Training is also important and should be a priority, but the real challenge is identifying and hiring people who possess the core characteristics of a good underwriter.

Let's start with a basic rule: Not every bright, energetic candidate will be a good underwriter. Learning this by experience is expensive in both training and staff morale. Therefore, the process for selecting good underwriters should be no less rigorous than that followed to select insureds. I suggest following these steps:

STEP 1: Identify Characteristics of Good Underwriter

Some managers seek "technicians," analytical types with an underwriting manual tucked in one hand and a calculator in the other. Technical skills are important, but they can be taught, unlike many of the other important characteristics an underwriter must possess.

Some attributes to look for in a candidate include good judgment and ability to deal with "gray" issues; strong decision-making skills; excellent oral and written communication skills; good problem-solving skills; flexibility and open-mindedness; strong sense of marketing; excellent teamwork skills and ability to interact with a variety of personalities; and working knowledge of computers and technology.

STEP 2: Educate Résumé Screeners

Educating your human resources representatives on identifying candidates with ideal underwriter characteristics is very important. Invite recruiters to the underwriting department. Encourage them to talk with experienced underwriters so they learn how the risk-selection function has changed in recent years. Allow them to observe the range of skills used in performing the job. Recruiters will understand that successful underwriters can come from a variety of educational and professional backgrounds, including marketing, communications, nursing and pre-med. Don't let an inaccurate perception of underwriting prevent you from seeing the candidates you need.

STEP 3: Use Interview to Validate Candidate Interest

Once you develop a pool of strong candidates, the next challenge is the interview. It's usually not difficult to determine if applicants truly have the characteristics they claim on their résumés. But how do you know which ones will like the job and stay on your underwriting team?

Few candidates, other than those with insurance experience, have even a vague idea of what underwriting is, and even fewer have underwriting listed as their job objective. The majority interview because "the HR representative thought I might be qualified." How do you sell them on the underwriting career path?

When you interview candidates, include a case underwriter—someone from the "trenches" who can offer a positive, yet realistic, description of the day-to-day duties.

Look for candidates with the interest in and confidence and judgment for making decisions that impact the company's bottom line. These candidates will enjoy the challenge of selling their decisions to producers and will be motivated to develop their skills and knowledge in a respected profession.

STEP 4: Offer Training to Build Underwriting Skills

Once selected, the right candidates will need training to turn them into underwriting professionals. Here are some training suggestions:

Ensure the training is well rounded. Although medical-impairment training is important, there are other important issues, such as financial underwriting, legal aspects of insurance, communication and negotiation techniques. Show trainees what the marketing department does and how products are sold. Help them see how their underwriting decisions fit into the big picture.

Have new underwriters begin casework early. The best way to learn is by doing. It's not necessary for them to know every disease or physical impairment before picking up a case. But make sure the framework exists for new trainees to receive help on cases beyond their abilities.

Mentoring is highly worthwhile To be successful, new underwriters need someone who can guide, encourage and offer advice. Mentoring is more than simply signing off on cases beyond the new underwriter's authority limit. An experienced underwriter can help a trainee develop judgment and communicate decisions effectively.

Companies should choose good candidates and then use training to make them even better.

Source: Excerpted from Greg Linde, "Build a Strong Underwriting Team," *Best's Review* (March 2000): 119. © A.M. Best Company, Inc.; used with permission of the publisher.

gradually receive more case approval authority as their demonstrated ability and quality of judgment improve. New underwriters are typically allowed to examine and approve only small-amount cases, and their work is reviewed by other, more experienced underwriters. By contrast, experienced underwriters and chief underwriters usually have authority to approve large-amount cases and to make decisions on more difficult, detailed cases without review by a more experienced underwriter.

An underwriter's level of authority is specified by (1) the face amount that the underwriter can approve and (2) the degree to which the underwriter may rate or decline a policy without approval or review by a more experienced underwriter.

Authority to Approve Specified Coverage Limits

Most insurers develop charts or schedules of underwriting authority to specify the highest amount of coverage that can be approved by each level of underwriter. Figure 2-4 provides an example of levels of case approval authority. The dollar amounts stated in the figure are used for illustration only. Specific amounts and number of levels of case approval authority vary from one insurer to another.

FIGURE 2-4. An Example of Levels of Case Approval Authority for Underwriters.

Underwriter Level	Standard	Substandard & Exclusions	Declined
Junior Underwriter with Less Than1 Year's Experience	$100,000 to $400,000, Clear Case	Not authorized	Not authorized
Junior Underwriter with 1 Year's Experience	$400,000	$100,000	Not authorized
Intermediate Underwriter with Less Than 1 Year's Experience	$500,000	$200,000	Not authorized
Intermediate Underwriter with 1 Year's Experience	$750,000	$500,000	Not authorized
Senior Underwriter with Less Than 1 Year's Experience	$1,000,000	$500,000	$200,000
Senior Underwriter with 1 Year's Experience	$1,500,000	$1,000,000	$500,000
Chief Underwriter	ALL AMOUNTS	ALL AMOUNTS	ALL AMOUNTS

Authority to Rate or Decline Cases

Some insurers require underwriting decisions to be reviewed and approved by a higher-level underwriter when an underwriter makes a decision to rate or decline a case, even if that underwriter has authority to approve the same type of case without a rating. In other words, the underwriter's authority to approve a case as applied for does not also permit the underwriter to rate or decline the case without consulting a higher-level underwriter. Generally, an underwriter's authority to approve a rated case decreases as the level of risk—represented by a substandard or special risk rating—increases.

In some insurance companies, all rated and declined cases are reviewed by an underwriter one level higher than the original underwriter. Other insurers require that only the chief underwriter performs this kind of review. The review is performed not only to ensure that the original underwriting decision is appropriate, but also to ensure the consistency of underwriting actions, to serve as a measure of an underwriter's job performance, and to enhance agents' confidence in the insurer's underwriting practices.

Key Terms and Concepts

risk assessment
impairment
mortality
morbidity
antiselection
risk class
preferred class
standard class
substandard class
declined class
underwriting philosophy
underwriting guidelines
industry experience
block of policies
undeliverable
rating
field underwriting
agent's statement
table of underwriting requirements
nonmedical basis
personal history interview (PHI)
case assignment system
work division system
team underwriting
jet unit underwriting
committee underwriting
exclusion rider

Endnotes

1. ACLI, *Life Insurers Fact Book 2000* (Washington, D.C.: American Council of Life Insurers, 2000), 17.
2. CLHIA, *Canadian Life and Health Insurance Facts* (Toronto: Canadian Life and Health Insurance Association, 2000), 8.
3. Ibid., 9.

CHAPTER 3 Legal Issues Affecting Underwriting

Chapter Outline

Legal Implications of Underwriting
- Processing Applications
- Acting Promptly upon Applications
- Documenting Underwriting

Antidiscrimination Statutes
- Sex
- Physical and Mental Impairments
- Marital Status
- Subjects of Abuse
- Sexual Orientation
- Canadian Antidiscrimination Statutes

Privacy and Confidentiality Laws
- U.S. Privacy Guidelines and Laws
- Canadian Privacy Guidelines and Laws
- State and Provincial Privacy Protection
- AIDS and Genetic Testing

Replacement Regulations

Premium Receipts

Statutory Requirements for Group Insurance
- Requirements in the United States
- Requirements in Canada

Objectives

After reading this chapter, you should be able to

- Describe the underwriter's role in processing and acting promptly upon applications and in documenting underwriting
- Identify two legally acceptable bases for discriminating among risks, and describe five types of risk factors that are specifically mentioned in antidiscrimination legislation
- Summarize the provisions of the Fair Credit Reporting Act (FCRA) concerning protection of consumers' privacy and confidentiality
- Explain three types of notice that an insurer must provide to applicants concerning consumer reporting agency reports
- Explain the general requirements of replacement regulations
- Distinguish between a conditional premium receipt and a temporary insurance agreement (TIA)
- Identify provisions of the NAIC Group Life Insurance Definition and Group Life Insurance Standard Provisions Model Act and the CCIR Group Insurance Guidelines

All businesses are subject to laws and regulations. So, if an underwriter for an insurance company were unaware of the legal issues affecting underwriting, the result could be large financial losses and legal penalties, as well as harm to the insurer's reputation and to its ability to continue doing business in one or more jurisdictions. In addition, some of an underwriter's day-to-day actions in processing applications and assessing risks can affect an insurer's legal position if the insurer is brought to court.

In this chapter, we will look first at an underwriter's responsibility to handle cases so that if a file should later be subjected to court scrutiny, all underwriting decisions and actions would be judged appropriate and would be clearly documented. Then we will consider specific laws and regulations that affect underwriting: antidiscrimination statutes, privacy laws, replacement regulations, and legal interpretations of premium receipts. Finally, we'll review regulations that affect group insurance underwriting.

Legal Implications of Underwriting

To protect the insurer from legal complications, when evaluating a case, an underwriter should

- Process the application carefully
- Act promptly upon the application
- Accurately and fully document every step in underwriting the case

Processing Applications

When an underwriter receives a completed application for insurance, he checks for incomplete, inaccurate, or altered information. In some instances, an underwriter will discover a need for further investigation.

Incomplete, Inaccurate, or Altered Information

Sometimes, missing or inaccurate information on an insurance application results from human error. For instance, suppose a proposed insured knows that he had surgery, but can't remember exactly what year that happened. He feels sure that it was longer than 10 years ago, and answers questions on the application accordingly. During underwriting, however, an APS shows that the applicant had the surgery nine years ago. In this case, the applicant mistakenly provided incorrect information on his application. Sometimes, however, repeated instances of incorrect information on one application or significant errors or omissions may indicate a misrepresentation.

A ***misrepresentation*** is the presence of false or misleading statements on an application for insurance. A misrepresentation can be made either intentionally or unintentionally. An intentional misrepresentation is known as ***fraud*** and typically is considered to be far more serious than an unintentional misrepresentation. Unscrupulous applicants or agents may falsify information about an applicant's age, medical history, or other facts because they realize that truthful answers would result in higher premiums or denial of the application. When an applicant or agent provides false dates of an applicant's active employment or omits critical information such as a known impairment or additional sources of income, the underwriter is permitted by law to (1) require the applicant to revise the false or misleading statements prior to underwriting or (2) deny the coverage. Figure 3-1 lists some of the warning signs of possible misrepresentation that underwriters look for when they review an application.

If an underwriter does not discover the misrepresentation and issues a policy based on the information provided in the application and other underwriting documents, the false information may be discovered during an investigation of a claim submitted on that policy. If the discovery occurs during the policy's contestable period (usually within two years after policy issue), the law permits an insurer to take the action of rescission. ***Rescission*** is a legal action by which the insurer seeks to void a policy or have it declared void. The basis for such a rescission is ***material misrepresentation***, which is a misstatement that is relevant to the insurer's acceptance of a risk. The test as to whether misrepre-

FIGURE 3-1. Misrepresentation Warning Signs.

Indications of possible misrepresentation on an application for insurance:

- The applicant has requested an amount of coverage that is slightly less than the amount of coverage that requires the applicant to undergo a medical examination or test.
- The applicant's signature on the application does not match the applicant's signature on other documents, such as a medical examination report.
- Answers to questions on the application have been changed or covered by correction fluid.
- The applicant is requesting an unusually large amount of coverage based on her occupation and income.

Source: Excerpted from Barbara Foxenberger Brown and Jane Lightcap Brown, *Life and Health Insurance Underwriting* (Atlanta: LOMA, © 1998), 50.

sentation is material is whether, if the truth had been known about the misstatement, the insurer would have declined to issue the policy or issued it on a different basis.

For example, suppose that underwriter Jeannine LaFleur received an application for $500,000 of life insurance coverage. When Ms. LaFleur reviewed the application, she found that it contained complete and appropriate information. In addition, the blood and urine tests that she ordered came back negative. Therefore, Ms. LaFleur issued the policy. Six months later, Ms. LaFleur read that the applicant/insured had been convicted of drug trafficking. Further investigation revealed that the applicant/insured apparently earned a living as a drug dealer and was not a car salesperson, the occupation that he had listed on his application. Under these circumstances, the insurer can legally rescind the policy because of the applicant's material misrepresentation of his occupation. If Ms. LaFleur had known that the applicant lied about his occupation, she would not have issued the policy. In the case of fraud, the insurer can take the action of rescission at any time, even after the contestable period has expired.

Generally, an underwriter does not accept an application containing ditto marks, dashes, or question marks. The insurer would probably be held by a court to have given up its right to challenge the accuracy of the information in an application or to ask for more information if an underwriter, in approving coverage, had overlooked unanswered questions or had not resolved conflicting information. The insurer's defense of material misrepresentation, then, would not be valid if the beneficiary sues the insurer for denying a claim under the policy.

Unless the applicant affirms the change in writing, underwriters avoid making alterations on a completed application. Insurance applications cannot be changed except by appropriate legal procedures. Many jurisdictions provide that an application presented in court must be the original application signed by the applicant and that no modification of the document is valid without the applicant's signed (or, sometimes, initialed) consent. Generally, an insurer cannot use a life or health insurance application as evidence in court unless a valid copy of that application was attached to the insurance contract when the policy was issued. Furthermore, without the applicant's signature or initials, the entire application is usually invalid and, therefore, inadmissible as evidence in a court of law. However, recent federal legislation relating to electronic signatures will undoubtedly affect the characteristics of applications considered admissible as evidence.

Investigation of Applications

An underwriter also considers the need to further investigate the information recorded in an application so that the insurer cannot be held to have waived the right to obtain certain information. Obtaining detailed information for every underwriting decision is often not cost-effective. However, the underwriter also needs to understand the possible outcomes of not obtaining sufficient information to support his decision.

Acting Promptly upon Applications

The amount of time an underwriter takes to process an application is important for two reasons. First, the longer an insurer takes to handle an application, the more difficult delivering the policy to the policyowner may be for the agent because the applicant might be considering policies offered by other insurers. Second, the courts of many jurisdictions have held that insurers that do not act upon an application within a relatively short period of time may be held liable—that is responsible—for paying benefits if the proposed insured dies or suffers an illness or a disability before an underwriting decision is made. If the insurer is held liable under these circumstances, it will have to pay benefits under the policy regardless of the proposed insured's insurability. The courts have been especially strict in holding an insurer liable when an applicant submits a premium with the application. If the insurer does not respond to such an application in a timely way, the company may be held by a court to have accepted the application.

Documenting Underwriting

The information an underwriter obtains forms a history of the way the insurer has handled the case. A well-documented case file provides evidence to justify a risk classification decision. In investigating a proposed insured, an underwriter typically makes telephone calls and receives letters, memos, faxes, and electronic documents from many different sources. The underwriter must fully document in the applicant's file all such communications and other information related to risk classification so that all facts will be available in the event of a legal challenge.

Most insurers require underwriters to use a worksheet to keep track of the information requested and received, as well as to record the final decision on each case. An ***underwriting worksheet*** is a document that contains records of telephone calls, letters and other communications, documentation of requests for reinsurance, lists of reports and other information requested, and other notations that will explain clearly the manner in which the underwriter has handled the case beginning with the submission of the application to the insurer. If the underwriter responsible for the case is out of the office, another underwriter will usually be able to answer inquiries on the case by reviewing the underwriting worksheet. The worksheet also explains to the insurer's internal auditors unusual or exceptional handling of a case. Figure 3-2 illustrates a typical underwriting worksheet.

FIGURE 3-2. Underwriting Worksheet.

MEMO FROM UNDERWRITING DEPARTMENT

TO	AGENCY	NAME
	AGENT	POLICY NUMBER

Req'd	Rec'd			
		PART I		
		PART II ❑ Non Med	❑ Paramedical	❑ Doctor's Exam
		BLOOD PROFILE		
		HOME OFFICE SPECIMEN		
		RECHECK SPECIMEN	❑ 1	❑ 2 Separate days
		RESTING ECG		
		TREADMILL—ECG		
		INSPECTION REPORT		
		MVR		
		QUESTIONNAIRE		
		FINANCIAL STATEMENT	❑ PERSONAL	❑ BUSINESS
		SEEKING REINSURANCE		
		SPECIAL TESTING:		
		APS—DR.	to whom we/you have written.	
		APS—DR.	to whom we/you have written.	
		UNDERWRITING MEMO		

CLOSE OUT DATE ________

❑ VP, Underwriting
❑ Senior Underwriter
❑ Senior Underwriter
❑ ________________

Source: Excerpted from Barbara Foxenberger Brown and Jane Lightcap Brown, *Life and Health Insurance Underwriting* (Atlanta: LOMA, © 1998), 54. Used with permission; all rights reserved.

Telephone Conversations

Because a telephone conversation about a case can place a legal obligation on an insurer, underwriters document every telephone discussion in a clear and accurate written record. Documentation of telephone conversations should include several types of information:

- The full name of the person and/or company contacted
- The exact date and time of the telephone conversation
- Client information, specifying the client's name and other identifying information, such as file or policy number
- A summary of the conversation, which should cover not only what issues were discussed and what questions were asked, but the responses and the actions the underwriter decided to take
- The underwriter's full name and signature, not just his initials

The Applicant's File

Every action an underwriter takes in classifying the risk represented by a proposed insured is recorded in the application file. The underwriting comments in the file provide a diary of each underwriting decision, from the first review of the application to its approval or rejection. The underwriter notes all results of the initial review of the application and/or supplemental information, rate calculations, new information obtained from telephone calls and correspondence, and other relevant information.

Each of the underwriting comments includes the date and time, the specific action taken or requested, and the underwriter's signature, not just her initials. Other information or documentation pertaining to the underwriting decision should also be in writing and should become a permanent part of the case file.

In addition, underwriters make sure that all comments included in an applicant's file are appropriate and free of any content that could be interpreted as indicating personal bias against an applicant or a proposed insured. Because the entire file can be placed into evidence in a court of law, the presence of such comments can embarrass and damage the insurer. Such comments could be used to support an assertion that the insurer did not deal in good faith with an applicant.

Insight 3-1 lets you check your understanding of the types of comments that underwriters should and should not include in applicants' files.

Insight 3-1. Check Yourself: What Would You Write?

Assume you're an underwriting supervisor checking some of the life and health insurance case comments written by junior underwriters. Decide which of the following notations are acceptable to include in a case file. Then compare your decisions with the explanations below.

Note 1. Mr. Jones from an agency in Tucson, AZ, telephoned to ask why the case on Hiram P. France has not been given a preferred rating. I told him the applicant's avocation of deep-water scuba diving and his tobacco status prevented our assigning the case a preferred rating. [Signed] BP

Note 2. June 23, 2000, 10:17 A.M.—Ethel Janacek called again about receiving a letter from underwriting re: her application for health insurance. She acted rude and impatient this time, as usual. I told her I'd check on it and get back to her. [Signed] M. Grimsby

Note 3. 4:15 P.M. 9/17/00—Parkerson Insurance Agency, Wichita, KS. Wayne Parkerson (316-555-1234) called to check on the status of Marion and Walter Upson's life policy #AB1064-ZW and to see if more tests were required. I said I'd call back before noon on 9/19/00. [Signed] A. Perryman

Note 1 Explanation. *Unacceptable.* The first name of the caller and the name of the agency, as well as the date and the time of the call and the policy number, should be included. The last name of the underwriter, or at least the first initial and surname, should be added to the note.

Note 2 Explanation. *Unacceptable.* The note omits the policy number. In addition, the underwriter's comments about Ms. Janacek's "being rude and impatient" are irrelevant and do not demonstrate a positive customer service attitude. In addition, the comment "as usual" might be interpreted to imply a bias against this applicant.

Note 3 Explanation. *Acceptable.* The notation contains all necessary information, including the telephone number, and is objective and clear.

The documentation in a case file could be critical if the underwriter is ever called to provide testimony about a specific underwriting decision because the underwriter needs a solid, objective basis for the underwriting decision. Furthermore, months or years may have passed between the time the underwriting decision was made and the time of a hearing or trial. In such a situation, the underwriter may not remember all the details associated with a case; therefore, accurate documentation is crucial.

Antidiscrimination Statutes

An underwriter's responsibility is to distinguish—that is, to discriminate fairly—among risks that are acceptable and risks that are unacceptable by carefully examining the facts about proposed insureds and classifying the risks into appropriate, equitable risk classes.

Discrimination among risks is usually legal when it is based upon (1) recognized actuarial principles or (2) actual or reasonably anticipated experience. Antidiscrimination policies and laws restrict or prohibit insurance discrimination based on certain factors, such as specific physical or mental impairments, marital status, and sexual orientation. In this section, we'll look briefly at five risk factors specifically mentioned in U.S. antidiscrimination laws, and then we'll discuss Canadian antidiscrimination laws.

Sex

Most states and provinces have passed laws based on the Model Regulation to Eliminate Unfair Sex Discrimination, which was adopted by the National Association of Insurance Commissioners (NAIC). These laws prohibit the restriction or denial of coverage solely on the basis of whether a person is female or male. However, most states and provinces allow insurers to use sex-based actuarial tables.

> **FAST FACT**
>
> In the United States in 1997, 38% of life insurance policies were purchased by adult women; 45% of life insurance policies were purchased by adult men.[1]

In addition, most states have adopted the NAIC's model regulation permitting insurers to use sex-blended or unisex mortality or morbidity tables that merge risk-related information from both males and females to produce figures that can be applied to both sexes equally. However, many insurers oppose the use of unisex tables because statistical and actuarial data clearly show that women as a group live longer than men. Insurers contend that different premium rates based on sex allow insurance costs to reflect risks more accurately.

Physical and Mental Impairments

U.S. state laws based on the Model Regulation on Unfair Discrimination in Life and Health Insurance on the Basis of Physical or Mental Impairment and the Model Regulation to Prohibit Unfair Discrimination on the Basis of Blindness or Partial Blindness prohibit insurers from discriminating against people solely on the basis of physical impairments—including total or partial blindness and deafness—or mental impairments.

Typically, these laws specifically prohibit insurers from (1) limiting or refusing insurance coverage or (2) charging different premium rates based solely on a physical or mental impairment or blindness, unless such action is based either on recognized actuarial principles or on actual or reasonably anticipated experience. In addition, a number of states have passed laws making discrimination in underwriting against people solely on the basis of deafness or other hearing impairments illegal.

Marital Status

Many state laws prohibit discrimination solely on the basis of an applicant's marital status. One exception to this general rule is in family coverage policies, which cover all family members under one contract. These laws generally allow an insurer to decline an application for family coverage on cohabiting single people. Some insurers, however, do offer coverage to cohabiting single people who have children and a clear insurable interest in each other. Recent legislation in some states prohibits an insurer from declining coverage for an applicant who is a partner in a civil union.

Subjects of Abuse

Many states prohibit insurers from discriminating against applicants—including spouses and children—who are subjects of abuse. According to many of these laws, life and health insurers cannot (1) decline, restrict, or refuse to renew insurance coverage or (2) charge an additional premium solely on the basis of the proposed insured's status as a subject of abuse. In addition, life insurers cannot request information about acts of abuse or abuse status—that is, whether a person is or has been abused. Moreover, life insurers cannot make use of such information, however it was obtained, when they assess the risk represented by a proposed insured.

Under such laws, an underwriter cannot treat abuse status as a medical condition or an underwriting consideration. If an underwriter makes an unfavorable underwriting decision that affects an abused person, the underwriter must be able to demonstrate that the action is based on sound actuarial principles and is the same decision that would have been made if the applicant were not a subject of abuse. For example, the underwriter can underwrite using a permanent injury as a factor, even if an abuser caused that injury.

In addition, these laws permit underwriters to decline an application for coverage on the life of an abused person if the proposed policyowner is known to have abused the proposed insured or if the proposed insured has an objection to the issuance of the policy on the grounds that the policy would benefit the abuser.

Sexual Orientation

Most states have enacted regulations prohibiting underwriters from discriminating against an applicant based solely on the applicant's sexual orientation. Such regulations mean that, if an applicant is known to be homosexual, the insurer cannot deny coverage, charge a higher premium, or require any medical test solely on the basis of the applicant's sexual orientation. Many states prohibit underwriters from using sexual orientation to influence underwriting decisions and from basing underwriting requirements on a person's actual or perceived sexual orientation, including making inferences based on a person's stated occupation, area of residence, or choice of beneficiary.

Canadian Antidiscrimination Statutes

Underwriters in Canada generally may not discriminate among life and health insurance applicants on the basis of whether a person is male or female. Provincial regulation for most other types of discrimination varies. Because of this disparity in regulations, an underwriter handling business subject to Canadian laws usually needs to know about relevant laws in all Canadian jurisdictions in which his company does business. Some provinces specifically prohibit discrimination on the basis of physical and mental impairments, marital status, and sexual orientation.

Privacy and Confidentiality Laws

To conduct business, insurers need to acquire and store a great deal of personal information about their customers. Such personal information can include facts about a person's health and medical history, financial situation, credit history, and occupation or avocations. To protect the privacy of customers and the confidentiality of personal information, most jurisdictions have established extensive laws regulating the use and disclosure of that information. Insurance underwriting is subject to these laws. In this section, we will look at federal privacy laws in both the United States and Canada. Although privacy laws enacted at the state and provincial level vary from one jurisdiction to another, most such laws are patterned on model laws and guidelines proposed by the NAIC in the United States and by the Canadian Life and Health Insurance Association (CLHIA) in Canada.

U.S. Privacy Guidelines and Laws

Countries around the world have attempted to establish ways to prevent personal information from being misused. Internationally, the Organization for Economic Cooperation and Development (OECD) in 1980 developed guidelines to protect the privacy of personal information that flows between countries. European members of OECD and the United States and Canada endorsed these guidelines, and the CLHIA incorporated the guidelines into its "Right-to-Privacy Guidelines." CLHIA's guidelines are presented in Insight 3-2.

Insight 3-2. CLHIA's "Right-to-Privacy Guidelines."

In providing life and health insurance to Canadians, insurance companies require significant amounts of detailed information about individuals. This information, much of which can be regarded as "personal," is required both for risk evaluation and for claim adjudication under both individual and group contracts. Indeed, it could be said that personal information is the principal raw material for the life and health insurance process.

In recognition of this fact, and of the potentially sensitive nature of such information, insurance companies must adhere closely to strict rules governing the protection of the confidential information they hold.

These Guidelines set a minimum standard. Insurance companies may adopt these Guidelines or may develop their own guidelines, which are at least as protective as these minimum standards.

1. Scope and Purpose of Guidelines

These Guidelines apply to the collection, verification, possession, protection, use, and disclosure of personal information acquired by a life and health insurance company in the course of its Canadian operations.

2. Definitions

"Company" means a life and health insurance company and includes its life and health insurance subsidiaries and benefit-plan-administration subsidiaries.

"Personal information" means any information relating to an identified or identifiable individual, including, but not limited to, health and financial information.

3. Collection Limitation

Only lawful means will be used to collect personal information. To the extent appropriate

(a) Such personal information will be obtained directly from the individual

(b) Prior to collecting such information from any other source, the individual concerned will be notified or his/her written authorization obtained

Parts (a) and (b) of this section do not apply to information supplied to the company by a group plan sponsor for the purpose of risk evaluation, administering a group plan, or claim adjudication.

4. Data Quality

Every reasonable effort will be made to ensure that personal information obtained by the company is

(a) Pertinent to the effective conduct of the company's business

(a) As accurate and complete as possible, consistent with the purpose(s) for which it was obtained

5. Purpose Specification

The purpose(s) for which personal information is collected from an individual will be specified on or before the collection of information, and any change of purpose will be communicated to the individual.

6. Use and Disclosure

Personal information will not be disclosed or used for purposes other than those specified to the individual in accordance with Section #5, except

(a) With the consent of the individual concerned; or

(b) Where required by law; or

(c) Where reasonably necessary, to determine eligibility for an insurance benefit or to protect the interests of the company against criminal activity, fraud, and material misrepresentation in connection with an insurance contract; or

(d) In the discharge of public duty

7. Individual Access to Information

Each company will adopt a general policy of openness about the company's practices and policies with respect to the use and protection of personal information. In particular

(a) Upon appropriate identification and written request satisfactory to the company, an individual will be advised of personal information about him/her retained in the company's records. A company may charge a reasonable administration fee to supply the information. Some medical information may be made available only through the individual's designated physician.

(b) Where information cannot be disclosed to the individual, he/she will be given the reasons for not disclosing information.

(c) An individual may clarify or correct erroneous personal information retained by the company. Incorrect or incomplete information will be amended, and differences as to the correctness of the information will be noted.

8. Compliance and Complaint Resolution

In order to ensure compliance with the protection of privacy guidelines, each company will

(a) Designate an officer to receive complaints

(b) Establish procedures for receiving and resolving complaints

Individuals dissatisfied with the complaint resolution of a company can contact the office of the insurance regulators in their province.

9. Security Safeguards

Personal information will be considered confidential, and comprehensive safeguards will be established by the company to protect that confidentiality.

A company will take the necessary measures to ensure that all employees of the company are required to conform to the company's applicable privacy guidelines.

All agents, brokers, plan sponsors, and other persons or organizations acting for or on the behalf of the company will be required to comply with the guidelines.

Source: Canadian Life and Health Insurance Association. Reprinted with permission.

In the United States, a federal regulation—the Fair Credit Reporting Act (FCRA)—helps ensure the privacy and confidentiality of personal information, including insurance records.

The Fair Credit Reporting Act

The 1970 ***Fair Credit Reporting Act (FCRA)*** helps ensure that credit reporting agencies act fairly, impartially, and with respect for the consumer's right to privacy when preparing reports on individuals. Under the FCRA, only individuals are considered to be consumers; corporations and other types of businesses are not protected by this act.

The FCRA affects underwriting when, in assessing the risk represented by a proposed insured, the underwriter obtains a report from a consumer reporting agency. A ***consumer reporting agency*** is a person or an organization that regularly prepares consumer reports and furnishes them, either for profit or on a cooperative, nonprofit basis, to other people or organizations. According to the FCRA, underwriters must follow specific procedures when obtaining consumer reports and investigative consumer reports.

A ***consumer report*** is a communication from a consumer reporting agency that contains information relating to a person's creditworthiness, credit standing, or credit capacity, as well as information about the person's general reputation or personal characteristics.

An ***investigative consumer report*** is a type of consumer report that includes information gathered during interviews with people such as friends, neighbors, business associates, and others who are associated with or who have knowledge of the consumer. An inspection report, which we will discuss in Chapter 5, is a type of investigative consumer report.

The FCRA requires underwriters who use the reports generated by consumer reporting agencies to notify applicants that such a report may be used in connection with underwriting.

An insurer uses a ***pre-notice*** to disclose clearly and adequately to an applicant that an investigative consumer report may be made. The insurer must use the term *investigative consumer report* in its disclosure. Such disclosure must (1) be in writing, (2) be mailed or otherwise delivered to the proposed insured no later than three days after the date on which the report was first requested, and (3) include a statement informing the proposed insured of her right to obtain a disclosure of the nature and scope of the investigation requested. Figure 3-3 provides an example of a pre-notice typically included in an application for insurance.

In certain circumstances, insurers must also provide two other types of notice. A ***supplementary notice*** must be sent within five days of a consumer's request for information about the nature and scope of the

FIGURE 3-3. Pre-Notice Typically Included in an Application for Insurance.

The Federal Fair Credit Reporting Act requires that you be given a copy of this notice.

This is to inform you that as part of our procedure for handling your insurance application, an investigative consumer report may be prepared whereby information is obtained through personal interviews with your neighbors, friends, or others with whom you are acquainted. This inquiry includes information as to your character, general reputation, and personal characteristics. You have the right to make a written request within a reasonable period of time to receive additional, detailed information about the nature and scope of this investigation.

Source: Excerpted from Barbara Foxenberger Brown and Jane Lightcap Brown, *Life and Health Insurance Underwriting* (Atlanta: LOMA, © 1998), 59. Used with permission; all rights reserved.

investigation specified in the pre-notice. Also, a ***post-notice*** must be sent to an applicant if an underwriter denies an application or rates a policy based wholly or partially on information contained in a report from a consumer reporting agency. The post-notice must (1) inform the proposed insured of the adverse decision and (2) supply the name and address of the consumer reporting agency that made the report so that the applicant may obtain a copy of the report and correct any erroneous information. The post-notice does not include details contained in the report from the consumer reporting agency.

The FCRA states that a consumer report regarding an applicant who has applied for less than $150,000 of insurance cannot contain certain adverse information that predates the report by a specified period (usually 7 to 10 years). The excluded information includes comments about bankruptcies, suits and judgments, tax liens, and arrest and conviction records. These types of information, however, may be included in a consumer report if the policy applied for has a face amount of $150,000 or more.

Canadian Privacy Guidelines and Laws

Canadian underwriters follow many of the same practices as U.S. underwriters when dealing with personal and confidential information. The CLHIA's member companies have agreed to follow the association's "Right-to-Privacy Guidelines" (see Insight 3-2) to ensure privacy and to protect the confidentiality of their customers' personal information. The guidelines instruct underwriters to

- Obtain personal information only from the individual concerned whenever practicable
- Obtain the individual's authorization before collecting personal information from any source other than the individual concerned
- Refrain from using misleading practices or a ***pretext interview***, which is an information-gathering interview conducted by a person misrepresenting himself as someone other than who he really is

State and Provincial Privacy Protection

Many states have enacted privacy laws based on the NAIC Insurance Information and Privacy Protection Act, better known as the Model Privacy Act. The ***NAIC Model Privacy Act*** is a model law that establishes standards for the collection, use, and disclosure of information gathered in connection with insurance transactions by insurance institutions, agents, and insurance-support organizations. A state law patterned on the model act protects only people who are residents of that state and who are applying for personal insurance. The NAIC Model Privacy Act does not protect people who are applying for insurance for business purposes or corporations.

The NAIC Model Privacy Act has the following stated purposes:

1. To minimize intrusions on individuals' privacy
2. To establish a mechanism that allows people to determine what information about them relevant to insurance transactions is currently being collected or has already been collected
3. To enable such people to have access to information collected in order to verify or dispute its accuracy
4. To limit the disclosure of collected information
5. To enable applicants and policyowners to obtain a justification for adverse underwriting decisions

To achieve these purposes, the NAIC Model Privacy Act stipulates a number of procedures that insurers must follow when a person applies for coverage, whether that coverage is a new policy or a renewal or an expansion of existing coverage. The act also specifies enforcement procedures and prohibits insurers or agents from conducting pretext interviews.

In addition to understanding state privacy laws modeled after the NAIC Model Privacy Act, underwriters stay informed about other state and provincial laws affecting the collection and use of personal information. Many jurisdictions have enacted statutes that protect medical records and tax returns.

Even in jurisdictions that have not enacted privacy legislation, many insurers voluntarily observe the following practices for protecting the privacy of their customers:

1. Safeguarding the confidentiality of records
2. Conducting periodic evaluations of recordkeeping practices
3. Allowing applicants access to information obtained during a background check
4. Reviewing the operating practices of consumer reporting agencies

Underwriters—and other financial services employees—should know to whom medical information may be released. Figure 3-4 lists the people or entities to whom various state and provincial laws either *mandate* or *allow* insurers to release medical information.

Not all states and provinces mandate or allow all of the people listed in Figure 3-4 to receive medical information. State and provincial laws vary considerably, but the overriding principle governing the release of medical information is that only people with a legitimate business need-to-know or some other legitimate need-to-know—such as the proposed insured himself or his physician or guardian—should receive the information. Underwriters, therefore, must know what is allowed or mandated in each state or province in which their companies conduct business.

FIGURE 3-4. People and Entities Authorized to Receive Medical Information.

- ✓ The proposed insured
- ✓ The proposed insured's physician
- ✓ Another health care provider designated by the proposed insured
- ✓ MIB, Inc. (which we will discuss in Chapter 4)
- ✓ A reinsurer
- ✓ Certain employees of the insurer
- ✓ A legal guardian of the proposed insured
- ✓ A person authorized by the proposed insured to receive such information
- ✓ A law enforcement official
- ✓ A state department of health
- ✓ The insurer's legal counsel

AIDS and Genetic Testing

Insurers have struggled with how best to respond to the public concern over confidentiality of medical records containing the results of genetic testing or information on such diseases as acquired immune deficiency syndrome (AIDS). For example, insurers must determine to whom they may release test results indicating the presence of human immunodeficiency virus (HIV) and what procedures insurers must follow to inform an applicant that his blood tests indicate the presence of HIV.

Insurers treat information about AIDS with the same level of confidentiality with which they have treated all medical information. In short, following the laws of relevant jurisdictions, insurers generally do not release such personal information without permission from the HIV-positive person. Many states have adopted the NAIC Guideline for Notice and Consent Form Model Act. This act provides a sample notice and consent form to be used as a guide by insurers in states that allow HIV testing and requires insurers to inform applicants when their blood would be tested for AIDS and to obtain their consent to the test. Figure 3-5 presents this sample notice and consent form.

Insurers are also monitoring developments in the complicated and controversial area of genetic testing. Genetic testing can indicate a person's predisposition to a certain illness or disease. Specifically, insurers are responsible for protecting confidential information revealed by genetic tests.

> **FAST FACT**
>
> A Time/CNN poll found that 75% of 1,218 Americans surveyed did not want insurance companies to know their genetic code, and 84% wanted that information withheld from the government.[2]

Some states have passed laws that restrict the use of genetic-test results by life insurance companies. Although they vary, most such laws prohibit life insurers from considering genetic conditions in determining policy rates and terms, *unless* claim experience or actuarial projections establish that substantial differences in claims are likely to result from the genetic condition.

If a proposed insured for insurance does have a disease caused by a genetic trait, that disease ordinarily can legally be taken into account during underwriting. For instance, an underwriter may not rate or deny coverage solely on the basis that the proposed insured possesses a gene associated with diabetes, but may rate or deny coverage if the proposed insured also exhibits evidence of diabetes.

Replacement Regulations

Surrendering an insurance policy or part of the coverage of an insurance policy in order to buy another policy is known as ***replacement.*** Policy replacements are subject to regulation. Although replacement of an existing life insurance policy is not illegal, the replacement may not be in a policyowner's best interest. Insurers typically establish programs

FIGURE 3-5. NAIC Guideline for Notice and Consent Form Model Act.

Although the NAIC has not taken a position on testing to determine the presence of antibodies or antigens to the HIV virus, for those states that allow testing and that require notice and consent, the following form may be used as a guideline.

To evaluate your eligibility for insurance coverage, it is requested that you consent to be tested to determine the presence of antibodies or antigens to the Human Immunodeficiency Virus (HIV). By signing and dating this form, you agree that these tests may be performed and that underwriting decisions will be based on the test results.

Pre-Testing Consideration: Many public health organizations have recommended that before taking an AIDS virus (HIV) antibody/antigen test a person seek counseling to become informed concerning the implications of such tests. You may wish to consider counseling, at your expense, prior to being tested.

Disclosure of Test Results: All test results will be treated confidentially. The results of the tests will be reported to the insurer identified on this form. Results of the tests will not otherwise be disclosed except as required or allowed by law.

Meaning of Positive Test Results: While positive HIV antibody test results do not mean that you have AIDS, they do mean that you are at increased risk of developing AIDS or AIDS-related conditions. The tests are tests for antibodies to the HIV virus, the causative agent for AIDS, and show whether you have been exposed to the virus. Positive HIV antibody/antigen test results will adversely affect your application for insurance. This means that your application will probably be declined.

Consent: I have read and I understand this Notice and Consent Form. I voluntarily consent to testing and disclosure as described above. I understand that I have the right to request and receive a copy of this form. A photocopy of this form will be as valid as the original.

The results of these tests will be released to: ______________________________

DATE ______________________ ______________________________

Signature of Proposed Insured or Parent/Guardian

Source: Excerpted from NAIC, *Guideline for Notice and Consent Form*, 1996. Reprinted with permission from the National Association of Insurance Commissioners.

for agency training and home office education to help ensure that a replacement is carried out ethically and legally, with full disclosure to policyowners.

An agent must clearly inform the policyowner of the difference between the two policies and the financial consequences of the replacement. To help prevent unethical replacement, most states have adopted some version of the NAIC's Replacement of Life Insurance and Annuities Model Regulation, which states that replacement of policies is generally permissible if the replacing insurer provides full and fair disclosure and no deceptive practices are involved. State replacement regulations usually do not govern certain types of policies, including term policies, group policies, conversion policies, and temporary policies issued under a premium receipt.

If the application for insurance indicates that the policy requested will replace existing coverage, the replacing insurer—and, thus, the underwriter in many instances—has a number of significant duties to perform. Depending on the jurisdiction involved, these duties can include

- Requiring that the agent prepare, either with or as a part of each application, a list identifying to the best of her knowledge all existing life insurance policies proposed to be replaced.
- Obtaining a copy of the "Notice to Applicants Regarding Replacement of Life Insurance" provided to the applicant. The replacing insurer keeps these forms on file for at least three years or until the state insurance department concludes its next regular examination of the insurer, whichever is later.
- Immediately notifying an insurer whose policy is being replaced and furnishing that insurer with a copy of a policy summary.

Premium Receipts

Underwriting some coverages, especially for large amounts or for proposed insureds with complicated medical histories, can take many weeks or even months. If the applicant has submitted the initial premium with the application, many insurers provide temporary life insurance coverage on the proposed insured if certain conditions are met. A ***premium receipt*** is a written acknowledgment that an insurer has received the initial premium submitted with an application for insurance.

One type of premium receipt is a ***conditional premium receipt***, which makes the applied-for insurance coverage effective from the date of the application, provided that the underwriter ultimately finds the proposed insured to be an insurable risk. An example would be an applicant for insurance on his own life who is issued a conditional premium receipt and then dies in a boating accident before the underwriting decision has been made on his application. The applicant's death will be covered under the applied-for coverage *if* the underwriter determines that on the date of the application the applicant was an insurable risk. If the underwriter finds that the applicant was not an insurable risk on the date of his application, his death will *not* be covered.

Some courts have rendered the intent of conditional premium receipts meaningless, interpreting them as providing unconditional, immediate coverage regardless of the intention of the company or the wording of the receipt. This interpretation, called the ***interim insurance law,*** generally holds that, if the agent has accepted payment, the proposed insured is covered until the insurer notifies the proposed insured that coverage has been terminated and returns the premium.

Because of the interim insurance law, conditional premium receipts often do not protect the insurer from temporarily assuming undesirable risks. Under the interim insurance law, even if the applicant is found to be uninsurable and would not have been granted coverage under a policy, the insurer may be liable for the full policy benefit amount if an applicant who paid the initial premium and received a conditional premium receipt dies before being notified of the rejection or before the initial premium has been refunded.

Many insurance companies have responded to the interim insurance law by issuing temporary insurance agreements. A ***temporary insurance agreement (TIA)***, also known as a *binding premium receipt*, provides insurance coverage of a specified amount for a specified time, usually for the time required to underwrite the case. The TIA also specifies that coverage under the TIA will end on the earliest of (1) the date the insurer returns the premium; (2) a specified number of days after the insurer mails a notice of termination to the premium notice address on the application; or (3) the date coverage begins under the issued policy. Coverage under the TIA does not depend on the proposed insured's insurability. However, this kind of receipt typically lists conditions under which the receipt provides no coverage, such as (1) material misrepresentation in the answers to the questions in the receipt or (2) death of the proposed insured from suicide or an intentionally self-inflicted injury. Figure 3-6 contains a typical TIA.

A TIA is a contract between an insurer and an applicant, but is not a part of the insurance policy. A TIA temporarily binds the insurer to the risk regardless of whether the insurer ultimately issues a policy to the applicant.

Statutory Requirements for Group Insurance

In the United States and Canada, group insurance is regulated by many of the same laws that regulate individual insurance. In addition, group insurance in the United States is regulated by legislation modeled on several NAIC model acts and in Canada is guided by Canadian Council of Insurance Regulators (CCIR) guidelines.

FIGURE 3-6. Temporary Insurance Agreement.

TEMPORARY INSURANCE AGREEMENT HEALTH QUESTIONS

If you qualify, do you wish to have temporary insurance on the life of the proposed life insured(s) before delivery of the policy being applied for by this application? ❐ Yes ❐ No

It is understood that any temporary insurance will be subject to the conditions of the temporary insurance receipt attached to this application including the maximum amount of $250,000. To qualify for this temporary insurance, you must (a) be able to answer "NO" to both parts of question 1) below; (b) be able to answer "NO" to question 2) below for any child (children) proposed for insurance; and (c) meet the requirements, including payment of the first premium, of the temporary insurance receipt below. Question 2) must be answered only if a child(ren) is/are proposed for insurance.

1) To the best of your knowledge and belief, have you:
   a) within the last four months, been admitted or been advised to be admitted to a hospital or other medical facility other than for childbirth? ❐ Yes ❐ No
   b) within the last two years, consulted a physician for, or had treatment for heart trouble, stroke, AIDS or cancer; or had an electrocardiogram for chest pain or for other physical complaint? ❐ Yes ❐ No
2) To the best of your knowledge and belief, does any child proposed for insurance have any congenital or current medical problem(s) not covered in question 1) b)? ❐ Yes ❐ No

The ABC Insurance Company acknowledges the receipt of $______________, which is to be applied in payment of the first premium for insurance on the lives of the proposed life insured(s) in the application having the same number as this receipt. The full names of the proposed life insured(s) are as follows:

Dated this ____ day of ____________, 20____, ________________________, Agent's Signature.

This receipt is not VALID to provide insurance coverage unless the requirements set out below are fulfilled. If the requirements set out below are fulfilled, the insurance coverage is subject to the conditions stated below.

The requirements necessary to render this receipt valid to provide insurance coverage are as follows:

1) Payment of the money must be made on or prior to the date of completion of the application. 2) The amount paid must be at least equal to a monthly premium for the policy applied for. 3) Any check, draft, money order, other instrument tendered in payment must be paid according to its tenor. 4) Questions 1)a), 1)b) and 2) (if applicable) of the temporary insurance agreement must have been answered "NO."

NO AGENT HAS AUTHORITY TO MODIFY OR WAIVE THESE REQUIREMENTS, OR THE CONDITIONS OF COVERAGE SET OUT BELOW.

TEMPORARY INSURANCE

The ABC Insurance Company agrees to insure the proposed life insured(s), based upon representations of health in the application, including the representations in the form of negative answers to questions 1)a), 1)b) and 2) (if applicable) of the temporary insurance agreement health questions section, subject to the following conditions:

1. Insurance restricted to death resulting from accidental bodily injury shall commence on the date of this receipt, but, unless previously replaced by insurance not so restricted, shall expire in 30 days.
2. Insurance not restricted to death resulting from accidental bodily injury shall commence on the date of completion of ABC's published initial underwriting requirements for the insurance applied for, consisting of the application including all medical examinations that may be required.
3. Insurance provided under this receipt shall be governed by the standard policy terms and exclusions, including exclusions relating to suicide, which would have been applicable had the policy applied for been in effect on the date of death of the proposed life insured(s).
4. Subject to a maximum aggregate liability of $250,000 under this and all other temporary insurance receipts in force at the death of the proposed life insured(s), the maximum amount payable under this receipt shall be the lesser of: (a) the amount applied for; and (b) $250,000. In applying the maximum aggregate liability limit, amounts payable as between this and other temporary insurance receipts shall be prorated.
5. Insurance hereunder which has not previously expired or terminated shall terminate on the earliest of (a) tender of a policy by ABC, whether such policy is accepted or rejected by the applicant; (b) notice by ABC terminating the insurance (if notice is sent by mail, it will be deemed to have been received by the applicant on the second day following mailing); (c) the 90th day following the date of this receipt.

   Upon termination of insurance hereunder, the applicant shall be entitled to refund of the money acknowledged by this receipt, except where the applicant has accepted a policy. However, termination of insurance shall take place notwithstanding that such refund has not yet been received by the applicant.

Source: Excerpted from Barbara Foxenberger Brown and Jane Lightcap Brown, *Life and Health Insurance Underwriting* (Atlanta: LOMA,

Requirements in the United States

In the United States, state laws specify

1. The nature of groups that are eligible for group insurance
2. Certain provisions that must be included in group contracts
3. Limitations on benefits that can be provided under group coverage
4. The types and level of taxes that may be levied on out-of-state insurers licensed to do business within a state

In assessing the risk represented by a group that includes people who work in different states, the underwriter considers the laws that are applicable to each state. Such an analysis of the group's risk can become complicated, particularly if the group members in one state are affected by laws that are significantly different from the laws affecting group members in another state. Underwriters processing such cases, therefore, receive timely updates as the laws are changed.

In the United States, employee benefits have been regulated by federal law for many years. More recent federal legislation now regulates *all* group insurance plans. One federal law is the ***Employee Retirement Income Security Act of 1974 (ERISA)*** that establishes (1) the rights of participants in pension plans, (2) standards for investing pension plan assets, and (3) requirements for disclosing plan provisions and funding. ERISA does not establish requirements that directly affect underwriting, but does require groups to file certain documents that underwriters can use in assessing the risk for group coverage. In Chapter 8, we will discuss documents filed under ERISA that underwriters use as an information source.

Certain elements of group insurance coverage are also regulated by U.S. federal laws, the most important of which include the Age Discrimination in Employment Act (ADEA), Title VII of the Civil Rights Act, Family and Medical Leave Act (FMLA), ERISA, Health Maintenance Organization (HMO) Act of 1973, Consolidated Omnibus Budget Reconciliation Act (COBRA), and the Health Insurance Portability and Accountability Act (HIPAA). Figure 3-7 summarizes key information about each of these laws.

Two NAIC model acts contain standard contract provisions for group life and health insurance policies. These acts are the (1) Group Life Insurance Definition and Group Life Insurance Standard Provisions Model Act (known as the Group Life Insurance Model Act) and (2) Group Health Insurance Definition and Group Health Insurance Standard Provisions Model Act (known as the Group Health

FIGURE 3-7. Some U.S. Federal Laws That Regulate Health Care Coverage.

Legislative Act	Who Must Comply	Protected Class	Effect of Legislation on Health Care
ADEA	Employers that have 20 or more employees	Employees age 40 and over	All active employees, regardless of age, must be eligible for the same health care coverages, and older employees cannot be required to pay more for that coverage than younger employees pay.
Title VII of the Civil Rights Act	Employers that have 15 or more employees and that are engaged in interstate commerce	All employees	Pregnancy Discrimination Act (an amendment to the Civil Rights Act) requires group health plans sponsored by employers subject to the act to provide coverage for pregnancy, childbirth, and related medical conditions on the same basis as they provide coverage for other medical conditions.
Family and Medical Leave Act workers	Employers that have 50 or more employees	Employees, upon the birth or adoption of a child, or who need to provide care for a seriously ill family member, or who are ill themselves	Workers must be allowed to take up to 12 weeks of unpaid leave during any 12-month period for qualifying events. Employers are required to continue to make group health benefits available to while they are on leave.
ERISA	Employers that sponsor welfare benefit plans to provide benefits listed in the act (medical, surgical, hospital, disability death, unemployment benefits, etc.)	Employees covered under welfare benefit plans	ERISA requires group health care plans have a written plan document, to have a summary plan description, and to file an annual report with the IRS, and establishes standards of conduct for plan fiduciaries.

Figure 3-7. Some U.S. Federal Laws That Regulate Health Care Coverage (continued).

COBRA	Employers that have 20 or more employees	Employees and certain dependents whose health care coverage is lost due to a qualifying event	COBRA requires that certain persons whose group health coverage would otherwise terminate be allowed to continue group coverage at their own expense for a stated period of time following a qualifying event.
HMO Act of 1973	Federally qualified HMOs and employers that have 25 or more employees and that make contributions to an employee health care plan	*Not applicable*	The HMO Act encouraged the establishment and development of HMOs by providing grants and low-interest loans to start up HMOs that met federal qualification requirements; created requirements for federal qualification; requires employers in certain situations to provide employees with the option of participating in either a federally qualified HMO or the employer's group health plan.
HIPAA	Employer-sponsored group medical expense insurance plans and insurers that issue individual medical expense insurance coverage	*Not applicable*	Individuals who own medical expense coverage generally have the right to renew that coverage by paying premiums as they come due. Specified individuals are guaranteed the right to purchase individual medical expense coverage. By limiting the pre-existing condition exclusion that group medical expense plans may include, HIPAA increased the portability of medical care coverages.

Source: Excerpted from Harriett E. Jones and Dani L. Long, *Principles of Insurance: Life, Health, and Annuities,* 2nd ed. (Atlanta: LOMA, © 1999), 425. Used with permission; all rights reserved.

Insurance Model Act). The standard provisions contained in these model acts relate to

- Incontestability
- Grace period
- Evidence of insurability
- Application being made a part of the policy contract
- Misstatement of age
- Required issue of a certificate to every insured person

In addition, the Group Life Insurance Model Act states that a group life insurance contract must make provision for conversion rights (including payment of proceeds during a conversion period), naming a beneficiary, and continued coverage during disability. The Group Health Insurance Model Act states that a group health insurance contract must provide for the insurer to receive notice of a claim within a reasonable period after the claim was incurred.

Requirements in Canada

In Canada, group insurance plans generally are regulated by the provinces. Most provinces have enacted an ***Insurance Act***, which is a general statute that contains most of a province's insurance laws and that regulates the conduct of insurers and agents within the province.

In the common-law jurisdictions of Canada, the model ***Uniform Life Insurance Act*** is legislation that governs both group and individual life insurance contracts, while the model ***Uniform Accident and Sickness Insurance Act*** is legislation that governs both group and individual health insurance contracts. These acts have been developed by the Canadian Council of Insurance Regulators (CCIR), a voluntary organization of the provincial Superintendents of Insurance that recommends guidelines for insurance practices.

Similarly, the ***Quebec Civil Code*** is a regulation that governs all life and health insurance contracts in Quebec and specifies what provisions must be included in insurance contracts. The required provisions vary according to whether the contract (1) provides life or health insurance and (2) is issued to a group policyholder or an individual insured. To ensure that group contracts fulfill the requirements of these acts and codes, group underwriters are knowledgeable about the provisions of each act.

In addition to these provincial laws, several aspects of group insurance are governed by the CCIR's Guidelines Governing Group Life Insurance (Group Life Guidelines) and the Guidelines Governing Group Accident and Sickness Insurance (Group A&S Guidelines). Quebec has insurance regulations similar to the Group Life and Group A&S Guidelines. Unlike regulations such as the Uniform Life Insurance Act, the CCIR guidelines do not have the force of law. However, most Canadian group insurance policies conform to these guidelines.

The Group Life Guidelines specify what kinds of groups are eligible for group coverage and require that insurance contracts contain provisions relating to group policy termination and conversion. The Group A&S Guidelines specify what kinds of groups can receive group health coverage and what kind of information must be included in the certificate issued to each group insured.

Canadian residents receive some insurance benefits through government-mandated insurance programs. For instance, the federal ***Canada Health Act*** is legislation that requires that each Canadian province provide its residents with health care coverage for hospital and medical services. Insurance companies offer group life, health, and disability income benefits that supplement these government insurance programs.

For health care coverage, Canadian provinces require that, if a certain medical service or treatment is covered under the provincial health care plan, then private insurance plans *cannot* offer benefits for that service or treatment. For instance, if a provincial health care plan provided coverage for inpatient hospital services such as radiological procedures, an insurer could not offer coverage for those procedures under a private health care plan. To know what supplemental benefits can be offered to prospective groups, underwriters become familiar with the provisions of provincial health care plans.

In addition to receiving provincial health care benefits, all Canadian employees are eligible for benefits through the ***Canada Pension Plan***, a federal insurance plan that provides disability income benefits and survivor benefits (life insurance) to Canadian employees, including those who are self-employed. The Canada Pension Plan is funded through mandatory contributions from employees and employers. The ***Quebec Pension Plan*** is a provincial plan that provides similar benefits to employees in Quebec.

In Canada, most group disability income benefit and life insurance plans are issued to employer-employee groups as supplemental coverage to the benefits provided by the Canada Pension Plan or the Quebec Pension Plan. It's important, therefore, for group underwriters in Canada to not only be familiar with the provisions of the Canada Pension Plan, but also to have a working knowledge of provincial and federal employment standards legislation. ***Employment standards legislation*** mandates certain employment standards relating to such issues as minimum wage rates, overtime pay, and maximum hours of work. Provincial legislation regulates standards for most employees, whereas federal legislation regulates standards for employees of businesses that operate between provinces, such as railways, highway transport, and telephone and cable systems.

Benefits provided by private group insurance plans must comply with the employment standards applicable to a group's province or type of occupation. Group underwriters consider these standards when evaluating a group's requested coverage. For example, when evaluating a group case in which an employer wishes to forego providing certain benefits to its employees, an underwriter needs to know if the employment standards regulating that employer permit such benefits to be excluded. Employment standards can affect the type of coverage offered by group plans in certain provinces; therefore, group underwriters are familiar with these standards.

Key Terms and Concepts

misrepresentation
fraud
rescission
material misrepresentation
underwriting worksheet
Fair Credit Reporting Act (FCRA)
consumer reporting agency
consumer report
investigative consumer report
pre-notice
supplementary notice
post-notice
pretext interview
NAIC Model Privacy Act
replacement
premium receipt
conditional premium receipt
interim insurance law
temporary insurance agreement (TIA)
Employee Retirement Income Security Act of 1974 (ERISA)
Insurance Act
Uniform Life Insurance Act
Uniform Accident and Sickness Insurance Act
Quebec Civil Code
Canada Health Act
Canada Pension Plan
Quebec Pension Plan
employment standards legislation

Endnotes

1. ACLI, *Life Insurers Fact Book 2000* (Washington, D.C.: American Council of Life Insurers, 2000), 12.

2. Paul Recer, "Gene Map Creates New Frontier for Discrimination, Experts Say," 12 February 2001, http://wire.ap.org (19 July 2001).

CHAPTER 4

Underwriting Individual Life Insurance

Chapter Outline

The Application for Individual Life Insurance
- The Field Underwriting Manual
- Part I and Part II of the Application

Sources of Medical Information
- MIB, Inc.
- Requests to Physicians
- Laboratory Tests

Assessing Medical Factors
- The Numerical Rating System
- The Table Rating Method
- The Flat Extra Premium Method
- Combining Methods
- Underwriting Manual

Assessing Age and Build

Objectives

After reading this chapter, you should be able to

- Describe the typical information presented in a field underwriting manual
- List the types of insurability information contained in Part I and Part II of an application for insurance
- List and describe medical factors for underwriting individual life insurance
- Describe the sources of information for medical factors used in underwriting individual life insurance
- Discuss the ways underwriters assess medical factors in underwriting individual life insurance

In this chapter, we will study individual life insurance underwriting. We will explain the agent's field underwriting manual and will discuss features of the insurance application. We'll explain how the underwriter evaluates the application, along with various kinds of medical information about an applicant's insurability. We'll conclude the chapter by discussing the approaches an underwriter uses to assess medical risk factors.

The Application for Individual Life Insurance

Underwriting a proposed insured often begins well before an application for insurance reaches the insurer. As we mentioned in Chapter 2, field underwriting is the process of gathering initial information about a proposed insured and screening applicants who have requested coverage. Agents typically interview applicants and proposed insureds to determine each proposed insured's suitability for the requested insurance coverage. When agents understand and properly fulfill their field underwriting responsibilities, the quality of business an insurer receives is greatly improved, and the response time of underwriting is faster.

The Field Underwriting Manual

To help agents perform field underwriting, most insurers develop a field underwriting manual. A ***field underwriting manual*** is a document developed by an insurance company for agents to use when making initial assessments of proposed insureds. A field underwriting manual typically presents

- The insurer's underwriting philosophy
- An outline of the agent's responsibilities, including compliance issues
- Specific guidance on completing applications and on submitting changes and reinstatements

- Brief definitions of common medical terms and common impairments to help the agent describe impairments revealed by a proposed insured

- A description of the evidence of insurability usually required for common impairments, as well as broad characteristics of whether the risk for those impairments is typically minimal, moderate, or high

- Lists of questions related to common impairments so that the agent can obtain sufficiently detailed information about them

- Extra premiums applied to certain impairments so that the agent can inform a proposed insured about possible additional premiums or limited coverage

- Other insurer-specific considerations—such as risk factors and age and amount limitations for specific insurance products—with which the agent should be familiar

A field underwriting manual shows clearly that underwriting is not a mysterious activity, but is based on well-reasoned principles and on facts relevant to each applicant. Reviewing the field underwriting manual can help an agent appreciate the need for submitting a detailed and accurate medical history for every proposed insured. Given such a complete medical history, an underwriter can assess the risk objectively and fully and, if the case meets the insurer's underwriting criteria, can then issue appropriate coverage.

Part I and Part II of the Application

The insurance application is one of the underwriter's most important risk assessment tools and serves as the basis of the contract between the insurer and the policyowner. The application that an agent submits to an insurer's home office contains information about two people with whom the insurer may do business: the agent and the applicant (or the proposed insured, if different from the applicant). Knowledge about a particular agent and that agent's way of doing business can help the underwriter assess the probable quality of the submitted business and the probable accuracy of the information contained in the application.

The life insurance application form has traditionally consisted of two sections: Part I and Part II. Nearly all insurers ask basically the same types of questions as those included in Part I and Part II. In this textbook, we'll discuss Part I and Part II of the insurance application as separate sections, but keep in mind that some insurers do not divide the insurance application into these sections.

Part I of the Application

Part I of the life insurance application identifies the proposed insured (and the policyowner, if different from the proposed insured), specifies the amount and type of coverage requested, and provides basic insurability information. The type of insurability information usually includes the following:

- Identification of the proposed insured by name, social security number (United States) or social insurance number (Canada), date of birth, country of birth, age, sex, address and telephone number, length of time at residence, occupation and current employer, and the length of time with the current employer
- Identification of the applicant, if the policy is applied for by someone other than the proposed insured
- Identification of the policyowner, if different than the applicant or the proposed insured
- The face amount, plan of insurance, and premium payment mode requested, and dividend options if appropriate
- Special features or riders desired
- Name of the beneficiary and secondary beneficiary and relationship to the proposed insured
- Signatures of the applicant, the proposed insured, and the agent

Part I also includes a series of questions concerning the proposed insured's avocations, or hobbies, and aviation activities, as well as questions about the proposed insured's insurance history. In addition, Part I includes questions concerning foreign residence and travel, driving record, and criminal convictions.

When an underwriter evaluates the information in Part I, she examines the relationship between the coverage requested and the proposed insured's age, occupation, and other characteristics that are important in evaluating the risk. If an applicant requests an unusually high amount of coverage in relation to his circumstances, the underwriter typically asks the agent why that amount was requested in order to determine whether the situation indicates antiselection.

Some insurers also include in Part I a section called the agent's statement, which we introduced in Chapter 2. The agent's statement is important when, after reviewing a completed case file, the underwriter has doubts about whether to accept a risk. The agent's statement can include details about how well the agent knows the proposed insured and if the agent saw the applicant in person, as well as information that the agent has about the proposed insured's financial worth and annual income and reason for requesting the insurance.

The agent's statement usually includes information concerning whether the agent is a full-time representative of another insurance company and whether the agent has submitted an application on the proposed insured to any other insurer within the past six months. In addition, the agent's statement sometimes has space for the agent to (1) indicate the types of medical proofs being submitted if the coverage requires a medical examination and (2) list the name and address of the paramedic or physician who will complete the medical examination, if any, and the date scheduled for the examination.

Insurance that is issued on a nonmedical basis is offered without requiring a proposed insured to undergo either a paramedical or medical examination. Typically, insurers require an exam on a face amount applied for that is above a set limit. ***Nonmedical limits*** are the total amounts of insurance that an insurer will issue to an applicant without requiring a paramedical or medical examination. For example, an insurer may specify the following nonmedical limits for a specific insurance product:

Age	Limit of Nonmedical Coverage
0–30	$250,000
31–40	$200,000
41–45	$100,000
46–50	$ 75,000
51–60	$ 50,000

Nonmedical limits usually apply to the total of (1) insurance being applied for and (2) insurance already in force with the insurer. That is, if a proposed insured already has a certain amount of life insurance coverage in force and applies for an additional amount of life coverage, the total of in-force and applied-for coverage cannot exceed the insurer's nonmedical limits if the applicant wants to apply on a nonmedical basis. For example, if a 43-year-old applicant already has $50,000 of life insurance coverage in force with an insurer and is applying for an additional $100,000 of coverage with that insurer, the total of $150,000 would exceed the nonmedical limits specified in the preceding table. In such a case, the proposed insured could either reduce the amount of life insurance coverage requested to $50,000 in order to apply on a nonmedical basis or undergo a medical examination to apply for the $100,000 additional coverage.

Part II of the Application

Part II of the life insurance application consists of medical information about the proposed insured. Part II may take one of three forms: (1) a nonmedical supplement, (2) a paramedical report, or (3) a medical report. Insurers provide agents with information about which type of Part II report (or which type of application form) to submit for each applicant.

The type of Part II application required depends primarily on the proposed insured's age and the amount of coverage requested. Generally, the higher the potential risk to the insurer according to the insurer's underwriting guidelines, the more extensive the medical information required. Although an insurer needs information about a proposed insured's health history to evaluate the degree of risk represented, the insurer also needs to balance the need for such information with the cost of obtaining it.

Nonmedical Supplement. The type of Part II application known as a ***nonmedical supplement*** contains health history questions that an agent asks of a proposed insured as a substitute for a physical examination. A nonmedical supplement typically is used for applicants requesting amounts of coverage up to $250,000 or $300,000. Because it is part of the application, the nonmedical supplement becomes part of the insurance contract. Based on information provided in the nonmedical supplement, the underwriter can decide to request additional information about the proposed insured.

Paramedical Report. The second type of Part II application is a ***paramedical report,*** which contains (1) the proposed insured's answers to the same medical history questions that are included in the nonmedical supplement and the medical report and (2) the results of a partial physical examination of the proposed insured conducted by a paramedical examiner. The section of the paramedical report that contains the proposed insured's answers to medical history questions is signed by the proposed insured and becomes a part of the insurance contract. However, the portion of the paramedical report containing physical examination results is not signed by the proposed insured and does not become a part of the insurance contract.

A paramedical examination is generally used when the face amount of coverage is too high for the insurer to rely on a nonmedical supplement alone. If the information on a paramedical report indicates a medical impairment, an underwriter can request a full medical examination of the proposed insured. More and more insurers use paramedical examinations instead of medical examinations because paramedical exams are less expensive and faster, more convenient for the proposed insured, and, in many cases, provide all the information needed for accurate underwriting.

Medical Report. The third type of Part II application is a ***medical report,*** which is the most extensive of the three types and is designed to be completed by both the proposed insured and a physician. In one section of a medical report, an examining physician records the proposed insured's answers to questions that are the same as or similar to those asked on the nonmedical supplement and the paramedical report. As is the case for the paramedical report, the proposed insured signs the medical report form to verify that the information given was correctly recorded by the physician. Because this section of the medical report is part of the application, it becomes a part of the insurance contract. Figure 4-1 shows an example of this section of a medical report.

In another section of the medical report, the physician records the results of the medical examination given to the proposed insured. It usually includes the proposed insured's height, weight, blood pressure, pulse rate, heart sounds, and other information. This section of the medical report is not signed by the proposed insured and does not become part of the insurance contract. Figure 4-2 presents an example of the section of a medical report showing the results of a physical examination.

> **FAST FACT**
>
> A sample of substandard life insurance policies bought in the United States in 1999 shows 94% of such policies were given substandard ratings for medical reasons, including cardiovascular-renal disease and weight problems.[1]

The main differences between a medical report and a paramedical report are (1) the medical report is more extensive (for example, a paramedical examiner does not listen to a proposed insured's heart and lungs, as does a physician who conducts an exam for a medical report) and (2) the medical report is completed and signed by a physician.

Sources of Medical Information

As we have indicated in our discussion of the application, a proposed insured's medical status is a critical factor in underwriting individual life insurance. Part II of the application provides a considerable amount of medical information. However, additional medical information is often critical to underwriting individual life insurance. The medical information necessary to evaluate a risk comes from a variety of sources. These sources include MIB, Inc., the attending or examining physician, and laboratory tests. The underwriter's goal in ordering information about an applicant's medical condition is to have enough data to assess the risk fairly without accumulating excessive or unnecessary information, incurring excessive costs, or taking too much time. In the following sections, we'll discuss the sources of medical information and explain how insurers assess an applicant's age and build.

FIGURE 4-1. Section of a Medical Report Form.

Please check the appropriate column.
(If yes, circle the appropriate disorder and give details in the section below.)

	YES	NO
HAS THE PROPOSED INSURED EVER HAD ANY KNOWN INDICATION OF OR BEEN TREATED FOR ANY DISORDER OF:		
16. A. The heart, blood vessels, such as heart murmur, poor circulation, phlebitis, stroke, heart disease, heart attack, angina, chest pain, or high blood pressure?		
B. The chest, lungs, nose, and throat, such as asthma, chronic bronchitis, or emphysema?		
C. The digestive system, including stomach, intestines, gall bladder, liver, or pancreas, such as ulcer, colitis, hepatitis, or bleeding?		
D. The kidneys, urinary, bladder, reproductive organs, such as sugar, albumin, pus, or blood in urine?		
E. The nervous system, eyes, ears, such as dizziness, seizure, paralysis, mental or nervous disorder, impairment of sight or hearing?		
F. The glandular system, blood, such as diabetes, thyroid, anemia, leukemia, disorder of the breast or skin?		
G. Acquired Immune Deficiency Syndrome (AIDS), persistent lymph gland enlargement, unusual infections, any other immune system abnormality, or had a positive test related to AIDS?		
H. Musculo-skeletal system, such as arthritis, sciatica, amputation, injury, pain or defect of the neck, back, bones, or joints?		
I. Any other illness, disease, operation, tumor, injury, or congenital defect not mentioned above?		
17. Is any individual proposed for coverage currently under observation, taking medication, or receiving treatment?		
IN THE LAST FIVE YEARS, HAS THE PROPOSED INSURED:		
18. A. Applied for or received compensation or been off work because of illness, injury, or disability?		
B. Been advised about or treated for use of alcoholic beverages?		
C. Used marijuana, mood-altering drugs, narcotics, barbiturates, amphetamines, cocaine, heroin, etc?		
D. Had a checkup, operation or test, or been hospitalized or advised to have an operation or further investigation?		
E. Consulted or been referred to a specialist?		
19. Details to "Yes" answers in questions 16–18.		

Question Number	Give nature of disorder, diagnosis, test made	Results	Date	Duration	Name and addresses of doctors, hospitals, etc.

Source: Excerpted from Barbara Foxenberger Brown and Jane Lightcap Brown, *Life and Health Insurance Underwriting* (Atlanta: LOMA, © 1998), 114. Used with permission; all rights reserved.

FIGURE 4-2. Results of Physical Examination.

1. HEIGHT (IN SHOES)	WEIGHT (CLOTHED)	CHEST (FULL INSPIRATION)	CHEST (FORCED EXPIRATION)	ABDOMEN, AT UMBILICUS RELAXED	Details of "Yes" answers. (Identify Item.)
FT. IN.	LBS.	IN.	IN.	IN.	

Did you weigh? ❐ Yes ❐ No Did you measure? ❐ Yes ❐ No

Weight change in past year? ____ lbs. ❐ Gain ❐ Loss — Cause?

Is appearance unhealthy or older than stated age? ❐ Yes ❐ No

2. Blood Pressure (Record all readings)

	AT REST	AFTER EXERCISE	3 MINUTES LATER
Systolic			
Diastolic			

3. Pulse:

	AT REST	AFTER EXERCISE	3 MINUTES LATER
Rate			
Irregularities Per Min.			

4. Heart: a. Is there any cyanosis, dyspnea, edema, arteriosclerosis, peripheral vascular or other cardiovascular disorder? ❐ Yes ❐ No

b. Is heart enlarged? ❐ Yes ❐ No (if yes, describe)

c. Is murmur present? ❐ Yes ❐ No (if yes, complete 4d)

d. Murmur is:

		❐ Systolic	❐ Apical	❐ Soft (Gr. 1–2)
❐ Constant	❐ Transmitted	❐ Presystolic	❐ Basal	❐ Mod. (Gr. 3–4)
❐ Inconstant	❐ Localized	❐ Diastolic	❐ Other	❐ Loud (Gr. 5–6)

After exercise: ❐ Unchanged ❐ Increased
❐ Decreased ❐ Absent

Show Location Of:
- Apex by X
- Area of murmur by ◌
- Point of greatest intensity by O
- Transmission by →

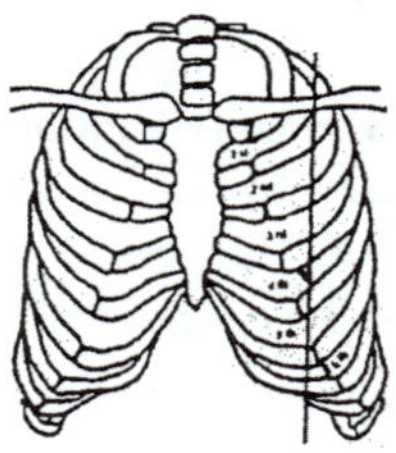

Your impression?

5. Is there on examination any abnormality of the following: (Check applicable items and give details.)

	YES	NO
a. Eyes, ears, nose, mouth, pharynx? (If vision or hearing markedly impaired, indicate degree and correction.)	❐	❐
b. Skin (incl. scars); lymph nodes, blood vessels (incl. varicose veins)?	❐	❐
c. Nervous system (include reflexes, gait, paralysis)?	❐	❐
d. Respiratory system?	❐	❐
e. Abdomen (include scars)?	❐	❐
f. Genitourinary system (include prostate)?	❐	❐
g. Endocrine system (include thyroid and breasts)?	❐	❐
h. Musculoskeletal system (include spine, joints, amputations, deformities)?	❐	❐
6. a. Are there any hernias?	❐	❐
b. Any hemorrhoids?	❐	❐
7. Have you any pertinent information not brought out above?	❐	❐

MIB, Inc.

An underwriter can request information about a proposed insured from MIB, Inc., formerly known as the Medical Information Bureau. ***MIB, Inc.*** is a nonprofit organization established to provide coded information to insurers about impairments that applicants have admitted to or that other insurers have detected in connection with previous applications for insurance. Such coded information received from MIB only alerts member companies of the need for further investigation of an applicant's insurability. MIB strictly prohibits its member companies from using MIB information as the sole basis of an unfavorable underwriting decision.

MIB furnishes its members with a confidential list of factors that are considered important to risk selection and a three-digit code that identifies each factor. Member companies report back to MIB any of a proposed insured's underwriting information that involves impairments listed in the MIB Code Book, regardless of the underwriting decision. Member companies do *not* send MIB information about (1) specific amounts of insurance applied for or issued, (2) underwriting decisions, or (3) claim decisions.

Before an underwriter at a member company can ask MIB to search its files for coded information about a proposed insured, the company must

- Obtain the proposed insured's written consent on a form that specifies that only MIB member companies are allowed to obtain MIB information

- Furnish the proposed insured for individual life or health insurance with a written pre-notice that describes MIB, its member services, and the proposed insured's right to request that MIB disclose information according to procedures described in the Fair Credit Reporting Act

If this search shows that a different insurer previously reported coded information resulting from an underwriting evaluation of the proposed insured, the codes are sent to the inquiring insurer. If the information in the codes is not revealed in the underwriting documents submitted by the applicant and the agent to the inquiring insurer, that insurer makes its own investigation if such an investigation appears necessary.

Underwriting on the Basis of MIB Information

If an underwriter's investigation does not verify the information received from MIB, the underwriter can request details through MIB, which asks the reporting insurer for further information. The reporting insurer is not obligated to furnish such details.

Information received from MIB can be used in considering a proposed insured's insurability when, and only when, the underwriting member company can verify the following information:

- No further investigation is needed to ensure that the application being considered and MIB-coded medical information refer to the same person.
- The underwriting insurer has obtained from the reporting member company either (1) the documents or summaries of the documents that are the basis of the reporting member's report to MIB or (2) advice from the reporting member that MIB information is verified by information from either a medical source or the proposed insured.

The Fair Credit Reporting Act (FCRA) and MIB rules require that, when MIB-coded information is used to consider a proposed insured's insurability, the insurer must (1) provide notice to the applicant that such information may be used in connection with the evaluation of the application and (2) ask the applicant to authorize the insurer to use the information. Such a notice is illustrated in Figure 4-3.

FIGURE 4-3. Authorization to Obtain Information.

To determire my eligibility for insurance, I authorize the release of information concerning (1) the diagnosis, treatment, or prognosis of any past or present physical or mental condition and drug or alcohol condition and (2) any nonmedical data that relates to insurability.

The parties authorized to release such information include (1) any physician or medical practitioner, (2) any hospital, clinic, or other medically related facility, (3) any insurance or reinsurance company, (4) MIB, Inc., or any consumer reporting agency, and (5) any employer of those proposed for insurance.

The information may be released to (1) the ABC Insurance Company and (2) the legal representative or any agent of the ABC Insurance Company.

Any data obtained will not be released by the ABC Insurance Company to any person or organization except (1) reinsuring companies, (2) MIB, Inc., (3) people performing business or legal services in connection with my application, and (4) any physician named in my medical declarations (as required for my medical care). Moreover, any data obtained will not be released by the ABC Insurance Company except as required by law or as I further authorize.

I agree that a photocopy of this authorization will be as valid as the original. I know that I may request a copy of this authorization. I agree that this authorization shall be valid for 24 months from the date shown below. I know that I may revoke this authorization at any time except to the extent that action is taken in relying on it.

Date ______________ Signature of proposed insured ______________________

Signature of witness ______________________

Source: Adapted from Barbara Foxenberger Brown and Jane Lightcap Brown, *Life and Health Insurance Underwriting* (Atlanta: LOMA, © 1998), 121. Used with permission; all rights reserved.

This notice typically is made a part of the insurance application and is, therefore, part of the insurance contract if coverage is approved and issued. Most insurance applications also include a section that briefly explains how MIB works and informs the applicant that he can contact MIB to obtain any information that MIB might have about him.

Confidentiality and Consumer Protection Procedures

Current MIB rules require that all MIB information be kept strictly confidential. Access to MIB information must be restricted to authorized medical, underwriting, and claim personnel of each member company. Further, member companies must maintain internal security procedures to prevent the exposure or release of MIB information to any unauthorized person or organization.

In order to ensure the accuracy of MIB information, member companies are required to (1) maintain internal procedures to cancel, correct, or supplement information submitted to MIB and (2) notify MIB if the insurer has reason to believe that a report received from MIB contains inaccurate or incomplete information.

Requests to Physicians

A physician who has provided medical care for a proposed insured is usually called an ***attending physician***. A physician who performs an examination of a proposed insured at the request of the insurance company is usually called an ***examining physician***. When an underwriter reviews an application on which the health history requires clarification, the underwriter can request a statement from the attending physician, can ask the examining physician for more information, or can request information in a specialized medical questionnaire or a physician interview.

The ***attending physician's statement (APS)*** is a report by a physician who has treated, or who is currently treating, the proposed insured. An APS is one of the most frequently ordered additional sources of medical information for underwriting purposes. Underwriters most frequently order APSs when (1) the application reports a visit to a doctor as a routine checkup, (2) the application mentions a specific illness or medical history, (3) the amount of insurance requested is very large, (4) information about the proposed insured from MIB is unfavorable, or (5) the proposed insured is of an advanced age.

An underwriter who needs detailed information about an impairment asks an attending physician for a history statement. A ***history statement*** is an APS concerning a specific health condition that a proposed insured has admitted having. Some conditions—such as nervous disorders, cancer, heart conditions, and diabetes—call for a history statement in almost every instance.

An underwriter also usually orders a history statement when there is evidence of overinsurance. ***Overinsurance*** refers to an amount of applied-for insurance that is excessive in relation to the potential loss for which coverage is being purchased. Evidence that a proposed insured would be overinsured if the applied-for coverage were approved may suggest a problem such as an unadmitted health history or an intent to commit suicide. Underwriters do not approve excessive amounts of insurance.

An underwriter also might request more detailed information about certain conditions such as coronary artery disease, chest pain, or diabetes by asking an attending or examining physician to complete a ***specialized medical questionnaire,*** a document that requests detailed information on a specific illness or condition. Figure 4-4 is an example of a specialized medical questionnaire requesting detailed information about a neuropsychiatric condition.

An underwriter sometimes speaks directly with an attending or examining physician to gather additional information on a proposed insured's specific disorder, to verify dates and details of treatment, and to clarify the reasons for certain diagnoses and medications. Sometimes an underwriter finds that information obtained from a source such as an APS or an MIB report discloses a medical impairment or a condition that was not reported on the application for insurance. Because the third-party information may be incorrect, the underwriter is careful not to reach a conclusion before interviewing the physician.

Laboratory Tests

Laboratory tests are usually ordered by the agent in accordance with the insurer's published underwriting requirements (recall the chart of such requirements in Figure 2-1). The required specimens of blood and urine are collected when the medical or paramedical examination is conducted, and the results are produced by commercial laboratories. Some insurers now use oral specimen (saliva) tests, for which the agent collects the specimen at the time of application and sends it to the laboratory to be tested. An underwriter may also order laboratory tests in addition to those ordered by the agent. A urinalysis is ordered on all medical examinations, and a blood profile is routine for many examinations. In addition, an electrocardiogram (ECG) is required at various age and amount levels. Figure 4-5 provides a brief description of four common tests.

Insurers keep the results of laboratory tests confidential to all parties except for those with a legitimate need to know the results. In testing

FIGURE 4-4. Specialized Medical Questionnaire for a Neuropsychiatric Condition.

NEUROPSYCHIATRIC QUESTIONNAIRE

Please complete from patient's existing medical records. A current medical exam is NOT required.

Patient's Name ________________ Application Number ________________

1. Please classify the disorder.
   - ❒ Affective Disorder
   - ❒ Personality Disorder
   - ❒ Anxiety Disorder
   - ❒ Psychotic Disorder
   - ❒ Organic Brain Disorder
   - ❒ Other (please specify) ________________
2. What is the appropriate DSM III American Psychiatric Association Diagnostic Code? _______
3. Date of onset? ____________
4. Please classify the degree of impairment.
   ❒ Mild ❒ Moderate ❒ Severe
5. Please indicate if any of the following have occurred.
   ❒ Substance Abuse ❒ Suicide Ideation ❒ Suicide Attempt
6. Indicate dates of psychiatric care.
   In-patient (hospitalization) ________________
   Out-patient ________________
7. Please specify the type of treatment prescribed.
   - ❒ Individual Counseling
   - ❒ Group Counseling
   - ❒ Electroconvulsive Therapy
   - ❒ Other (please specify)
   - ❒ Medication (include name and dosage of drug)
8. Is the condition under effective control? ❒ Yes ❒ No If yes, for how long? __________
9. Date of full recovery and return to work or school? ________________
10. Is there any reason to believe that psychiatric care may be necessary in the future? __________

Date ______________

Physician's Name (signature not required) ________________________

Source: Excerpted from Barbara Foxenberger Brown and Jane Lightcap Brown, *Life and Health Insurance Underwriting* (Atlanta: LOMA, © 1998), 128. Used with permission; all rights reserved.

FIGURE 4-5. Four Tests Commonly Ordered for Underwriting.

Electrocardiogram. An electrocardiogram (ECG) is a graphic record of the electrical forces produced by the heart and is a diagnostic tool for detecting a disease or an abnormality of the heart.

- A resting ECG is one taken when a proposed insured is at rest and the heart is beating at its normal rate.
- An exercise ECG (or stress ECG) is the same test taken during and after a proposed insured has engaged in a strictly defined amount of exercise. The duration of the exercise depends on the person's age and build.

In cases that call for ECGs, general industry practice is to obtain a resting ECG. A resting ECG reveals past heart damage while an exercise ECG signals potential future heart problems. Although an exercise ECG provides a more detailed analysis of a proposed insured's cardiac condition, underwriters usually request it only at higher age and amount combinations because the test is expensive and time-consuming.

Urinalysis. Analysis of a urine specimen is frequently required because it can detect protein, sugar, blood cells, hypertension and diabetic medication, and certain drugs of abuse. Because urinalysis can also detect cotinine (nicotine) in urine, insurers use this test to verify whether a declared nonuser of tobacco is qualified for nontobacco rates. When urinalysis is performed in a laboratory chosen by the insurer or in the insurer's home office, the requirement is usually referred to as a home office specimen (HOS).

Blood chemistry profile. A blood chemistry profile is a group of laboratory tests that identify various aspects of possible chronic and acute disease in a sample of blood. Most insurers require glucose, cholesterol, and liver function tests for certain ages and coverage amounts. The standard blood profile has 15 to 18 components related to liver function, kidney function, glucose/diabetes, blood lipids, and serum proteins. In addition, a test for human immunodeficiency virus (HIV) is included in all insurers' requirements.

Oral specimen (saliva) test. Oral specimen testing is a method of screening applicants for habitual use of nicotine or cocaine, and for the presence of HIV antibodies. The specimen is usually collected by the agent and sent to a laboratory to be tested. Oral specimen testing is usually more convenient and less expensive and invasive than blood or urine testing, although fewer tests can be performed because of the small specimen size.

the blood, saliva, or urine of a proposed insured for the presence of HIV antibodies, insurers obtain permission from the proposed insured for such testing and provide advance notice to the proposed insured concerning (1) the purpose of the test, (2) the meaning of normal and positive test results, and (3) the fact that test results will be sent to MIB and may be disclosed to any MIB member company to which the proposed insured applies for life or health insurance coverage. This notice usually informs the proposed insured that positive HIV antibody or antigen test results or other significant blood abnormalities will adversely affect the underwriting decision and that the application may be declined, an increased premium may be charged, or changes may be made in the applied-for policy. Insight 4-1 discusses the importance of information obtained from blood tests.

Insight 4-1. Don't Take Shortcuts with Risk.

Before the AIDS epidemic, blood testing and paramedical exams were thought to provide unnecessary information and cause needless expense, particularly for younger applicants. When the AIDS epidemic hit, the Food and Drug Administration approved a blood-test protocol for the detection of HIV antibodies. It was the only definitive method of detection. Now, tests exist that detect the HIV status of an individual via saliva or urine.

What some are forgetting is that during blood's evolution as a source of data, other information obtained through blood has led to an entirely new market—the preferred market. This is a whole new world of products that oral fluids alone cannot support.

If an underwriter's goal is to obtain the most information possible without overspending for additional information, consider the marginal cost of blood over oral fluids. After incurring the time and expense of verifying HIV status, it costs little more for further analysis of the blood, urine and vital signs, unless the agent is employed to do the collection.

Numerous alternative underwriting requirements have been attempted as surrogates for conventional tests. The motor vehicle report, for example, may offer some additional useful information to predict the likelihood of violent death at younger ages. But although violent deaths represent the most common cause of death in the first five policy durations among males underwritten in their 30s, they do not represent the majority. Roughly 66% of deaths under the age of 40 can be attributed to nonviolent causes. Another issue is motor vehicle report interpretation. It is common for the information about the frequency and seriousness of the violations that occurred to be incomplete or erroneous.

On the other hand, there has been tremendous progress in the refinement of the personal history interview process. This approach asks the prospective insured a host of scripted questions. In an electronic underwriting format, when a positive response is given, a series of drop-down questions appear to probe for more specific details on the response. This approach will have widespread use in the years to come. Yet as with any means that uses the prospective insured as the primary source of information—a source with a vested interest in the outcome—something is lost. In this case, that something is the "sentinel effect" (an early warning of possible problems from not requiring an exam and/or body fluid collection by a health professional. Again the real cost savings come when the agent collects the specimen, either saliva or urine, personally, even though the possibility of specimen substitution exists with this method of collection.

One final point to bear in mind: Most companies currently offer preferred-risk premium rates for amounts of $100,000 and up. They rely heavily upon blood-test results and findings from a paramedical exam to distinguish the favorable from the less favorable risks within the traditional standard class. Companies always have been able to choose from a wide range of opportunities to attract certain markets and meet the needs of potential customers in whatever ways that are deemed attractive. The premium that is charged must reflect the savings from reduced underwriting costs, and it must cover the loss of the sentinel effect, antiselection and, ultimately, increased mortality.

Source: Excerpted from Barry A. Wilkinson, "Don't Take Shortcuts with Risk," *Best's Review* (May 2000): 136. © A.M. Best Company Inc.; used with permission of the publisher.

Assessing Medical Factors

Medical factors are critical in underwriting decisions. To be consistent in evaluating the risk represented by medical factors, insurers depend on statistical information developed during large-scale studies of medical impairments. These studies have generally compared the relative mortality experience of impaired people to that of unimpaired people and have revealed mortality patterns by age, sex, and other factors. The medical impairment studies have guided actuaries in establishing rate classes for insurance.

Underwriters assess the medical risk represented by a proposed insured by using the numerical rating system, the table rating method, the flat extra premium method, or some combination of these approaches.

The Numerical Rating System

The ***numerical rating system*** is a method of assigning numbers to individual proposed insureds according to the degree of risk they present to the insurer. These numbers are then used to determine the appropriate risk class in which to place each proposed insured. The numerical rating system assigns a positive or negative number to characteristics that have been determined statistically to have a positive or negative impact on the mortality risk presented by proposed insureds. The total numerical rating a proposed insured receives determines his risk classification. The higher the total, the higher the degree of risk presented by the proposed insured.

The numerical value of the average, or standard, mortality risk is set at 100, indicating 100 percent of standard mortality. A proposed insured's medical, personal, and financial characteristics that have a favorable effect on mortality are assigned "minus" values (such as –25) and are called ***credits.*** The net effect of credits is to lower the number indicating an applicant's predicted percent of standard mortality. Therefore, the lower a proposed insured's numerical value, the lower the risk he represents to the insurer.

In contrast, a proposed insured's medical, personal, and financial characteristics that have an unfavorable effect on mortality are assigned "plus" values (such as +25) and are called ***debits.*** The net effect of debits is to increase the number indicating an applicant's predicted percentage of standard mortality. In other words, the higher a proposed insured's numerical value, the greater the risk he represents to the insurer.

Combining debits and credits with the basic standard value of 100 produces the numerical value of the risk presented by an individual applicant. For example, suppose Alfredo de Santo's medical records indicate that he has a slightly enlarged heart. The insurer from which Mr. de Santo is requesting coverage typically assigns a debit of +50 to such an impairment, indicating that a person with this type of impairment represents 150 percent of the mortality rate for standard risks. If Mr. de Santo's other characteristics indicate no other impairments and if he has no characteristics that decrease his predicted mortality, then the number representing his predicted percent of standard mortality is 150 (100 points representing standard mortality plus 50 points representing the additional risk). Figure 4-6 presents a typical life underwriting worksheet showing debits and credits assigned.

In developing premium charges for substandard risks, insurers assume that the mortality pattern of a given impairment or characteristic will remain constant, increase with age, or decrease with age. Insurers charge for substandard risks by charging a premium based on a table rating, charging a flat extra premium, or combining these two methods.

The Table Rating Method

Insurers adjust premium rates to compensate for extra mortality by using the ***table rating method,*** an approach to charging for substandard risks by dividing those risks into broad groups according to their numerical ratings. The extra mortality for each substandard group is expressed as a percentage added to standard mortality as has been shown by the insurer's actual mortality experience and is presented in an ***extra-percentage table.*** The table rating method is appropriate when a risk shows a pattern of extra mortality that increases with age, as is found in hypertensive and overweight people. Table ratings are used for the majority of extra risks and are generally the same from one insurer to another. Figure 4-7 shows an example of an extra-percentage table.

According to Figure 4-7, the total mortality for each class is figured as 100 (representing standard mortality) plus the total of debits (representing extra mortality). Each table represents an increase in extra mortality of 25 debits. Therefore, a case rated Table 1 has a mortality rating of 125, or 1.25 times the standard mortality; a case rated Table 2 has a mortality rating of 150, or 1.5 times standard mortality, and so on.

An easy way to remember the amount of extra mortality represented by each table is to multiply the table number by 25, then add 100 (which represents standard mortality). For instance, a case rated Table 4 has a mortality rating of 200 [(4 × 25) + 100] or two times the standard mortality, and a case rated Table 5 has a mortality rating of 225 [(5 × 25) + 100] or 2.25 times the standard mortality.

The Flat Extra Premium Method

The ***flat extra premium method*** is an approach to charging for substandard risks that provides that, for every $1,000 of insurance, a specified extra dollar amount will be added to the standard premium. The flat extra premium method is used mainly in cases involving extra

FIGURE 4-6. Underwriting Worksheet.

Life Underwriting Worksheet

Life app $ 250,000
ELR $

☑ WP ☑ AD ☐ GB ☐ VB ☐ PUA

Personal		+/–
☑ Male ☐ Female	☑ Non-Smoker ☐ Smoker	
Age: 47		
Height: 5'11"	Weight: 255	+75
Family History: both parents alive 75 71		–10
MB ☐ YES ☐ NO		
General		
Diabetic onset age 40 control by diet only		+50
good control by both blood result + APS. Normal ECG.		-25
		+90
☐ ELR/CTB ☐ Male ☐ Female	☐ Non-Smoker ☐ Smoker	
Age:		
Height:	Weight:	
Family History:		
MB ☐ YES ☐ NO		
General		

Request	Requirements	Receive	Clear	Waive
✓	Para	✓	✓	
	Med			
✓	Ecg	✓	✓	
	Spec ☐ 1 ☐ 2			
✓	Blood Profile	✓	✓	
	Insp. ☐ MVR47 ☐			
✓	Aps/Dr Smith	✓		
	Aps/Dr			
	EP 18 ☐ 1 ☐ 2			
	23 ☐ 25 ☐ 28 ☐ F37 ☐			
	Smoking Q F170			
	Fin. Ques. 17			
	Reinsurance 45			
	Branch Reply 02			
	Replacement 29			

Financial Calculation	Life	A.D.
In Force (all Co's)		
New (all Co's)		
Total		

Income:	Required Income
Factor:	$

FIGURE 4-7. Typical Extra-Percentage Table.

Table (or Substandard Class)	Total Mortality (Standard Mortality + Extra Mortality)
1 or A	125
2 or B	150
3 or C	175
4 or D	200
5 or E	225
6 or F	250
8 or G	300
10 or H	350
12 or J	400
16 or K	500

For example, Table I (A) total mortality of 125 equals 100 debits for standard mortality *plus 25* debits for the extra mortality.

mortality that is considered to be either constant (such as occupation or avocation) or decreasing with age. This method contrasts with the table rating method, which is used in cases involving extra mortality that is expected to increase with age.

The amount of extra premium derived by this method varies according to the amount of risk represented by the impairment or characteristic, but does not vary from year to year during the time the extra premium is charged. For example, an insurer may charge $2 per $1,000 for a mild impairment, but $7 or $15 per $1,000 for a more serious impairment. Whatever the amount charged, it will remain the same ($2 or $7 or $15) throughout the period that the flat extra premium is charged.

An insurer may charge a ***temporary flat extra premium*** for an impairment for which the extra mortality risk is expected to decrease and eventually disappear over a limited time period. A temporary flat extra premium is charged for such impairments as cancers in remission and heart conditions from which the insured is recovering. Most insurers program their information systems to automatically remove this type of premium at the appropriate time.

When insurers do impose a flat extra premium for a medical impairment, the extra premium is almost always temporary. A ***permanent flat extra premium*** is charged, however, for cases in which a

FAST FACT

Of the 4% of individual life insurance policies purchased by Canadians during 1999 that were rated extra risk, less than one half of one percent were due to dangerous occupations.[2]

nonmedical risk is expected to remain constant throughout the life of the policy. This type of rating is most commonly used for hazardous occupations, dangerous avocations, or unfavorable driving records.

Combining Methods

Insurers often use a combination of a flat extra premium and a numerical or table rating when the risk of death is expected to increase during a certain period and to decrease after that period. For example, experience has shown that a person who has already had a heart attack is more prone to heart attacks than is a person who has never had one. This increased risk is greatest during the first 10 years following the initial attack. After 10 years, the risk is much lower, although it still exists. Thus, a proposed insured who suffered a heart attack two years before applying for life insurance might be accepted with a percentage table rating of 200 percent, plus a $10 flat extra premium per $1,000 of coverage for each of the next eight years. After eight years, the $10 flat extra premium would automatically be removed, but the table rating would continue.

Underwriting Manual

The debits and credits and the extra ratings that insurers assign to insurance risks vary from one insurer to another because of differences in assumptions about expected mortality. The information an insurer uses to assign relative values to life insurance risks is contained in an ***underwriting manual,*** which may exist in paper or electronic form. An underwriting manual typically provides descriptive information on impairments and serves as a guide to underwriting action. An underwriting manual is not to be confused with a field underwriting manual, which we have described as a document used by agents to make initial assessments of proposed insureds.

The underwriting manual typically includes

1. A description of various impairments and diseases associated with each organ and system of the body

2. A list of debits or credits, or both, for specific impairments and characteristics

3. A statement of the amount of flat extra premium to be charged for certain impairments and characteristics

4. Extra-percentage tables to be used for table ratings

Each underwriting manual also includes an index listing synonyms and derivative terms for characteristics, with page references. Most manuals also include a laboratory section that lists basic laboratory test data and a "normal" range of values for the most commonly used laboratory tests. To help underwriters interpret medical information, many manuals contain a glossary of symptoms and medical terms, as well as a list of medical and insurance abbreviations and definitions. Most insurers emphasize that the suggested actions and ratings listed in their underwriting manuals are intended to be flexible and may be modified by an underwriter according to individual circumstances.

Assessing Age and Build

Underwriters consider a person's age and build to assess the medical risk represented by a proposed insured.

Placing each applicant for life insurance into the correct risk classification involves assessing information on every factor that might affect that person's longevity. The most important single factor affecting the length of time a person is likely to live is that person's current age. Because of its importance in assessing risk, age can render a person ineligible regardless of other factors affecting insurability. Nearly all insurers establish upper age limits beyond which the insurers will not issue life insurance. The upper age limits usually vary according to the insurance product applied for and are generally lower for term insurance (an average upper-limit age is about 75) and higher for whole life insurance (an average upper-limit age is 85 to 90). Some insurers are revising these age limits as the number of active and healthy people at older ages continues to grow. We will discuss age as an underwriting factor in more detail in Chapter 5.

In addition to age, underwriters also assess an applicant's build. ***Build*** is the shape or form of a person's body, including the relationship among height, weight, and distribution of the weight. To evaluate build, an underwriter typically uses a ***build chart,*** which is based on established studies and indicates average weights for various heights for each sex, along with the mortality debits associated with increases in weight.

An underwriter also considers recent gains or losses in a proposed insured's weight, because substantial or rapid gains or losses in weight may indicate medical impairments. Figure 4-8 illustrates part of a typical build chart.

FAST FACT

Weight problems accounted for 38% of substandard ratings on individual life insurance policies purchased in the United States in 1999.[3]

FIGURE 4-8. Build Chart.

Adult Build Chart
Age 16 and over (feet and inches/pounds)

Ht.	Avg. Male Wt.	Avg. Female Wt.	+25	+50	+75	+100	+125	+150	+200	+250	+300
4'8"	121 lbs	105 lbs	180 lbs	190 lbs	200 lbs	215 lbs	220 lbs	230 lbs	240 lbs	245 lbs	255 lbs
4'9"	124	108	185	195	205	215	225	235	245	255	260
4'10"	127	112	190	200	210	220	230	240	250	255	265
4'11"	130	116	195	205	215	225	235	245	255	260	270
5'0"	133	118	195	205	220	230	240	250	255	265	275
5'1"	136	122	205	210	225	235	245	250	260	270	280
5'2"	139	125	205	215	230	235	245	255	265	275	285
5'3"	143	129	210	220	230	245	255	265	275	280	290
5'4"	147	132	220	225	240	250	260	270	280	290	300
5'5"	151	135	225	235	245	255	265	275	285	295	305
5'6"	155	138	230	240	250	260	270	285	295	305	315
5'7"	159	143	235	245	255	270	280	290	300	310	320
5'8"	163	146	240	250	265	275	285	300	310	320	330
5'9"	167	151	250	260	270	285	295	305	320	330	340
5'10"	172	154	255	265	280	290	305	315	325	335	345
5'11"	176	158	260	275	285	300	310	325	335	345	355
6'0"	181	162	270	280	295	305	320	330	340	355	365
6'1"	185	166	275	290	300	315	325	340	350	360	370
6'2"	190	169	285	300	310	325	335	345	360	370	380
6'3"	195	173	290	305	320	330	345	355	365	380	390

Key Terms and Concepts

field underwriting manual
Part I
nonmedical limits
Part II
nonmedical supplement
paramedical report
medical report
MIB, Inc.
attending physician
examining physician
attending physician's statement (APS)
history statement
overinsurance
specialized medical questionnaire
numerical rating system
credits
debits
table rating method
extra-percentage table
flat extra premium method
temporary flat extra premium
permanent flat extra premium
underwriting manual
build
build chart

Endnotes

1. ACLI, *Life Insurers Fact Book 2000* (Washington, D.C.: American Council of Life Insurers, 2000), 15.
2. CLHIA, *Canadian Life and Health Insurance Facts* (Toronto: Canadian Life and Health Insurance Association, 2000), 9.
3. ACLI, 15.

CHAPTER 5

Personal Factors and Financial Factors for Individual Life Insurance

Chapter Outline

Personal Factors for Individual Life Insurance

Sources of Personal Information
Assessing Personal Factors

Financial Factors for Individual Life Insurance

Sources of Financial Information
Assessing the Need for Insurance
Assessing Financial Factors
Large-Amount Cases

Objectives

After reading this chapter, you should be able to

- Describe the sources of personal information used in underwriting individual life insurance
- Discuss personal factors used in underwriting individual life insurance
- Explain how underwriters assess personal information used in underwriting individual life insurance
- List and describe financial factors used in underwriting individual life insurance
- Describe the sources of financial information used in underwriting individual life insurance
- Explain how underwriters assess financial need for individual life insurance

We have seen the importance of medical factors in assessing insurance risks. However, the activities a proposed insured pursues also can significantly affect the quality and probable length of the person's life. In addition, the proposed insured's financial status affects the underwriting process. In this chapter, we will look at how personal and financial factors affect risk evaluation for individual life insurance.

Personal Factors for Individual Life Insurance

We'll begin this chapter by discussing the sources of personal information about a proposed insured. Then we'll examine each of the personal factors that are considered in underwriting. Figure 5-1 includes a list of the personal factors we will discuss.

Sources of Personal Information

To assess the risks posed by a proposed insured's personal activities, underwriters access many sources of information, including the application for insurance, the motor vehicle record (MVR), the inspection report, the personal history interview, and personal questionnaires. In this section, we'll define each of these sources and explain how they are used in underwriting.

The Application for Insurance

Some of the questions asked on the application for insurance are so personal that they could not be asked in other situations—for example, during a job interview, direct queries cannot be made about marital status, height, weight, physical handicaps or defects, past illnesses, number and ages of children, net worth, and outstanding loans. During underwriting, however, such personal information helps the underwriter not only to make an accurate assessment of the risk, but also to view the proposed insured as an individual rather than just as another request for coverage. In order to make a sound judgment on the risk represented by that person, the underwriter needs to know and assess all relevant information.

FIGURE 5-1. Personal Factors Considered in Underwriting.

- Insurable interest
- Moral hazard
- Persistency
- Age
- Sex
- Occupation
- Driving history
- Avocations and professional sports
- Tobacco use
- Alcohol use
- Substance abuse
- Subjects of abuse
- Criminal history
- Civilian and military aviation
- Military status
- International travel and residence

Source: Excerpted from Barbara Foxenberger Brown and Jane Lightcap Brown, *Life and Health Insurance Underwriting* (Atlanta: LOMA, © 1998), 173. Used with permission; all rights reserved.

The insurance application typically requests such personal information as

- Date and place of birth
- Marital status
- Occupation and any intent to change occupation
- Net worth, annual earned income, and sources of other income
- Length of time at current and former residences
- Aviation activities other than as a passenger on scheduled airlines
- Avocations that could result in physical injury (including motor vehicle racing, scuba or sky diving, hang gliding, parachuting, mountain climbing, rodeos, and others)
- Driving record information, including driver's license suspension or revocation, driving convictions, pending charges, or more than a specified number (usually three) of moving traffic violations
- Criminal history information, including conviction for any criminal offenses
- Travel or residence outside the country in which coverage is being sought
- Tobacco use
- Family death from any disorder of the heart or from cancer

The answers to these questions form the basis for the underwriter's evaluation of the case. If any of the questions indicate the possibility of an increased risk—for example, if the information shows the presence of a dangerous avocation, tobacco use, or family disease history—the underwriter is obliged to look further at those aspects of the case and to gather sufficient information to decide whether to issue the coverages applied for, to rate the requested coverage, or to decline coverage. Also, if information on the application appears inconsistent—for instance, if a person's annual earned income seems inconsistent with the person's occupation—the underwriter seeks additional information to clarify the apparent inconsistencies. An underwriter might also seek additional information if answers on the application indicate that the applicant has changed addresses several times in a short period of time or has unexplained gaps in her employment history.

Motor Vehicle Record

A ***motor vehicle record (MVR)*** typically contains information about a person's driving history, including information about traffic violations and arrests and convictions for driving-related incidents. The MVR is usually available from consumer reporting agencies and, in most jurisdictions, from public records. The underwriter uses information in the MVR to assess the degree of risk represented by a proposed insured's driving habits.

Inspection Report

An ***inspection report*** is a type of investigative consumer report that is developed by a consumer reporting agency and that contains information about a proposed insured's personal life, activities, occupation, and financial status. To compile an inspection report, an inspector uses public records and sometimes interviews the proposed insured and some of the proposed insured's friends, neighbors, and business associates.

Before an underwriter can order an inspection report, the proposed insured signs a release form that is part of the application and that authorizes various people to release information for the inspection report. Some insurers provide only the notice required by the Fair Credit Reporting Act informing a proposed insured that an inspection report may be requested.

Because gathering information for an inspection report is expensive, underwriters carefully weigh the value of an inspection report against its cost. Typically insurers establish a coverage amount—such as $1 million—above which inspection reports are routinely ordered. Insurers also reserve the right to order, at the underwriter's discretion, inspection reports on applications for lower amounts. Inspection reports are seldom ordered on small-amount policies because the cost of such a report is too high to be cost-effective.

Personal History Interview

You'll recall from Chapter 2 that the personal history interview allows the underwriter to clarify information by talking to the proposed insured. In addition to obtaining information about the proposed insured's health history, a personal history interview allows the underwriter to clarify information provided by the proposed insured on the application for insurance regarding his personal activities.

Personal Questionnaires

Insurers have developed many different kinds of specialized questionnaires designed to allow underwriters and other investigators to gather information needed for complete and accurate underwriting of risks. These questionnaires generally fall into two types: those concerning medical impairments—such as diabetes, heart attack, and chest pain—and those concerning personal factors—such as aviation, avocation, residence, and occupation.

Personal questionnaires typically ask for information that tells the underwriter the extent of the proposed insured's participation in a specified activity that is known to be related to additional mortality or morbidity. In addition, these questionnaires ask for proof that the proposed insured is qualified or certified to take part in the specified activity.

All of the questions on a personal questionnaire are designed to gather information related to the risk that exists when a person takes part in a certain activity, such as scuba diving or mountain climbing. The questions are based on statistical information about the relationship of specific activities to injuries and death. Many insurers rely on standard questionnaires that have been used in the industry for years and have been proven to be accurate in gathering information needed for underwriting. Figure 5-2 is an example of a personal questionnaire requesting information about a proposed insured's participation in ballooning/hang gliding.

Assessing Personal Factors

In underwriting individual life insurance applications, an underwriter looks carefully at several personal factors that can have an impact on a proposed insured's risk classification. These personal factors include the presence of insurable interest and the appropriateness of beneficiaries, the possibility of moral hazard, probable persistency, age,

FIGURE 5-2. Ballooning/Hang Gliding Questionnaire.

BALLOONING/HANG GLIDING QUESTIONNAIRE

Construction of balloon or hang gliding craft:

❒ Home assembled ❒ Factory assembled ❒ Home built

❒ Rigid wing ❒ Motorized ❒ Not motorized

Type of flying:

❒ Student ❒ Carrying passengers ❒ Pleasure

❒ Advertising ❒ Instructing ❒ Other (explain)

Date of first flight: ______________________

Date of last flight: ______________________

Flight hours during last 12 months: ______________________

Average height: ______________________

Average distance: ______________________

Average duration: ______________________

Greatest height: ______________________

Greatest distance: ______________________

Greatest duration: ______________________

Have you ever had accidents or mishaps? ❒ Yes ❒ No

If yes, please explain:

Describe types of terrain over which you fly:

Do you currently hold a DOT or FAA pilot's license? ❒ Yes ❒ No

I declare that the above information is true and complete and shall form part of my application to ABC Assurance Company.

Signature ______________________

Source: Excerpted from Barbara Foxenberger Brown and Jane Lightcap Brown, *Life and Health Insurance Underwriting* (Atlanta: LOMA © 1998), 94. Used with permission; all rights reserved.

sex, occupation, driving history, avocations and professional sports, tobacco and alcohol use, substance abuse, subjects of abuse, criminal history, civilian and military aviation, military status, international residence and travel, and immigrants and citizens of foreign countries. We'll consider how each of these personal factors affects underwriting.

Insurable Interest

At inception, contracts of insurance are considered to be binding only if the insured, the policyowner (if different from the insured), or the beneficiary would suffer a genuine, foreseeable economic loss if the event insured against were to occur. The condition in which a person or an entity would suffer a genuine economic loss if the event insured against were to occur is called ***insurable interest.*** If insurable interest is not present where required, the contract is void. Note that insurable interest must be present at the time the insurance is issued, regardless of whether it exists at a later date. For example, a married couple that subsequently divorces may no longer have an insurable interest in each other, although insurable interest was present when they were married. However, a policy taken out at the time of their marriage is not voided at the time of the divorce because of the lack of insurable interest.

Insurable interest often exists where the insured and the beneficiary share a close relationship by blood, marriage, or dependency. An underwriter generally assumes that the proposed insured's spouse, parent, child, grandparent, grandchild, and siblings have an insurable interest in the life of the proposed insured. The underwriter assumes, however, that no insurable interest exists between the proposed insured and an aunt, uncle, niece, nephew, cousin, or relative by marriage, unless a dependent relationship exists between them. For example, a child who is dependent on a cousin or an aunt for financial support has an insurable interest in that person's life.

Because the death of a child usually results in only funeral expenses, but not a loss of income to a family, most underwriters anticipate that insurance on the life of a child is being purchased for the future benefit of the child, such as to provide the child with an early start on a life insurance program when premiums are low. Marriage usually establishes an insurable interest of either spouse in the life of the other.

Beneficiary Designation. In regards to the beneficiary designation in an application, the underwriter checks for the presence of insurable interest and the phrasing of the beneficiary designation.

A person legally can apply for as much insurance coverage on her own life as an insurer is willing to issue and can name anyone she wishes as the beneficiary. On the other hand, if one person submits an application for insurance on the life of another person, the underwriter determines whether the named beneficiary has an insurable interest in the life of the insured, according to the prevailing laws. If the underwriter determines that insurable interest is questionable or not present, further investigation is necessary to determine the existence of insurable interest.

Third-party Applicants. A person who applies for coverage on the life of another person is called a ***third-party applicant.*** In general, a third-party applicant must show evidence of insurable interest in the life of the person to be insured. Some jurisdictions make exceptions for a spouse who wishes to purchase insurance on the life of the other spouse, for a parent who wishes to purchase insurance on the life of a minor child, and for a grandparent purchasing coverage on the life of a grandchild.

Often, the third-party applicant is also the beneficiary of the policy. Sometimes, however, a third-party applicant names another person as the beneficiary. Because this situation creates the possibility of speculation or antiselection, some insurers and some states require that a third-party beneficiary have an insurable interest in the life of the insured at the time the insurance is issued.

Business Relationships. Businesses often purchase insurance coverage on certain people for business purposes. Such coverage is a type of third-party insurance and requires the presence of insurable interest. An insurable interest is considered to be present in coverage requested for business purposes if the premature death of one person in a business relationship would cause serious financial loss to the surviving person or persons or to the business. In such a situation, the person or organization that would suffer a financial loss has an insurable interest in the life of the person whose death would cause the loss. We'll discuss underwriting for business insurance in more detail in Chapter 6.

Moral Hazard

Moral hazard is a characteristic that exists when the reputation, financial position, or mental state of an applicant or a proposed insured indicates that the person is likely to cause a loss intentionally or is likely not to limit a loss after it has occurred. If an underwriter finds, after an appropriate investigation, that an applicant or a proposed insured has been involved in dishonest practices or otherwise exhibits behavior that might lead to intentional or prolonged losses, the underwriter either limits the coverage or denies it.

Persistency

Another factor an underwriter considers is ***persistency,*** which refers to how well a policy or group of policies remains, or persists, in force. A policy or group of policies that remains continuously in force for a long time is considered to have good persistency. An insurer's persistency experience is a major factor in achieving the insurer's desired financial results. However, an insurer that experiences poor persistency loses money because the insurer does not make up the policy's first-year expenses, which usually exceed the policy's first-year premium.

Underwriters generally consider any of the following to be indications that a policy may have poor persistency:

- The applicant has a low income.
- The applicant has an occupation that requires little skill or training.

FAST FACT

In the United States, for policies in force less than two years, the 1999 voluntary termination rate was more than 14%; for those in force two years or longer, the voluntary termination rate was just over 4%.[1]

- The applicant has previously allowed one or more policies to lapse.
- The application requests that premiums be paid monthly by check rather than by an automatic payment method.

An underwriter who decides that an application indicates a high probability of poor persistency usually declines to issue a policy.

Age

Underwriters also consider the proposed insured's age when making an underwriting decision. In most cases, physical impairments become more severe and more complex with advancing age. In addition, the age of the proposed insured, coupled with the amount of coverage already in force and the amount applied for, help the underwriter resolve questions of possible antiselection.

For example, a 60-year-old man purchasing life insurance for the first time is statistically a greater risk for possible antiselection than is a 60-year-old man who has purchased insurance throughout his adult life. The fact that the first man has decided to purchase coverage only at an older age, perhaps as a result of sudden concern for his declining health, indicates the possibility of antiselection.

Considerations for Young, Middle-Aged, and Older Proposed Insureds. Young proposed insureds, generally aged 15 through 39, typically present few underwriting problems. In considering applications from young people, an underwriter normally has all the selection tools needed to identify unacceptable levels of extra mortality, which usually concern factors relating to accidental death, such as driving history, avocations, and alcohol or substance abuse. Middle-aged proposed insureds, generally aged 40 through 65, are of more concern from a medical standpoint because many people begin having physical problems after age 40. The underwriter, therefore, examines more closely the possibility of antiselection in applications from such people, even for lower amounts of coverage.

For older proposed insureds, generally aged 66 and older, an underwriter considers several additional aspects of insurability. In general, the older the proposed insured, the greater the chance that the person will have developed a physical impairment or limitation. A 68-year-old woman who does not admit to having seen any doctors during the previous five years or who lists only minor or very few injuries or illnesses is not typical. For such a proposed insured, the underwriter tends to conduct a very thorough review.

The underwriter may find many reasons for approving coverage for older people. Some beneficiaries are not adequately supported by savings, government benefits, and other means. Also, some older people who previously lacked the financial means to purchase life insurance may finally apply for it to pay their last expenses or to pay estate taxes.

Sex

Insurers' experience, the pressure of competition, and state, provincial, and federal laws have caused insurers to generally disregard the sex of the proposed insured in determining the amounts and types of insurance coverage issued. However, because females tend to live longer than males, many insurers do use sex-based actuarial tables to determine premiums.

Occupation

A proposed insured's occupation is usually not a factor in underwriting unless it could be considered hazardous by the insurer's standards. In most cases, occupations that are not listed in an insurer's underwriting manual are not considered hazardous regardless of their nature. Sometimes, however, an unlisted occupation is evaluated as to the extent of its hazard, especially if it resembles one that is listed.

An underwriter typically assesses two kinds of occupational hazards: accident hazards (such as working on high-rise construction) and health hazards (such as exposure to toxic chemicals). Accident hazards are more common among some workers, such as lumber workers and demolition experts, while health hazards are more common among other workers, such as those involved in radium analysis. Moreover, some workers—coal miners, for example—are subject to both types of hazards. Figure 5-3 lists a number of occupations that many insurers consider hazardous.

A rating for occupation may be reduced or removed when the insured's occupation changes. Generally, insurers require that an insured person who has previously been in a hazardous occupation must work for at least one year in a less hazardous occupation and must not be likely to return to the former, more hazardous occupation.

Driving History

Because accidental deaths frequently result from motor vehicle accidents, underwriters pay considerable attention to a proposed insured's driving history. Underwriters consider the number, type, and recency of traffic violations, as well as whether alcohol or other drugs were involved in any of the violations. Proposed insureds who have many

FIGURE 5-3. Occupations That Many Insurers Consider Hazardous.

Occupation	Description of Risk
Aquanautics	Work in an alien environment with experimental equipment at considerable water depths
Building demolition	Unsound structures that may be likely to collapse; blasting and other use of explosives may be dangerous
Firefighters and smoke jumpers	Smoke inhalation, equipment malfunction, and entrapment
Mining and quarrying	Accident hazard, rock falls and cave-ins, fire and explosions, asphyxiation and poisonous gases
Stunts in films	High exposure to accidents resulting from high-speed driving, leaps and dives, exposure to fire and explosives
Radium analysis	Exposure to risk of radioactive poisoning and potential carcinogenic effects

Source: Adapted from Barbara Foxenberger Brown and Jane Lightcap Brown, *Life and Health Insurance Underwriting* (Atlanta: LOMA, © 1998), 189. Used with permission; all rights reserved.

traffic violations pose generally greater risks for fatal motor vehicle accidents and for nonfatal accidents that produce serious injuries.

For people who have unfavorable driving histories, most insurers use flat extra premiums. In order to obtain information about a proposed insured's driving record, an underwriter may request an inspection report and/or an MVR, both of which we described earlier in this chapter.

Avocations and Professional Sports

A proposed insured's choice of leisure activities, or avocations, influences risk appraisal. To gather information about an applicant's avocations, underwriters use specialized personal questionnaires. Such a questionnaire may focus on just one activity or may gather information on several avocations.

FAST FACT

In the United States, sports-related injuries to adults ages 35 to 54 increased 33% from 1991 to 1998.[2]

In underwriting avocations, an underwriter relies on the rating schedules that are provided in an insurer's underwriting manual and that are typically derived from the insurer's experience. Underwriters also consider the proposed insured's age and other personal factors to determine whether an extra premium should be charged for participation in an avocation that may add to an applicant's risk. Underwriters usually distinguish between people who pursue ratable avocations as an occupation (professional) and those who do it as an avocation (amateur). As examples, automobile racing, boxing, wrestling, and rodeo riding can be either avocations or occupations. Insight 5-1 discusses Americans' increased participation in certain risky avocations, such as snowboarding and scuba diving.

Insight 5-1. Study of the Extreme.

Americans have more recreation choices today, but few actively participate in traditional sports, let alone extreme sports, say Rodney B. Warnick and John R. Kelly, authors of *Recreation Trends and Markets: The 21st Century*, which looks at the way Americans spend their leisure time. Warnick is a faculty member in the department of hotel, restaurant and travel administration at the University of Massachusetts in Amherst. Kelly is a professor emeritus at the University of Illinois at Champaign–Urbana.

In writing the book, the two studied participation trends in 103 leisure activities, drawing their data from annual market-research surveys of 15,000 to 23,000 households. They concluded that despite the mountain biking and snowboarding images that abound on television and in glossy magazines, American adults are far more likely to golf, walk or gamble in their spare time.

A lot of the activities they looked at have participation rates of less than 10% of the population, Warnick said. One reason could be the fragmentation of leisure activities. For example, activities once classified under the general heading of "bicycling" now would be broken down into the categories of "road or tour cycling," "off-road mountain biking" or "on-road biking." "However, within selected activities and within the actual portion of people who do participate, you could have a very committed core of participants," Warnick said. That may be true of certain extreme sports, where the number of participants also has increased in recent years. Warnick cited these examples:

- **Snowboarding:** During the 1990s, the number of snowboarders rose from about 1.8 million to 3.6 million.
- **Skin diving and scuba diving:** From 1979 to 1996, participation in these activities rose from 2.6 million to 7.5 million enthusiasts.
- **Rock climbing:** An estimated 5 million Americans were rock climbing in 1993, and their numbers grew to 8.3 million in 1997.
- **Mountain biking:** During the 1990s, the number of people engaged in off-road mountain biking rose about 15% a year, increasing from less than 4 million in the early 1990s to more than 8 million in 1997–98.
- **Riding personal watercraft:** An estimated 7.2 million Americans ride personal watercraft, but a large percentage of them (72%) do so infrequently, often while they are on vacation, Warnick said.

Source: Excerpted from Barbara Bowers, "Risky Sports Gain in Popularity," *Best's Review* (March 2000): 37.

Tobacco Use

People who use tobacco in any form show greater morbidity and mortality at every age than people who do not. Using tobacco causes or contributes to many impairments and aggravates other health problems. As a result, insurers generally provide lower premiums for tobacco nonusers than for tobacco users. Under this approach, tobacco use and nonuse are considered risk factors that require mortality debits or credits, respectively.

Alcohol Use

Because alcohol use can lead to alcoholism, which is considered a disease, underwriters investigate both alcohol abuse and alcoholism just as they would investigate any other health history or disease. Current evidence of excessive alcohol use may indicate a more serious problem in the future, as the person increases his alcohol consumption or suffers from the cumulative effects of many years of abuse.

Obtaining information about a proposed insured's use of alcohol can be very difficult. Underwriters usually gather information from inspection reports, personal interviews, alcohol usage questionnaires, MVRs, APSs, and liver function tests.

An alcohol usage questionnaire usually asks a proposed insured to provide information on his consumption of alcoholic beverages, as well as details about any conditions that may have resulted from or be related to alcohol use. Some insurers obtain answers to an alcohol usage questionnaire that the proposed insured must sign. The questionnaire is then attached to the policy for possible use if the insured's death occurs during the contestable period.

Substance Abuse

Substance abuse generally refers to the excessive use of any of a variety of several substances, including narcotics, hallucinogens, stimulants, and sedatives. People who abuse these substances may have or may develop psychological impairments, physical dependence, or personality disorders that can constitute additional risk. When evaluating the possibility of substance abuse, underwriters consider many of the same factors considered in cases involving excessive alcohol consumption.

Gathering information about an applicant's substance abuse is often difficult, especially because positive answers to questions concerning a person's use of illegal substances can be incriminating. In using tests to check for the presence of illegal substances, an underwriter verifies that the tests are conducted properly and that the test results are kept confidential. A medical examination by a doctor, medical history information including an APS, a urine test to screen for the presence of drugs, and an inspection report focused on substance abuse are generally included in the underwriting process when substance abuse is suspected and when the amount of insurance applied for is sufficient to warrant such an extensive investigation.

The fact that an applicant uses illegal substances also raises the question of moral hazard. An underwriter is generally persistent in seeking detailed information in every case in which substance abuse is suspected because such abuse can add substantially to the degree of risk that a proposed insured represents.

Subjects of Abuse

The risk that results from the physical abuse of a spouse, partner, or other family member by another is a sensitive issue for underwriters. Recall from Chapter 3 that several jurisdictions have enacted legislation that prohibits insurers from requesting or using information about whether an applicant is abused in making an underwriting decision. However, in states where the law permits insurers to consider abuse status when making an underwriting decision, considering the risk posed by potential abuse requires the underwriter to impartially evaluate the level of risk that the abuse represents and to determine the degree to which the risk is acceptable or unacceptable to the insurer.

Criminal History

Underwriters carefully investigate proposed insureds who have a history of criminal or illegal activities. Ranging from arson and assault to fraud and vandalism, criminal activity in the history of a proposed insured usually causes underwriters to rate or decline the case. Although underwriters cannot predict that criminal activity will recur, such a case requires a thorough review of the facts, an extensive inspection report, and detailed interviews with people who are likely to know the current activities and character of the proposed insured.

Civilian and Military Aviation

Because the federal government has kept statistics on aviation accidents and fatalities since the early days of aviation, underwriters and actuaries have a reliable database from which to assess the degree of risk involved in aviation activities. Although civilian and military aviation are underwritten somewhat differently, the primary sources of information for both include the application for insurance, the aviation questionnaire, the medical examination, the APS, the inspection report, and the personal history interview.

Civilian aviation includes air ambulance, ballooning, commercial aviation, crop dusting, fire fighting, power line and pipe inspecting, mail service, mapping, policing, racing, sightseeing, and weather or traffic control. Civilian aviation also includes flying for pleasure.

Many insurers consider civilian aviation to be a standard risk. Some insurers charge an extra premium for civilian aviation risks. Another approach is to issue the policy with an aviation exclusion rider. Generally, aviation exclusion riders are used only in cases in which the aviation hazard (1) is too great for any coverage or (2) cannot be measured.

Many of the factors considered in underwriting civilian aviation are also considered when underwriting military aviation. Underwriters look carefully at the age and duty area of all proposed insureds who are military aviators, as well as the type of aircraft in which they fly. Generally, the flat extra premiums for military aviation are higher for people younger than 30 than for people age 30 and older. Also, the flat extra premiums charged for pilots are usually higher than the premiums charged for aviation crew members. In most military aviation cases, people who serve in hazardous places are not acceptable risks and are declined.

Military Status

Underwriters generally treat military status as a separate area of risk assessment. If a country is not at war or involved in a military conflict, most insurers approve military personnel for coverage at standard rates. Career military personnel in particular are generally considered good risks and are underwritten as if they were civilians.

Most insurers do not include war exclusions in their policies. If an armed conflict broke out, most insurers would refuse an application from military personnel for as long as the conflict lasts. Some insurance companies, however, issue individual life insurance coverage at standard rates to all military personnel who do not exhibit extraordinary risk other than that associated with military service.

International Residence and Travel

Many insurers in the United States and Canada do not approve coverage for proposed insureds whose permanent residence is in a foreign country because of the difficulty of gathering complete underwriting information and, if coverage is issued, of conducting an adequate, cost-effective claim investigation. Insurers that conduct considerable business in foreign countries and that have established foreign offices, however, typically charge special premium rates for coverages in those countries and do issue insurance to people residing there either temporarily or permanently.

In considering international travel and residence as a risk selection factor, underwriters are usually concerned with extended residence abroad. Vacation trips of up to six months' duration are usually of no concern to the underwriter unless a proposed insured plans to travel to an area with great political unrest, military activity, or known deadly disease. The coverage may be approved at higher premiums or declined, or the decision to issue coverage may be postponed until the proposed insured returns to her home country. Most insurers remove extra premiums after an insured has returned to the United States or Canada and has remained there for one to two years.

One of the most important factors in all applications in which foreign travel and residence are involved is the type of insurance requested. In general, when an applicant requests the cheapest possible term insurance and wishes to make monthly payments for it, the underwriter considers the coverage to be "trip insurance" with probable poor persistency. Therefore, the underwriter usually declines the risk.

Some cases involve proposed insureds who travel internationally for business or diplomatic reasons. An employer may purchase insurance on an important employee as a means of inducing the employee to travel internationally by providing protection for the employee's family. Career foreign service personnel may present varying risks for an insurer because these people typically spend a great deal of time away from their home country and are subject to relocation from one country to another, perhaps to a politically unstable area.

Immigrants and Citizens of Foreign Countries

Underwriting immigrants and citizens of foreign countries is based on individual consideration of the class of risk presented, the reason for the insurance purchase, the reputation of the submitting agent, and the quality of the agent's previously submitted business. Generally, insurers give favorable consideration to immigrants and foreign countries' citizens who

- Intend to become permanent residents of the country in which the insurer does business
- Possess a permanent resident visa
- Do not travel at all or travel only infrequently to their country of origin

If an immigrant or a citizen of a foreign country has lived in the new country for less than six months to one year, most insurers require a medical examination and a complete blood profile for any amount of life insurance coverage.

Most insurers do not issue coverage to foreign nationals who are only visiting or temporarily living in North America because of a concern that the policy may lapse upon the person's departure. Such a person has little apparent reason to own a policy issued outside the native country.

Financial Factors for Individual Life Insurance

Besides considering medical and personal factors, underwriters usually also look at the proposed insured's financial information. Insurers have learned from experience that if people buy more life insurance than they can afford and need, they may not be able to pay the premiums. In addition, purchasing excess coverage may indicate the possibility of speculation and antiselection. Underwriters, therefore, approve insurance coverage on the basis of an applicant's real need for insurance, including the presence of a genuine potential financial loss in the event of the proposed insured's death.

Although financial factors are relevant in underwriting both personal and business insurance, we'll postpone discussion of business insurance to Chapter 6. In this section, we'll focus on financial factors for personal insurance. ***Personal insurance*** can be defined generally as insurance purchased by individuals for income replacement, family needs and expenses, and payment of estate taxes.

Underwriters assess an applicant's financial status to see that the amount of life insurance applied for is consistent with the anticipated amount of loss upon the proposed insured's death. A person's ***financial status*** is defined as a person's current income expressed in terms of amount, sources, and permanency, and by the person's ***net worth***, which is the difference between the person's assets and liabilities.

To examine the financial factors underwriters consider for personal insurance, we'll begin by discussing sources of financial information. Next, we will look at the ways underwriters evaluate an applicant's need for personal life insurance, and we will examine the significance of insurable interest, antiselection, and speculation. We'll conclude by showing how underwriters assess financial factors that help justify the underwriting decision.

Sources of Financial Information

Underwriters rely on three main sources of information to assess an applicant's financial situation: (1) the application for insurance, (2) the agent, and (3) the inspection report. The amount and type of financial information requested are generally determined by the amount of coverage requested. To manage and organize financial information, an underwriter may use a ***financial worksheet***, which is a document that enables an underwriter to organize financial information and to develop a clear picture of a person's financial situation.

FAST FACT

In 1999, the average amount of life insurance coverage per insured household in the United States was $189,800, equal to 36 months of disposable personal income for the insured household.[3]

The Application for Insurance

The application for insurance provides the underwriter with an initial picture of the proposed insured's financial status. The application shows the proposed insured's age, occupation, and income; the amount of other insurance in force; the cost and amount of the coverage requested; and the relationship between the proposed insured and the proposed beneficiary.

In examining this information, the underwriter looks for consistency before making a judgment regarding the appropriateness of the amount of insurance requested. For example, if a proposed insured already has several small-amount life insurance policies that have been in force for years and now wishes to purchase a large additional amount of coverage, the underwriter determines whether or not the new coverage can be justified according to the proposed insured's current income and ability to pay for the coverage.

The Agent

The agent's business relationship with the insurance company also influences whether or not the underwriter asks for additional information about a proposed insured's financial status and the reason for the insurance purchase. An agent who has established a strong relationship with an insurer and who generally requests coverage only for qualified applicants is likely to be considered a reliable source of financial information during underwriting. If the underwriter has questions or doubts about the justification for requested insurance, the underwriter typically talks to the agent to clarify the submitted information. If doubts persist, the underwriter may then request more information from the agent, the proposed insured, or an inspection agency. If an underwriter doesn't know the agent well and needs to check on the quality of business submitted, the underwriter typically orders an inspection report.

Inspection Report

Another of the underwriter's sources of financial information is the inspection report. The information in an inspection report can be important to an underwriter in verifying information from the applicant and the agent. The underwriter may request that the inspection report cover the finances of the proposed insured, including

- Cash, stocks, and bonds
- Earned and unearned income
- Real estate
- Automobiles and personal possessions
- Business equity
- Other sources of assets and liabilities
- Credit history

Many insurers do not use an inspection report for financial underwriting on applicants requesting less than $500,000 of personal life insurance. For cases above $500,000, the underwriter may interview the proposed insured's accountant or bank to verify information in the application and other documents.

Further, for large-amount cases, the agent usually is required to complete a financial questionnaire that the applicant must sign or provide an audited financial statement to show the income, net worth, and sources of income. If the questionnaire or the audited financial statement reveals that an applicant's finances are not consistent with the amount of coverage requested, and if the case file doesn't already include an inspection report, the underwriter may order an inspection report.

The bankruptcy of a proposed insured poses certain underwriting problems. The increased risk associated with bankruptcy includes persistency problems and the possibility of antiselection resulting from suicide. If the inspection report reveals that a proposed insured is currently involved in a bankruptcy, many insurers deny coverage until the proposed insured has been released from bankruptcy for a certain period of time, usually one to seven years. Some insurers, however, approve applications for moderate amounts of term insurance from people involved in certain types of bankruptcies.

Tax Forms

Underwriters can gather valuable information from an applicant's W-2 form (in the United States) or T4 form (in Canada), as well as from federal, state, or provincial income tax returns. Such forms enable underwriters to verify financial information obtained from the application and other sources. The W-2 form in the United States provides the underwriter with information about the amount of money paid to the proposed insured by an employer. In Canada, the T4 form provides information that is similar to that provided by the W-2.

Underwriters also can request copies of income tax returns from the agent or the proposed insured to verify financial information. Particularly when a tax return contains itemized information and various schedules, it can provide a great deal of financial information about a proposed insured.

For example, when a proposed insured's tax return shows unemployment compensation, the underwriter might question whether the applicant is steadily employed and can pay for insurance. If an applicant's tax return shows a considerable deduction for medical or dental expenses, the underwriter likely will seek further information about the applicant's health, especially if other information indicates that the applicant may have a significant health impairment.

For large-amount applications, some insurers use statements from a proposed insured's banker or certified public accountant instead of or in addition to information from tax forms. The statements typically cover several years and report gross income, net income, net worth, and financial losses. When available, such statements have credibility because they have been compiled by professionals, who submit with the statements a certificate that the statements are accurate.

Financial Questionnaire

Underwriters can also obtain financial information about an applicant by using a financial questionnaire that requests specific details about the financial situation of the proposed insured and that is signed by the proposed insured. In handling financial questionnaires, the underwriter is especially careful to adhere to the insurance company's rules of confidentiality. An example of a financial questionnaire is shown in Figure 5-4.

If an applicant is requesting personal life insurance as a means of paying a future estate tax liability, the underwriter can use a financial questionnaire to ask about the value of the applicant's estate, the composition of the estate (for instance, property, investments, and other sources of assets), the estimated value and the dates of all gifts made from the estate, the applicant's estimated liability for estate tax, and the name of the person who is liable for paying the estate tax after the applicant's death.

Financial Statements

When a proposed insured who owns a business wishes to purchase a considerable amount of personal life insurance, the underwriter can

FIGURE 5-4. Financial Questionnaire.

FINANCIAL QUESTIONNAIRE

To be completed by Proposed Insured

Name:	Birthdate: (Day/Month/Year)	Amount applied for: $

Annual Personal Income (prior 3 years) and Net Worth Calculation

Income	Year______	Year______	Year______
Salary	$	$	$
Business profits reported as personal income	$	$	$
Bonus	$	$	$
Commission	$	$	$
Pension/profit sharing	$	$	$
Other (describe) --------------	$	$	$
Total Earned Income	$	$	$
Annual Unearned Income			
Dividends	$	$	$
Interest	$	$	$
Net rentals	$	$	$
Capital gains	$	$	$
Other (describe)	$	$	$
-----------------------	$	$	$
-----------------------	$	$	$
Total Unearned Income	$	$	$

ASSETS		**LIABILITIES**	
Cash	$	Mortgages	$
Real estate	$	Loans	$
Business equity	$	Liens	$
Stocks	$	Bonds	$
Other (describe)	$	Other (describe)	$
-----------------------	$	-----------------------	$
-----------------------	$	-----------------------	$
-----------------------	$	-----------------------	$
-----------------------	$	-----------------------	$
Total Assets	$	**Total Liabilities**	$
Net Worth	$		

I understand that my answers to this questionnaire are material to my application for insurance and will be relied upon by the insurance company in determining my insurability.

I understand that any material misrepresentation in this questionnaire, or elsewhere in my application for insurance, will permit the insurance company to decline my application or rescind the policy.

I declare that the above answers are complete and true, and shall form part of my application to the insurance company.

Date ____________________

Witness ______________________________ Proposed Insured's Signature ______________________

Source: Excerpted from Barbara Foxenberger Brown and Jane Lightcap Brown, *Life and Health Insurance Underwriting* (Atlanta: LOMA,

request financial statements relating to the business to help determine the stability of the business and to rule out possible antiselection.

In assessing financial statements for a personal business, an underwriter usually considers the following information:

- The historic trend of profit or loss in the business, typically for a period of at least the three to five years prior to the date of application for insurance

- The relative performance of the business in its industry during the same three- to five-year period

- Financial obligations to which the business is or will be committed

- Evidence of plans to expand, restructure, or sell the business

The underwriter keeps in mind that the debt of a business can rise and fall substantially during the year. Therefore, the underwriter typically uses annual financial statements, not recent quarterly reports, in determining the amount of debt a company carries. Using a recent quarterly report could present a distorted view of the company's financial strength or weakness.

Assessing the Need for Insurance

Evaluating a proposed insured's financial situation includes an assessment of that person's need for insurance. Underwriters are justifiably wary of an application requesting coverage that is far in excess of the proposed insured's expected needs because such an application may indicate antiselection.

Generally accepted financial purposes for purchasing personal life insurance include

- Family income protection

- Estate settlement

- Charitable contributions

In the context of insurance coverage, ***family income*** is defined as funds needed to replace the ordinary living expenses formerly paid by the income of a deceased person whose wages or other income supplied the needs of a family. Underwriters generally approve coverage for family income if the need for that income in the amount requested is clearly shown.

Estate settlement is the process of paying debts after a person's death. Estate settlement typically requires funds to pay taxes, as well as medical expenses not covered by other insurance, funeral costs, attorneys' fees and other costs incurred to settle the estate, and repayment of debts owed by the deceased person. Life insurance can provide the funds needed to pay these costs. Underwriters usually approve coverage intended to pay such expenses when evidence of the likely obligations is clear.

Sometimes the beneficiary listed in an application for life insurance is a charitable institution. If a person has been making regular contributions to a charitable organization, the contributions will cease when that person dies. Life insurance proceeds can be used to replace that person's lost future contributions. Even if a person has made no previous contributions, using life insurance proceeds to benefit a charity is a legitimate and widely recognized way of making charitable gifts.

Insurable Interest, Antiselection, and Speculation

We have already introduced the topics of insurable interest and antiselection. In assessing financial factors, the underwriter protects both the insurer and other insureds by making certain (1) every case has a valid insurable interest, especially in relationship to the amount of insurance requested, (2) antiselection is not present, and (3) speculation is not a factor, particularly for cases in which a large amount of insurance is involved.

In assessing insurable interest, the underwriter often projects the loss into the future, particularly if the proposed insured provides a considerable amount of financial assistance to a beneficiary, as a parent would provide for a child, or one spouse would provide for the other spouse. The underwriter checks carefully to be sure that each beneficiary has an insurable interest in the continued life of the proposed insured, that the amount of coverage requested is justified in relationship to the insurable interest of the beneficiary, and that the reasons for purchasing coverage are justifiable. Note that, in most jurisdictions, a proposed insured who is also the applicant can name anyone as the beneficiary.

Some applicants have a strong financial need that they do not disclose when they apply for insurance and that they hope will not be discovered during underwriting. In such cases, the possibility of antiselection arises, with resultant potential financial harm to the insurer and its other insureds.

Underwriters also are aware of possible antiselection on the part of elderly applicants. Whereas life insurance may not be suitable for income protection for an elderly person whose spouse dies, many elderly people have sizable estates for which insurance can provide estate tax protection. Underwriters usually approve coverage for such people after investigation to be sure that antiselection is not a factor in the case.

The possibility of speculation arises when the amount of insurance exceeds the potential financial loss that a beneficiary might suffer if an insured person were to die. In insurance, ***speculation*** is the purchasing of insurance with the expectation of making a profit on the proceeds. For example, an application made by an adult child for insurance on an aged, dependent parent requires special examination, because such an application may present an element of speculation. Upon the death of the proposed insured, the adult child not only would receive the death benefit, but would also be relieved of support expenses. The underwriter might, however, approve coverage on the life of an elderly parent who was providing a service, such as babysitting for grandchildren.

Assessing Financial Factors

Financial underwriting for life insurance is based on the assumption that the coverage an insurer issues will compensate for a loss, but will not be so great that the money will represent a profit to the beneficiary or beneficiaries. Most proposed insureds demonstrate a clear need for the requested amount of coverage. In a few cases, however, the amount of coverage requested does not seem appropriate, at least not initially. In these cases, the underwriter judges the appropriateness of the amount of insurance requested according to three financial factors: the applicant's (1) net worth and income, (2) ability to pay for insurance, and (3) insurance in force. After discussing these factors, we'll look at the special challenge of underwriting large-amount cases.

Net Worth and Income

From an underwriting perspective, a person's net worth—the difference between that person's assets and liabilities—represents the estimated economic value of that person's life. Income is one of the elements used to determine the amount of financial loss that would occur in the event of a person's death. Elements that the underwriter considers include current income, potential income, and taxes.

A proposed insured's income has a specific relationship to the amount of loss that person's death could cause and to the amount of coverage that an underwriter probably would approve. The underwriter's job includes determining the proposed insured's approximate income and its importance to the named beneficiaries. The underwriter keeps in mind that a person may have income from various sources, some of which are fairly permanent and some of which are temporary or occasional. The underwriter also decides which source or sources of income can be used to determine whether the applicant can afford to buy the amount of insurance requested.

The underwriter also considers the potential earning power of a proposed insured. The person might have just begun her career and not yet reached her full earnings potential. If a proposed insured has an irregular or insecure income—for instance, someone who has no business experience and is starting a new company, or someone whose sole income is derived from participation in a minor league sport—the underwriter could have difficulty estimating the person's potential income. In such cases, consulting the chief underwriter and additional research can help the underwriter make a fair decision on the case.

Taxes complicate the underwriter's assessment task because usually a substantial difference exists between an applicant's pre-tax income and after-tax income. Usually, underwriters use pre-tax figures, making the necessary adjustments for taxable income in cases in which the inclusion of taxes produces a significantly different picture of an applicant's finances.

Ability to Pay for Insurance

Another task of the underwriter is to determine whether an applicant can afford to pay the premiums required to purchase the amount of insurance requested. In making this determination, the underwriter considers all sources of available income, some of which are fairly permanent and others of which are temporary. Possible sources of income include salary from a full-time job, salary from a part-time job, spouse's salary, bonuses, commissions, stock options, expense allowance, profit sharing, investment income, capital gains, dividends, and inheritance.

In this section, we'll discuss factor tables as well as two other methods of determining ability to pay: the percentage-of-income rule and the 20 percent rule. These rules are used as guidelines, not as rigid decision-making tools. Therefore, an underwriter usually looks at the insurance amounts suggested by one or more of the rules, but may consider other factors as well in coming to a decision about an appropriate amount of insurance for a specific case.

Factor Tables. Factor tables prescribe the amount of life insurance coverage for which an applicant is eligible. A ***factor table*** is a chart that shows the maximum amount of insurance, expressed in multiples of a person's salary or total income, that an insurer will typically approve in each of several age ranges. An insurer's factor table is updated every five years or so to reflect changes in the economy and in the insurer's underwriting guidelines, which generally change according to revisions in the insurer's product line and claim experience.

Because each insurer develops its own factor tables, the amount of insurance a person can buy may vary widely from one insurer to another. Figure 5-5 shows a typical factor table for life insurance; the table specifies the amount of insurance, figured as a multiple of a proposed insured's current gross income, that may be purchased at specified ages.

An underwriter is usually not bound absolutely by the numbers in a factor table. Higher amounts of coverage can be approved for applicants whose current income is low, but who can be expected to have higher earnings in later years. For example, young doctors, attorneys, financial consultants, and sales people generally can be expected to earn considerably more money as they gain experience and develop larger practices and more clients. For such applicants, underwriters often request documentation indicating the applicant's potential future earnings.

Percentage-of-Income Rule. An underwriter can determine the amount that can be spent on insurance by using a ***percentage-of-income rule***, which stipulates the amount of money an applicant can afford to spend on insurance according to the applicant's income. The percentage generally varies between 6 percent and 20 percent, depending on the level of the person's gross income and the type and amount of coverage requested. Each insurer stipulates its own percentages for each insurance product.

As an example, one insurer's percentage-of-income rule specifies that an applicant for a certain life insurance product can afford premiums of no more than 7 percent of the first $10,000 of her gross annual income, 11 percent of the next $15,000, and 18 percent of the remainder. According to this insurer's percentage-of-income rule, an applicant who

FIGURE 5-5. A Typical Factor Table for Whole Life Insurance.

Age	Multiple of Current Income
20–24	20
25–29	18
30–34	17
35–39	15
40–44	12
45–49	11
50–54	9
55–59	8
60–64	6
65 and older	5

earns \$100,000 a year can afford to pay a maximum premium of \$15,850 annually for life insurance coverage, computed as follows:

\$ 700	[0.07 × \$10,000]
+\$1,650	[0.11 × \$15,000]
+\$13,500	[0.18 × \$75,000]
\$15,850	

20 Percent Rule. Another similar method of determining the amount of coverage an applicant can afford to purchase is known as the 20 percent rule. Under the ***20 percent rule***, a maximum of 20 percent of the applicant's gross earned income can be used to buy life insurance. For example, according to the 20 percent rule, an applicant who earns \$100,000 annually could afford to spend a maximum of \$20,000 (\$100,000 × 0.20) each year for life insurance coverage.

As you review these three methods of determining an applicant's ability to pay for coverage, remember that each rule may result in slightly different amounts of coverage for any given insured. If a 45-year-old proposed insured who is in good health and who earns a gross annual income of \$85,000 is evaluated by each of the three rules as specified in our discussion, the amounts of coverage that would be considered appropriate based on his ability to pay would differ, as shown in Figure 5-6.

Insurance in Force

In order to rule out the elements of speculation and antiselection, the underwriter makes certain that the proposed insured is not overinsured. Therefore, the underwriter evaluates the amount of insurance that a proposed insured currently has in force with all insurers and the amount of insurance for which the person is applying. To determine this amount, the underwriter uses information on the application. If the proposed insured is replacing one policy with another, the underwriter subtracts the amount of the policy being replaced from the proposed insured's total amount of coverage. Each insurer sets its own limits for the total acceptable amount of in-force coverage. The following example shows one insurer's total in-force coverage limits:

Age	Acceptable Total Amount of Insurance
18–29	Total amount ≤ 25 × income
30–39	Total amount ≤ 20 × income
40–49	Total amount ≤ 15 × income
50–59	Total amount ≤ 10 × income
60+	Total amount ≤ 6 × income

FIGURE 5-6. Methods of Determining a Person's Ability to Pay for Coverage.

Rule	Example	Amount of coverage considered appropriate based on ability to pay
Factor table	Age — Multiple of Current Income 30–34 — 17 35–39 — 15 40–44 — 12 45–49 — 11 50–54 — 9	$935,000 in coverage ($85,000 × 11)
Percentage-of-income rule	To buy life insurance, an applicant for a certain product can spend no more than 7 percent of the first $10,000 of her gross annual income, 11 percent of the next $15,000, and 18 percent of the remainder.	The amount of coverage that can be purchased for a maximum premium of $13,150: $700 (0.07 × $10,000) $1,650 (0.11 × $15,000) +$10,800 (0.18 × $60,000) $113,150
20 percent rule	A maximum of 20 percent of the applicant's gross earned income can be used to buy life insurance.	The amount of coverage that can be purchased for a maximum premium of $17,000 ($85,000 × 0.20)

Source: Excerpted from Barbara Foxenberger Brown and Jane Lightcap Brown, *Life and Health Insurance Underwriting* (Atlanta: LOMA, © 1998), 169. Used with permission; all rights reserved.

In some insurance companies, the calculation for the amount of insurance in force includes an accidental death benefit (ADB), which doubles or triples the face amount of the policy if the insured dies in an accident as defined in the policy. Some insurers establish separate limits for face amount coverage and for ADB coverages.

Also, when calculating a proposed insured's total amount of in-force insurance, the underwriter considers personal insurance and business insurance separately. Life insurance coverage paid for by a proposed insured's employer is typically not included as in-force coverage. Such insurance is usually requested and owned by the employer, and the insured does not choose the benefit amount. For example, suppose a proposed insured has $250,000 of personal life insurance and $500,000 of business life insurance. The proposed insured's employer purchased the business coverage because the proposed insured is considered important to the company's future success. If the proposed insured applies for an additional $100,000 of *personal* life insurance, the underwriter would consider the existing $250,000 of *personal* life coverage to be the total amount of in-force coverage when assessing the proposed insured's total amount of personal insurance coverage.

Large-Amount Cases

Underwriting life insurance applications for unusually large amounts of coverage presents the underwriter with a special challenge. Insurers' experience has shown that the possibility of antiselection tends to be greater for large policies. In underwriting an application for a substantial amount of coverage, the underwriter needs to know considerably more about the applicant's financial background than is necessary for smaller-amount cases. For instance, for underwriting large-amount cases, an insurer might require the following:

- A letter from the agent explaining the applicant's need for a large amount of insurance
- Financial documents for the past five or more years
- Detailed inspection reports, including a check of court records and motor vehicle records, and information obtained from conversations with people who know the proposed insured

Generally, insurers use more conservative underwriting guidelines when assessing risk for a large-amount policy than they use when assessing other risks. Often, applications for such policies are reviewed by several underwriters, including senior underwriters, before a decision is made.

Key Terms and Concepts

motor vehicle record (MVR)
inspection report
insurable interest
third-party applicant
moral hazard
persistency
personal insurance
financial status
net worth
financial worksheet
family income
estate settlement
speculation
factor table
percentage-of-income rule
20 percent rule

Endnotes

1. ACLI, *Life Insurers Fact Book 2000* (Washington, D.C.: American Council of Life Insurers, 2000), 11.
2. U.S. Consumer Product Safety Commission, "CPSC Reports Sports-Related Injuries Boom Among Baby Boomers," 7 April 2000, http://www.cpsc.gov/CPSCPUB/PREREL/prhtml00/00094.html (20 July 2001).
3. ACLI, 12.

CHAPTER 6

Underwriting Specialized Policies and Supplemental Coverages

Chapter Outline

Underwriting Business Insurance
- Insurable Interest
- Medical, Financial, and Personal Factors
- Estimating the Value of a Business
- Business Solvency, Liquidity, and Profitability
- Assessing Risk

Underwriting Multi-Life Products

Underwriting Juvenile Insurance

Handling Guaranteed-Issue Products
- Direct Response Products

Underwriting Policy Replacements
- Antiselection in Policy Replacements
- Underwriting Standards in Policy Replacements
- Possibility of Churning or Twisting
- Tax Consequences of Policy Replacements

Underwriting Supplementary Coverages
- Waiver of Premium for Disability
- Accidental Death Benefit
- Family Benefit
- Guaranteed Insurability

Objectives

After reading this chapter, you should be able to

- Describe the types of information an underwriter gathers by using a business financial supplement
- List and explain the criteria an underwriter uses in estimating the value of a business
- Discuss the underwriting considerations for the following types of business coverages: creditor insurance, partnership insurance, sole proprietorship insurance, key-person insurance, and split-dollar plans
- Explain the typical underwriting approach for multi-life products, juvenile insurance, individual guaranteed-issue products, and direct response products
- Discuss the importance of antiselection and underwriting standards in connection with policy replacements
- Describe the procedures for underwriting supplementary coverages

In this chapter, we'll examine the underwriting considerations for certain specialized life insurance coverages. You'll see that many of the same factors that are assessed in underwriting individual life coverages are also used to determine the degree of risk represented by applicants for specialized coverages. In addition to specialized coverages, we'll discuss supplemental coverage. ***Supplemental coverage*** is an amount of coverage that adds to the amount of coverage specified in a basic insurance policy.

We'll begin by discussing the underwriting considerations for business insurance, multi-life products, juvenile insurance, and guaranteed-issue and direct response products. We'll also examine the underwriting approaches for policy replacements and for certain supplementary coverages including waiver of premium for disability, accidental death benefit, family benefit, and guaranteed insurability.

Underwriting Business Insurance

Business insurance provides coverage for the insurance needs of a business organization rather than those of an individual. Underwriters examine the same factors—medical, financial, and personal—in underwriting business insurance as they consider in underwriting individual life insurance. In addition, business insurance underwriters also consider financial factors related to the business for which the coverage is intended. After we explain these factors, we'll look at underwriting approaches used for specific types of business insurance, including creditor insurance, partnership insurance, sole proprietorship insurance, key-person insurance, and split-dollar plans. Figure 6-1 briefly summarizes these specific types of business insurance.

Insurable Interest

Unlike most personal life insurance, business insurance is usually third-party insurance, so the proposed insured is not the applicant and will not be the policyowner if a policy is issued. An exception is sole proprietorship insurance for which the proposed insured and the policyowner are the same.

In assessing the risk for business insurance, underwriters usually consider insurable interest to be present if the premature death of one party in a business relationship would cause serious loss to the surviving parties or to the business. For example, insurable interest generally is considered to exist when a business wishes to insure the lives of

FIGURE 6-1. Types of Business Insurance.

Creditor Insurance	Creditor insurance is issued to a lender or to a borrower to cover the life of the borrower for the amount of an outstanding loan—for example, to cover the amount of a mortgage on a building in which a business is establishing its headquarters. If the borrower dies before the loan is repaid, the policy benefits pay the remaining debt. The face value of creditor insurance decreases to match the amount of unpaid debt.
Partnership Insurance	Partnership insurance is designed to provide funds so that the remaining partners in a business can buy the business interest of a deceased or disabled partner. A variation of this type of coverage is *stock repurchase insurance*, which provides funds so that other stockholders in the company can buy stock from the estate of a deceased stockholder.
Sole Proprietorship Insurance	Sole proprietorship insurance provides coverage on the life of the sole proprietor of a business—and may be used to pay the salary of a person hired to run the business if the sole proprietor dies—or provides funds for a trusted employee or another person to buy the business at the death of the owner (as agreed upon in a buy-sell agreement signed by the company's owner and the prospective purchaser.)
Key-Person Insurance	Key-person insurance is coverage purchased by a business on the life of a person (usually a high-ranking executive in the business or an employee with special skills) whose continued participation in the business is judged necessary to the firm's success and whose death would cause financial loss to the company.
Split-Dollar Plan	Split-dollar insurance covers the life of an employee and is paid for jointly by the employee and the employer. The employee names the beneficiary. Each year, the employer pays the portion of the premium that is equal to the increase in the policy's cash value for that year, and the employee pays the rest of the premium. If the employee dies, the employer receives the amount of the proceeds equal to what it paid for the policy, and the beneficiary of the policy receives the remaining policy proceeds.

certain key employees who are essential to the continued success of the company; the owners of a business wish to insure each other's lives; and a creditor wishes to insure the life of a debtor.

Medical, Financial, and Personal Factors

Using many of the same sources and procedures as when gathering information for personal insurance, business insurance underwriters collect and assess medical, personal, and financial information.

Medical Information

The underwriter usually gathers medical information about a person whose life is to be covered by business insurance in the same manner as when underwriting a personal insurance policy. The underwriter reviews the application and may order an APS and laboratory tests. Medical underwriting requirements for business insurance coverage usually are the same as those for personal insurance coverage.

FAST FACT

At the end of 1999, $213 billion of creditor insurance was in force in the United States.[1]

Financial Information

Financial assessment for business insurance focuses on the finances of the business more than on the finances of the proposed insured. The underwriter examines the financial condition of the business to ensure that a legitimate need for the insurance exists and that the business will be able to pay the premiums.

To collect financial information about a business, the underwriter typically uses many of the same sources used to collect financial information for personal insurance, such as the application for insurance, the agent's statement, an inspection report, W-2 or T4 forms, business income tax returns, a specialized financial questionnaire, and business financial statements. In addition, if a lender has required the proposed insured to be covered by a specific amount of insurance, the underwriter usually asks the agent to obtain copies of relevant personal and business loan documents.

An underwriter also can use a specialized questionnaire called a ***business financial supplement***, which is a document that requests information about the type of business, the current financial condition of the business, and the purpose for which the insurance is being requested. This type of supplement is also occasionally used for underwriting personal insurance when the value of a proposed insured's business is important in assessing that person's financial worth. Figure 6-2 shows a typical business financial supplement.

The underwriter assesses financial documents in much the same way as for personal coverage applications. However, one special consideration for business coverages is that a business's audited financial statements sometimes need investigation because acceptable methods of valuing assets and liabilities, and of reporting profits and earnings, vary widely. Underwriters may consult with people in the insurer's legal, investment, and accounting areas to help investigate and understand business-related financial documents.

The financial health of a business is often difficult to assess. Underwriters who specialize in business insurance are trained to look for indications that a business is in financial difficulty. Such indications include

- Negative cash flow from operations and inadequate financing
- Excessive debt that probably cannot be paid within a reasonable time and without reducing the funds that the business needs for maintenance and expansion

FIGURE 6-2. Business Financial Supplement.

BUSINESS FINANCIAL SUPPLEMENT

I. NAME OF COMPANY ______________________________

II. TYPE OF ORGANIZATION ❒ Corporation ❒ Partnership ❒ Sole Proprietorship

III. Please attach a copy of your company's latest audited financial statements (Balance Sheet and Profit & Loss). If not available, complete the following questions:

A. CURRENT COMPANY BOOK VALUE

Assets $__________
Liabilities $__________
Net Worth $__________

B. CURRENT COMPANY MARKET VALUE

Market Value $__________
Insured's % Ownership $__________
Market Value of Insured's % Ownership $__________

C. COMPANY NET PROFIT—Past Two Years
(Before taxes and bonuses)

20____ $__________
20____ $__________
This Year (Est.) $__________

D. What other stockholders, partners, or key persons are also being insured in favor of the company? (Please name)

IV. (Check at least one box and provide details)

❒ **KEY PERSON**

A. Why is the person to be insured important to the company? What special skills, knowledge, or abilities does he/she possess that make insurance necessary? ______________________________

____

____

B. How is it expected that the proceeds will be utilized? ______________________________

____

❒ **STOCK REDEMPTION/BUY AND SELL**

A. Is there a written agreement: In effect? (Attach signed copy)
Contemplated? Give expected finalization date ______________

B. How is the business being valued in the agreement? ______________________________

____

❒ **BUSINESS LOAN**

A. Name and address of the lender: ______________________________
B. Amount of loan $______________ **C.** Date of loan: ______________
D. The repayment terms are: ______________________________
E. The purpose of the loan is: ______________________________
F. Is lender requiring the insurance? ❒ Yes ❒ No

I understand that ABC Life Insurance Company will rely on the above statements in determining the need and justification for the insurance applied for, and I represent that all answers are true and accurate statements to the best of my knowledge and belief as of the date of application for life insurance. A photographic copy of this statement may be attached to and made part of any insurance contract issued.

Signature of Proposed Insured ______________ Date ______________
Signature of Owner ______________ Date ______________
Witnessed by ______________ Date ______________

- Unusual financing arrangements, such as loans from family members, subsidiaries of the business, or clients of the business
- Dependence on only a few projects or clients instead of a wide variety of projects or clients
- A trend of declining sales or revenues
- A history of defaults on loans or debts, denial of credit by lenders, or recent financial restructuring
- Unexplained or illogical sale of substantial assets
- Bankruptcy
- Labor strife
- Recent or substantial litigation
- Large losses that were not covered by insurance

Personal Information

The same kinds of personal information required for underwriting personal coverage generally are considered in underwriting business insurance. That is, underwriters evaluate a proposed insured's age, sex, occupation and avocations, driving history, tobacco and alcohol use, substance abuse, criminal history, civilian and military aviation, military status, and international travel and residence. In addition, underwriters examine any indications of moral hazard in connection to the proposed insured as well as any evidence that persistency of the coverage may be problematic.

The sources of personal information for business insurance are generally the same as for individual insurance. For example, underwriters examine information from such sources as motor vehicle records (MVRs), inspection reports, personal history interviews, or specialized personal questionnaires.

Estimating the Value of a Business

Underwriting an application for business insurance requires the underwriter to analyze the financial strength of the business by assessing a number of criteria, including the following:

- Tangible assets (such as buildings, equipment, and inventory)
- Intangible assets (such as goodwill, an established customer base, favorable industry reputation, market presence, franchise value,

name recognition, desirable location of the business, trademarks, logos, and patents)

- Historic trend of profit or loss in the business, especially its average earning capacity over a period of at least three to five years prior to the date of application for insurance
- The relative performance of the business in its industry during the same three- to five-year period
- Current economic conditions and the future outlook of the business sector in which the business operates and of the economy as a whole
- Probable ability of the business to be self-sustaining by (1) hiring and retaining employees and (2) retaining current customers and attracting new ones
- Book value and recent sales of the company's stock, if any, and the dividend-paying capacity of the business
- Financial obligations to which the business is or will be committed
- Evidence of plans to expand, restructure, or sell the business

One of the challenges for every underwriter in estimating the value of a business is knowing enough about the business to make an equitable and accurate assessment of its worth. Because industries grow, change, merge, and diversify, underwriters continually update their knowledge not only of business in general, but of specific industries.

Business Solvency, Liquidity, and Profitability

To avoid antiselection, business insurance underwriters examine a business' solvency, liquidity, and profitability. Considered in isolation, the figures concerning solvency, liquidity, and profitability mean little, if anything. Underwriters typically compare these figures for a business to the norms established by the insurance industry and to the figures of other businesses in the same or similar industries.

Solvency

A company's ***solvency*** is the company's ability to pay its debts on time. A business that is unable to maintain sufficient funds to pay its debts not only may be unable to pay insurance premiums, but also may be likely to suffer financial failure. In either situation, such a company is not a sound candidate for business coverage. The norm typically used by insurers for underwriting purposes is that a financially sound company has a total debt less than its net worth.

Liquidity

Liquidity refers to the ease with which a company can convert its assets into cash for an approximation of their true value. A company's ***current assets*** are usually the items that the company presently has or owns, and that can be easily converted to cash. Examples include short-term investments, and cash and cash equivalents. A company's ***current liabilities*** are usually all the debt that is due and payable within the next accounting period, typically one year. Current liabilities include salaries payable and interest payable.

To determine a company's liquidity, an underwriter compares the company's current assets to its current liabilities. If a current appraisal of asset value is available, the underwriter uses it. If such information is not available, the underwriter estimates the market value of assets. Although the desired ratio of current assets to current liabilities varies among industries, insurers generally consider a business to have acceptable liquidity if the business has at least $2 in current assets for every $1 in current debt. That is, the firm's current assets should be at least two times as great as the firm's current debts.

Profitability

A company's ***profitability*** measures the productivity of the company's assets and its return on investment. Companies operating in higher risk businesses expect a higher return, whereas companies operating in lower risk businesses are satisfied with a smaller return. In general, most insurers consider a company with a return on its investment of 10 to 20 percent (depending on the industry) to be financially sound.

Underwriters can have difficulty assessing the financial strength of nondomestic corporations whose accounting practices and business strategies differ considerably from those generally applied to domestic organizations. Determining the financial integrity of nondomestic companies requires that the underwriter develop a thorough understanding of financial statement practices in other countries. Governmental organizations and attorneys' organizations in foreign countries usually maintain and publish records of business legal problems and can provide information that is useful for underwriting purposes.

By gathering as complete information as possible on a business, the underwriter seeks to approve coverage for appropriate risks and to deny coverage to businesses that are financially unstable or that are involved in commercial fraud. Some of the warning signs of possible business fraud include

- Evidence that the ownership of a company is being concealed
- A partner or other key person who has worked for a considerable period in a foreign country or who has worked for a number of companies that are no longer in business
- A partner or other key person who is unable to provide information concerning his or her business history and past associations
- Failure of a business that otherwise seems healthy—the failure may be the result of questionable operations that can include diversion of funds, sale of assets, and excessive use of credit
- An overly complex organizational or partnership structure, or a confusing web of subsidiaries and conglomerates
- Trade, bank, or business references that appear fraudulent or unbelievably positive
- Financial statements that have been issued at irregular intervals or that list assets that cannot be confirmed by other sources, that use round figures instead of specific amounts, or that list accounts receivable that are inconsistent with other figures such as inventory and purchasing records

Assessing Risk

The underwriter uses basically the same approaches to assess the risk for every type of business insurance. However, each type of business insurance coverage has slightly different requirements. We'll examine the primary underwriting considerations for several types of business coverages and riders. These types of business insurance were defined briefly in Figure 6-1 and will be discussed in more detail in this section.

Creditor Insurance

Creditor insurance is coverage that is designed to alleviate the economic loss suffered by a creditor when one of its borrowers dies before the debt is repaid. In this discussion, we are considering only business loans, not consumer loans that finance the purchase of a house or a personal vehicle. Creditor insurance provides the creditor with proceeds that are no greater than the unpaid debt so that the principle of insurable interest is maintained. The creditor is legally entitled to only that portion of a loan that has not been repaid.

The underwriter also determines whether a borrower has means other than insurance to repay the debt. One issue to be considered in underwriting a creditor insurance application is whether money from the loan is being used to purchase something that can serve as collateral for the loan. Another issue is whether the collateral will continue to produce income to pay off the loan. If it seems likely that the borrower only will be able to repay the loan with the life insurance benefit, then the underwriter declines the case. In such a situation, the application for creditor insurance represents an undesirable risk and possible antiselection. The underwriter may want to see the loan repayment schedule in order to obtain a better idea of the proposed insured's financial situation. Another element to consider is that a short-term creditor policy may lapse before the insurer can recover its costs or realize a profit. Generally, issuing creditor insurance for short-term loans is not in an insurer's best interest.

FAST FACT

The number of creditor insurance policies in the United States increased from 1 million in 1935 to 46 million in 1999.[2]

Over the years, large-amount creditor coverage has consistently demonstrated the poorest mortality experience. Usually, 50 percent to 75 percent of the loan is the maximum an underwriter approves. The allowable amount depends upon whether the loan is collateralized by other assets. An application submitted after a significant period of time has passed since a loan has been granted can indicate that a debtor's financial situation or health has deteriorated since the loan was granted, so the debtor or the creditor wishes to ensure that the debt will be paid. The underwriter verifies, therefore, that loan payments have been made in a timely fashion and that the debtor's financial condition and health remain sound.

Partnership Insurance

A business partnership is formed when two or more people voluntarily join together as co-owners of a business. The death of a business partner can cause severe loss to a company. Under the laws of most jurisdictions, a partnership is dissolved when a change occurs in its membership. The remaining partners are bound by law to close the business and to pay an equitable share of the value of the business to the estate or the heirs of the deceased partner.

Partnership insurance is coverage that provides cash with which surviving partners can purchase the business interest of a deceased partner from that partner's heirs. The partnership owns the partnership insurance policy and is the beneficiary of the coverage. To underwrite partnership insurance, the underwriter assesses the insurability of each partner covered by the policy. If one partner is uninsurable, generally the coverage can still be issued, although at a higher premium. Most insurers, however, consider that the fewer the number of partners in a business, the more conservatively the application is handled.

In gathering information to underwrite an application for partnership coverage, underwriters typically use a financial questionnaire that focuses on the partnership. Figure 6-3 illustrates such a partnership insurance questionnaire.

A variation of partnership insurance is stock repurchase insurance. If a person who owns a significant amount of stock in a company dies, the stock goes into that person's estate. In some situations, however, other stockholders want to buy that stock. The money to pay for the stock purchase can come from life insurance proceeds, and the coverage that provides the money is called ***stock repurchase insurance*** or *stock redemption insurance.*

In underwriting applications for stock repurchase insurance, the underwriter's main concern is that the people who plan to buy the stock owned by the proposed insured have an insurable interest in the insured's life. The underwriter also learns (1) the present and projected value of the stock in order to determine the amount of coverage required and (2) the net worth of the business. Many insurance companies establish a rough figure of seven times the business's net worth as a maximum amount for stock repurchase coverage.

Another underwriting concern for stock repurchase insurance is the proportion of the total amount of stock owned by a proposed insured.

FIGURE 6-3. Partnership Insurance Questionnaire.

1. Name of applicant (partner) ____________________
2. How many partners are there?____________________
   2a. What are the partners' names?________________
3. What is the nature of the business transacted?_________
4. How long has the partnership been in existence?________
5. What has been the profit/loss of the partnership over the last three years?____________
6. What has been the applicant's salary/share of profits over each of the last three years?________
7. What is the current value of the partnership?____________
   How was the value established?____________________
8. What is the applicant's percentage share of the partnership?______________________
9. Does a buy/sell agreement exist?__________________
   If not, is one to be executed in the near future?_________
10. Are policies to be purchased on the lives of all other partners?______________________
    If not, please give reasons.____________________

No real need to insure purchase of the stock exists unless the proposed insured's stock holdings represent a significant portion of the company's equity. The underwriter makes sure that the lives of other major stockholders are also covered by insurance in order to rule out the possibility of antiselection.

Sole Proprietorship Insurance

A sole proprietorship is a business owned by one person (or, in some jurisdictions, by a husband and wife). By law, the business assets of the sole proprietor are not kept distinct from his personal assets. ***Sole proprietorship insurance*** provides coverage on the life of the sole proprietor of a business—and can be used to pay the salary of hiring someone to run the business if the sole proprietor dies—*or* provides funds for a trusted employee or other person to buy a business at the death of the owner. The arrangements to sell the company and to use the insurance proceeds to pay for it are typically provided in a buy-sell agreement between the company's owner and the prospective buyer of the company.

For example, suppose that Perry Davidovich owns his own business. Because he has no partners, he alone is responsible for the success of the company. If he were to die, no one would be available to continue running the business. Therefore, Perry may apply for sole proprietorship coverage that will enable his family, if he dies, either to hire a person to head the business or to receive an amount to compensate them for the loss of income that was provided by Perry's business. Alternatively, if Perry has arranged for a buy-sell agreement, the person designated to buy the company is the beneficiary of the sole proprietorship insurance and uses the policy benefits to buy the company.

Underwriting sole proprietorship applications requires the underwriter to make the same sort of inquiries into the proposed insured's medical, personal, and financial condition as would be made for personal life insurance. In addition, the underwriter examines the financial health of the business, checking to be sure the company has not incurred large debts. If a buy-sell agreement is involved, the underwriter also verifies the ability of the prospective purchaser to run the business and otherwise ensures that the buy-sell agreement represents a good faith attempt to continue the business.

Key-Person Insurance

An owner or employee may be so important to a company that if that person dies or leaves, the company will suffer a severe loss—of customers, investors, technical skills, or management skills, for example. The term ***key person*** refers to a person whose absence would cause a serious loss to a business. ***Key-person insurance*** is coverage that protects a business from the losses that occur when a key person dies. Figure 6-4 illustrates a typical questionnaire used to gather information necessary to assess the risk for key-person insurance.

Because a large percentage of new businesses fail within the first two to three years, underwriting key-person coverage for a new company is more conservative than for businesses with a longer history of operation. The insurer is concerned that a new business might fail before the insurer has collected enough premiums to cover the expenses of underwriting, issuing, and administering the policy.

Similarly, the size of a business is important for underwriting key-person coverage. Generally, as a business grows larger, losing one person is less likely to produce a significant loss to the business. If a business appears to have other equally valuable employees or partners who are not being proposed for key-person coverage, the underwriter usually questions why only the proposed insured is being singled out.

Although the insurable interest that a business has in the life of a key person is usually obvious, certain situations may prompt the underwriter to look more closely for insurable interest. If the proposed insured is nearing retirement age and has not previously been insured by that business, the underwriter questions why that person has become important to the company. If a company applies for a large amount of coverage on a proposed insured who holds what appears to be only a moderately important position in the company, the underwriter may investigate further to determine insurable interest.

In evaluating the amount of coverage requested on a key person, the underwriter tries to determine the dollar value of the proposed insured to the company. This amount is usually set at 5 to 10 times the proposed insured's salary, but the underwriter can also include the dollar value of other compensation, whether in cash (such as bonuses) or in fringe benefits (such as employer-provided health insurance or use of a company car). The underwriter can also include the dollar amount of sales attributed to the key person and the cost of recruiting and training that person's replacement.

Underwriters pay particular attention to applications for insurance for key persons in multinational companies—those that operate in two or more countries. The financial documents may be written in another language, may be abridged or unaudited, and/or may use accounting terms with different meanings from those in the underwriter's country.

Insight 6-1 comments further on underwriting considerations for key-person insurance.

Split-Dollar Plans

A ***split-dollar plan*** is a type of business insurance that covers the life of an employee and is paid for jointly by the employer and the employee.

FIGURE 6-4. Key-Person Insurance Questionnaire.

1. Name of applicant (key person)____________________
2. What is the key person's precise occupation?__________
3. What is the nature of the business transacted by the key person's employer?____________________________
4. How long has the employer been in business?_________
5. How many other employees are there?______________
6. How long has the key person been employed by the employer?__________________________________
7. What has been the key person's gross salary over each of the last three years? This figure should include bonuses and commission.______________________________
8. What has been the net profit/loss of the employer over each of the last three years?_________________________
9. Is the key person a shareholder in the employer's business?____________________________

   If so, what percentage of shares does the key person hold?____________________________
10. What special abilities does the key person possess to justify classification as a key person?______________________
11. What existing coverage is in force on the applicant's life?______________________________
12. Why has the amount of insurance applied for been chosen?___________________________
13. What is the nature of the risk that is subject to loss?
    - Future earnings or sales jeopardized_____________
    - Investment jeopardized_______________________
    - Forced liquidation of assets____________________
    - Jeopardized working capital___________________
    - Management expertise________________________
    - Other_____________________________________
14. Will the employer insure the lives of other employees as key persons? If so, how many lives and what amounts of coverage are proposed? Include lives already insured under key-person coverage.______________________

Insight 6-1. What to Consider in Key-Person Coverage.

Many companies of all sizes and types have life insurance on their top executives. From the company's point of view, the purpose of this insurance is "Key Person" indemnification. These executives may very well be key to the ongoing success of the organization. In the event of the untimely death of one or more of these top people, the company could suffer a significant economic loss.

The following are factors that could determine the impact of such a loss:

- The key employee is an active, managing owner.
- The key employee may be a top salesperson or sales manager.
- The potential loss of goodwill.
- The entity is a one-person operation.
- Any corporate debt needs to be collateralized.
- The business relies on the personal services of the key person.

Large multi-billion dollar corporations frequently own key person life insurance on the CEO, the COO, the CFO, the Chairperson of the Board and others. These corporations recognize the potential loss in leadership of the top people in the organization. Their loss could have a huge impact on the price of publicly held stock.

In the case of smaller corporations, the loss could be even more critical. In fact, the loss could even cause the corporation's demise. If this were to happen, for estate tax purposes would the IRS value the business as a going concern or a liquidating asset? Chances are, it would be the former.

Source: Excerpted from Alan L. Fry, "What to Consider in Key Person Coverage," *National Underwriter*, Life & Health/Financial Services ed. (27 September 1999): 8. Reprinted with permission from *National Underwriter.*

The insured is the employee, and the owner of the policy is either the employer or the employee. Each year, the employer pays the portion of the premium that is equal to the increase in the policy's cash value for that year, with the rest of the premium being paid by the employee. At the employee's death, the proceeds are split according to the agreement previously made between the employer and the employee; the employer receives an amount equal to the policy's cash value or the sum of the premiums paid by the employer, and the insured's beneficiary receives the remainder of the policy proceeds.

Although split-dollar plans are considered business insurance, they are underwritten in the same manner as personal insurance. The split-dollar approach is often used for partnership and key-person coverages.

Underwriting Multi-Life Products

A life insurance contract that is written on more than one life is a multi-life product. The most common type of multi-life product is a ***joint-and-last-survivor policy***, which is a life insurance contract that provides coverage on two or more lives. If the policy provides that proceeds will be paid when the first of two or more insured people dies, the contract is called a ***first-to-die policy.*** If, by contrast, the policy provides that proceeds will be paid when the second of two or more insured people dies, the contract is called a ***second-to-die policy*** or *survivorship policy.* Some contracts provide that proceeds are paid to the named beneficiary on the death of each insured, and some contracts waive premiums after one person dies, a provision that protects a surviving spouse from the burden of paying premiums. Some insurers write policies that cover as many as 10 to 20 lives.

Underwriters make a separate evaluation of each life to be covered under a multi-life policy. If an underwriter determines that one of the proposed insureds represents a ratable risk or is uninsurable, the policy can still be issued at an increased premium for that person. However, if one person is uninsurable, the contract usually does not contain a provision that premiums will be waived upon the death of the first insured person to die.

Underwriting Juvenile Insurance

A ***juvenile insurance policy*** is a life insurance policy purchased by an adult to cover the life of a child. The owner of a juvenile insurance policy is usually the adult. Some jurisdictions limit the amount of coverage that can be issued on a juvenile.

Underwriters can use the same information sources to assess a juvenile proposed insured as those used to assess an adult. Some insurers offer a special, nonmedical juvenile application that is similar to an adult nonmedical application and that is completed by the adult applying for coverage on the child's life.

To evaluate an application for juvenile insurance, underwriters consider many of the same factors that are needed for risk appraisal of an adult's life. These factors include the age, sex, and medical history of the child, as well as the financial status of the applicant. However, underwriters regard the face amount of the insurance and policy ownership differently when evaluating an application for juvenile insurance.

In evaluating the appropriateness of the face amount requested, an underwriter considers whether other children in the family are similarly insured. If only one child of several is insured, or if one child is being insured for a larger amount of coverage than are the other children, the underwriter investigates the reason for such unusual treatment of one child. The underwriter's approval of the amount and plan of insurance requested on a child is based on the financial situation of the policyowner, rather than on the child's financial situation.

Underwriters also consider who will be the owner and the beneficiary of a juvenile policy. Usually, only parents, grandparents, or legal guardians are considered to have an insurable interest in the life of a child. Therefore, insurers usually require that one of these parties be either the owner or the beneficiary of the policy, or both.

When parents are not the owners of a policy covering a child, most insurers obtain the written consent of the parents. In addition, parents are required to attest to the correctness of responses to medical questions because grandparents who are purchasing the policy, for example, may live far away and may not have knowledge of the child's current state of health. Such parental permission is kept on file with the application or is made a part of the policy in order to record the validity of the transaction. For adopted children, no coverage is issued until the adoption legally is final, but then they are treated the same as children whose biological parents purchase the juvenile insurance.

Insurers seldom require a medical examination for juvenile insurance for two reasons: (1) after the first year of life, the mortality rate for children is very low and (2) most juvenile insurance applications do not involve large sums of money and therefore do not justify expensive and complex medical examinations. If the information provided on the juvenile application indicates that the child has a health problem or if the parent or legal guardian cannot complete the nonmedical portion of the application, then the underwriter usually requests an APS, generally from the child's physician. Most insurers approve coverage after a child has been released from a hospital after birth. However, for infants born prematurely, coverage is generally declined, but can be considered as soon as the infant's weight is normal for his age.

Some juvenile policies include a ***waiver of premium for payor benefit***, which provides that an insurer will waive payment of the policy's premiums if the adult policyowner becomes disabled or dies prior to the insured child's attainment of a specified age, usually 21. For this benefit, the insurer requires modest evidence of insurability from the payor. Typically, the payor's age, sex, occupation, height and weight, and a brief medical history are sufficient evidence of the payor's insurability. This information is typically provided as part of the regular application for juvenile coverage. A medical examination of the payor is seldom required unless the payor's medical history indicates that an examination is warranted. The waiver of premium for payor benefit is usually issued only if the payor is considered to be a preferred, standard, or slightly substandard risk.

Handling Guaranteed-Issue Products

Not all insurance requires the extensive underwriting that we have described. Insurance products that are sold on a guaranteed-issue basis do not require much underwriting, and some products require none.

Guaranteed-issue products are insurance products designed so that each applicant who meets certain conditions established by the insurer is automatically issued a policy. Although most guaranteed-issue products are issued to groups, a few are issued to individuals.

The most common conditions for individual life insurance products sold on a guaranteed-issue basis include the following:

1. Uniform face amount of coverage—the applicant cannot select a different face amount
2. Strict eligibility requirements, such as limiting coverage only to people within a certain age range
3. Enrollment periods or deadlines, such as a specified date by which the enrollment application must be submitted
4. Maximums imposed on the face amounts of guaranteed-issue policies issued to one person. These maximum amounts of coverage usually decrease as the age of the insured increases. In most jurisdictions, guaranteed-issue policies cannot be issued to people over age 85 or 87. Some state regulations forbid selling this type of coverage to people over age 74.

Direct Response Products

Many individual insurance products sold on a guaranteed-issue basis are sold through the direct response method. ***Direct response products*** are insurance products sold to consumers by an insurer without the help of an agent, usually through direct mail, advertising in print and other media, telephone solicitation, or, increasingly, the Internet. Many guaranteed-issue policies limit the benefit amount payable—often to a return of premiums—if the insured dies from natural causes during a specified period.

Marketing guaranteed-issue coverage through direct response allows an insurer to target certain markets, such as retired people over age 65, or people who are between 40 and 60 years old and who are earning over $30,000 a year. If offered on a guaranteed-issue basis, most direct response products have no underwriting requirements at all. Few direct response life insurers use substandard rates, and the standard risk class for guaranteed-issue coverage generally includes people whose anticipated mortality is assessed as high as 150 to 200 percent of standard mortality.

Proposed insureds for guaranteed-issue direct response coverage usually do not have to undergo a medical examination, although the application typically asks several basic medical history questions, such as the following:

- Check each condition you have had or for which you have received medical treatment. (A list follows, containing impairments such as high blood pressure, heart trouble, chest pains, cancer, tumors, convulsions, and diabetes.)

- Within the last five years, have you tested positive for the human immunodeficiency virus (HIV) or been told you have acquired immune deficiency syndrome (AIDS)?
- Within the last three years, have you consulted a doctor, been hospitalized, or taken prescription medication?

The answers to these questions identify proposed insureds whose medical history may place them outside of the parameters established for the insurance product. The vast majority of people solicited for coverage qualify for direct response products solely on the basis of their answers to the questions on the application. If the direct response insurer's underwriter determines that further information is needed, the applicant or the applicant's physician may be asked to complete a medical questionnaire. In difficult cases, medical examinations, inspection reports, or both may also be required.

Underwriting Policy Replacements

In Chapter 3, you learned that replacement involves surrendering an insurance policy or part of the coverage of an insurance policy in order to buy another policy. While replacement of existing life insurance policies is not illegal, it may not be in a policyowner's best interest.

To be eligible for a replacement without evidence of insurability, the proposed insured must be covered by a policy that was fully underwritten and that was issued within a certain recent period, usually five years. For policyowners who own coverage that was not fully underwritten or who are covered by policies issued more than five years ago, insurers generally require minimal evidence of insurability, such as answers to these two simple health questions:

1. Is the insured now so disabled by sickness or injury that he is unable to perform all the duties of his normal job?
2. During the last five years, has the insured had high blood pressure, heart disease, diabetes, or cancer?

In insurance companies that require some underwriting for policy replacements, underwriters have the options of issuing the policy as requested, issuing the policy with a substandard rating, or declining to issue coverage.

In evaluating applications for policy replacements, the underwriter is essentially concerned with

- The possibility that antiselection has motivated the request for the replacement

- The underwriting standards of the insurer that issued the original policy
- The possibility of churning or twisting
- The tax consequences to the policyowner of the replacement

Antiselection in Policy Replacements

Particularly for proposed insureds at older ages, underwriters check for antiselection in policy replacements. An insured whose health has deteriorated may have an incentive to obtain a new policy at a lower premium and without evidence of insurability. Moreover, a person may wish to replace one policy for another if the new policy offers a comparatively higher interest rate on its cash value.

Underwriting Standards in Policy Replacements

Underwriters also consider the underwriting philosophy and guidelines of the insurer that issued the original policy because, by making a policy replacement, the replacing insurer is accepting the original insurer's standards as its own. If the original insurer's underwriting philosophy and guidelines are liberal and the replacement insurer's are conservative, the policy proposed for a replacement may not be acceptable as it was originally written. In such a situation, accepting the policy as written can lead to increased mortality results for the accepting insurer. For this reason, some insurers usually exclude from their policy replacements all policies originally issued by insurers that specialize in providing coverage for substandard risks.

Possibility of Churning or Twisting

Two undesirable activities that can occur during replacement are churning and twisting. ***Churning*** is an unethical activity by which an agent induces a policyowner to cash in a policy and buy another, even though the replacement is not in the policyowner's best interest. An agent engages in churning to collect the high first-year commissions that are paid when any new policy is issued. ***Twisting*** is the illegal practice of misleading a policyowner about replacement or providing an incomplete comparison of the two policies to the disadvantage of the policyowner. Underwriters have a responsibility to be aware that churning or twisting may be occurring when an agent does a high volume of replacement business.

Tax Consequences of Policy Replacements

A policyowner who surrenders a policy and receives its cash surrender value in a lump sum may be required to pay income tax on the gain. Any portion of the cash surrender value that exceeds the cost basis for the policy is considered a gain and is taxable as ordinary income. Usually, the ***cost basis*** of an insurance policy is equal to the total net premiums paid *plus* accumulated dividends and *minus* certain specified costs. To avoid incurring income taxes when an insurance policy is replaced, many insurers use a ***1035 exchange***, a transaction in which the cash surrender value of a replaced policy is used as the initial premium for a new policy. The policyowner receives no financial gain on the transaction because the cash surrender value is used to pay a premium. Because the policyowner experiences no gain, no tax is due.

Generally, a 1035 exchange is underwritten in the same manner as a new business application. However, underwriters usually take two additional precautions. First, to prevent a gap in coverage during the time underwriting is taking place, the original policy is not surrendered until the new policy has been approved for issue. Second, if the new policy must be issued with a substandard rating, the underwriter obtains from the applicant a letter stating that the applicant understands that a higher premium will be required if the face amount of the new policy remains the same as that of the original policy.

Underwriting Supplementary Coverages

Supplementary benefit riders expand the insurance protection provided by most life insurance policies. Such riders provide additional benefits and allow existing contracts to be adapted to the needs of insureds without the expense of redrawing the contracts. If a proposed insured requests such supplementary coverage, the request is considered during underwriting. If a person who is already insured asks for supplementary coverage, the request is usually considered first by the insurer's policyowner service staff. When such a request involves only a slight increase in the insurer's risk, policyowner service staff can approve the request. However, if revising the coverage may cause the insurer to bear a greater degree of risk, the policyowner service staff forwards the request to underwriting for more detailed consideration.

In the next sections, we'll discuss four important supplementary coverages:

- Waiver of premium for disability
- Accidental death benefit (ADB)

- Family benefit
- Guaranteed insurability (GI)

Waiver of Premium for Disability

A ***waiver of premium for disability*** rider provides that, in the event an insured is totally disabled as defined in the rider, the insurer will waive the payment of all premiums that become due during the period of disability. The waiver of premium for disability rider eliminates the possibility of the insured's having to drop the basic life insurance protection when he experiences a loss of income from disability. The insurer pays the premiums waived by the rider.

When underwriting the waiver of premium for disability rider, underwriters consider such factors as the proposed insured's age, avocation, occupation, health, and finances. Because insurance studies and Social Security reports indicate that the risk of disability increases with age, issue of the rider is normally limited to proposed insureds below age 55 or 60.

If a proposed insured's mortality rating is standard according to health history and physical condition, the rider is usually granted. In some situations, however, even if the policy was issued as standard, the insured's avocation or occupation may present enough of an extra hazard that the insurer must require an extra premium for the rider or decline to issue it.

The applicant's financial circumstances rarely affect underwriting for the waiver of premium for disability rider. However, on very large amounts of insurance with high cash value plans, the cash values can accumulate fast enough for the policy loan provision to provide the insured with a significant source of income during a disability. Loans on the cash value of the policy could provide the insured with such a large disability income that the insured might have no incentive to terminate a period of disability. In such a situation, the underwriter generally does not approve the rider.

Accidental Death Benefit

An ***accidental death benefit (ADB)*** rider provides an additional death benefit above the face amount of a policy if an insured's death occurs as the result of an accident. This additional amount can be a multiple of the amount of the basic life coverage, or it can be an unrelated amount.

For ADB coverage, the underwriter usually adheres to the same principles used in underwriting basic life coverage. In certain business insurance cases, the ADB may not be justified. For example, if a business needs $100,000 to fund a buy-sell agreement, the amount is fixed and specific. The business has no reason to receive double that amount simply because the insured's death is accidental. However, individual insurance needs—as well as some business insurance needs, such as key-person coverage—are not fixed and specific and are not as easily measured.

Age is an important factor considered in underwriting an ADB rider. Most ADB riders expire when the insured reaches age 65 or 70, and insurers rarely issue ADB riders to people over age 55 or 60. One reason for these restrictions is that accidents are more likely to happen to older people.

Rather than trying to assess each case individually, most insurers specify that ADB riders can be issued at standard rates to low substandard life risks, such as those rated to 200 percent mortality, but will be denied to or rated for those that exceed 200 percent mortality. ADB riders are usually not available to applicants rated for substance abuse, particularly alcohol abuse.

People with certain hazardous occupations or avocations may be charged an extra premium for ADB coverage or may be denied the rider. For example, most insurers exclude coverage for death resulting from an aviation accident if the insured had duties aboard the airplane.

The underwriter decides how much coverage can be included in the ADB approved for a case. The amount usually depends on the amount of life insurance in force, the amount of coverage requested, and the beneficiary designation. The underwriter also examines the appropriateness of the designated beneficiary.

Family Benefit

A ***family benefit*** rider insures the lives of an insured's spouse and children. The amount of underwriting necessary for a family benefit is limited.

To underwrite a family benefit rider, the underwriter requires insurability information for all family members, but usually the basic information on the application fills this need. A spouse and children, including those with slight impairments, are generally accepted as standard risks if the mortality rating of each family member is no higher than 200 percent. Higher mortality risks are usually declined.

Some insurers establish age requirements for family benefit riders. For example, an insurer might require that a spouse be at least 17 years old and no more than 10 to 15 years younger than the insured. The insurer might also establish an upper age limit for a spouse. To be accepted for coverage, children typically must be under 18 years old at the time of issue. Furthermore, unless a child has a physical disability and is a dependent, coverage on the child ends when the child reaches age 21 or 25.

Guaranteed Insurability

A policy rider for ***guaranteed insurability (GI)*** gives a policyowner the right to buy additional insurance up to a specified amount at a specified premium rate and at specified times without providing new evidence of insurability. If the policyowner does not exercise the option under the GI rider to buy additional insurance at the time specified, that opportunity is lost; the policyowner cannot purchase the amount of insurance available under those circumstances at a subsequent option date. The purpose of the requirement to exercise options promptly is to avoid antiselection.

If the GI rider is not included in the basic policy when the policy is issued, the rider usually may be added up to 60 days after issue. The underwriter's main concern is to determine the probability of a change in insurability during the 60-day post-issue period. Some insurers allow an insured to add the GI rider more than 60 days after issue by presenting evidence of insurability.

An important underwriting factor for the GI rider is age. Usually, the maximum age for issue of the GI rider is 40 or 45. Aside from the age factor, the risk selection factors involved in underwriting the GI rider are typically the same as those considered in underwriting the basic policy. The additional coverage provided by the GI rider has the same risk class rating as the policy.

Key Terms and Concepts

supplemental coverage
business insurance
business financial supplement
solvency
liquidity
current assets
current liabilities
profitability
creditor insurance
partnership insurance
stock repurchase insurance
sole proprietorship insurance
key person
key-person insurance
split-dollar plan
joint-and-last-survivor policy
first-to-die policy
second-to-die policy
juvenile insurance policy
waiver of premium for payor benefit
guaranteed-issue products
direct response products
churning
twisting
cost basis
1035 exchange
waiver of premium for disability
accidental death benefit (ADB)
family benefit
guaranteed insurability (GI)

Endnotes

1. ACLI, *Life Insurers Fact Book 2000* (Washington, D.C.: American Council of Life Insurers, 2000), 18.
2. Ibid., 20–21.

CHAPTER 7

Underwriting Individual Health Insurance

Chapter Outline

Information Sources for Health Underwriting
- Insurance Application and Agent's Statement
- Medical Examination and APS
- Inspection Report
- Specialized Questionnaires

Underwriting Substandard Risks
- Higher Premium Rate
- Modifications and Exclusions

Elements Important to Underwriting Individual Health Insurance
- Insurable Interest
- Antiselection
- Health History
- Other Factors

Underwriting Individual Disability Income Insurance
- Moral Hazard
- Health
- Occupation
- Finances and Portion of Income Insured

Underwriting Critical Illness Insurance

Underwriting Long-Term Care Coverage
- Considerations About Aging
- Antiselection
- Field Underwriting
- Tools for LTC Underwriting

Objectives

After reading this chapter, you should be able to

- Describe the information sources a health insurance underwriter uses
- List five ways an underwriter can modify medical coverage for a substandard risk
- Explain the function of impairment riders
- Discuss the importance of insurable interest, antiselection, health history, and other factors in underwriting health insurance
- List and explain the four elements considered in underwriting individual disability income coverage
- Explain the factors involved in underwriting critical illness insurance
- Distinguish between an impairment guide and a long-term care field underwriting manual
- Discuss the differences between the tools used for underwriting long-term care insurance and those used for underwriting other types of health insurance

By this point in your study of insurance administration, you've looked at many aspects of underwriting individual life coverages, including the medical, personal, and financial considerations involved in assessing the risk presented by a proposed insured. Now we'll examine the underwriting issues connected with individual health coverages.

In some insurance companies, an underwriter reviews applications not only for individual life insurance, but for individual health insurance as well. As you have learned, underwriting for life coverages concerns *mortality*, which is the relative incidence of death occurring among a given group of people. Underwriting for health insurance, sometimes called sickness/accident insurance, involves *morbidity*, the relative incidence of sickness and injury occurring among a given group of people.

Although health underwriters emphasize morbidity in risk assessment, they also look at any indication of increased risk of mortality as a result of an impairment. For instance, a proposed insured is considered obese when the body weight is more than 30 percent higher than the weight established as normal for that person's height and sex. Most insurers would not issue health insurance at standard rates to an obese person, and nearly all insurers would decline to issue disability income coverage because obese people are statistically more likely to have higher morbidity and mortality rates than are people of average weight.

Health insurance underwriters need to learn a great deal of medical terminology and to understand typical treatments for a wide variety of medical conditions. In addition, health underwriters continually expand their knowledge as medical information changes and increases. Discovery of new medical conditions and knowledge of medical advances enable health underwriters to recognize and assess new types of impairments and to understand new means of treatment.

In this chapter, we'll first look at the information sources that health underwriters use most frequently. After examining the underwriting considerations for substandard health risks, we'll discuss underwriting of several types of individual health insurance, including the following:

- ***Medical expense insurance***, which pays benefits for treatment of sickness or injury

- ***Disability income (DI) insurance***, which helps replace income lost as a result of sickness or injury

- ***Critical illness (CI) insurance***, also known as *critical diagnosis insurance*, which pays a lump sum benefit when the insured is diagnosed with a specified illness

- ***Long-term care (LTC) insurance***, which pays for medical or other health-related services required in a person's home or in a nursing facility

Information Sources for Health Underwriting

In assessing risks, the health underwriter uses the same kinds of tools that the life underwriter uses, including the insurance application and the agent's statement, the results of a medical examination (if one is required), an APS, an inspection report, and specialized questionnaires. Some insurers also require a blood profile and urinalysis from adults applying for medical expense coverage. Just as for life underwriting, the health underwriter considers the cost involved in relation to the underwriting benefit when seeking additional information about a proposed insured.

Insurance Application and Agent's Statement

The questions on an individual health insurance application typically place more emphasis on the proposed insured's occupational duties and income than do the questions on a life insurance application. Disability income applications, in particular, request extensive information on the applicant's occupation and income. Other information requested on a health insurance application is similar to that requested for life insurance coverages.

The agent's statement can be very useful to a health underwriter. An agent usually has an opportunity to observe a proposed insured and may have personal knowledge of that person's health history and possible impairments. For instance, an agent may notice that a proposed insured moves with difficulty from one chair to another or has trouble communicating verbally. Sharing such observations with the underwriter helps ensure that risk assessment is done cautiously and that the person's medical history, in particular, is investigated fully. By communicating this type of information to the underwriter, the agent plays a key role in helping an insurer evaluate each risk appropriately.

Information that an applicant or an agent withholds on a health insurance application can indicate antiselection and the possibility that, when covered by insurance, the insured may file an early claim. The underwriter, therefore, checks all apparently omitted information or unanswered questions. If an application has been initiated by a proposed insured rather than by an agent, the health underwriter scrutinizes the application with special care in order to guard against antiselection.

Most insurance companies instruct their agents to obtain a detailed health history through careful questioning of each applicant. To help agents gather complete information, most insurers provide agents with an ***impairment guide***, which is a list of common impairments and the probable underwriting decision for each. By using the impairment guide, an agent can inform a proposed insured about coverage types and amounts for which that person is most likely to be approved.

For example, suppose an agent is completing a health insurance application for a proposed insured who previously suffered an attack of appendicitis. The impairment guide notes that if the appendicitis was not medically resolved, the probable underwriting decision will be to add an impairment rider to the policy. (We'll explain impairment riders later in this chapter.) However, if at least one month has passed since successful, uncomplicated surgery for appendicitis (and if the proposed insured has no other significant impairments), the application will probably be considered a standard risk. Figure 7-1 presents sample entries in one insurer's impairment guide, which contains information for underwriting both health and life applications. Note that the health underwriting decisions for a specific impairment differ from the life underwriting decisions for the same impairment.

For coverage that does not require a medical examination, insurers generally instruct agents to furnish the following information about each impairment that a proposed insured acknowledges on the insurance application:

- Precise medical term for the impairment
- Date and duration of each attack or episode
- For a chronic or recurrent condition, the date of the first attack, frequency of episodes, and date of most recent attack
- Aftereffects and complications, if any
- Nature of treatment or medication, and date of last such treatment or medication
- Names and addresses of physicians consulted, dates of visits, and sequence in which physicians were consulted

FIGURE 7-1. Entries in One Insurer's Impairment Guide.

Impairment	Type of Coverage	Typical Underwriting Decision
APPENDICITIS	Health	Unoperated—impairment rider Operated within one month—decline One month after successful, uncomplicated operation—probably standard
	Life	Usually standard
ASTHMA	Health	Mild, occasional—usually standard Moderate to severe—rate to decline
	Life	Mild—usually standard Moderate to severe—rate to decline
DIABETES	Health	Mild—individual consideration Others—decline
	Life	Standard to decline, depending on age, duration, and other medical factors
EPILEPSY	Health	Individual consideration
	Life	Depends on history—rate to decline Some types standard after five years
FRACTURES	Health	According to location, severity, complications, and recovery—standard, impairment rider, or both
	Life	After recovery—standard

- If hospitalization occurred, dates of hospitalization, length of hospital stay, and name and location of hospital

This information is usually included in the agent's statement or in a letter attached to the application.

Medical Examination and APS

Medical or paramedical examinations are less frequently required for health insurance than for life insurance, except for disability income applications that often do require a medical exam, as we'll explain later in this chapter. Generally, health underwriters rely more on the information contained in the application and other documents than on information revealed by a medical examination. However, if the underwriter notices that a proposed insured for health coverage has undergone recent treatment for a serious impairment or appears to have a significant medical condition, the underwriter usually orders an APS from every doctor who diagnosed or treated the impairment or condition.

Some insurers require a blood profile and a urinalysis if results from these tests are not included in a recent APS. Blood and urine tests are usually required on applications for disability income coverage.

Inspection Report

Health underwriters generally order inspection reports more frequently than do life underwriters. Particularly for disability coverages, a health underwriter needs to know much more about an applicant's occupation and finances than a life underwriter needs to know to assess the risk for insurance. The results of an inspection report can verify financial information submitted on the application.

Specialized Questionnaires

Health underwriters use specialized questionnaires or supplements more often than do their life insurance counterparts. Most insurers use similar kinds of specialized questionnaires covering specific physical disorders and diseases, as we have discussed in the chapters on underwriting life insurance.

Underwriting Substandard Risks

Each insurer that sells health insurance has a health underwriting manual that contains information needed to underwrite such coverage. Typically, the manual explains many impairments similar to those found in a life underwriting manual. Like a life underwriter, a health underwriter can accept, rate, or decline an application according to the degree of risk the proposed insured presents to the insurance company. If a proposed insured represents a risk greater than standard and if the risk is not so great that the underwriter must decline the application, the underwriter can rate the application and accept the risk with a rated policy. A ***rated policy*** is a policy issued to a person considered to have a greater-than-average risk of loss. A rated policy may be issued with (1) a premium rate higher than the rate for a policy issued to a person with an average or less-than-average risk of loss, (2) modifications and exclusions, or (3) any combination of a higher premium rate, modifications, and exclusions.

Higher Premium Rate

A health underwriter evaluates the risk represented by a proposed insured by using a numerical rating system based on standard morbidity. The standard premium for health coverage is usually based on 100 percent of standard morbidity. The health underwriter indicates degrees of extra risk as debits, which are converted to rating percentages. After assigning debits to a proposed insured, the underwriter consults a ***rating schedule,*** which is a table that shows the conversion of total rating debits to a rating percentage. Each insurer develops its own rating schedule. A typical rating schedule is shown below.

Rating Debits	Rating Percentage
0–5	0
10–15	10
20–35	25
40–60	50
65–85	75
90–110	100
115–135	125
140–165	150
170–185	175
190–220	200
220 and up	Declined

To calculate the premium to be charged for the coverage, the underwriter adds the rating percentage to the standard percentage (100), then multiplies that figure by the standard premium amount.

For example, suppose a proposed insured has 30 rating debits and is assigned a rating percentage of 25. This proposed insured will be charged a premium that is 125 percent of standard premium (100 percent for standard premium + 25 percent for the rating = 125 percent). If the standard premium for the applied-for coverage is \$300 a year, the premium this proposed insured will be charged for the coverage is \$375 (\$300 × 1.25).

When a proposed insured has more than one ratable impairment and when no other instructions are given in the health underwriting manual, the health underwriter usually sums the debits. If the sum of debits appears to overstate the risk anticipated, the underwriter may decide that only a portion of the debits for the second or third impairment is appropriate for the total risk presented. For certain impairments occurring together, however, the risk is higher than the sum of the debits. For instance, diabetes occurring with hypertension presents a much higher risk than either diabetes or hypertension alone. Other combinations of impairments may not represent an increased risk. For some proposed insureds with combinations of impairments, for example those who have continuing impairments such as epilepsy in addition to impairments that typically improve with time, the underwriter may assign a rating for the continuing impairment and an impairment rider for any impairment that tends to improve with time.

Certain medical impairments may also work in combination with nonmedical factors such as occupation or avocation to increase risk significantly. For example, a proposed insured who has a respiratory disease and smokes or a cosmetologist who is sensitive to certain chemical solutions used in performing her job present significantly increased risks because their habits/jobs directly affect their medical impairments. The underwriter considers such combinations of medical and nonmedical factors to reach an equitable rating.

If a proposed insured is assessed as having a rating above +150, which represents a 50 percent greater morbidity than standard, most insurers do not offer a benefit period beyond five years. At progressively higher ratings, insurers typically reduce the length of the benefit period and the amount of benefits. An insurer might charge extra premiums for only a certain length of time—for example, in a case in which an impairment is not expected to be permanent—or for the entire period for which coverage is being purchased.

Insurers typically use percentage ratings for impairments that increase the risk as the age of the proposed insured increases. For impairments for which the extra risk does not increase with age, insurers generally use ***flat rating,*** which is a rating method used for impairments that present an accident hazard but no additional health hazard. Flat rating is typically used for such conditions as a loss of a limb as a result of an accident, not disease.

Modifications and Exclusions

Like life underwriters, health underwriters can also modify the coverage originally requested so that the applicant becomes insurable on some basis. The health coverage issued to an extra-risk proposed insured can be modified using one or more of the following techniques:

1. Reduce the policy's benefit-paying period—for example, from two years to one year

2. Reduce the benefit amount

3. Increase the deductible amount

4. Increase the ***waiting period***, which is the period of time that must pass before benefits are payable to an insured

5. Attach an impairment rider (defined below) to the contract excluding coverage for an identified, prior health impairment

Let's look more closely at the last two of these techniques.

The waiting period for medical expense coverage is a specified length of time, counted from the date of policy issue, during which the insured's medical expenses are not covered. Increasing a waiting period of 30 days to 60 days reduces the insurer's risk on a substandard policy. For disability income coverage, the waiting period (also called the *elimination period*) is a specified length of time, beginning with the onset of a disability, during which benefits are not payable. Often, an insurer uses a ***split elimination period***, which is an increased waiting period for only the impaired problem, while the usual waiting period is applied to other claims.

An ***impairment rider,*** also known as an *impairment waiver* or an *exclusion rider,* is a policy attachment that excludes from coverage (1) a loss arising from a specified disease or physical impairment or (2) a specific body part. An impairment rider is typically used with a health policy if a proposed insured's health history presents the possibility of the recurrence of a disabling illness or if the applicant has a chronic condition for which future treatment seems likely.

When a medical or an actuarial determination justifies the impairment rider, an insurer has the right to use the rider for a condition not manifested but indicated as being strongly possible in the future. Suppose that a proposed insured with a family history of breast cancer has no identified breast cancer, but has developed fibrocystic disease, certain forms of which are associated with a higher risk of breast cancer. In this circumstance, the underwriter typically requires a waiver of coverage for diseases of the breasts because the proposed insured currently has a condition that can increase risk.

An impairment rider excludes from coverage a medical condition, a disease or disorder of a specified body part, or both. The impairment rider is worded in simple, straightforward terms so that a proposed insured may understand what condition is being excluded from coverage. The insurer's medical director and legal department can help an underwriter draft a rider to suit the circumstances of a specific case. A sample impairment rider that specifies the limits of coverage is shown in Figure 7-2.

FIGURE 7-2. Sample Impairment Rider.

Impairment Rider

Name of Insured____________________

Policy Number____________________

Effective Date of Coverage____________________

This Impairment Rider is attached to and forms a part of the above-referenced policy number.

It is agreed and understood, anything in the printed part of the policy notwithstanding, that the proposed insured expressly waives any benefits for any loss or disability resulting directly or indirectly, in whole or in part from **arterial hypertension disease or disorder of the heart or stroke** on behalf of the proposed insured, and no benefits shall accrue on account of any loss resulting therefrom. Said waiver is a permanent waiver for the entire duration of this policy.

ABC Insurance Company

Signature of insured ____________________

Date rider signed ____________________

Signature of owner, if other than insured ____________________

Date rider signed ____________________

Source: Excerpted from Barbara Foxenberger Brown and Jane Lightcap Brown, *Life and Health Insurance Underwriting* (Atlanta: LOMA, © 1998), 254. Used with permission; all rights reserved

To save the underwriter time in completing an impairment rider, most underwriting manuals provide the wording for many conditions that might warrant the use of an impairment rider. Samples of such suggested wording for riders covering certain medical conditions are shown in Figure 7-3.

Elements Important to Underwriting Individual Health Insurance

The elements of insurable interest, antiselection, and health history are important in underwriting health coverages, and they are often considered in different ways than they are for underwriting life insurance. We'll first discuss these elements and then several other factors important to health insurance underwriting. We will look at the primary elements that an underwriter assesses for individual medical expense insurance, commenting on how those factors also apply to disability income coverage and long-term care insurance where appropriate. In later sections, we'll look at additional elements an underwriter evaluates for disability income coverage and for long-term care insurance.

FIGURE 7-3. Examples of Wording for Standardized Impairment Riders.

Condition Involved	Suggested Wording for Riders
Cataract	Cataract or disease of, or partial or complete loss of sight of, one or both eyes; a complication thereof, treatment or operation thereof.
Phlebitis	Phlebitis, varicose veins, thrombosis, a complication thereof, treatment or operation therefor.
Raynaud's disease	Raynaud's disease or other peripheral vascular disease, a complication thereof, treatment or operation therefor.
Rheumatic fever	Rheumatic fever including a complication or residual effects thereof, treatment or operation therefor.

Insurable Interest

Health insurance underwriters do not have to establish insurable interest to the extent that life underwriters do. For health insurance, the requirement for insurable interest is met if the applicant can demonstrate a risk of economic loss if the proposed insured requires medical care or becomes disabled. When an applicant seeks health insurance coverage for family members, the underwriter verifies that each person proposed for coverage has a family relationship to the applicant.

Family relationships that require an underwriter to check with the agent include cousins, in-laws, grandparents, aunts and uncles, and common-law spouses. Most insurers require an agent to certify that a couple living as common-law spouses have maintained the relationship for a specified period of time, usually two years or longer, before coverage can be issued.

Antiselection

In underwriting for health coverages, insurers are aware that antiselection can be a factor in some applications if the proposed insureds have certain types of impairments, such as nervous conditions and chronic depression or chronic pain. These types of impairments do not necessarily result in undue numbers and amounts of claims, but some of them do, and insurers often have difficulty in determining the validity of such claims. Some insurers exclude coverage for conditions like these by using riders, whereas other insurers do not issue health insurance contracts to applicants with these or other serious impairments.

In contrast, health insurance does not usually exclude benefits for impairments that are considered temporary, because such impairments are not statistically indicative of possible antiselection. For instance, if a proposed insured has sprained her shoulder or has undergone shoulder surgery a month before applying for coverage, but has no previous history of shoulder problems (and if any surgery is considered to have resolved the current problem), most insurers would issue health insurance coverage without excluding shoulder or joint problems. Other temporary conditions that are generally not excluded by riders include eye and ear injuries that do not permanently impair sight and hearing, and nonmalignant skin tumors that can be successfully removed and that do not require more extensive treatment.

Health History

A proposed insured's health is a major factor in underwriting both life and health insurance, but health underwriters pay special attention to certain health histories that life underwriters would consider less significant. Certain impairments that are not typically considered life-threatening can be of considerable significance in health underwriting because those impairments have been shown statistically to result in higher-than-average health claims. Such conditions as arthritis, back injuries, spinal curvature, asthma, certain kidney impairments, and mild neuroses are examples. The health underwriter focuses especially on impairments associated with two types of concerns: (1) probable accidents and (2) future medical treatment or disability.

Probable Accidents

Health underwriters consider medical conditions that may present a higher-than-average probability of accidents. Some impairments, such as epilepsy, vertigo, paralysis, and impaired eyesight and hearing are often associated with accidents and are examined thoroughly in health underwriting.

Future Medical Treatment or Disability

In addition to looking at the probable effects of impairments, health underwriters also examine all information relating to health conditions that have been diagnosed or treated recently. Some conditions, especially certain types of cancer, are considered more serious when they have been recently discovered or treated. Many insurers specify in their underwriting manuals that some conditions that have been stable for a number of years may not negatively affect a proposed insured rating because the condition is not considered to have a significant potential effect on the proposed insured's future health. Even a history of acute illness, such as pneumonia, may not be significant in health underwriting if the proposed insured has recovered fully.

Health underwriters can accept some proposed insureds for coverage after a period of time following treatment for an impairment. Moreover, health underwriters do not consider each impairment in isolation, but try to obtain a clear understanding of the possible connections between various impairments and their combined effect on the proposed insured's health.

Finally, health underwriters pay special attention to factors in a proposed insured's life that can decrease or increase the probable effect of an impairment on the person's health. For example, a proposed insured who has been diagnosed with mild to moderate asthma and who also smokes or who has abnormal lung function test results between asthma attacks is underwritten more cautiously than one who has asthma but does not smoke.

Other Factors

In addition to the elements above, health underwriters consider several other factors, including the proposed insured's finances, existing health coverage, occupation, avocations, substance abuse, military status, driving history, foreign travel or residence, and foreign citizenship.

Finances

Most insurers that issue health coverage require that a proposed insured have a minimum level of annual income to qualify for certain types of insurance. Each insurer establishes its own eligibility requirements.

Existing Health Coverage

To ensure that an applicant is not overinsured, the underwriter checks the application to determine the amount and type of health insurance that the proposed insured already has in force. Verifying this information enables the underwriter to prevent duplication of coverage. Some insurers deny coverage or limit the amount of coverage issued if a proposed insured is already covered under another medical expense policy.

Occupation

Occupation is a major concern to health underwriters because it plays an important role in an insurer's assumptions about morbidity. A proposed insured's occupation is of much more significance in health underwriting than in life underwriting. Health underwriters are especially concerned about occupations that produce higher-than-normal accident rates and health hazards.

Avocations

The avocation risks to which many people are occasionally exposed are generally acceptable for health underwriting purposes. However, if a proposed insured participates more frequently than average in some avocations—for example, scuba diving, mountain climbing, and horse racing—the underwriter usually adds an impairment rider to the policy.

Substance Abuse

Health or disability income insurance applicants who have a record of abusing substances, including drugs and alcohol, are investigated thoroughly. If a proposed insured has been free of substance abuse for a considerable period of time—usually a minimum of five years—and has undergone treatment for substance abuse, most insurers issue a rated policy. Abuse of alcohol or drugs within the past five years, however, typically results in an underwriting decision to decline coverage. Underwriters who find evidence of past substance abuse typically obtain specific tests, including a urinalysis and blood profile, to check for current use.

Military Status

The military usually provides medical expense coverage for people who are in service. Insurance companies, therefore, typically do not approve health or disability income coverage for people currently serving in the military. TRICARE, formerly known as the Civilian Health and Medical Program of the Uniformed Services, or CHAMPUS, provides health care coverage in the United States for eligible active-duty and retired military personnel and their dependents. Under this system, the federal government shares with military families the cost of health care provided by military and civilian hospitals and doctors.

Some insurers offer supplementary insurance to retired military personnel that helps pay for medical expenses that TRICARE does not cover completely. This supplementary coverage includes some hospital, medical, and surgical services. Most applications for TRICARE supplementary policies are underwritten on a nonmedical basis.

Driving History

If a proposed insured has a poor driving record, as shown by numerous arrests or accidents, most insurers severely limit benefits or decline coverage. Underwriters pay special attention to any indication that a proposed insured has a record of driving under the influence (DUI) of alcohol or other substances.

Foreign Travel or Residence

Foreign travel and foreign residence mainly present problems of claims administration because gathering claim-related information can be difficult when the insured lives in another country. In handling applications involving foreign travel or residence, health underwriters generally follow the principles of life insurance underwriting, paying particular attention to the prevalence of diseases peculiar to a given area. For large-amount cases, most insurers require an inspection report that focuses on the location and frequency of the proposed insured's travel or duration of residence. Some insurers also require that a proposed insured who is a U.S. citizen and who travels in foreign countries spend at least nine months of each year in the United States, or, if the proposed insured is Canadian, in Canada.

Foreign Citizenship

Most insurers in the United States require proposed insureds who have foreign citizenship to

- Reside in the United States for two years before applying for health insurance
- Supply a copy of a visa or green card
- Provide the name of a medical practitioner in the United States who can supply adequate medical records
- Show intent to remain in the United States

Underwriting Individual Disability Income Insurance

Disability income (DI) insurance coverage presents somewhat different underwriting considerations from those presented by other types of health insurance coverages. DI coverage is intended to replace only a portion of income that is lost during a period of disability. The DI payment is not intended to replace income completely because full income replacement might discourage a recipient from returning to work. Rather, DI coverage is intended to provide a percentage of the insured's former income so that the disability will not cause the insured to become destitute. DI underwriters are primarily concerned with four elements: moral hazard, health, occupation, and the relationship between the proposed insured's finances and the portion of income to be insured.

FAST FACT

More than 43 million disability income insurance policies were in force in the United States in 1999.[1]

Moral Hazard

For DI coverage, moral hazard is the most important underwriting element. The potential for antiselection for DI coverage is greater than for life insurance and for other types of health insurance. Underwriters generally regard as suspicious any applicant who (1) intentionally includes erroneous information or withholds information on the application, (2) attempts to buy excessive amounts of DI coverage, or (3) is otherwise unethical. Such applicants may present moral hazard and are investigated with extreme care.

The underwriter determines as clearly as possible that each applicant is free of any indication of moral hazard. Being sure that the amount of DI coverage approved is appropriate for each proposed insured helps the underwriter reduce the possibility of antiselection.

Health

Generally, a health condition is more likely to result in disability than in death. DI coverage is usually not approved if the proposed insured has a physical condition that could make it difficult to determine whether a disability exists when a claim is made. Back pain and nervous system problems are examples of conditions that usually are not approved for DI coverage.

In assessing risk for DI insurance, underwriters typically order more reports—including medical records, blood profiles, urinalyses, and inspection reports—than do underwriters for life coverage. If a proposed insured for life coverage mentions in a questionnaire that she has a medical history of back sprains, for example, most life underwriters will not investigate further because back sprains do not usually result in death. A DI underwriter, however, typically investigates such a report because a history of back sprains is closely associated with disability.

Occupation

DI underwriters consider occupation in more detail than life underwriters do. DI underwriters especially assess the likelihood that a proposed insured may become disabled because of his occupation. To be considered an acceptable risk, an applicant for DI coverage should have a favorable employment record—that is, steady employment and regular attendance—in a nonhazardous occupation.

Applicants whose work environment presents potential hazards of diseases or accidents or whose employment is seasonal or otherwise irregular are generally viewed as undesirable risks for DI coverage. In addition, a person who works from her home is sometimes considered a questionable risk because if a disability occurs, the insurer can have difficulty determining if the person is continuing to work or if she has returned to work. In certain occupations, a self-employed person who works from home and who has no considerable net worth or other means of support is also considered a poor risk for DI coverage because the person may have little incentive to return to work.

In addition, the proposed insured's job duties or requirements affect the anticipated duration of a disability and, thus, affect the underwriting decision. Insurance industry statistics show, for instance, that a white-collar worker who has suffered a heart attack is more likely to return to work sooner than a blue-collar worker. Similarly, a relatively minor injury such as a broken wrist could prove incapacitating to a dentist or a doctor, but would not necessarily prevent a teacher, an office manager, or a minister from continuing employment.

All insurers establish ***occupational rating classes*** into which occupations are grouped according to the relative degree of risk they present for DI coverage. Occupations that are rated as presenting less relative risk include those that offer few physical dangers or psychological stresses and are stable, with little annual turnover. Occupational classes range from the least hazardous occupations to the most hazardous occupations, which are uninsurable. When assessing an applicant whose duties cross occupational lines, a DI underwriter usually applies the classification covering the most hazardous duties. One insurer's occupational rating classes are shown in Figure 7-4.

Finances and Portion of Income Insured

An applicant for DI coverage typically submits detailed information on finances. The underwriter examines each applicant's net worth, net earned income (gross income minus taxes), and unearned income, such as income from investments, interest, or a trust fund. Each insurer establishes limits on the amount of DI insurance—usually expressed as an amount of monthly benefit—it will issue based on an applicant's earned income. This limited amount of DI coverage is expressed in an ***income replacement table***, which is a chart that shows the amount of monthly net income earned by a proposed insured with a specified annual net earned income, as well as the total monthly DI benefit that

FIGURE 7-4. Occupational Rating Classes.

Class 1 (Standard)

This class includes people in the least hazardous occupations—for example, attorneys, auditors, bookkeepers, drafters, insurance agents, librarians, meteorologists, pharmacists, administrative assistants, and stockbrokers.

Class 2

This class generally includes (a) people in certain nonhazardous occupations in which even a minor injury can result in liability, such as most people working in medical professions, laboratory workers, and musicians for whom a minor injury could interrupt or end employment in that occupation and (b) people having office and overall supervisory responsibility in manufacturing plants or at construction sites. Examples include architects, building contractors who inspect construction, medical technicians, supervising plant managers, and surgeons.

Class 3

This class generally includes (a) blue-collar workers or people doing light manual labor, (b) people who drive passenger or light delivery vehicles, and (c) managers who directly supervise manual laborers on the job and who may occasionally assist in manual activity. Examples include athletic coaches, bus drivers, house painters, motor freight dispatchers, plumbers, taxi drivers, and waiters.

Class 4 (Most Hazardous)

This class includes people in the most hazardous insurable occupations, generally those in which the incidence of injury is high—for example, boilermakers, border patrol police, locomotive engineers, stevedores, structural steelworkers, and other heavy construction workers.

Uninsurable

This class includes people who are exposed to unusual hazards and are uninsurable for any disability income—for instance, certain professional and semiprofessional athletes, aerial photographers or surveyors, blasters, divers, underground miners, steeplejacks, test pilots, and war correspondents.

person could obtain. For example, according to Figure 7-5, which is a portion of one insurer's income replacement table, a proposed insured who has an annual net earned income of $40,000 and receives approximately $3,333 monthly after taxes is eligible for approximately $2,400 in monthly benefits under DI coverage.

In figuring the amount of income that a proposed insured is eligible to insure through DI coverage, the underwriter considers both primary and secondary income sources. Generally, if an injury prevents a proposed insured from earning income from both primary and secondary

FIGURE 7-5. Income Replacement Table.

Annual Net Earned Income	Monthly Net Earned Income	Total DI Benefit
$20,000	$1,667	$1,300
$30,000	$2,500	$1,950
$40,000	$3,333	$2,400
$50,000	$4,167	$2,900
$60,000	$5,000	$3,350
$70,000	$5,833	$3,750
$80,000	$6,667	$4,100
$90,000	$7,500	$4,400
$100,000	$8,333	$4,700

sources, then the proposed insured is eligible for insurance that covers both sources of income. If a proposed insured has income from a secondary occupation that requires skills similar to those required to perform the primary occupation, the underwriter includes the amount of secondary income in figuring the total amount of income that may be insured. If, however, the proposed insured has secondary income from an occupation that uses skills that are unrelated to the skills required to perform the primary occupation, the underwriter does not include the secondary income in evaluating the appropriate amount to insure.

For example, if a proposed insured who is a veterinarian also earns money by giving motivational speeches, an underwriter would not consider the income earned by speaking as part of the proposed insured's primary income because speaking requires a different set of skills than does the practice of veterinary medicine. If another proposed insured is employed as a high school Spanish teacher and also teaches Spanish to adults in the summer, however, the underwriter would include the secondary income in the total income eligible for DI coverage because both the primary and secondary occupations require similar skills.

The underwriter considers as favorable any indication that an applicant's income is consistent or increasing over a three-year period. Conversely, if a proposed insured has suffered severe, recent decreases in income, the underwriter looks at the sources and consistency of that person's income. A severe reduction in income is usually considered to be at least 40 percent of original income. A decrease in income level is considered to be recent if the decrease has occurred within the last three years, without recovery to the original level of income.

DI underwriters also look at a proposed insured's income stability. Funds earned through seasonal or temporary employment are generally not considered stable and are not included under DI coverage. For example, a person who delivers new telephone directories once a year or who works at a retail store only during a holiday season is typically ineligible to have income from those sources protected under DI coverage.

If an applicant has an unusually high unearned income—50 percent or more of his net earned income—the underwriter generally does not include the unearned income in figuring the amount of income to be covered. A person with substantial unearned income may not depend on an earned income to the same extent as would a person without high unearned income and might, therefore, be a greater risk for a DI claim. The amount of DI coverage cannot be so great as to remove an insured's financial incentive to return to work.

Similarly, if a proposed insured has a high net worth, the underwriter checks to be sure the applicant cannot completely replace the current net earned income by liquidating assets. For instance, if a proposed insured has a net worth of $3,000,000 and an annual net income of $20,000, most underwriters would conclude that this person does not need DI coverage. If this person were disabled so that she could not work, she has sufficient net worth to provide well for herself.

Underwriters also consider any other DI coverage protecting an applicant and use the income replacement table to assess whether an applicant is eligible for DI benefits. For instance, according to Figure 7-5, an applicant who has $60,000 in annual net earned income and who has no significant unearned income or excessive net worth would be eligible for $3,350 a month in DI benefits. If this applicant is already covered by some DI insurance offered by his employer, however, the underwriter usually reduces the benefit amount under the new policy so that the total of DI benefits paid—by any and all insurers—does not exceed $3,350 per month.

FAST FACT

Nearly one-third of all Americans will suffer a serious disability between ages 35 and 65.[2]

Underwriting Critical Illness Insurance

Critical illness (CI) insurance is offered as a stand-alone product or as a rider to a life or disability income contract. CI insurance typically provides coverage for three to five times annual salary and protects insureds against the financial hardship that can result from surviving a serious illness. Financial underwriting of critical illness is done to minimize the potential of an excessive windfall in the event of a critical illness claim. CI benefits are usually paid in a lump sum when the insured is diagnosed with a specified illness, such as heart attack, life-threatening cancer, stroke, major organ transplant, or kidney failure.

Under critical illness coverage, the lump sum benefit is paid to the insured regardless of expenses incurred as a result of the illness, the insured's ability to work, or the loss of income. The insured can use the benefit in any way, such as building a wheelchair ramp for a residence, seeing an out-of-network doctor, undergoing an experimental treatment, replacing a spouse's income so that the spouse can care for the insured, paying for childcare during recuperation, continuing a business, paying off a mortgage, or even taking a vacation.

Some insurers also offer an accelerated death benefit rider to CI insurance policies for insureds with certain critical illnesses. ***Accelerated death benefits*** are a portion of a policy's benefits paid during life to a terminally ill policyowner-insured who has a remaining life expectancy of less than a specified period, usually ranging between six months and two years. Under an accelerated death benefit rider, the CI policy's lump sum benefit is payable upon either the death of the insured or the diagnosis of a covered condition, whichever occurs first. Some accelerated death benefit riders offer a percentage of the face amount (such as 50 percent) upon diagnosis, with the remainder payable upon death. Many accelerated death benefit riders for critical illness insurance also offer payments of a percentage of the face amount (such as 25 percent) for medical conditions or procedures such as coronary artery bypass surgery or angioplasty.

Because CI coverage is designed to provide protection for survivors of critical illnesses, most critical illness products include a survival requirement, stating that no benefits will be payable if the insured dies within 30 days of the diagnosis of illness that results in death. Accelerated death benefit plans do not include a survival requirement because the benefit is paid at the time of diagnosis or upon the death of the insured, whichever occurs first. Many CI products also include a waiting period or limited benefit period, designed to keep premiums affordable and to combat antiselection.

Risk selection for critical illness coverages requires increased attention to a number of both medical and financial aspects of the potential risk. Underwriting critical illness coverage or riders differs considerably from underwriting life insurance because underwriting life insurance focuses on prospective mortality or the risk of dying. On the other hand, underwriting for critical illness focuses on the potential of future incidence of a particular impairment or group of impairments. Before an underwriter can begin to underwrite critical illness coverage, the underwriter must become very familiar with the nature of and details regarding the impairments covered by the plan or rider. The number of impairments covered can range from a minimum of 3 or 4 to 30 or more.

While the maximum extra mortality rating for life risks can exceed 400 percent, the level of extra risk for critical illness typically does not exceed 150 percent for a total of 250 percent. Debits typically are added for both build and blood pressure. Family history is also significant in the determination of the likelihood of the future incidence of the impairments covered by critical illness products. The most important and most frequently occurring impairments included under CI coverage are cardiovascular diseases and cancer, both of which have a significant genetic component. Underwriters typically assign larger debits to applicants whose family histories include cardiovascular diseases or cancer.

Underwriting Long-Term Care Coverage

Long-term care (LTC) insurance covers expenses that are not paid for by medical expense insurance or Medicare. LTC insurance provides benefits to pay for medical and other services to people who need assistance in their own home, a nursing home, or other facility. Insight 7-1 describes how the need for LTC insurance will increase in the future.

The benefit period for LTC insurance can be set for any length of time, starting at one year and extending to a maximum of lifetime coverage. Possible underwriting actions on most LTC products are to issue the coverage at standard rates, modify the amount of coverage available, increase the premium amount, or decline to issue the coverage.

Insight 7-1. Longer Lives Require More Care.

More of us living into our 80s and 90s probably will mean more of us will need long-term care. "It's like that Beatles' song, 'Will you still need me, will you still feed me, when I'm 64,'" said David Holland, president of Munich American Reassurance in Atlanta. "Only now it should be 84. That was a really prescient song, given the situation today."

Actuaries who responded to the Society of Actuaries' 1999 Delphi Study predicted that babies born in the United States in 2010 could expect to live to be 79, and those born in 2050 can make plans for their 82nd birthday parties. At the same time, death rates in the United States from heart disease, cancer, AIDS, and accidents will steadily decrease, the actuaries said.

But even though we'll be living longer and healthier lives, as we get into our 80s and 90s, health care costs will go up, said Alastair Longley-Cook, corporate actuary for Aetna Inc., Hartford, Connecticut.

There'll be some serious concerns about whether we'll have enough money to continue a comfortable lifestyle and what will happen when we start to lose our faculties, Holland said. Consequently, the need for long-term care insurance and recognition of the need will grow.

Source: Excerpted from Sally Whitney, "Longer Lives Require More Care," *Best's Review,* Life and Health ed. (November 1999): 35.

Considerations About Aging

Underwriting LTC coverage requires a great deal of information about the ways that aging affects people. Generally, the minimum age for proposed insureds for whom insurers will accept LTC applications is 40, and the maximum age is 85. LTC underwriters, therefore, develop a thorough knowledge of the kinds of physical and mental disorders that are part of the aging process. Specifically, LTC underwriters develop detailed knowledge of many elements of ***geriatrics***, which is the branch of medicine dealing with the diseases and conditions of aging.

Accurate underwriting for LTC insurance also requires consideration of the proposed insured's physiological age in relation to his chronological age. A person's ***physiological age*** refers to the relative age or youthfulness of his vital organs and their functioning. A person who has a chronological age of 75 years may be in far better health than the average person of that age, so his physiological age may be closer to 60 or 65 than to 75. Conversely, another person who has a chronological age of 75 may be in such poor health that his physiological age may be closer to 85 or 90 than to 75.

Many older people exhibit signs of ***cognitive impairment***, which is a reduction in a person's ability to think, reason, or remember. Cognitive impairment includes several mental conditions, such as the following:

- Forgetfulness
- Memory loss
- Decreased ability to think clearly
- Reduced mental keenness
- Confusion or disorientation
- Delirium or amnesia

LTC underwriters typically understand the probable effect each impairment has on a proposed insured's ability to live independently. One of the most common types of cognitive impairment is ***dementia***, a general term used for mental deterioration that is characterized by loss of certain intellectual abilities—such as memory, judgment, and abstract thinking—of such a degree as to interfere with social functioning. People who have any type of dementia typically experience decreased longevity and increased dependence and eventually may require confinement in a long-term care facility. Another common type of cognitive impairment is ***Alzheimer's disease***, also called *primary degenerative dementia,* which causes deterioration of a person's intellectual and cognitive functions—including memory, orientation, intellect, and judgment—and can cause deterioration of a person's speech and motor functions.

In underwriting most LTC coverages, the underwriter checks for medical conditions that, over time, will probably cause a disability in one or more of the activities of daily living so that the proposed insured requires personal, one-on-one assistance in performing those activities. The ***activities of daily living (ADLs)*** generally include

- Eating
- Bathing
- Dressing
- Mobility (transferring from bed to chair or getting out of bed)
- Toileting

Generally, insurers deny coverage to anyone who, at the time of application, cannot personally perform all ADLs, but some insurers do offer limited coverage to people who are unable to fulfill only one or two such functions.

Certain types of cognitive impairment can limit one's ability to perform ADLs significantly. For example, a person suffering from dementia may be physically able to feed himself, but may not remember to eat or may forget how to feed himself. He may be able to put on his own clothes, but may wear the same clothes day after day. People with significant cognitive impairment usually require assistance with ADLs.

FAST FACT

Long-term care expenditures for the elderly in the United States were projected to amount to over $120 billion in 2000.[3]

Some people can manage the ADLs, but have difficulty with other, usually less essential types of activities that are called ***instrumental activities of daily living (IADLs)***. Managing one's own finances, cooking and doing laundry, and shopping for food and clothing are a few IADLs. Some insurers consider IADLs in underwriting proposed insureds for LTC coverage, but others consider only ADLs.

Antiselection

An LTC underwriter helps prevent antiselection by determining whether an applicant currently has acquired, or is in imminent danger of acquiring, any significant physical, mental, social, or behavioral reason to seek institutional care. A person who is disposed to seek such care is usually not accepted for LTC insurance. LTC coverage is designed and priced to provide for institutional care at a future time when a proposed insured develops conditions or impairments that require the care. LTC coverage is not designed and priced to provide such care for people who are already suffering from incapacitating conditions or impairments at the time of application.

Field Underwriting

To help agents perform effective field underwriting of LTC applicants, many insurers develop special field underwriting manuals that focus specifically on the requirements for this type of insurance. Generally, an ***LTC field underwriting manual*** is an insurer's guidebook that lists several medical conditions associated with aging and provides general underwriting criteria for those conditions. For each medical condition, the LTC field underwriting manual describes characteristics and complications and includes questions that the agent is expected to ask in gathering information from the proposed insured.

An LTC field underwriting manual is similar to an impairment guide in that both these publications list impairments. The publications differ in that an impairment guide provides very general information on a wide variety of impairments, whereas an LTC field underwriting manual provides more specific information on the types of conditions that people applying for LTC can exhibit. In addition, an impairment guide gives very general information about the probable underwriting decision for each impairment, whereas an LTC field underwriting manual cites more specific information about the underwriting decision for specific types of impairment.

Look again at Figure 7-1 and examine the entry for fractures in one insurer's impairment guide. Note that the impairment guide states only that, according to the location, severity, complications, and recovery from a fracture, coverage can be issued at standard rates, with an impairment rider, or both. By contrast, the listing for fractures in one insurer's LTC field underwriting manual, shown in Figure 7-6, provides more specific information for certain types of fractures (hip, spinal column, pelvic, and so on), and also lists specific fractures for which no coverage will be issued. Unlike the impairment guide, the LTC field underwriting manual also provides a general description of the characteristics and complications of fractures, as well as a list of questions that an agent may ask a proposed insured in gathering information to submit with the application.

Tools for LTC Underwriting

The tools an LTC underwriter uses for assessing a proposed insured differ considerably from the tools used for underwriting other types of individual health coverages. For example, underwriters for LTC coverages do not use information from MIB, Inc. because that

FIGURE 7-6. Section of One Insurer's LTC Field Underwriting Manual.

Fractures

Fractures are more common in women than in men, probably because of post-menopausal osteoporosis and the tendency for women to outlive men. The presence of osteoporosis often determines whether a fall results in a fracture. Pathological fractures—those associated with a fall or trauma—are common in the elderly.

The most common sites of fractures in our claim experience have been the hips, followed by compression fractures of the spinal column and fractures of the pelvis, shoulders, and wrists. Healing of fractures in the elderly is often delayed because of reduced blood supply to the area, arthritis, reduced nutrition, and decreased physical activity.

If an applicant has suffered a fracture, you should find out

- What bone was fractured, and when?
- Has surgery been recommended?
- Has osteoporosis been diagnosed?
- Is there evidence of functional or movement limitations, or is human assistance required?
- Are narcotics such as Demerol, morphine, Percodan, or Talwin being used to control pain?
- Is physical therapy currently required?
- Are assistive devices such as a wheelchair, walker, or crutches used?
- Does the applicant have a history of imbalance with falls and fractures?

These are the underwriting criteria for fractures:

- Fractures of the hip, tibia, or hip replacement are acceptable 6 months after the person regains full functional status and release from medical follow-up
- Fractures of the pelvis or vertebra are acceptable 12 months after recovery

The following fractures are not acceptable for coverage:

- Three or more long bone, vertebral, or pelvic fractures due to falls or osteoporosis
- Any fracture where assistance is still required or wheelchair or walker is used
- Curvature of the spine with secondary pulmonary problems

information is typically too general to be useful for the kind of detailed investigation necessary to underwrite LTC insurance. Few insurers use inspection reports for LTC underwriting because other sources reveal more specific and useful information.

LTC underwriters assess each risk by using information from the application along with the results of a paramedical examination and an APS from each physician who has treated the applicant within the last three to five years. Checking for possible cognitive impairment is also an essential part of LTC underwriting. The underwriter is not concerned with projecting the amount of cognitive impairment that will develop after coverage is issued, but is concerned with any cognitive impairment that exists prior to issue of coverage. In addition to the information from the APS and the paramedical examination, the LTC underwriter checks for possible cognitive impairment by using a personal history interview, a face-to-face assessment, and a cognitive screen.

You'll recall from Chapter 2 that a personal history interview (PHI) is a conversation between the underwriter—or another insurance company employee—and the proposed insured. For an LTC policy, the PHI may take place between the underwriter and the proposed insured's medical caregiver. Before consulting with medical caregivers, the underwriter verifies that each caregiver has been given permission to discuss medical information with the insurer. During the PHI—which usually takes place over the telephone—the parties discuss items on the application and on any other documents used in evaluating the risk. The underwriter's purpose in conducting a PHI is to check facts that have been provided and to elicit facts that may not have been included. During a conversation with a proposed insured, the underwriter may ask a short list of questions designed to indicate the presence of cognitive impairment. For example, the underwriter may ask the current date, season, location of the proposed insured, and other questions that people without a cognitive impairment would find simple to answer.

A ***face-to-face assessment*** involves a meeting between a proposed insured and an interviewer who represents the insurance company and who is usually employed by a vendor. During a face-to-face assessment, the proposed insureds physical and mental condition are observed and, to some extent, examined. Most insurers require a face-to-face assessment for proposed insureds aged 76 and older, although if an application reveals the possibility of significant medical conditions, or if current medical records are unavailable, an insurer may require a face-to-face assessment for a proposed insured who is younger than 76. Typical questions asked during a face-to-face assessment are shown in Figure 7-7.

FIGURE 7-7. Typical Questions Asked During Face-to-Face Assessment.

To assess a proposed insured's mobility:

- Do you go outside your house at any time? If so, where do you go? Do you go alone or with someone else?
- Do you drive? If so, where do you drive? How often?
- Do you need support or help from another person when you go outside within walking distance of your home?
- Do you need to use any equipment such as a cane, walker, or wheelchair?

To assess the ability of a proposed insured to dress himself:

- Do you need help to dress or undress yourself?
- Are you able to get your clothes from the closet?
- Can you manage dressing with someone standing by in case you need help, or do you need frequent assistance?

As part of the face-to-face assessment, the interviewer may also use a ***cognitive screen,*** which is a test designed to determine a person's powers of recollection or short-term memory recall. One type of cognitive screen is a ***delayed word recall (DWR) test***, which examines the ability of a proposed insured to remember several common words. The inability to recall between 3 and 5 words correctly from a list of 10 words is indicative of a cognitive impairment. If a proposed insured shows a significant degree of forgetfulness, the underwriter generally declines the application. Another type of cognitive screen is a ***backward number sequence test***, which examines the ability of a proposed insured to recall a series of numbers and name them in reverse sequence. For example, if an interviewer gives the numbers "45, 78, 17," the proposed insured is supposed to recall the numbers in this order: "17, 78, 45."

Certain health conditions and treatments put such severe limitations on a person's ability to function independently that most insurers automatically decline LTC applications submitted by proposed insureds who exhibit these conditions or treatments. Figure 7-8 provides a partial listing of such conditions and treatments.

FIGURE 7-8. Partial Listing of Conditions and Treatments Preventing LTC Coverage.

- Alzheimer's disease
- Amputation resulting from disease (for instance, from diabetes or atherosclerosis)
- Blindness resulting from disease or with ADL/IADL limitations
- Cancer with evidence of distant metastasis within past 10 years
- Cystic fibrosis
- Dementia, irreversible
- Emphysema, on oxygen
- Gangrene resulting from diabetes or peripheral vascular disease
- Hospital or nursing home, current confinement, or current use of home or adult day care
- Kidney dialysis within past 6 months
- Memory loss within 12 months, including confusion, delirium, or disorientation, and any current use of medication for same
- Multiple sclerosis
- Muscular dystrophy
- Organ transplants (excluding kidney transplant 5 or more years ago)
- Oxygen use, current
- Paralysis, paraplegia, or quadriplegia
- Senility, all forms
- Spinal cord injury
- Stroke (cardiovascular accident)
- Surgery, scheduled or anticipated (except cataract surgery under local anesthesia)

Key Terms and Concepts

medical expense insurance
disability income (DI) insurance
critical illness (CI) insurance
long-term care (LTC) insurance
impairment guide
rated policy
rating schedule
flat rating
waiting period
split elimination period
impairment rider
occupational rating classes
income replacement table
accelerated death benefits
geriatrics
physiological age
cognitive impairment
dementia
Alzheimer's disease
activities of daily living (ADLs)
instrumental activities of daily living (IADLs)
LTC field underwriting manual
face-to-face assessment
cognitive screen
delayed word recall (DWR) test
backward number sequence test

Endnotes

1. ACLI, *Life Insurers Fact Book 2000* (Washington, D.C.: American Council of Life Insurers, 2000), 57.
2. Ibid., 53.
3. Ibid., 62.

CHAPTER 8

Underwriting Group Coverage

Chapter Outline

Principles of Group Underwriting

Risk Assessment Factors: The Proposed Group
- Reason for Existence
- Type of Group
- Stability
- Size
- Nature of Business
- Geographic Location
- Employee Classes
- Level of Participation
- Age
- Sex
- Dependents
- Expected Persistency
- Prior Coverage and Claims Experience

Risk Assessment Factors: The Proposed Coverage
- Plan of Insurance
- Plan Administration
- Mode of Commission Payment

Procedures for Group Underwriting
- Information Sources for Group Underwriting
- The Proposal for Insurance
- The Master Application
- Rating Methods for Group Cases
- Post-Issue Underwriting for Group Insurance

Objectives

After reading this chapter, you should be able to

- List and describe risk assessment factors of the proposed group that affect underwriting group coverage
- Describe how risk assessment factors of the proposed coverage affect underwriting group coverage
- Discuss the procedures underwriters use for group coverage
- List and discuss the sources of information for group underwriting
- Explain the purpose, contents, and attachments that are normally submitted with a Request for Proposal
- Explain the purpose and the general contents of a master application
- Distinguish among manual rating, experience rating, and blended rating
- Define and explain three types of post-issue underwriting used in group insurance

A group insurance policy provides coverage for a number of people under one contract. The insurance contract is formed between the insurer and the group policyholder, which typically is an organization, such as an employer or an association. The people who are insured under a group policy are not parties to the insurance contract and are usually underwritten as a group, rather than as individuals, although the members of some small groups are usually underwritten individually.

Many employee benefit plans provide group health care coverage through a plan of ***managed care***, a method of integrating both the financing and delivery of health care within a system that seeks to control the cost, accessibility, and quality of care. Under a managed care plan, certain medical services are provided to plan subscribers in exchange for a prepaid fee. In contrast, traditional health care plans provide ***indemnity benefits***, which are medical expense benefits stated as a maximum dollar amount that is payable for each covered service. The principles of risk assessment are similar for both kinds of group health care plans, although underwriting procedures and the processes for developing premium rates under each plan differ. In this text, we'll focus our discussion on the established principles and procedures for underwriting traditional group insurance plans.

Group policies are generally marketed by (1) agents, (2) brokers, or (3) representatives who are employees of an insurance company and who work cooperatively with agents or brokers to sell group products. Some insurers use all three. Group insurance marketing usually follows certain steps. First, an agent gathers information about the insurance coverage requested for a proposed group. The organization that the agent and the insurer hope will become the policyholder for a proposed group is generally called a ***prospect.*** After the agent sends the information to the insurer, the group underwriter assesses the risk. If the proposed group represents an acceptable risk, the rates necessary to provide the requested coverage are calculated. Then the insurer develops a proposal, which the agent presents to the prospect. If the prospect accepts the coverage at the stated rates, the group coverage is then issued and administered.

The underwriting principles and procedures for all types of group insurance are essentially the same. Instead of approaching the discussion of group underwriting by product, therefore, we'll examine the overall principles and procedures of assessing group risks; we'll mention underwriting guidelines for specific products as necessary.

We'll begin our discussion with the principles of group underwriting. We will also examine the risk assessment factors considered in evaluating applicants for group insurance. Then we'll conclude the chapter by discussing the procedures used for underwriting group coverage.

Principles of Group Underwriting

Successful group underwriting seeks to achieve the same goal as individual underwriting: to assess risk accurately and equitably and to calculate an appropriate premium to pay for the coverage. In striving for this goal, underwriters assess and accept proposed groups whose members, plan designs, and administrative processes fall within the parameters established by the insurer for the group product. In general, a group underwriter

- Reviews the characteristics of the proposed group
- Evaluates the coverage and services requested
- For renewal and transfer cases, assesses the proposed group's premium and claims experience

If the requested coverage is within the insurer's parameters, the underwriter calculates the cost of the coverage and of the services the insurer will provide to the proposed group. The cost includes the expenses of administering the plan, establishing reserves, funding claims, and providing for commissions and profits. The premium rate charged for group coverage may be increased or decreased when the policy is renewed at the policy anniversary.

If the coverage requested is *not* within the insurer's parameters, the underwriter modifies the coverage and the premium so that the plan more closely meets the insurer's guidelines. If the underwriter cannot adjust the coverage to the proposed group's satisfaction, then coverage for that group is declined.

In assessing the risk represented by a group, the underwriter ensures that the group and the plan meet all legal requirements. In addition, if group members are allowed to elect the type of coverage they will receive, the underwriter assesses the characteristics of the portion of the group that will be insured by each kind of coverage.

For example, suppose that the Sunshine Software Company applied for two basic types of health coverage—an indemnity plan and a managed care plan—and that Sunshine employees can choose to be covered by either plan, but not both. For this case, the underwriter evaluates the risk represented by each subgroup—that is, the people covered by each plan—rather than the risk represented by the entire group of Sunshine employees. If most of the older employees or most of the medically impaired employees have selected one plan over the other, claim costs could be adversely affected. The underwriter considers this possibility and takes it into account when assessing the risk and determining premium rates.

For group insurance, underwriters generally do not require evidence of insurability for each group member; rather, they assess the entire group according to two factors: (1) characteristics of the proposed group and (2) characteristics of the coverage. Figure 8-1 summarizes these two types of risk assessment factors, each of which we will discuss in detail in this chapter.

FIGURE 8-1. Risk Assessment Factors for Group Insurance.

Characteristics of the Proposed Group

- Reason for Existence
- Type of Group
- Stability
- Size
- Nature of business
- Geographic location
- Employee classes
- Level of participation
- Age
- Sex
- Dependents
- Expected persistency
- Prior coverage and claims experience

Characteristics of the Coverage

- Plan of insurance
- Plan administration
- Mode of commission payment

Risk Assessment Factors: The Proposed Group

Underwriters examine several characteristics of a proposed group. Keep in mind that because underwriting involves gathering and evaluating several types of information at once, a group underwriter typically examines and assesses many of a group's factors simultaneously.

Reason for Existence

Most insurance companies in the United States and Canada generally adhere to the principle that an eligible group must have been formed for a purpose other than to purchase insurance coverage. This requirement protects insurance companies from antiselection that would result if a number of people, all of whom were poor insurance risks, were to join together for the purpose of obtaining insurance.

Some insurers do underwrite groups that have been formed solely for the purpose of obtaining insurance, but such groups typically exhibit many of the characteristics of a standard, employer-employee group. For example, several small businesses may form a group so as to buy insurance. If all members of the group work steadily in an industry or occupation that presents an acceptable level of risk, and have a regular income, some insurance companies would accept the group for coverage even though the group formed to buy insurance.

Professional associations that apply for coverage are assessed to ensure that the reason for their existence is not solely to purchase group insurance. If a majority of the members of a profession belong to the association, most insurers assume that the group has a valid purpose aside from obtaining insurance.

Type of Group

The types of groups that generally are considered for group insurance include employer-employee groups (including private employers and public employers such as municipalities, county governments, and state governments), multiple-employer groups (including trade associations, trusts, and labor unions), professional associations, and debtor-creditor groups. For each of these types of groups, specific underwriting considerations influence risk assessment. Figure 8-2 provides a brief explanation of the distinctions between types of groups.

FIGURE 8-2. Type of Groups.

Employer-Employee Group

The most common type of group insured under group coverage, it consists of an employer, who is the policyholder, and its employees, who are the insureds.

Multiple-Employer Group

Two or more employers in the same industry who join together to provide insurance for their employees through one group plan.

Professional Association

A group composed of people who have the same type of occupation or who share a common interest. Educator, health care professional, real estate agent, and police officer are some of the professions that typically form professional associations.

Debtor-Creditor Group

A group that consists of a credit-granting institution, such as a bank, and its debtors.

Stability

From an underwriting perspective, an ideal group is relatively stable in composition, with a steady flow of younger, newer members to replace or at least balance the gradual aging of older members. Underwriters typically do not look favorably upon a group whose composition either changes too frequently or remains static for a long period of time. An unusually high turnover rate produces unexpectedly high administrative costs and may indicate that people are joining the group for the purpose of obtaining insurance coverage for a short time period. This type of antiselection generally produces an undesirably high claims cost. Similarly, an unusually low turnover rate produces an increase in the average age of group members. Because mortality and morbidity tend to increase as people grow older, a group with low turnover is likely to experience higher-than-average claims costs.

Insurers try to encourage stability within a group by setting eligibility requirements that define which employees can be covered under a group policy. If a group has experienced a high degree of turnover, for example, an insurer may establish a service requirement for the group. According to a ***service requirement,*** a person must be employed for a certain length of time—usually three to six months—before being covered under the group insurance plan. If a proposed plan includes a service requirement, the underwriter determines which employees are eligible under the plan.

FAST FACT

In Canada at the end of 1999, 102,200 group contracts covered about 5.9 million workers and their 8.3 million dependents for supplementary major medical expenses.[1]

Size

Fluctuations in a group's claims experience tend to decrease as the size of the group increases. Moreover, the larger a group, the lower the level of its administrative expenses as a percentage of the total premium amount the group pays. In the early days of group insurance, most insurers believed that a group with fewer than 100 insureds was too small for reliable estimation of likely mortality or morbidity. Today, because of increasing information about mortality and morbidity experience, the minimum group size has been reduced considerably. Some insurers, in fact, underwrite groups with as few as two members.

However, the smaller a group, the less predictable or credible the estimate of future claims costs. Therefore, the underwriter may have difficulty determining an appropriate premium for a small group. To assist the underwriter in estimating a small group's probable claims costs and in calculating an equitable premium, most insurers use pooling and manual rating for small groups. ***Pooling*** is the practice of considering a number of small groups as one large group for risk assessment purposes. The larger the number of proposed insureds in the pooled group, the more likely that the underwriter can arrive at a fair estimate of the whole group's claims costs. ***Manual rating*** involves establishing premium rates for broad classes of groups, especially for those with no credible claims experience. We'll discuss manual rating in more detail later in the chapter. Figure 8-3 summarizes the effects of group size on underwriting.

FIGURE 8-3. Effects of Group Size on Underwriting.

Smaller Group

- Relatively larger fluctuations in claims experience increase the difficulty of assessing the group's experience
- Relatively larger fluctuations in claims experience require that manual rating be used to determine premiums
- Relatively higher expense level as percentage of total premium can increase the premium amount for coverage

Larger Group

- Relatively stable claims experience makes it easier to assess the group's experience
- Relatively stable claims experience often permits rating on the basis of the group's claims experience
- Relatively lower expense level as percentage of total premium can decrease the premium amount for coverage

Nature of Business

The type of industry in which a group works influences the underwriting decision. Information on occupational hazards and experience information concerning the likelihood of people in certain jobs to make excessive claims assist insurers in setting appropriate underwriting guidelines. The occupations of a majority of the participants in the group can be a significant underwriting factor, especially for accident or sickness hazards.

The strength and financial condition of a business are also important in underwriting. Usually, a business or an organization must have been operating on a sound financial basis for at least one year in order for an insurance company to approve a group plan. General economic conditions and their relationship to the profitability of that business or organization may be another factor in determining the desirability of a specific group risk.

Geographic Location

Morbidity and mortality rates differ in various areas of the world and tend to be higher in areas that are susceptible to natural disasters. The underwriter takes these factors into consideration and also looks at the living conditions and the economic level of the proposed insureds, as well as the availability and cost of adequate health care in the area.

In some proposed groups, all members of the group are not located in the same place—for example, an organization may have multiple offices in a number of states, provinces, or countries. In assessing such groups, an underwriter considers all applicable laws and regulations concerning each of the locations involved.

Employee Classes

The people to be insured by group coverage may be classified in various ways. An ***employee class*** is a group of employees categorized by position, earnings, or rank. The amount of insurance available to each employee class may vary.

In order for a group to be approved for coverage, assignment to a class must be established on a nondiscriminatory basis according to conditions pertaining to employment, and the policyholder may not select specific people to be in any particular class. Moreover, laws in some jurisdictions prohibit classes based on marital status, sex, or age. Figure 8-4 illustrates some typical nondiscriminatory classes established for group insurance.

FIGURE 8-4. Typical Nondiscriminatory Classes for Group Insurance.

Classes Based on Salary

All salaried employees

All salaried employees earning up to $X per year

All employees earning more than $X per year

Classes Based on Hours Worked

All salaried employees working X hours per year

All employees working X hours per year

OR

All employees working X hours per year

All employees working fewer than X hours per year

Classes Based on Occupation

All officers, managers, and supervisors

All officers and managers

All officers

Classes Based on Length of Service

All salaried employees with X years of service

All employees with X years of service

OR

All employees with X years of service

All employees with fewer than X years of service

In groups other than employer-employee groups, people proposed for coverage may be assigned to classes according to their membership in the group, their debtor relationship to a bank or other lending institution, or some other nondiscriminatory basis.

Level of Participation

Insurers categorize group plans as either noncontributory or contributory. A ***noncontributory plan*** of group insurance provides that the insureds pay no part of the premium for their coverage. The group policyholder pays the entire premium, and coverage is automatic for all eligible members of the group. In a noncontributory plan, the level of participation is usually required to be 100 percent of all eligible group members. By contrast, a ***contributory plan*** of group insurance provides that the insureds pay some part of the premium for their insurance coverage and may choose whether to participate in the group insurance plan. In a contributory plan, the more closely participation in the plan approaches 100 percent, the more the standard risks in the group tend to compensate for the impaired lives and potential morbidity and mortality in the group, thereby reducing the effects of antiselection.

Consequently, for all but the largest groups enrolled in contributory plans, insurers normally require a minimum participation level of between 75 and 100 percent of eligible group members, depending on the size of the group. The larger the group, the more the participation requirement can be reduced because of the increased spread of risk. The following table illustrates minimum participation requirements established by one insurer for groups of various sizes enrolled in contributory insurance plans:

Number of Eligible Employees	Minimum Participation Requirement
Less than 250	75 percent
250–499	65 percent
500–749	60 percent
750–999	55 percent
More than 1,000	Case-by-case evaluation

Ideally, a group applying for life coverage exhibits a wide range of expected mortality (or, for health and disability coverages, a wide range of expected morbidity) so that the overall mortality or morbidity of the group approaches 100 percent of standard, which is the assumed mortality or morbidity for the product at the premium rates established for it. The higher the level of participation in a plan—that is, the larger the number of eligible group members enrolled in it—the more likely the group's mortality or morbidity will approach standard and the more acceptable the group becomes as an insurance risk.

Age

The age spread of a proposed group should be sufficiently broad to produce a wide range of risks. Underwriters are concerned about groups with a large proportion of older members who tend to experience high rates of morbidity and mortality. A group with low turnover tends to increase in average age, but ensuring a steady flow of new entrants can help to maintain the desired age spread in a group, particularly if the new entrants are young.

Sex

Underwriters also consider the ratio of males to females in a group. Women as a group tend to experience lower mortality, but higher morbidity, than men as a group tend to experience. All other factors being equal, a group with a large proportion of females represents a statistically lower risk for life coverage than does a group with a large proportion of males. Conversely, a group of males represents a statistically lower risk for health and disability insurance than does a group of females.

Dependents

Most insurance companies define a ***dependent*** as (1) a spouse or (2) an unmarried child—including an adopted child, stepchild, or foster child—who is under age 19 or to age 25 if disabled or a full-time student and who relies on the insured person for support and maintenance. Most insurers consider a common-law spouse to be included within the definition of *spouse* for the purposes of group insurance coverage. Some insurers also recognize the same-sex partner of an insured person as that person's spouse. Generally, a dependent cannot be insured unless the eligible group member is also insured.

Expected Persistency

In order to help control the financial loss resulting when business is canceled during the first year, most insurers evaluate the degree to which a prospect will probably continue coverage over a period of years past the first few years, when commissions and the cost of adding the group business to the insurer's books reduce or eliminate the insurer's profit on the case.

Persistency is also important because, even if a group has unusually high claims costs in a given year, the group's experience may improve during the following years; a policy in force for a sustained period is more likely to overcome the effects of a single bad year of claims. A group that has frequently changed insurers is likely to be charged a higher-than-average premium to compensate the insurer for the additional risk of losing the business early.

Prior Coverage and Claims Experience

When a group requests that its existing coverage be transferred to a different insurer, the underwriter at the new insurance company thoroughly assesses the case. The underwriter looks at the reason for the transfer, the amount of premium the group paid to the previous insurer, the claims experience of the group, the underwriting philosophy and guidelines of the previous insurer, and how much the rates for the group coverage have increased since the coverage began.

Group members who currently have claims on file with the previous insurer must be protected from loss of benefits when the group changes insurance carriers. Most insurers defer coverage on people who are not actively at work on the date the new coverage becomes effective. In addition, most insurers do not collect premiums on absent group members until those employees have returned to work on a full-time basis at their regular place of business.

Underwriting transferred business requires evaluation of the group's claims experience under the previous group policy. Most insurers require three years' documented experience of benefit changes and their effective dates, and of rates billed, premiums paid, claims incurred, and claims paid.

Risk Assessment Factors: The Proposed Coverage

In assessing the degree of risk represented by a prospect, insurers generally consider the plan of insurance, including its eligibility requirements and benefits; plan administration arrangements; and the mode of commission payment.

Plan of Insurance

Important elements of plan design include eligibility requirements and benefit levels. Details of these elements vary from one plan to another.

Eligibility Requirements

Most insurers stipulate that only full-time, permanent employees and their dependents may enroll in a group plan of insurance sponsored by an employer. The underwriter is responsible for checking the eligibility of each person to be insured under a plan.

Benefit Levels

Benefit levels determine in large part whether a plan will be financially successful for both the insured and the insurer. A plan with excessive benefits may be overutilized so that claims experience will be too high, whereas a plan with too few benefits or with inequitable benefits for one or more classes may not appeal to group members and will, therefore, not achieve the desired percentage of group member enrollment.

FAST FACT

At the end of 1999, group life insurance provided $6.1 trillion of protection in the United States.[2]

Plan Administration

Unlike individual insurance policies, many group plans require the active involvement of the group policyholder to manage and administer benefits. Effective plan administration is critical to keeping plan costs low and helping ensure the long-term satisfaction of the policyholder—and the group insureds—and, thus, the persistency of the coverage. Underwriters evaluate the willingness and ability of a group policyholder to cooperate in administering the plan. Specifically, a group policyholder should be able to promote the plan and encourage all eligible group members to enroll, maintain accurate and complete records of each group member's status and contributions to the plan, and assist group members with claim submissions.

Mode of Commission Payment

If the persistency of a proposed group is in question, the underwriter may determine that the agent's commission should be spread over several years instead of being paid as a single first-year commission. An extended mode of commission payment enables the insurer to lower the first-year cost associated with a plan and to experience less loss if the plan lapses at the end of the first year.

Procedures for Group Underwriting

The procedures that group underwriters follow in assessing risks generally include the same kinds of activities performed in underwriting individual coverages—that is, gathering information, assessing the risk, and making a decision on whether to approve the policy. If the group underwriter decides that the insurer can accept a risk, the underwriter also calculates the rate to be charged for the requested coverage. Insight 8-1 provides one expert's view of the challenges of medical underwriting for employee groups.

Information Sources for Group Underwriting

The underwriter uses various resources to assess the risk represented by a group proposed for coverage. These resources may include a Request for Proposal, attachments submitted with the proposal, an agent's statement, and documents filed according to ERISA requirements. We'll discuss each of these resources in the following sections.

Request for Proposal

After talking with a proposed policyholder and obtaining a Request for Proposal form, an agent completes the ***Request for Proposal (RFP)***, a document that provides detailed information about the requested coverage and requests a bid from an insurer for providing that coverage. The information in the RFP enables the underwriter to assess the risk represented by the group and to make an accurate estimate of the premium required to pay for the requested coverage. If for some reason the requested coverage cannot be offered to the group, the underwriter can propose alternate coverage. If the insurer cannot offer coverage to the group, the underwriter declines the RFP.

Proposal Attachments

An RFP is normally submitted with a number of attachments, including a benefit transmittal, a rate transmittal, and an employee census. Some of the information in an RFP typically refers to the groups of employees, or employee classes, to be insured. Recall that earlier we defined an employee class as a group of employees categorized by position, earnings, or rank.

A ***benefit transmittal*** provides details concerning the insurance benefits being requested for each employee class, the effective date of coverage, how premium billing and claims will be administered, and

Insight 8-1. The Art of Medical Underwriting.

Matching rate to risk: It's the essence of all insurance, and the group medical business is no exception. But it's one of the most difficult tasks we face. While we'd like the rating of cases to be an exact formula, it's often more art than science. What gets in the way of matching rate to risk? There are several barriers, but two stand out:

State regulations that place upper (and lower) limits on rates an insurer can charge for new cases and at renewal. These are sometimes called "rating band limits" and apply in most states.

Lack of quality information. Privacy laws, competitive pressures or difficulty in retrieving case history or other information from current carriers or third-party administrators contribute to this problem.

The states' reform laws on small groups attempt to assure access to affordable insurance and to ease volatility of rates for smaller groups (fewer than 50 in most states). These laws limit the rate levels that can be charged and the amount of annual rate change that insurers can apply to smaller cases. The rating limits can range from liberal ("wide") bands that allow considerable flexibility to strict regulations requiring "community rating"—charging the same rate for all groups with similar characteristics.

The more variance allowed, the closer a specific case's rates may be to the assumed risk determined by the insurer's underwriter. With less variance, insurers try to assess the risk of their entire block of business and the individual case's medical risk factors don't impact rates. Demographic differences, however, do.

In a perfect world, a medical underwriter would have in-depth medical information and history on each individual to be insured—employees and dependents. Then, the rates for the group to which those individuals belong would be a "roll up" of the assumed risk for each of the individuals. Instead, underwriters use various "tools" to gather information to assess risk for a specific case. The tools include:

- **Company-level risk questionnaire.** An individual at the company, theoretically knowledgeable about the medical-risk makeup of the group, fills this out. It often includes questions about the current carrier, the employer's current rates and benefits, and the employer's business and financial history. The information provided by this type of questionnaire isn't of great value because it's rare that one person would know about all employees and dependents. When provided with this type of information, insurers tend to rate groups based more on their block of business than on the questionnaire.
- **Individual health statements.** Individuals complete these about themselves and their dependents. Accurate information is valuable in identifying potential claims exposures. This method may provide the most credible information, but it complicates the enrollment process, especially for larger cases.
- **Review of claims experience.** Opinions vary on the value of using individual health statements on larger cases. Some argue that, over time, larger cases will tend to have "normal" claims experience year after year. A better indicator for assessing claims risk for a larger group may be to look at its claims experience with the current carrier. This is where the art of underwriting may play a big role. Plan benefits, provisions, network scope and discount arrangements contribute to a group's claims experience. The underwriter must consider all these items to determine rates under the new plan.

So what are the problems with the tools underwriters use? The tools vary depending on the information available. Claims experience may not be easily obtained or based on current benefits. Equally important is the competitive situation. Company-level risk questionnaires are easiest for employers to complete, but provide the least amount of information—and the least valuable. They also expose employers to greater potential for rate volatility at renewal. It's sort of like the old saying, "pay me now, or pay me later."

Most of these tools look at the past. Looking into the future, sometimes called "prospective underwriting," may well be the most accurate way to rate a case. But that's another story, with many other issues, not the least of which is the privacy of the individual.

Source: Excerpted from Gary Cain, "The Art of Medical Underwriting," *Best's Review* (March 2001): 103. © A.M. Best Company, Inc.; used with permission of the publisher.

other information concerning the type of plan being requested for the group. A ***rate transmittal*** specifies the agent's proposed rates for each type of insurance coverage for each class of employees. The final rates that the underwriter determines to be necessary for a group may differ from those proposed by the agent. An ***employee census*** lists demographic information about the proposed group as a unit and about individual people within the proposed group. Figure 8-5 shows a portion of a typical employee census.

FIGURE 8-5. Portion of a Typical Employee Census.

DOB	M/F	Salary	Division	Dependents	Life	*LTD	**WI
05/57	F	$33,904	0001	Y	$68,000	$1,800	$435
01/67	M	$27,050	0001	N	$55,000	$1,503	$347
10/49	M	$26,520	0002	Y	$54,000	$1,474	$341
09/47	F	$41,600	0001	Y	$84,000	$1,800	$534
03/52	M	$30,680	0003	Y	$62,000	$1,705	$394
11/65	M	$33,280	0001	Y	$67,000	$1,800	$427
10/45	F	$30,680	0003	Y	$62,000	$1,705	$394
07/39	M	$70,000	0001	N	$70,000	$1,800	$600

*The numbers in this column represent the amount of monthly long-term disability income benefits requested for the employee.

**The numbers in this column represent the amount of weekly income coverage (for short-term disability) requested for the employee.

Agent's Statement

The group agent usually attaches to the Request for Proposal an agent's statement, with a recommendation concerning the appropriateness of the requested coverage and the feasibility of providing that coverage to the specified group. The agent's statement is important to the group underwriter in deciding whether to submit a bid for providing the coverage. An agent who has consistently submitted sound business to an insurance company is likely to have his recommendation considered favorably during underwriting. Moreover, insurers generally place a great deal of confidence in the comments of an agent who specializes in the group market and who makes a considerable number of group sales of the type offered by the insurer. Figure 8-6 shows a sample agent's statement for group coverage.

ERISA Documents

In Chapter 3, we noted that documents filed according to requirements of the Employee Retirement Income Security Act (ERISA) can be

FIGURE 8-6. Agent's Statement for Group Coverage.

This company has been in business for 47 years manufacturing and assembling movable windows. Its annual net profit has increased during the past 5 years from $1.3 million to $4.4 million. The current carrier has been underwriting coverage for 7 years; the anniversary date is June 1, 2002. Major claims over $10,000 in the past 24 months have been nonexistent. I feel that the strength of the business and the stability of the group, coupled with its moderate claims experience, make it a prime candidate for coverage under our policy.

helpful to the underwriter in evaluating the risk represented by a proposed group. Generally, underwriters use documents filed under ERISA reporting requirements only to assess the risk for groups previously covered by a self-insured group insurance plan. In a self-insured group insurance plan, also known as self-funded group insurance plan, the group sponsor, not an insurance company, is financially responsible for paying claims made by group insureds.

The Proposal for Insurance

After underwriting on a Request for Proposal is complete and if coverage has not been denied, the underwriter develops a proposal for insurance for the agent to present to the proposed policyholder for consideration. A ***proposal for insurance*** provides a number of specifications for the insurance coverage approved by an insurer for a proposed group. A proposal for insurance enables a proposed policyholder to examine the coverage that the underwriter has approved for the group and to compare the cost and benefits of plans offered by several insurers.

Although each insurer develops its own format for a proposal for insurance, such a document usually includes the following information:

- The name of the proposed group, the eligible employee groups and dependents (if applicable), and the number of eligible employees and dependents (if applicable).

- A schedule of benefits that will be included in the group policy. Under a group insurance plan, a ***schedule of benefits*** is a table that specifies the amount of coverage provided for each class of insureds. If an insurer has been able to approve exactly the type of coverage listed in the group's Request for Proposal, the proposal for insurance specifies that type of coverage. If the insurer has not been able to approve the requested coverage, but has been able to offer another type, the proposal for insurance notes the differences between the requested coverage and the offered coverage.

- A list of rates used and the premium amounts quoted for each type of coverage. This information usually includes an ***illustration of net cost***, which is an explanation of rates that typically covers two or more years, and shows possible future ratings and premiums, provided the group's claim experience remains within the parameters assumed for the insurance product.

- Underwriting principles and assumptions for the proposed coverage.

- Details concerning plan administration, including the responsibilities of the policyholder and the insurer.

The Master Application

By means of a master application, a group prospect submits information required for underwriting. The ***master application*** contains the specific provisions of the requested plan of insurance being applied for and is signed by an authorized officer of the proposed policyholder. If the insurer approves the coverage, information from the master application is used to develop the ***master contract***, which is the legal document certifying the relationship between the insurer and the group policyholder. The master application contains more detailed information than the Request for Proposal, including the name of the ***correspondent***, a person in the policyholder's organization who serves as liaison with the insurer. In employer-employee groups, the correspondent is often a member of the human resources department.

Along with the master application, the proposed group submits an ***enrollment card***, also called an *enrollment application,* completed by each eligible employee. In addition to providing the employee's personal data, the enrollment card includes a statement that the employee signs to indicate that he understands the coverage offered and agrees to have his portion of the premium deducted from his salary if the plan is contributory. An employee who chooses not to participate in the group plan signs a statement to that effect. Figure 8-7 illustrates a typical employee enrollment card.

The underwriter examines the master application and the enrollment cards to ensure that all information is complete and is consistent with the applied-for plan of insurance. If a group has been given tentative approval pending receipt of these information sources, the underwriter uses the information either to give final approval to the case or, if the information contains discrepancies or presents other underwriting problems, continues evaluating the case to arrive at a sound

FIGURE 8-7. Typical Employee Enrollment Card.

EMPLOYEE APPLICATION TO **ABC Life Insurance Company**

NAME OF EMPLOYEE (LAST) (FIRST) (MIDDLE)	GROUP NO.	SECTION NO.	CERT NO.

ADDRESS OF EMPLOYEE	(STREET NO.)	(CITY)	(STATE)	(ZIP)

NAME OF EMPLOYER	SUBSIDIARY, AFFILIATE, OR MEMBER OF

DEPT.	DATE OF BIRTH (MO) (DATE) (YR)	DATE EMPLOYEED (MO) (DATE) (YR)	SEX ❒ MALE ❒ FEMALE	BASIC SALARY FROM EMPLOYER $	❒ SEMI-MONTHLY ❒ HOURLY ❒ WEEKLY	❒ MONTHLY ❒ ANNUALLY

JOB TITLE—IF AMOUNT OF INSURANCE IS BASED ON TITLE, BE SURE THAT TITLE GIVEN AGREES WITH POLICY.	SOCIAL SECURITY NO.	NO. OF HOURS WORKED IN NORMAL WEEK	MARITAL STATUS ❒ MARRIED ❒ WIDOWED ❒ SINGLE ❒ DIVORCED

BENEFICIARY'S LAST NAME	FIRST NAME	INITIAL	RELATIONSHIP	AGE

IF MORE THAN ONE BENEFICIARY IS DESIGNATED, INTEREST WILL BE EQUAL UNLESS OTHERWISE INDICATED

CLASS	OPTIONAL COVERAGE ENROLLED FOR (IF APPLICABLE)		
	DEPENDENT LIFE	OPTIONAL LIFE INSURANCE	LTD
	❒ YES ❒ NO	❒ YES ❒ NO IF YES AMOUNT $ _______	❒ YES ❒ NO

I hereby apply for group insurance as indicated above and authorize my employer to make the necessary deductions from my earnings to apply toward the premiums, if required. I understand that all insurance coverages will become effective according to the terms of the contract.

DATE ______________________________ SIGNATURE ______________________________

GROUP ENROLLMENT CARD

Source: Excerpted from Barbara Foxenberger Brown and Jane Lightcap Brown, *Life and Health Insurance Underwriting* (Atlanta: LOMA, © 1998), 350. Used with permission; all rights reserved.

decision. Figure 8-8 shows the sequence of documents typically used during group insurance underwriting.

Rating Methods for Group Cases

An underwriter is usually responsible for arriving at an adequate, equitable rate that the insurer will charge proposed and renewal policyholders. The rate needs to be adequate so that the insurer's costs of doing business and of settling claims are covered. The rate needs to be equitable so that each insured group pays a premium amount that fairly reflects the group's risk. At the same time, the rate must be competitive enough to attract prospects.

FIGURE 8-8. Sequence of Typical Group Underwriting Documents.

	Request for Proposal	Proposal for Insurance	Master Application
Person who prepares document	Agent, on behalf of group prospect	Underwriter	Agent, on behalf of group prospect
Purpose of document	To provide general information about the proposed group and to request a bid from the insurer for specified group coverage, including plan benefits and rates	To propose a plan for group coverage; may or may not match coverage or rates requested by group	To provide detailed information about the proposed group and coverage being requested
Specific information provided with document	• List of current open claimants • Benefit transmittal • Rate transmittal • Employee census • Agent's statement	• Benefit schedule • Illustration of net costs	• Name of correspondent • Enrollment card for each employee

Source: Excerpted from Barbara Foxenberger Brown and Jane Lightcap Brown, *Life and Health Insurance Underwriting* (Atlanta: LOMA, © 1998), 351. Used with permission; all rights reserved.

Determining the premium that a specific group will be charged for requested coverage involves two steps:

1. Determining a ***premium rate,*** which is the amount an insurer charges for a specified amount of coverage. Note that this term does *not* refer to the total amount that a group prospect will pay for the requested coverage; rather, it refers to the rate charged for one ***benefit unit***, or specific amount of coverage. For instance, the benefit unit for term life insurance is usually $1,000. If an insurer charges a certain group 17 cents per month per $1,000 of term life coverage, then the premium rate for that coverage is 17 cents and the benefit unit is $1,000.

2. Determining the ***annual premium***, which is the amount that the group policyholder will be charged for the total amount of coverage requested.

Most insurers now use computer-based rating systems to determine group premium rates. However, an underwriter may have information about a case that cannot be entered into a computer. For example, the underwriter may know that the agent submitting a case has a long history of submitting quality business to the insurer. This knowledge might enable the underwriter to charge the group a lower rate than the rate calculated by the automated system. It is also important for underwriters to understand how group rates are calculated because then they can analyze the rate determined by the automated system and recognize anomalies when they occur.

In calculating the premium rate to charge for group coverage, insurance companies generally use manual rating, experience rating, or a combination of the two. We will discuss these approaches and will then comment on the rating approaches used for small groups.

Manual Rating

Earlier in the chapter, we defined manual rating as a method of establishing premium rates for broad classes of groups, especially for those with no credible claim experience. Sometimes the underwriter performs manual rating by considering the aggregate claim experience of a class of insureds, but does not consider the claim experience of a specific group.

Manual rates usually stay in effect for a group for a specified period of time—usually 12 months for medical expense, disability income coverage, and life insurance coverage—until the insurer develops enough experience information for that group to be able to calculate rates based on the group's experience.

Experience Rating

Experience rating is the process of using a group's claim experience to calculate premium rates. This type of rating is generally used for large groups that have previously been insured and have a history of claims. An important assumption underlying experience rating is that a group's claim experience is likely to remain relatively constant from one year to another. In some years, a group may have higher or lower numbers of claims and dollar amounts of claims. Nevertheless, the likelihood is high that a group whose composition remains relatively constant is likely to experience about the same level of claims from one year to another. Experience rating is used to establish initial premiums for groups requesting coverage for the first time from the insurer, as well as to calculate renewal premiums for groups that the insurer already covers.

Experience rating helps an insurer charge equitable premiums to each insured group. Using a group's own experience to assess the premium due from that group is a fair way to charge each group for the amount of benefits it is likely to claim. Experience rating also enables an insurer to compete successfully with other insurance companies. In a free marketplace with adequate competition, a seller who most closely matches the cost of a product to the benefits of that product is more likely to succeed than are sellers who overprice their products.

In addition, experience rating helps insurers to avoid the effects of antiselection. An insurer that offered all groups the same premium rate would probably find that lower-risk groups would resist paying more for the coverage, seeking coverage from other insurance companies that would charge a lower premium. Meanwhile, higher-risk groups would tend to seek coverage from the insurer offering one premium rate because those groups could not obtain the same coverage at the same cost from other insurers that used experience rating. The resulting antiselection would probably harm the insurer's business, both present and future.

Blended Rating

Insurers sometimes use both manual and experience rating to calculate premiums. Sometimes adequate experience information is unavailable to permit an underwriter to base premiums solely on a group's history. However, including a measure of a group's prior experience helps to ensure that the premium is equitable and accurate. Therefore, ***blended rating*** is performed by assigning a credibility factor to the group's experience and including that factor in the premium calculations. A ***credibility factor*** is a percentage that represents the degree to which the underwriter has estimated that the available underwriting information accurately shows the risk represented by a group.

Suppose an underwriter assigns a 15 percent credibility factor to a group's experience. As a result, the underwriter assumes that 15 percent of the group's future claim cost will be based on the group's experience. The remaining 85 percent of the group's future claim cost will be based on the insurer's manual rating. The blended rate is determined by multiplying the premium calculated by manual rating and experience rating by the factor assigned to each, and adding the two products.

For example, suppose that an underwriter compiles the following information for a group:

- Premium calculated by experience rating = $250
- Credibility factor for experience rating = 15%
- Premium calculated by manual rating = $300

The underwriter calculates the premium using blended rating as follows:

$$(\$250 \times 0.15) + (\$300 \times 0.85) = \$37.50 + \$255.00 = \$292.50$$

As in this example, the premium calculated by blended rating is typically lower than the premium calculated by manual rating alone, but higher than the premium calculated by experience rating alone.

Rating Approaches for Small Groups

Because small-group underwriting for life insurance and short- and long-term disability income coverage is similar to individual underwriting for these products, many companies send such small-group cases to an individual underwriter. After assessing the risk, if the case is acceptable, the individual underwriter forwards the case to a group underwriter, who performs the rate calculations.

Developing equitable rates for small groups requires the underwriter to exercise particular caution. Individual variations in age, health, and other risk factors increase in importance as group size decreases. In a group of eight people, for example, one person who represents a high level of risk can have a strong effect on the risk represented by the group. However, that same person, as part of a group of 500 people, would have much less effect on the group's level of risk.

Each insurer establishes its own numerical limits for a small group. When a proposed group falls within those limits, the insurer may require that each person in the group show evidence of insurability. The evidence required ranges from a simple health questionnaire completed by each group member to APSs and other medical evidence. An underwriter may require APSs and additional evidence on only those group members whose health questionnaires indicate the presence of possibly greater risk.

Risk factors that underwriters typically examine for each individual in a small group are age, sex, dependents, and the type of benefits for which the group requests coverage. Some insurers also consider the geographic location and the type of industry in which a group's employees are involved.

Post-Issue Underwriting for Group Insurance

Group underwriters are involved not only in approval of new risks, but in several kinds of underwriting that occurs only after a group policy has been issued. In this section we'll explain post-issue underwriting: approval of late entrants, approval of benefit changes, and renewal underwriting.

Approval of Late Entrants

Employees who choose not to enroll in a group plan when it is first offered may decide to enroll later. Sometimes these employees defer enrollment until they develop a health condition that would be covered by the plan. To avoid this kind of antiselection, insurers usually require late entrants to provide evidence of insurability. Such evidence is also submitted for a dependent whom the employee wishes later to enroll. Employees who are enrolled in a group plan and who then withdraw while still employed are usually required to submit evidence of insurability when they apply to re-enroll in the plan.

Approval of Benefit Changes

When an insured group wishes to increase the type or extent of benefits offered under a plan of insurance, the underwriter examines the group's claim experience. If that experience indicates that the group's rate should be increased to cover the additional benefits, the underwriter calculates the increase. On the other hand, the underwriter may find that a group that has had lower-than-expected claim experience is eligible to increase benefits without an increase in premium. Similarly, a group that wishes to reduce its benefits can be eligible for a reduction in premium unless the group's experience has been unfavorable. The underwriter is also involved when a policyholder wishes to offer insurance to employee classes that were previously excluded from certain types or amounts of coverage.

Renewal Underwriting

Unlike individual life policies, group policies are subject to annual renewals, during which underwriting takes place. In ***renewal underwriting***, the underwriter reviews all the risk assessment factors considered when the group was originally underwritten and all changes in the group and its coverage between the previous underwriting and the current time. In addition, the underwriter assesses how efficiently the policyholder has administered the plan during the year. Problems identified are usually brought to the attention of the group policyholder along with suggestions for corrective action. In the United States, the Health Insurance Portability and Accountability Act (HIPAA) of 1996 requires insurers to guarantee renewal of all group policies, except under certain conditions. Even though an insurer generally must renew a group's policy, group underwriters review the policy each year to determine if changes to the group or the group's claim experience require a premium adjustment.

Each year when the policy is renewed, the insurer uses experience rating to calculate a new premium rate that reflects the group's expected claim experience for the coming year. The ***expected claim experience*** is the dollar amount of claims that the insurer estimates the group will submit. The expected claim experience is calculated according to (1) the group's claim experience during the prior year, (2) changes in the group's average age and sex distribution that occurred during the previous year, and (3) changes in benefit payments that occurred during the previous year. The underwriter also takes into account any changes in the business segment occupied by an insured group or economic conditions affecting the financial strength of the insured group.

If a group's claim experience and administrative expenses have fallen within the parameters established for the policy when it was written, the underwriter may renew coverage at the same premium rate as for the previous period. If, on the other hand, a group's claim experience or administrative expenses have exceeded the established parameters, the underwriter is likely to (1) increase the premium rate or (2) suggest a revision in benefits. Typical proposed revisions in benefits include increasing the amount of premium that each employee pays and adding programs to monitor the type of care delivered. Other approaches insurers may take to help underwrite a group with questionable claim experience are to pool the group's risk with the risk from other groups, to require premiums to be paid earlier in the year, and to institute some degree of self-insurance.

A group whose claim experience has been considerably less than the established parameters is likely to receive approval of future coverage and may receive a reduction in its premium rate or an ***experience refund***, which is a return of a portion of a group insurance premium to a group policyholder whose claim experience is better than had been expected when the premium was calculated. Calculation of renewal premiums follows the same approach as that used to calculate initial premiums.

Key Terms and Concepts

managed care
indemnity benefits
prospect
service requirement
pooling
manual rating
employee class
noncontributory plan
contributory plan
dependent
Request for Proposal (RFP)
benefit transmittal
rate transmittal
employee census
self-insured group insurance plan
proposal for insurance
schedule of benefits
illustration of net cost
master application
master contract
correspondent
enrollment card
premium rate
benefit unit
annual premium
experience rating
blended rating
credibility factor
renewal underwriting
expected claim experience
experience refund

Endnotes

1. CLHIA, *Canadian Life and Health Insurance Facts* (Toronto: Canadian Life and Health Insurance Association, 2000), 14.
2. ACLI, *Life Insurers Fact Book 2000* (Washington, D.C.: American Council of Life Insurers, 2000), 16.

CHAPTER 9

Scope and Organization of Reinsurance

Chapter Outline

The Reinsurance Relationship
- Buyers and Sellers of Reinsurance
- Providers of Reinsurance

Reasons to Buy Reinsurance
- Increasing Capacity
- Easing Surplus Strain
- Minimizing Claim Payment Fluctuations
- Obtaining Underwriting Expertise
- Obtaining Product, Claim, and Administrative Information
- Issuing Policies Through Fronting

Limitations of Reinsurance

Reinsurance Underwriting
- The Application for Reinsurance
- Reinsurers and MIB

Legal Issues Affecting Reinsurance
- Licensing
- Monitoring Financial Condition

Objectives

After reading this chapter, you should be able to

- Describe the reinsurance relationship
- Discuss the reasons that insurers buy reinsurance
- Describe the limitations of reinsurance
- Explain reinsurance underwriting
- Discuss the legal issues that affect reinsurance

Now that you're familiar with the principal activities and responsibilities of underwriting, we'll consider the subject of reinsurance. In Chapter 1 we defined *reinsurance* as insurance that reimburses the insurer in the event of covered losses claimed under insurance policies it has issued. Briefly, reinsurance is insurance for an insurer.

In this chapter, we'll examine the scope of the relationship that an insurance company establishes with a reinsurance company. We'll discuss the reasons that insurers use reinsurance and the limitations of using reinsurance. Finally, we'll present some of the legal issues that affect the reinsurance relationship.

The Reinsurance Relationship

An insurance company—the insurer—uses reinsurance to transfer part or all of a risk to another insurance company—the reinsurer. In exchange for the reinsurance coverage, the insurer pays reinsurance premiums to the reinsurer. The amount of the reinsurance premiums is based on the reinsurance arrangement negotiated between the two companies. The company transferring the risk retains its financial relationship with and legal obligations to the policyowner. This type of reinsurance is called ***indemnity reinsurance*** because one company indemnifies another for losses incurred. The policyowner for whom the risk is being transferred is not a party to the exchange, and, in most cases, is not aware that the insurer has transferred part or all of the risk for his policy to a reinsurer. As long as the reinsurance arrangement is in effect, the reinsurer reimburses the insurer for claims covered under the agreement.

Another type of reinsurance involves the total and permanent transfer of risk from one company to another. In ***assumption reinsurance***, a reinsurer purchases a block of in-force insurance, creating contractual relationships with all insureds and assuming responsibility for policy administration and all liabilities.

Every insured risk must be supported by ***reserves***, which are accounts that an insurer maintains for meeting future business obligations, including paying claims. An insurer is responsible for setting up sufficient reserves to cover its risks. When risks are reinsured, the reinsurer also agrees to establish reserves for its proportionate share of each risk.

Sometimes the reinsurer also pays the insurer an allowance. An ***allowance*** is a reinsurer's proportionate share of the agent commissions, underwriting costs, administration costs, policy issue costs, and other expenses that an insurer incurs in acquiring a policy. An allowance is generally stated as a percentage of the gross premium that a policyowner pays for a policy. The parties to a reinsurance agreement may also agree to share more unusual expenses, such as costs of litigation. Figure 9-1 illustrates the reinsurance relationship.

FIGURE 9-1. The Reinsurance Relationship.

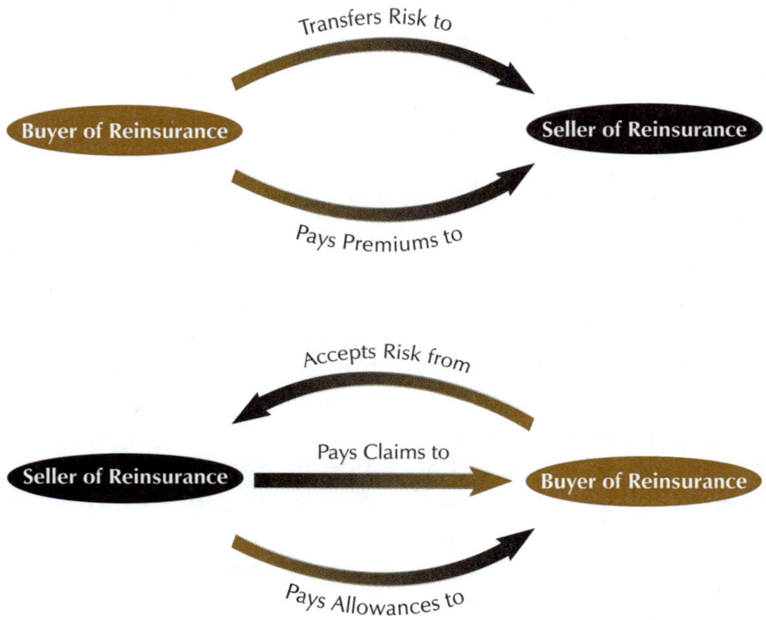

Buyers and Sellers of Reinsurance

An insurer that buys reinsurance is known as a ***ceding company*** because it is transferring, or ceding, insurance risk to a reinsurer. Most often, the ceding company insurer is a ***direct writing company***, also called a *direct writer* or a *direct insurer*, which is an insurer that sells coverage to consumers. The ceding company buys reinsurance from a ***reinsurance company***, also called a *reinsurer*, which is an insurer that sells reinsurance coverage.

An insurer that sells reinsurance is also called an ***assuming company*** because it is accepting, or assuming, insurance risk from a direct writer. So, in a reinsurance relationship, the ceding company purchases reinsurance from an assuming company.

A reinsurer can also cede some of the risks it has assumed by buying reinsurance from another reinsurer. In such a situation, the reinsurer that accepts risks from—and sells reinsurance to—another reinsurer is known as a ***retrocessionaire***. Figure 9-2 illustrates the roles of reinsurance buyers and sellers.

FIGURE 9-2. Distinguishing Among the Reinsurance Buyers and Sellers.

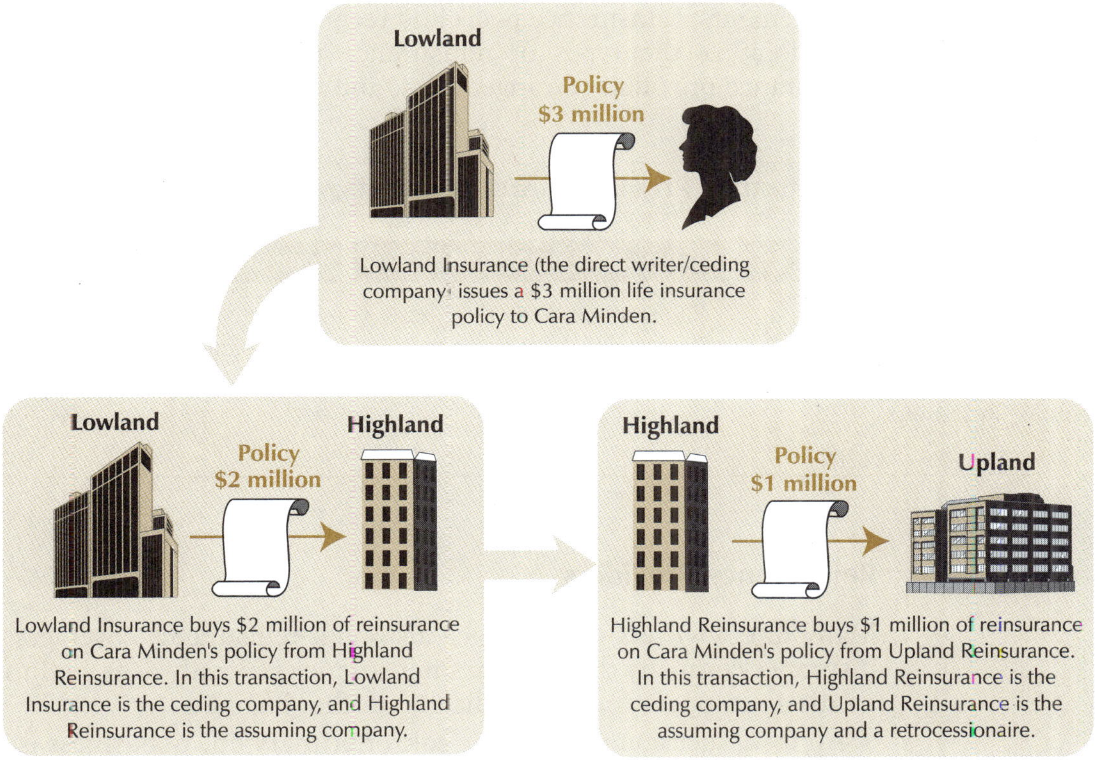

Source: Adapted from Jane Lightcap Brown and Jennifer W. Herrod, *Reinsurance Administration* (Atlanta: LOMA, © 2000), 5. Used with permission; all rights reserved.

Providers of Reinsurance

Insurers and reinsurers, including retrocessionaires, buy and sell reinsurance in various ways. In general, a provider of reinsurance must be either an authorized reinsurer or an accredited reinsurer in order to sell insurance. An ***authorized reinsurer,*** also known as an *admitted reinsurer,* is a reinsurance company that is licensed or otherwise recognized by the insurance department in the jurisdiction of the ceding company. An ***accredited reinsurer*** is a reinsurance company that is not licensed in the ceding company's jurisdiction, but (1) meets specified financial and reporting requirements of that jurisdiction and (2) holds a license in and is domiciled in at least one other jurisdiction. Requiring reinsurers to be authorized or accredited allows an insurer's home state insurance department to monitor the financial condition of the reinsurer and to help ensure that it will be able to pay claims when they become due.

In this section, we'll first discuss the providers of reinsurance, which include insurers, professional reinsurers, professional retrocessionaires, and captive reinsurers. Then we'll discuss two types of reinsurance arrangements: reinsurance pools and reciprocity arrangements. Finally, we'll look at the types of reinsurance marketers. Figure 9-3 lists reinsurance providers, arrangements, and marketers.

FIGURE 9-3. Reinsurance Providers, Arrangements, and Marketers.

Reinsurance Providers	Reinsurance Arrangements	Reinsurance Marketers
Insurers Professional Reinsurers Professional Retrocessionaires Captive Reinsurers	Reinsurance Pools Reciprocity Arrangements	Reinsurance Marketing Officer Reinsurance Intermediary

Reinsurance Providers

Many direct writers of insurance also offer reinsurance coverages. An insurance company that provides reinsurance generally does so through a unit or an operating area dedicated to that business.

An insurance company whose sole or primary line of business is selling reinsurance to direct writers is known as a ***professional reinsurer***. Similarly, a ***professional retrocessionaire*** is an insurance company whose primary business is providing reinsurance to reinsurers. Generally, a professional reinsurer or a professional retrocessionaire is licensed to do business in multiple jurisdictions, often on an international basis.

FAST FACT

In 1999, 30% of all life and annuity reinsurance premiums assumed in the United Sates were assumed by captive reinsurers.[1]

A ***captive reinsurer*** is a reinsurance company that is formed and controlled by an insurance company or another type of insurance marketer for the purpose of providing reinsurance to that insurer or marketer. Depending on its charter, a captive reinsurer may offer coverage only to the organization that formed it, to other insurers within the same line of business—for example, life insurance or disability insurance—or to a broader range of other insurers.

Reinsurance Arrangements

To establish a reinsurance arrangement, the insurers and reinsurers exchange cessions and/or retrocessions. A ***cession*** is both the unit of insurance that an insurance company cedes to a reinsurer and the document used to record the transfer of risk from a ceding company to an assuming company. A ***retrocession*** is both the unit of insurance that a reinsurance company cedes to a retrocessionaire and the document used to record the transfer of risk from a reinsurer to a retrocessionaire.

Insurers typically use two types of reinsurance arrangements. The first type of reinsurance arrangement is a reinsurance pool. A ***reinsurance pool*** is an arrangement where an insurer cedes risk, and a group of reinsurers assumes the risk. The risk is usually spread among the pool members according to specified shares. The portion of risk assumed by each reinsurer is known as the ***quota share***. Reinsuring risk through a pool can help smooth the fluctuations in the claim experience of each company participating in the pool. Rather than only one insurer bearing the full financial burden of paying a large claim alone, each insurer accepts a portion of the risk and, if a claim is submitted, pays part of the claim.

The second type of reinsurance arrangement is reciprocity. ***Reciprocity*** is an arrangement in which certain insurers and reinsurers agree to cede business to each other and assume risk from each other. Insurers usually base their reciprocity arrangements on either premiums or results. Premium-based reciprocity involves the exchange of business purchased for approximately the same amount of premium. Results-based reciprocity involves exchanging business for which the projected claim experience is approximately the same.

The insurers involved in reciprocity may be of several types: a direct writer and a reinsurer, a reinsurer and a retrocessionaire, two reinsurers, and so on. Two direct writers can reciprocate only if they are also authorized reinsurers; one of them acts as a reinsurer and the other acts as a direct writer.

One purpose of reciprocity is to increase the spread of risk. For example, suppose that the Sonora Insurance Company and the Western Hemisphere Insurance Company enter into a reciprocity agreement. Both direct-writing companies are authorized reinsurers. The two insurers agree to reinsure some proportion or specified amounts of each other's risks of a certain type, up to a designated amount per cession. An advantage of this arrangement is that each insurer is responsible for paying only a part of each claim submitted under the reciprocally reinsured coverage. In effect, each of the insurers is increasing its business and reducing its risk on each case. Figure 9-4 shows the reciprocity arrangement between Sonora Insurance Company and Western Hemisphere Insurance Company.

FIGURE 9-4. A Reciprocity Arrangement.

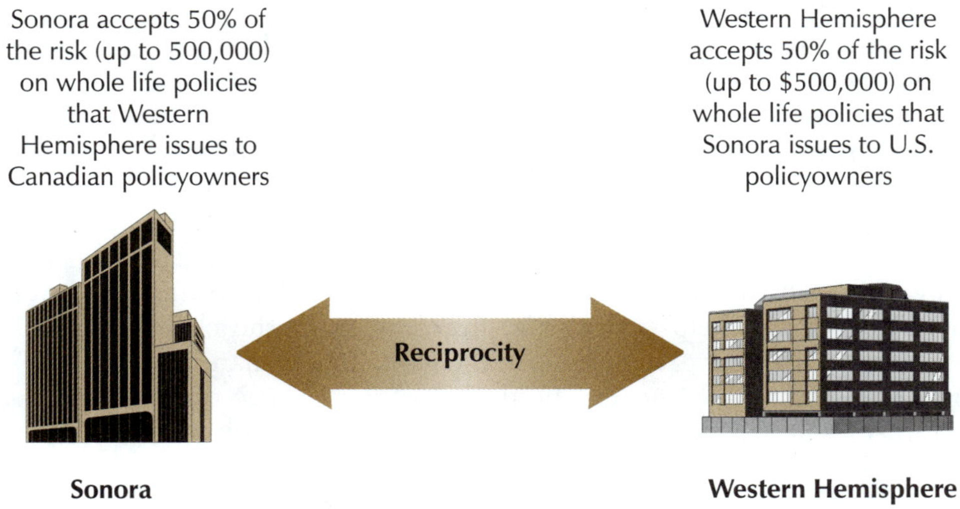

Reinsurance Marketers

Life insurers generally use two types of marketers to help them establish reinsurance arrangements: reinsurance marketing officers and reinsurance intermediaries.

Reinsurance Marketing Officers. A professional reinsurer normally maintains a staff of reinsurance marketing officers. A ***reinsurance marketing officer***, also known as a *reinsurance account executive*, is an employee who sells reinsurance and coordinates the marketing process for a reinsurer. Such employees visit the home offices of current and potential clients—usually direct writing companies and other reinsurers—and gather information about new reinsurance arrangements that clients need or adjustments they would like to make to existing arrangements. Reinsurance marketing officers work with other employees of their companies to develop or modify reinsurance arrangements with clients.

Reinsurance marketing officers are agents of their employer. Although they are not required to be licensed, most reinsurance marketing officers have extensive backgrounds in the insurance industry. Typically, they are considered by ceding companies to be valuable sources of information and advice about developments in the market that affect direct insurance and reinsurance.

Reinsurance Intermediaries. A ***reinsurance intermediary***, also called a *reinsurance broker*, is a third party who helps ceding companies find appropriate coverage for risks they want to reinsure and, for large-amount and unusual cases, to arrange for sufficient reinsurance from multiple reinsurers if no single reinsurance company will accept the entire risk. Reinsurance intermediaries are typically used when a ceding company lacks reinsurance expertise in a particular area.

Reinsurance intermediaries, who must be licensed in the jurisdictions in which they do business, typically handle reinsurance for health coverages. They occasionally handle reinsurance for life cases, particularly for cases involving very high face amounts, unusual underwriting characteristics, or complex designs.

Reasons to Buy Reinsurance

The principal reason for buying reinsurance is to spread the risk represented by an insurance policy. Other reasons to buy reinsurance include

- Increasing capacity by issuing larger amounts of insurance
- Easing surplus strain
- Minimizing claim payment fluctuations
- Obtaining underwriting expertise
- Obtaining product, claim, and administrative information and expertise
- Issuing policies through fronting

Increasing Capacity

Rather than turn away well-qualified new business, most insurers turn to reinsurance as a way of strengthening their financial position. Reinsurance expands an insurer's ***capacity***, which is the highest dollar amount of coverage that the company is financially able to accept on a specified risk. Therefore, when an insurer wishes to issue coverage beyond its current capacity, it turns to reinsurance to expand its capacity.

An insurer's capacity is determined primarily by an insurer's financial worth, but is also affected by the amount and nature of the insurer's in-force coverage. Capacity includes (1) the amount of risk an insurer transfers to reinsurers and (2) the insurer's ***retention limit***, which is the maximum amount of coverage per life that the insurer will carry at its own risk. When an insurer wishes to issue a policy whose face amount exceeds its retention limit, the amount over the retention limit can be covered by reinsurance.

When a ceding company purchases reinsurance, the company, in effect, adds to its own capacity the capacity of the reinsurer and, therefore, is able to accept a greater amount of financial risk than it could accept alone. In this way, reinsurance enhances an insurer's ability to expand the marketing for its products and to satisfy the needs of agents and applicants for large policy amounts.

Suppose that a well-qualified applicant applies for $2 million of life insurance coverage, but the insurer's retention limit for each life insured under that type of coverage is $500,000. If the insurer cannot accept the full $2 million of risk, the applicant will go elsewhere to buy the coverage, and the insurer will lose a customer. However, if the insurer buys reinsurance to cover the $1.5 million in excess of its retention limit, the insurer can accept the application and issue the policy. Figure 9-5 presents some of the factors considered by an insurer when establishing its retention limits.

Easing Surplus Strain

You have learned that an insurer that issues an insurance policy is required to establish reserves to pay claims under the policy. In the early years of a policy, the premium payments are not adequate to cover the expenses associated with selling the policy and maintaining the reserves.

To establish the required reserves during the early years of the policy, the insurer must use some of its surplus. ***Surplus*** is the net amount of money earned from an insurer's operations and left to accumulate. State laws in the United States and federal and provincial laws in Canada establish minimum surplus standards that insurers must maintain to conduct business in each jurisdiction. In some situations, the use of surplus to establish reserves can cause an insurer's surplus level to fall dangerously close to the minimum level.

FAST FACT

Surplus funds of life insurers in the United States amounted to $179 billion in 1999.[2]

FIGURE 9-5. Factors Affecting an Insurer's Retention Limits.

An insurer's retention limit for each life—and in some instances, for each insurance product—is usually set after considering the:

Insurer's financial resources

Volume of coverage in force

Average age of insureds and type of group expected to buy the coverage

Amount of claim experience information available to the insurer

Expertise of the insurer's underwriting staff

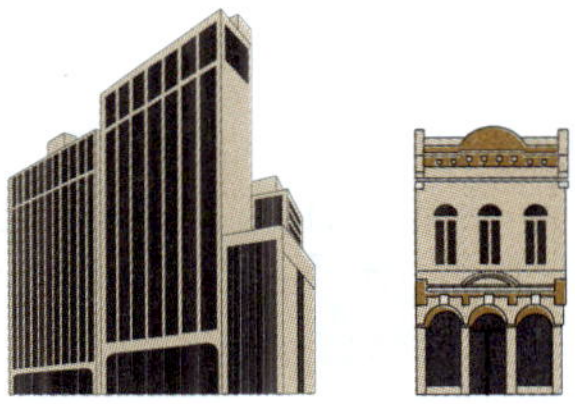

Effect of new business on existing business

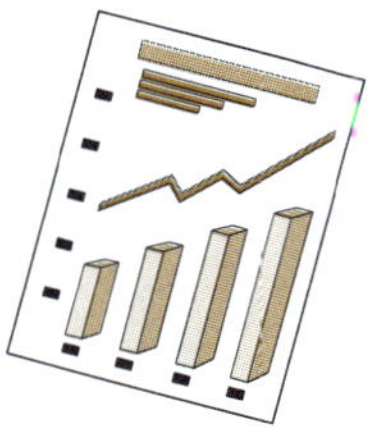

Insurer's desired level of risk

Cost of reinsuring the product

This decrease in surplus caused by the high initial costs of new policies and the reserve requirements for them is called ***surplus strain***.

One way that ceding companies can reduce surplus strain is by using reinsurance. Under certain reinsurance agreements, when the reinsurance company assumes a portion of the insurer's risk, the reinsurer also agrees to establish reserves for the part of the assumed risk that it retains. Thus, by engaging in specific types of reinsurance transactions with reinsurers that meet specific requirements, the insurer can decrease the amount of reserves it must establish, reduce potential strain on its surplus, and consequently maintain its financial strength.

Minimizing Claim Payment Fluctuations

In maintaining financial strength, an insurer needs to be able to anticipate claim levels so that it has enough money available to pay claims. Sometimes, however, the actual level of claims is unexpectedly higher than the level projected when an insurance product was developed.

No amount of reinsurance can eliminate fluctuations in submitted claims—if a claim is due, it must be paid, regardless of the timing or the number of other claims submitted at or near that same time. But reinsurance can help *reduce* the fluctuations in claim payments because the reinsurer helps pay some of the benefits due. Reinsurance, therefore, protects an insurer from the negative financial effects of unexpectedly early claims and large numbers of claims. If an insurance company had to pay all such claims by itself, it might have less money available for business operations, product research and development, client acquisition, and claim reserves. By reinsuring some of its issued policies, a ceding company ensures that, even if a larger-than-expected number of claims are incurred during a period, the ceding company will have the funds necessary to pay the claims without suffering financial stress and possible competitive disadvantage.

Obtaining Underwriting Expertise

Not only do reinsurers have access to the claim experience information of some of their client insurance companies, but reinsurers also develop experience statistics based on their own cases. In addition, some reinsurers develop considerable expertise through many years of underwriting risks, some of them quite complicated. Some reinsurers, for example, specialize in issuing coverage on insureds who have experienced cardiovascular bypass surgery or who have specific severe forms of diabetes. A reinsurer can, therefore, advise an insurer about establishing sound underwriting principles and procedures for impairments about which the reinsurer has extensive knowledge.

For example, proposed insureds who suffer from hypertension generally represent a higher level of risk than do those who do not. Yet an underwriter would be inaccurate in concluding that all applicants with hypertension represent the same level of risk. Many other factors in combination with hypertension may change the level of risk represented by an applicant. Because reinsurance companies maintain enormous banks of statistics on the claims submitted by insureds who suffer from hypertension—as well as many other impairments—the reinsurers can help insurers underwrite these cases accurately.

A new insurance company usually establishes a relationship with a reinsurer in order to benefit from the reinsurer's underwriting expertise and to receive advice on such matters as premium rates, policy wording, and claims. Moreover, an insurer that is developing a new product usually considers reinsurance during the product design process, particularly if the product has unusual features or must be priced very competitively. Most insurers prefer to establish a reinsurance relationship before they bring a new product to the market. If the insurer decides to offer the product and to obtain reinsurance for it, a reinsurer can assist the insurer in assessing the strength of the product by evaluating the product's underwriting standards, administration method, system capabilities, premium structure and pricing assumptions, commission plan, and marketing approach.

Just as direct writers benefit from such underwriting consultations, so do the reinsurers. A reinsurer that can help its insurer clients make more accurate underwriting decisions also helps preserve its own financial security by ensuring that the business it reinsures is thoroughly evaluated prior to acceptance.

Obtaining Product, Claim, and Administrative Information

When an insurance company is designing a new type of coverage or modifying an existing insurance product, the broad-based knowledge of its reinsurers can help prevent mistakes, such as offering too much or too little coverage for a certain premium, or including product features that experience has shown may result in unexpectedly high claims.

Further, a reinsurer can help an insurer make a sound determination regarding the validity of claims submitted under reinsured coverage. While the intent of all insurance companies is to pay appropriate claims in full, every insurer also has an obligation not to pay inappropriate claims. When a problematic claim is submitted, an insurer can consult with its reinsurer to help determine whether the claim is appropriate under the coverage.

An insurer can also refine its administrative workflow in any area, from information systems to customer service, by gathering information from its reinsurers. After doing business with a number of insurance companies, a reinsurer generally becomes familiar with the most commonly used systems, efficient workflows, key risk areas, and control mechanisms. Although the need to protect client confidentiality and proprietary information prevents a reinsurer from sharing the specific details of any insurer's business practices, the reinsurer can advise its clients about general procedures that have been successful—or unsuccessful—in conducting the business of insurance.

For instance, in order to enhance its interactions with insureds, an insurance company can learn from its reinsurers some effective ways to deliver rapid responses to customers' questions. Collaboration of this type between insurers and reinsurers serves to improve the quality of the insurance industry and, therefore, to make higher quality services available to consumers.

Issuing Policies Through Fronting

Sometimes an insurance company wants to issue policies in a jurisdiction in which the insurer is not currently licensed to do business. In such a situation, the insurer may use reinsurance for ***fronting***, which is a procedure by which an insurer that is not licensed in a jurisdiction arranges to have another insurer that is licensed in the jurisdiction issue requested coverage and then cede the coverage to the unlicensed insurer.

Fronting enables insureds to obtain insurance from an insurer that offers appealing premiums, terms, or customer service, but that is not licensed in the customer's jurisdiction. Some jurisdictions have adopted legislation designed to (1) limit the dollar amount or the percentage of fronting business allowed and (2) establish audits and other monitoring procedures for fronting.

Limitations of Reinsurance

Despite the many advantages of using reinsurance, this approach to sharing risk has certain limitations. First, insurers cannot transform an uninsurable risk into an insurable risk by using reinsurance to cover the potential loss. Similarly, an insurer cannot change an inadequately investigated and underwritten risk into a well-underwritten risk by using reinsurance. Although reinsurance can help to control the severity of an insurer's losses, it cannot help to control the frequency of those losses.

In addition, an insurer that overuses reinsurance to reduce its amount of risk can be harmed financially. Paying claims is a cost of doing business in the insurance industry. Attempting to avoid or excessively reduce claim-settlement costs by setting low retention limits will also reduce the amount of premium received, reducing the amount of an insurer's working capital and, ultimately, reducing the insurer's capacity to accept new business.

Reinsurance also does not transfer or eliminate the contractual legal liability that the ceding company has under a policy it issued to an insured. The reinsurance arrangements are separate and are not attached to a policy; no agreement exists between the reinsurer and the insured. For example, if for some reason, such as a dispute or insolvency, a reinsurer does not pay its part of a claim, the ceding company is still liable for the full claim. Therefore, reinsurance allows a ceding company to transfer risk, but not to transfer the legal liability under the policy.

Reinsurance Underwriting

Underwriting reinsurance risks is essentially the same as underwriting any risks, although reinsurance underwriters tend to work with more unusual or problematic cases—such as financial underwriting or high profile cases involving celebrities—than do other underwriters. Ceding company underwriting, also known as primary underwriting, and reinsurance underwriting differ in two important ways.

First, in primary underwriting, the underwriter's judgment of an agent's integrity plays a role in the underwriting decision. In reinsurance underwriting, the underwriter is concerned primarily with the quality of the ceding company's underwriting department and is less concerned about an agent's integrity.

Second, reinsurance underwriters try to accept their ceding colleagues' judgment. Occasionally, if a file has not been sufficiently developed to satisfy a reinsurance underwriter, the reinsurer's underwriter may request additional information or may ask the ceding company's underwriter to consult on the case. However, such requests not only delay policy issue, but also appear to question the thoroughness of the ceding company's underwriter. Insight 9-1 discusses the concerns that reinsurers have about underwriting.

The Application for Reinsurance

The application for reinsurance is the basic tool of reinsurance underwriting. The application identifies the ceding company, the insured(s),

Insight 9-1. Reinsurers Worry About Underwriting Practices.

Many U.S. life insurers protect themselves against underwriting surprises by splitting some of the risk of selling new life policies with reinsurers. Assuming recurring risk is a great business, but a reinsurer that accepts large amounts of recurring risk needs to pay close attention to its partners' underwriting practices, according to Larry Roy, senior vice president for strategic business development at Lincoln National Reassurance Company, Fort Wayne, Ind. "You're giving away your pen," Mr. Roy said. "That's a tremendous problem for the industry."

Reinsurers can help direct life writers by assuming either portfolio risk or recurring risk. When a reinsurer says it is assuming portfolio risk, it usually means it is taking responsibility for closed blocks of business—groups of customer accounts based on discontinued policies. When a reinsurer says it is assuming recurring risk, it usually means it's promising a direct insurer it will assume a specified amount of risk on all new policies of a specified type during a specified period of time.

Reinsurers accept small policies involved in recurring reinsurance arrangements automatically. Some reinsurers are trying to attract and keep recurring reinsurance clients by raising the size of the policies they will accept automatically. Others are raising the maximum size of the jumbo policies they'll take after a careful review, Mr. Roy said. Now that reinsurers are assuming large amounts of life underwriting risk, they are extremely interested in seeing that partners use the right criteria to evaluate applicants, Mr. Roy said. "You are going to see a lot more audits," he predicted.

Source: Excerpted from Allison Bell, "Reinsurers Worry About Turning over Pens," *National Underwriter*, Life & Health/Financial Services ed. (6 November 2000): 6. Reprinted with permission from *National Underwriter.*

the plan of reinsurance, and the amount to be reinsured. It also specifies preferred rating, tobacco use status, issue date, prior policy information, and any special benefits or riders involved. Generally, the application also asks for the ceding underwriter's assessment of the risk.

Reinsurers and MIB

Like primary insurers, reinsurers use coded information supplied by MIB as an alert to the possibility that a proposed insured has undisclosed impairments that could materially affect the mortality or morbidity assessment of the case. Most reinsurers are members of MIB, although some of their clients are not.

Legal Issues Affecting Reinsurance

Because a reinsurance agreement is formed between two businesses that are assumed to be able to protect themselves, the laws and regulations governing reinsurance are fewer and less detailed than those governing insurance. Rather than being heavily regulated by jurisdictional requirements, reinsurance is largely self-regulated. General reinsurance practice, based on a long-established reliance on the best practices of the parties to a reinsurance agreement, tends to guide the performance of insurers and reinsurers in their reinsurance relationships. Therefore, if an insurer and a reinsurer were to disagree about an issue relating to their mutual undertaking, they typically would try to resolve the issue through arbitration.

However, because of concern about potential reinsurer insolvency and about the legitimacy of claims submitted by insurers under reinsured contracts, both insurers and reinsurers are increasingly careful about the relationships they form. Furthermore, state and provincial regulators, auditors, and other parties consider reinsurance agreements as binding contracts that ought to be regulated. Regulators are especially concerned about ensuring that both insurers and reinsurers are financially strong and that sufficient information is available to evaluate their financial strength.

Many jurisdictions require insurers to pay a tax on the full amount of collected premiums, even if part of the business has been reinsured. Reinsurers sometimes reimburse the ceding company for all or part of the tax that applies to the reinsured business.

Two areas in which reinsurance is specifically regulated are licensing and financial condition.

Licensing

Licensing is one of the ways in which state and provincial governments (and the federal government, for federally regulated insurers in Canada) seek to guarantee the solvency of ceding companies and assuming companies. Licensing requirements apply to insurance companies in the United States and Canada and to reinsurance intermediaries in the United States.

Insurer and Reinsurer Licensing

Each jurisdiction requires ceding companies and assuming companies to meet certain requirements related to solvency and business operations in order to be licensed. The insurance department and/or legislature of each jurisdiction establishes its own standards for licensing. Typically, the licensing requirements for insurers and reinsurers are designed to (1) make sure that the companies can meet their financial obligations when they become due and (2) establish a mechanism by which the jurisdiction can oversee insurers' operations. Figure 9-6 lists some of the typical licensing requirements in many states in the United States.

In Canada, an insurer must be incorporated by the federal government or a provincial government and be licensed in each territory in

FIGURE 9-6. Licensing Requirements in the United States.

State licensing laws and regulations typically require that an insurer

- Hold a minimum dollar amount of capital and surplus funds.
- Deposit in trust a specified minimum amount of securities or other liquid assets. The trust will be used to pay policyowner claims in the event that the insurer becomes insolvent.
- Name the insurance commissioner of that state as the insurer's attorney in fact for the purpose of accepting on the insurer's behalf written notice that a lawsuit or other legal action has been filed against the insurer in that state.

which it conducts business. In order to be federally incorporated, a company must meet a variety of statutory requirements set out in the Insurance Companies Act. Most of these requirements are designed to ensure that insurers are financially sound and can meet their financial obligations. The Insurance Companies Act requires federally incorporated insurers and foreign insurers to obtain from the Superintendent an "order to commence and carry on business." For assuming companies, the order specifies that the insurer can conduct reinsurance business.

In general, provincial laws regarding the incorporation of insurers are similar to federal laws. For example, provincial statutes specify the minimum amount of capital a business must have before it can incorporate. A provincially incorporated insurer has the right to operate in a province other than the province in which it was incorporated as long as the insurer obtains the necessary licenses from the other province.

Licensing of Reinsurance Intermediaries

Most life reinsurance is marketed by reinsurance marketing officers who, as employees of a reinsurer, are not required to be licensed. In cases involving complex portfolios of risk or situations requiring high levels of expertise and strong industry contacts, life reinsurance is sometimes marketed by a reinsurance intermediary. Generally, reinsurance intermediaries represent the ceding company; in some cases, they may represent the reinsurer.

In most states, U.S. reinsurance intermediaries are subject to each state's regulations, some of which are based on the ***NAIC Reinsurance Intermediary Model Act***, a model law that regulates the activities of reinsurance intermediaries and of ceding and assuming companies that use reinsurance intermediaries' services. The model law is designed to

(1) ensure that reinsurance intermediaries are qualified to perform their services and (2) enable regulators to account for any funds the intermediary may have handled in the event of the insolvency of an assuming company. This Model Act requires each intermediary to be licensed in each state in which the intermediary has an office.

This Model Act further provides that to sell reinsurance to a company domiciled in another state, the intermediary must be licensed in that state or be licensed in a state that has a law similar to the Model Act.

The NAIC Reinsurance Intermediary Model Act imposes certain requirements on the contract between the ceding or assuming company and the reinsurance intermediary. For example, the contract must state that the insurer can terminate the intermediary's authority at any time. The contract must also require that the intermediary carefully adhere to prescribed record-keeping and reporting rules. Finally, the contract must require that the ceding or assuming company have access to the intermediary's records and annual financial statement.

Monitoring Financial Condition

Regulators monitor the solvency of ceding and assuming companies in their jurisdiction by (1) examining required financial reports from each company, (2) setting capital and surplus requirements and monitoring compliance with those requirements, and (3) doing on-site examinations. Each jurisdiction specifies the exact accounting and financial reporting systems to be used in the monitoring process.

Regulators generally use these accounting and financial reporting systems to look at two specific areas of an insurer's financial condition:

- *Adequate capitalization*: Does the insurer have enough financial resources to conduct business into the future?
- *Adequate liquidity*: Does the insurer have enough cash available to pay bills and meet other obligations as they become due?

In addition to meeting capital and surplus requirements, ceding companies must also meet regulatory requirements for reserves. You recall that reserves are accounts that an insurer maintains to set aside funds to meet its future business obligations. An insurer's reserves equal the amount that, together with future premiums from an insurer's in-force policies and interest earned, is expected to be needed to pay future benefits on those in-force policies.

The accounting entry used to record the reduction of reserves, due to the use of reinsurance, by the ceding company in its Annual Statement or Annual Return is called a ***reserve credit***. Some of the requirements for taking reserve credits in the United States are outlined in the NAIC

FAST FACT

In 1999, policy reserves for life insurance in the United States made up 27% of total insurance company reserves and amounted to $705 billion.[3]

Model Law on Credit for Reinsurance. An unlicensed reinsurer may be required to meet certain conditions before the ceding company is allowed to record a reserve credit in the Annual Statement or Annual Return.

Key Terms and Concepts

indemnity reinsurance
assumption reinsurance
reserves
allowance
ceding company
direct writing company
reinsurance company
assuming company
retrocessionaire
authorized reinsurer
accredited reinsurer
professional reinsurer
professional retrocessionaire
captive reinsurer
cession
retrocession
reinsurance pool
quota share
reciprocity
reinsurance marketing officer
reinsurance intermediary
capacity
retention limit
surplus
surplus strain
fronting
NAIC Reinsurance Intermediary Model Act
reserve credit

Endnotes

1. ACLI, *Life Insurers Fact Book 2000* (Washington, D.C.: American Council of Life Insurers, 2000), 152.
2. Ibid., 138.
3. Ibid., 136.

CHAPTER 10

Reinsurance Forms and Treaties

Chapter Outline

Dividing Risk in Reinsurance
- Proportional Reinsurance
- Methods of Ceding Proportional Reinsurance: Quota Share and Excess of Retention
- Nonproportional Reinsurance

Accepting and Rejecting Reinsurance Risk
- Automatic Reinsurance
- Facultative Reinsurance
- Facultative-Obligatory (Fac-Ob) Reinsurance

Reinsurance Treaties
- Reasons to Use Reinsurance Treaties
- General Characteristics of a Reinsurance Treaty
- Common Provisions

Defining Reinsurance Coverage
- Scope of the Agreement
- Termination of the Treaty

Reinsurance Coverages
- Reinsurance Coverage Provisions

Objectives

After reading this chapter, you should be able to

- Describe the way insurers divide risk in reinsurance
- Discuss the way insurers accept or reject reinsurance risk
- Explain why reinsurance treaties are used
- Describe the general characteristics of a reinsurance treaty
- Explain the reinsurance treaty provisions that define the parties to the agreement, the scope of the agreement, and the reinsurance coverage provided
- Describe the treaty provisions related to termination of a treaty

The reinsurance relationship between a ceding company and an assuming company is defined in a reinsurance treaty. A ***reinsurance treaty*** is a formal written agreement to establish a reinsurance arrangement, negotiated and signed by an insurer and a reinsurer. A reinsurance treaty typically provides that the ceding company will pay premiums to the reinsurer as payment for covering specified risks. It will become apparent as you read the next two chapters that the treaty is an extremely important document that shapes both the reinsurance relationship and the reinsurance administration activities.

Keep in mind that, when coverage is reinsured, the contractual relationship is between the direct writer and the reinsurer only. The reinsurance treaty has no effect on the contractual relationship between the direct writer and its policyowners, and the policyowners have no contractual relationship with the reinsurer.

Thus, if the reinsurer experiences financial difficulties and cannot reimburse the direct writer for claims submitted under the reinsurance coverage, the direct writer is still obligated to pay the claims. In addition, if a direct writer cannot pay its contractual obligations to its policyowners, those policyowners have no legal recourse against the reinsurer for indemnity at claim time.

Though the basic concept of reinsurance is relatively simple, the reinsurance product is far more complex. A ceding company and an assuming company can arrange for reinsurance coverage to take a variety of forms.

In a reinsurance arrangement, the parties negotiate several elements. Two of the most important elements are (1) the degree of the risk that each party will cover and (2) the obligation each party undertakes in ceding or assuming coverage. In this chapter, we'll discuss the most typical ways these elements can be arranged. First, we'll look at the ways that the parties define the risk obligation. Then we'll examine the ways the parties can agree to bind themselves to accept or reject risk. Finally, we'll explain why reinsurance treaties are used and how they help define reinsurance coverage.

Dividing Risk in Reinsurance

When making a reinsurance arrangement, an insurance company and a reinsurance company decide when and how much of each risk will be transferred to the reinsurer. In general, reinsurance can be structured as either proportional or nonproportional.

Proportional Reinsurance

FAST FACT

Almost $51 billion of reinsurance premiums were assumed in the United States in 1999.[1]

Proportional reinsurance is reinsurance coverage for which the ceding company and the assuming company agree to share premiums and claims according to a specified amount or a specified percentage of coverage. For example, an insurer and a reinsurer might agree that the reinsurer will accept 60 percent of the face amount of all whole life policies, up to a specified limit of $2 million. If a policy with a face amount of $1 million was insured under this agreement, the reinsurer would be responsible for $600,000 of risk (0.60 × $1,000,000), and the direct writer would be responsible for $400,000 of risk (0.40 × $1,000,000). Most life reinsurance provided in the United States and Canada is proportional reinsurance.

Proportional reinsurance plans can be of several types, including yearly renewable term (YRT), coinsurance, coinsurance with funds withheld, and modified coinsurance.

Yearly Renewable Term (YRT) Reinsurance

Yearly renewable term (YRT) reinsurance is a type of proportional reinsurance in which a ceding company buys an amount of insurance coverage that is equal to the net amount at risk on the reinsured portion of the policy for a one-year term premium rate. The ***net amount at risk (NAR)*** for a life insurance policy is the policy's death benefit minus the policy's cash value, or reserve.

Net amount at risk (NAR) = Policy's death benefit – Policy's cash value (reserve)

YRT reinsurance premium rates are not directly related to the premiums of the underlying policy. The ceding company pays for reinsurance covering only the amount reinsured. Under a YRT reinsurance plan, the ceding company alone pays policy dividends and cash values, as well as establishes most reserves for the entire policy; the reinsurer does not share these responsibilities. Thus, YRT reinsurance does not reduce surplus strain to the same degree that coinsurance does.

The cost of the YRT reinsurance, expressed as a one-year term rate, and the amount of YRT coverage the ceding company purchases change each year that the policy is in force. As reserve or cash value accumulates, the NAR declines, reducing the total amount of reinsurance the ceding company must buy. However, as the insured gets older, the cost per $1,000 of YRT reinsurance increases. If the policy remains reinsured and reaches maturity, the ceding company's reserves will equal the entire risk, leaving no NAR, and the reinsurance terminates. Figure 10-1 illustrates decreasing NAR.

FIGURE 10-1. Decreasing Net Amount at Risk (NAR).

Year	Date	NAR
1	11/26/02	$2,908,712
2	11/26/03	$2,734,559
3	11/26/04	$2,550,154
4	11/26/05	$2,354,676
5	11/26/06	$2,147,081
6	11/26/07	$1,926,305
. . . Maturity	11/26/XX	$0

Coinsurance

Coinsurance is a type of proportional reinsurance in which an insurer and a reinsurer share the obligations of a policy, including paying the death benefit and the nonforfeiture values, and establishing the reserves. The reinsurer receives a proportionate share of the ceding company's gross premiums less a coinsurance allowance that the ceding company withholds for commissions and expenses. The amount of risk that each party accepts is predetermined using a dollar amount or a percentage—say, the first $50,000 of a risk or 45 percent of a risk. The effect of coinsurance is to transfer to the reinsurer the surplus strain of the reinsured portion of newly issued policies. In addition, the reinsurer becomes responsible for a proportionate share of losses from early lapses on policies, investment risk, and mortality risk.

Under a coinsurance reinsurance agreement, the ceding company and the assuming company share responsibility for almost every aspect of each policy that comes under the agreement. The ceding company proportionately shares the gross premium paid by the policyowner with the assuming company, and the assuming company proportionately pays for policy benefits such as cash value, expenses, commissions, dividends, extended term insurance, claims, and reserve accumulation. Frequently, however, the assuming company does not help pay out amounts under policy loans. To cover commissions and expenses, the assuming company pays the ceding company an allowance, which is typically subtracted from the reinsurance premium so that only the net amount is paid to the reinsurer. Unlike YRT, coinsurance relieves strain on the ceding company's surplus.

Coinsurance with Funds Withheld

Coinsurance with funds withheld is similar to coinsurance, with the exception that funds due to the reinsurer are not transferred. ***Coinsurance with funds withheld*** is a type of proportional reinsurance in which the ceding company retains funds that are due to the reinsurer, usually in an amount equal to the reserve required by law. The ceding company and the assuming company maintain accounting records that allow the companies to track increases and decreases in the net balance of the withheld funds. Cash flow between the companies is minimized, and the risk of harm to the insurer should the reinsurer become insolvent is minimized. The ceding company and the assuming company do not exchange any funds until the net balance of the funds withheld is zero.

Modified Coinsurance (Modco)

FAST FACT

In 1999, 57% of top U.S. reinsurers' life and annuity premiums assumed from nonaffiliated companies was for coinsurance.[2]

Modified coinsurance (modco) is a type of proportional reinsurance in which the ceding company maintains the entire reserve for each policy. In a modco agreement, the reinsurer is required to deposit its share of the reserve in cash with the ceding company. The reserve is usually adjusted on a quarterly basis. The ceding company, however, must pay interest to the reinsurer to replace the interest that the reinsurer would have earned had it retained and invested its share of the reserve.

Modified coinsurance was developed primarily to enable ceding companies to retain control over more of the funds generated by their own policies while keeping many of the attributes of coinsurance. When a claim is made on a policy, the reinsurer pays the death benefit of the reinsured portion of the policy minus the reserve credited for that amount.

Methods of Ceding Proportional Reinsurance: Quota Share and Excess of Retention

A reinsurance agreement generally specifies a method to determine the amount of coverage to cede through proportional reinsurance. The two most common methods are quota share and excess of retention.

Quota Share

As we mentioned in Chapter 9, a quota share is the portion of a risk assumed by each of two or more reinsurers. When reinsurance parties use quota share to assign risk, the ceding company retains a certain percentage of the risk and cedes the remaining percentage to one or more assuming companies. The parties to a reinsurance arrangement generally use two forms of quota share arrangements: excess quota share and first dollar quota share.

In an ***excess quota share arrangement***, the ceding company keeps its full retention limit and cedes the remaining risk to two or more assuming companies on a percentage basis. For example, assume that the Montrose Insurance Company has a $200,000 retention limit on its whole life policies. Montrose negotiates reinsurance treaties with Heliotrope Reinsurance Company and Grandiflora Reinsurance Company. The treaties include excess quota share arrangements in which Heliotrope Re agrees to assume 40 percent of specified risks and Grandiflora Re agrees to assume 60 percent of the same risks in excess of Montrose's retention limit.

For a policy with a face amount of $500,000, Montrose would keep its retention limit of $200,000, leaving $300,000 in risk to be assumed by the reinsurers. Heliotrope Re would assume $120,000 (0.40 × $300,000), and Grandiflora Re would assume $180,000 (0.60 × $300,000). For a $600,000 policy, Montrose would keep its retention limit of $200,000, leaving $400,000 to be assumed by the reinsurers. Heliotrope Re would assume $160,000 (0.40 × $400,000), and Grandiflora Re would assume $240,000 (0.60 × $400,000). Figure 10-2 shows how the risk is divided in this excess quota share arrangement.

In a ***first dollar quota share arrangement***, the ceding company cedes a certain percentage of the entire risk to the assuming company or

FIGURE 10-2. Excess Quota Share Among Three Companies.

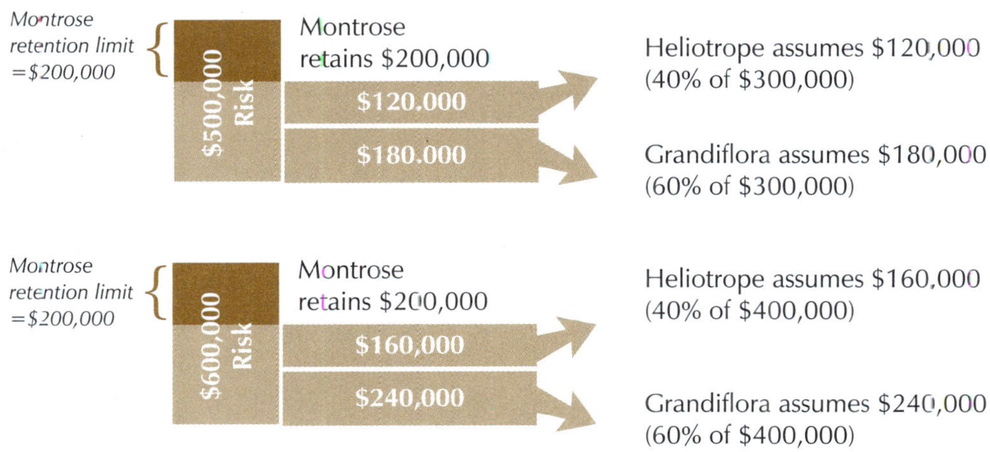

Source: Adapted from Jane Lightcap Brown and Jennifer W. Herrod, *Reinsurance Administration* (Atlanta: LOMA, © 2000), 26. Used with permission; all rights reserved.

companies despite the presence of a retention limit—that is, the ceding company cedes coverage from the first dollar. This kind of agreement limits the face amount of the policies to be covered by the agreement so that the ceding company will not exceed its retention.

For example, suppose Montrose has a first dollar quota share arrangement with Heliotrope Re and Grandiflora Re. In this arrangement, Montrose agrees to retain 20 percent of each risk, Heliotrope Re agrees to accept 35 percent of each ceded risk, and Grandiflora Re agrees to accept 45 percent of each ceded risk. On a $100,000 risk, Montrose would retain $20,000 (0.20 × $100,000), Heliotrope Re would assume $35,000 (0.35 × $100,000), and Grandiflora Re would assume $45,000 (0.45 × $100,000). On a $300,000 risk, Montrose would retain $60,000 (0.20 × $300,000), Heliotrope Re would assume $105,000 (0.35 × $300,000), and Grandiflora Re would assume $135,000 (0.45 × $300,000). Figure 10-3 illustrates this first dollar quota share arrangement.

First dollar quota share arrangements are used when the ceding company wants to increase the number of reinsurers participating in the risks. Under a first dollar quota share arrangement, the ceding company is able to achieve a better spread of risk for a better price, but the ceding company also cedes more of its risk than under an excess quota share arrangement.

Excess of Retention

In an ***excess of retention arrangement***, an insurer cedes specified amounts of coverage that exceed its retention limit. For example, the Shasta Insurance Company has a retention limit of $500,000 on its life insurance policies. Shasta has two reinsurance treaties in place: The

FIGURE 10-3. First Dollar Quota Share Agreement.

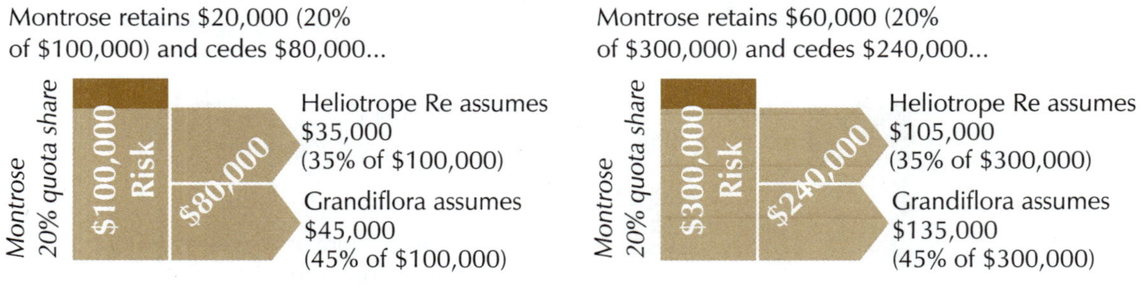

Source: Adapted from Jane Lightcap Brown and Jennifer W. Herrod, *Reinsurance Administration* (Atlanta: LOMA, © 2000), 29. Used with permission; all rights reserved.

Inyo Reinsurance Company has agreed to take the excess of retention up to $2 million of the face amount on Shasta's whole life products, and the Redding Reinsurance Company has agreed to take the excess of retention above $2 million, but not to exceed $5 million. If Shasta sells a $2.5 million policy, Shasta will retain $500,000 of the risk and Inyo Re will assume $2 million. If Shasta sells a $3 million policy, Shasta will retain $500,000, Inyo Re will assume $2 million, and Redding Re will assume the remaining $500,000 of the risk. The excess of retention method allows the ceding company to maximize its retention on each case and to minimize the amount of reinsurance that must be ceded. Figure 10-4 illustrates this excess of retention arrangement.

FIGURE 10-4. Excess of Retention Arrangement.

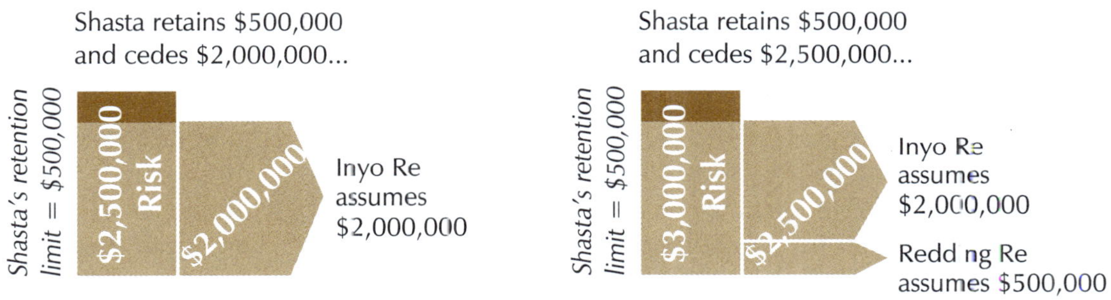

Source: Adapted from Jane Lightcap Brown and Jennifer W. Herrod, *Reinsurance Administration* (Atlanta: LOMA, © 2000), 29. Used with permission; all rights reserved.

As you can see, sometimes a ceding company needs reinsurance in a larger amount than one assuming company can provide. ***Layering*** is a method of dividing reinsurance coverage among multiple reinsurers by allowing one reinsurer or a pool of reinsurers to cover all cases in excess of an insurer's retention limit up to a specified amount. This amount is called the ***first excess***. The ***second excess***—a specified amount of the remaining coverage—is ceded by the insurer to a second assuming company (or to a second group of assuming companies). If there exists a ***third excess***—a specified amount of the coverage that remains after the first and second excesses have been ceded—it in turn is ceded by the insurer to a third company or group of companies. This process—the creation of further excesses and their ceding—continues until all the excess coverage has been accounted for.

Ceding companies and assuming companies often use a combination of quota share and excess of retention when determining the proportions used with each reinsurer. Layering arrangements can become quite complex with multiple reinsurers participating.

An alphabetic split can also be used to divide risk among reinsurers. In an ***alphabetic split,*** also known as an *alpha split*, risks are divided among a group of reinsurers by assigning part of the alphabet to each reinsurer and then sending that reinsurer all cases whose insureds' surnames begin with the assigned alphabet letters. As an example, Warner Reinsurance could assume the risk for all policies with insureds whose surnames begin with the letters A through L, and Jenkins Reinsurance could assume the risk for the policies with insureds whose surnames begin with the letters M through Z.

Nonproportional Reinsurance

In contrast to proportional reinsurance, ***nonproportional reinsurance*** is a type of reinsurance coverage on a segment of the ceding company's business, rather than on individual lives for specific amounts. In nonproportional reinsurance, the specific amount or proportion of the risk to be shared by the ceding company and the assuming company is not known at the time the reinsurance agreement is created. Instead, claims under nonproportional reinsurance are paid by a reinsurer when an insurer's losses exceed a certain limit.

For instance, a reinsurer might agree to pay all claims in excess of $50 million submitted under a certain type of coverage within a specified time period. In a nonproportional reinsurance agreement, the risk level for each party generally depends on the dollar amount or the number of claims submitted under the reinsured coverage. In this way, nonproportional reinsurance limits an insurer's total risk of loss.

Nonproportional reinsurance is generally sold under one of five plans: excess-of-loss, stop-loss, catastrophe, spread-loss, and extended-time. Figure 10-5 briefly describes these types of nonproportional reinsurance.

Accepting and Rejecting Reinsurance Risk

Risk in reinsurance arrangements can be accepted or rejected on an automatic, facultative, or facultative-obligatory (fac-ob) basis. The basis of the reinsurance agreement determines whether the insurer, the reinsurer, or both can choose whether to cede or accept risks.

Automatic Reinsurance

Automatic reinsurance is reinsurance under which the ceding company agrees to cede and the assuming company agrees to accept

FIGURE 10-5. Types of Nonproportional Reinsurance.

	What the Reinsurer Will Pay	Type of Insurance Covered	Top Limit of Reinsurance Specified?
Excess-of-Loss	Amount of a claim above a predetermined limit	Individual coverage	Yes
Stop-Loss	Claims that exceed (1) a specified percentage of the total loss incurred above a certain amount during a specified period and/or (2) a maximum dollar amount	Total percent or amount of claims incurred by ceding company	Yes
Catastrophe	Claims that exceed a minimum number or amount	Life claims from a single event	Yes
Spread-Loss	Benefits above amount specified; ceding company pays the reinsurer for benefits (plus interest) that the reinsurer has paid	Specified in reinsurance agreement	No
Extended-Time	Benefits after ceding company has paid for a specified amount of time	Disability income, generally	No

specified types of cases on the underwriting judgment of the ceding company alone, up to a specified amount. Automatic reinsurance allows a ceding company to bind a reinsurer to a risk without providing underwriting evidence for a case and without asking the reinsurer's approval in advance, provided all agreement requirements are met.

An automatic reinsurance agreement usually specifies the following elements:

- The maximum amount of coverage to be ceded
- The plan(s) of insurance
- The maximum rating for the policy
- The minimum and/or maximum age of the insured
- An effective date on or after which the policy must be issued

In most such agreements, the insurer establishes a retention limit for the amount of risk it will retain on an automatic case, and the reinsurer specifies an ***automatic binding limit***, which is the maximum dollar amount of risk on a life the reinsurer will accept without making its own underwriting assessment of the risk. If an automatic binding limit is established in an automatic reinsurance agreement, the reinsurer must accept the risk on all policies whose face value does not exceed the automatic binding limit. Cases exceeding the automatic binding limit can be submitted to the reinsurer on a facultative or fac-ob basis. (We discuss facultative reinsurance in the next section.)

Another limit that reinsurers use is the ***jumbo limit***, which is the maximum allowable dollar amount of total insurance in force and applied for with all insurers on any one life that will be automatically accepted by a reinsurer. The reinsurer is not required to automatically accept the risk on any case that exceeds its jumbo limit. The jumbo limit protects the reinsurer from excessive risk resulting from the accumulation of several policies on the same life—for instance, a person who already has insurance on her life for $15 million with various insurance companies and who has applied for $10 million more. Without a jumbo limit, a reinsurer that has several automatic treaties in effect may find itself bound to cover a huge total amount of coverage on one life. Jumbo limits help reduce the reinsurer's likelihood of becoming over-exposed to mortality risk on any one life.

In general, automatic reinsurance provides no choice about whether the ceding company will reinsure the coverage nor whether the reinsurer will accept it. To complicate matters somewhat, many automatic reinsurance treaties include a provision that allows a ceding company to submit certain applications facultatively to its reinsurance partner and to other reinsurers. The purpose of such a provision is to allow policies that do not comply with automatic limitations to be reinsured facultatively. In these situations, the reinsurer can review each case separately. Cases submitted facultatively could be submitted for extra-mortality, for exceeding age limitations, or for amounts of insurance over automatic binding limits or jumbo limits.

Shortly after an insurer issues a policy, the insurer notifies the reinsurer that automatic reinsurance coverage has been issued on the case. The premium rates for automatically ceded policies are specified in the agreement, so both the ceding company and the reinsurer can determine how much money is due for the reinsurance.

Facultative Reinsurance

In contrast to automatic reinsurance, ***facultative reinsurance*** allows a ceding company to choose whether to ask a reinsurer to consider coverage on a risk, the reinsurer to choose whether it wishes to accept or decline the risk, and the ceding company to choose whether to accept the reinsurer's offer on the risk, if an offer is made. The ceding company sends all underwriting papers to the reinsurer. In considering a facultatively submitted case, a reinsurer underwrites the case, assigns the case a risk classification, and makes an offer based on its own underwriting guidelines and terms. This approach differs from automatic reinsurance, in which the ceding company must cede specified business and the reinsurer must accept it.

Many insurance companies choose to submit cases facultatively for reinsurance because they receive the benefit of the reinsurer's underwriting judgment prior to making a decision on accepting or declining the case. The cost to an insurer of reinsuring cases facultatively is generally higher than the cost of automatic reinsurance. One reason for the higher cost is the practice of ***shopping***, that is, submitting cases to several reinsurers to obtain competitive quotes for reinsurance. A reinsurer is under no obligation to submit a quote for a case submitted facultatively. Also, because facultative reinsurance is often used for hard-to-place, complex cases involving multiple risk factors, a reinsurer may charge more to underwrite and evaluate such cases and builds these additional costs into the terms of the agreement. However, many reinsurers do not charge more because they consider these additional costs to be part of their cost of doing business.

Facultative-Obligatory (Fac-Ob) Reinsurance

Facultative-obligatory (fac-ob) reinsurance is based on an agreement that (1) allows a ceding company to choose whether to submit cases to a reinsurer and (2) requires the reinsurer to accept the cases based on the ceding company's underwriting, up to an amount defined in the agreement, if the reinsurer has available capacity. When a case is submitted to a reinsurer under a facultative-obligatory agreement, the reinsurer determines whether it has capacity to accept the risk. If the reinsurer lacks capacity and therefore cannot accept the risk, the insurer is notified in writing immediately; if the reinsurer fails to notify the insurer within a specified period, and the amount of reinsurance requested on the submitted case is within the agreed-upon acceptance limits, the reinsurer is automatically bound to the risk.

Reinsurance Treaties

Establishing a reinsurance relationship requires a high degree of mutual trust. Formerly, the bond between an insurer and a reinsurer was as much a "gentlemen's agreement" as a formal business arrangement.

However, reinsurance arrangements today are established by a reinsurance treaty, which you'll recall is a formal written agreement, negotiated and signed by an insurer and a reinsurer.

Reasons to Use Reinsurance Treaties

The reinsurance relationship depends on a treaty-based agreement on which both parties can rely. The principal reason for establishing a reinsurance treaty is to create and express a foundation for transferring risk and for conducting the financial transactions associated with reinsurance. Having a treaty in place also protects the financial security of the parties. Because risk transfers and information exchanges can affect the parties' financial strength, details of the transfers and their administration must be disclosed in the treaty provisions.

Having a treaty in place also ensures that the accountability of each party is clear and helps prevent misinterpretations and errors resulting from overlooked details. Unlike some insurance products, which offer essentially the same type of coverage to most applicants, reinsurance is not a "one size fits all" product. Each reinsurance agreement is tailored to fit the requirements of the ceding company and the assuming company; a reinsurance treaty can be dozens of pages long and can involve hundreds of details. Although treaties differ substantially in the details—such as plans covered, premium rates, and quota shares—the wording and the articles included are becoming increasingly standardized, in part due to guidelines created by groups such as the Society of Actuaries, the American Council of Life Insurance (ACLI), and the Canadian Reinsurance Conference. The ***Canadian Reinsurance Conference (CRC)*** is a meeting held each year by Canadian ceding companies and reinsurance companies to discuss current life and health insurance and reinsurance issues.

In addition, most insurers buy reinsurance from multiple assuming companies and need different types of reinsurance coverage for various kinds of insurance. Similarly, reinsurers conduct business with many insurers, each of which has different requirements and may be subject to different rules in different jurisdictions. Therefore, keeping track of all the details of each agreement without using a treaty would be extremely difficult.

A treaty not only helps clarify these details, but also helps prevent mistakes. Reinsurance companies use treaties to avoid errors and omissions that could result in costly, inefficient administration and adverse financial effects on the parties.

In the past, when insurance products were relatively straightforward and when nearly every insurer offered approximately the same types of products, handling reinsurance was relatively simple. Reinsurance parties knew what to expect, based on their experience with the products and their administration. However, the recent creation of new product designs and features, some of them quite complex, has required insurers and reinsurers to specify the ways they will handle the reinsurance of products with which they have little current experience. Many of the newer insurance products require innovative reinsurance arrangements and administrative practices that are best specified in a treaty. Under many treaties today, the reinsurer is involved in every policy issued, not just those in excess of the ceding company's retention limits.

Some reinsurance agreements remain in effect for many years, and the treaty allows the next generation of administrators to know how the policies should be handled. The treaty also allows companies affected by a merger or an acquisition to become familiar with the products the new company has acquired, easing the merger or acquisition transition. Figure 10-6 summarizes these reasons to use reinsurance treaties.

FIGURE 10-6. Reasons to Use Reinsurance Treaties.

- Create a basis for conducting reinsurance transactions
- Protect financial security of parties by defining liability
- Clarify each party's accountability
- Describe terms of the reinsurance agreement
- Protect parties from errors and misinterpretations
- Specify administration of new and complex insurance products
- Document agreement terms for future administration

General Characteristics of a Reinsurance Treaty

Some reinsurance treaties—particularly those between companies that have a long-term, ongoing relationship—are expressed in broad terms that give both parties considerable discretion in implementation and administration. Other treaties are quite specific about the accountabilities of each party and the procedures that each party is to follow. Regardless of the amount of detail expressed in a treaty, every reinsurance treaty contains certain provisions that protect the interests of the reinsurance parties.

These provisions generally take two forms. The body of the reinsurance treaty is made up of ***articles***, which are relatively standard provisions. The provisions that cover the more variable elements of a treaty are known as ***schedules***, *exhibits*, or *conditions*. Schedules typically address details such as the plans covered, retention limits, binding limits, and premium rates and allowances.

The treaty provides guidelines for reinsurance-related actions that take place between the parties. Every activity associated with administering the reinsurance agreement must be carried out according to the treaty's statements and provisions.

Regardless of the number of treaty provisions and schedules, unexpected events sometimes occur in a reinsurance partnership. The partners treat such events in a common-sense manner and work together to find a fair solution to the problem. In addition, if the treaty requirements cause unforeseen problems in the administration of the business, the parties can apply good judgment to the situation to develop a solution suitable to both.

Common Provisions

Because an insurer and a reinsurer negotiate a treaty to meet their specific needs, no two reinsurance treaties are exactly alike. Most reinsurance treaties, however, have similar versions of some basic provisions, which are listed in Figure 10-7.

Two of these basic provisions are unique to reinsurance treaties: the errors and omissions provision and the arbitration provision. These provisions allow ceding companies and assuming companies to correct mistakes and resolve disagreements without becoming involved in litigation. These provisions set the tone for a cooperative, mutually beneficial treaty.

As we have discussed, reinsurance treaties also contain schedules that provide key information such as retention limits, premium rates, allowances, and sample forms. Figure 10-8 lists information typically presented in schedules in a reinsurance treaty.

Defining Reinsurance Coverage

The treaty sections that define the reinsurance coverage include provisions describing (1) the scope of the agreement and (2) the termination of the treaty.

Scope of the Agreement

The provisions that describe the scope of the agreement include the parties to the agreement provision, the entire agreement provision, the duration of the agreement provision, and the recapture provision.

FIGURE 10-7. Basic Provisions in a Reinsurance Treaty.

Scope of the Agreement: Names the ceding company and the assuming company as the sole parties to the reinsurance agreement; states the effective date of the treaty; and specifies that the treaty articles, schedules, and amendments constitute the entire agreement between the parties. Includes

- Parties to the agreement
- Entire agreement
- Duration of the agreement
- Recapture

Termination of the Treaty: Identifies the terms and conditions under which the treaty may end; describes the procedures for notification of termination; and describes the handling of the reinsurance in force under the treaty.

Reinsurance Coverages: Identifies the basis of reinsurance, such as facultative or automatic; the type of coverage, such as YRT or coinsurance; the method of coverage, such as first dollar quota share or excess; and the plan of coverage, such as whole life, term, or universal life products allowed under the treaty. Also describes any riders covered and the limits on the reinsurance. Includes

- Plans of reinsurance
- Amounts of reinsurance and related limits

Reinsurance Rates and Payment: Describes how premiums and allowances are calculated and specifies when they are due. Also explains (1) in what ways the reinsurance coverage will change if the face amount of a reinsured policy changes or if the insurer changes its retention limits and (2) what procedures will be followed if the ceding company decides to take back some or all of the risks it has ceded to the reinsurer. Includes

- Premium payments
- Expense allowances
- Premium changes
- Modco reserve adjustment
- Premium reporting
- Policy dividends and cash values
- Experience refunds

Premium Taxes: Describes the manner in which the reinsurer will reimburse the ceding company for premium taxes the ceding company pays, if the treaty calls for such reimbursements. Includes

- Deferred acquisition costs (DAC) account and tax

Procedures to Begin Coverage: Describes the notification process for automatic, facultative, and facultative-obligatory reinsurance. Includes

- Notification for automatic reinsurance
- Notification for facultative reinsurance

Reporting: Describes the procedures for reporting reinsurance transactions and the types of reports required.

Records Inspection: States that either party to the agreement can inspect the records of the other relating to the agreement.

Changes to the Reinsurance: States the procedures required for notification and handling of changes to reinsurance such as increases, conversions, reinstatements, reductions, and terminations. Includes

- Change in retention limit and recapture
- Increasing death benefit products and riders
- Continuation
- Conversion
- Reinstatement
- Reduction and termination of reinsurance

Claims: States the circumstances under which a reinsurer will pay claims and outlines the procedures required for notification, settlement, and contest of claims. Also describes how claim expenses will be handled in various situations. Includes

- Contest or denial of a claim

Rescission: Describes the notification and handling procedures required when a policy is rescinded.

Errors and Omissions: States that if an unintentional error occurs because of misunderstanding, oversight, or faulty judgment, both parties are normally restored to the positions they would have occupied if the error had not occurred.

Arbitration: Describes the arbitration process to be used if an event arises that cannot be resolved to the mutual satisfaction of the parties to the agreement.

Insolvency: Describes the procedures that will be followed if either party to the agreement becomes unable to meet its financial obligations on time. Includes

- Ceding company insolvency
- Assuming company insolvency

FIGURE 10-8. Information Typically Found in Schedules in Reinsurance Treaties.

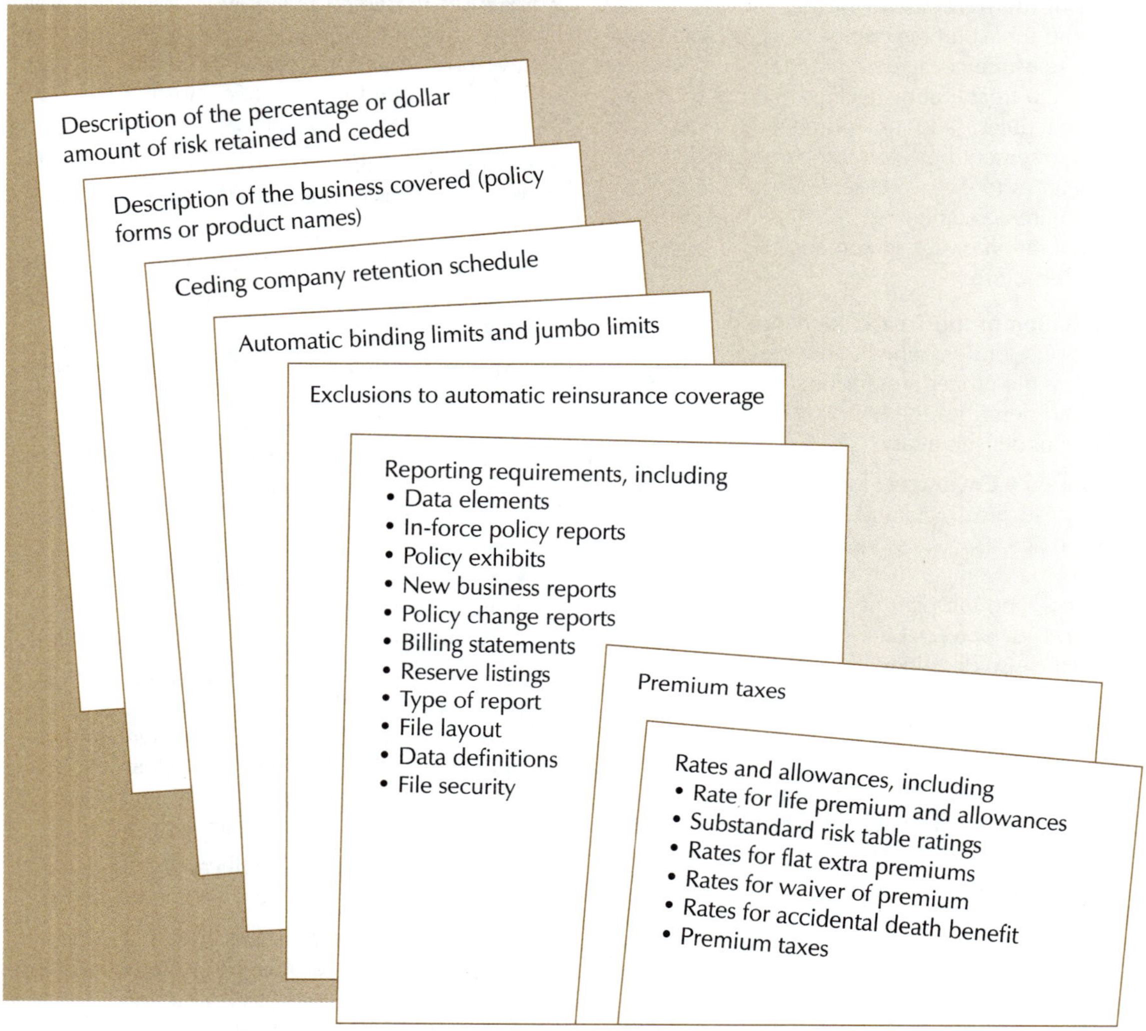

Source: Adapted from Jane Lightcap Brown and Jennifer W. Herrod, *Reinsurance Administration* (Atlanta: LOMA, © 2000), 86. Used with permission; all rights reserved.

Parties to the Agreement Provision

The ***parties to the agreement provision*** typically states that the reinsurance agreement exists solely between the ceding company and the assuming company. As you have learned, the reinsurance agreement does not create any legal relationship between the reinsurer and the insured, the policyowner, any beneficiary, any assignee, or any other party. Further, the agreement establishes a business relationship between the reinsurance parties *only* for the coverage to be reinsured and not for any other business dealings.

Entire Agreement Provision

The ***entire agreement provision*** states that the treaty and any amendments represent the whole agreement between the parties, which have no further agreement than that stated in the treaty. The entire agreement provision is intended to protect both parties from any liability implied, but not expressed, by the treaty. Thus, only the reinsurance arrangements that are specifically stated in the treaty and its amendments are binding on the parties.

If a reinsurer cedes to a retrocessionaire part of the risk it has assumed from a ceding company, such a retrocession does not affect the agreement between the original ceding company and the assuming company in any way. The entire agreement provision further specifies that any future changes or modifications to the treaty will be void unless the changes are made by amendments or in writing signed by appropriate representatives of both the ceding company and the assuming company.

In addition to these two provisions, some treaties state that neither the agreement nor the reinsurance covered by the agreement can be sold, assigned, or transferred by either party without prior written permission from the other party. This provision protects the ceding company from having the reinsurance coverage changed to another reinsurance provider without the ceding company's knowledge and consent. The provision also protects the assuming company from having the reinsured business sold to a direct writer that has less stringent underwriting guidelines and claim practices than the original direct writing insurer.

Duration of the Agreement Provision

Most reinsurance treaties provide that the agreement takes effect on an agreed-upon date, known as the ***treaty effective date***. The treaty effective date is any date agreed upon by the parties. Each treaty will also specify how the reinsurance effective date will be determined. The ***reinsurance effective date*** is the date on which the reinsurance coverage for a specific risk takes effect. Some treaties specify that coverage for a policy begins on the date of application; other treaties state that coverage begins on the policy issue date.

Sometimes a ceding company and an assuming company form a treaty that uses the application date as the determining factor for the beginning of reinsurance coverage. In a later treaty, however, these parties might use the policy issue date instead.

A facultative treaty provides that the responsibility of the assuming company will begin and end at the same time as that of the ceding company, provided that both

- The assuming company has given the ceding company an unconditional offer to reinsure.
- The ceding company has notified the assuming company in writing of its acceptance of the offer.

Most reinsurance treaties specify that, when a treaty has taken effect, it continues for an unlimited period. The intent of this specification is to release the parties from spending time and money to renew a treaty that is fulfilling its intended purposes. However, treaties typically specify that the treaty can be terminated for new business at any time when either party gives written notice to the other party, usually 30 to 90 days in advance of intended termination. We will discuss termination of treaties in more detail later in this chapter.

In addition, treaties usually provide that if amounts due are not paid within a specified period as provided by one party—except as stated under the errors and omissions provision—then the other party has the right to cancel all reinsurance in force under the agreement by giving written notice, usually 30 days in advance. Other treaties may provide that such cancellation applies only to policies for which the premium is in arrears.

Recapture Provision

Recapture is the process by which a ceding company takes back some or all ceded business from a reinsurer. A ceding company may increase its retention limit and then choose to recapture entire policies, groups of policies, or amounts of coverage from its reinsurers. The ceding company must notify the reinsurer of its intent to apply the new retention limit to its existing business. The recapture usually takes effect on the next policy anniversary.

Most reinsurance treaties provide that a ceding company cannot recapture coverage if it did not retain its maximum retention limit when the coverage was first ceded. If reinsurance on any policy is reduced, then reinsurance on all ceded policies of that type must be reduced in a similar manner. This provision protects the reinsurer from adverse selection by the ceding company in the event that the ceding company decided to recapture only the lowest risks and to leave the highest risks covered by the reinsurer.

Termination of the Treaty

As we have stated, most reinsurance treaties stay in effect indefinitely, but occasionally a reinsurance treaty is terminated. Each jurisdiction dictates the circumstances under which termination is acceptable and may limit reserve credit for ceding companies whose reinsurance treaties allow in-force coverage to be terminated by the reinsurer for other reasons.

The most common ways for a treaty to be terminated are through nonpayment of reinsurance premiums and by mutual agreement. Termination of a reinsurance treaty can also occur through

- The expiration of a treaty that contains a limitation on its term
- A notice of cancellation offered by either party at times specified in the treaty
- Termination of every policy reinsured under the agreement so that no policy remains in force
- Rescission or cancellation of the treaty by either party, brought about by fraud or failure to disclose material information
- Withdrawal of either party's insurance license
- Commencement of war
- Bankruptcy

Typically, the parties to the treaty go to great lengths to avoid terminating a treaty for reasons other than mutual agreement.

The parties to a reinsurance treaty can mutually agree to terminate the treaty at any time. If only one party wants to terminate the treaty, additional limitations apply. For example, if the termination is for nonpayment of reinsurance premiums, the reinsurer must provide the ceding company with adequate notice of the nonpayment so that the ceding company has the opportunity to pay any overdue reinsurance premiums and keep the reinsurance in force.

One party can terminate a treaty by sending the other party a written statement to that effect, known as a ***notice of cancellation***. The termination provision usually states that notices of cancellation can be tendered only at certain times, such as at the end of a quarter or year. The treaty generally specifies the date on which the notice becomes effective.

When a reinsurance treaty is terminated, the parties to the treaty consult the treaty to determine how to deal with the reinsurance currently in force. The treaty states which of several methods should be used to carry out the termination. Unless the parties mutually agree to end the reinsurance relationship, existing reinsurance remains in force until the natural termination or expiration of the policies. That is, a policy remains reinsured until a claim submitted under it is paid, or the policy terminates due to lapse or surrender, or, for term insurance, until the term of coverage has ended. Thus, termination of a reinsurance treaty ends the contractual relationship between the parties *only* for new business under that treaty. Reinsurance coverage issued earlier than the termination date is still in force, unless other arrangements are made to discontinue it.

The termination provision typically states that the reinsurer's obligation ends when the reinsured policy is terminated. The treaty requires the reinsurer to remain responsible for losses that have occurred prior to the termination, but that have not yet been settled.

Reinsurance Coverages

A reinsurance treaty describes in detail the plans of insurance to be retained and ceded and the reinsurance coverage to be provided. Unless the details of the ceded coverage and the reinsurance coverage are exactly stated from the beginning, the reinsurance parties run the risk of misunderstanding each other.

As an example of the need to be specific, suppose that a reinsurance treaty provides for coverage for universal life products. After the treaty is in effect for a number of years, the ceding company introduces a variable universal life product. In this situation, neither the ceding company nor the assuming company could be certain that the treaty, as written, covers the variable universal life product. The two companies would be likely to negotiate a change to their treaty to include the new coverage.

As you have learned, the parameters of the reinsurance coverage are often stated generally in treaty provisions and explained in detail in schedules attached to the provisions. Because each reinsurance treaty is unique, details about the reinsurance coverage could be found in a provision in one treaty, and in a schedule in another.

Reinsurance Coverage Provisions

The treaty provisions define in general terms the plans to be covered by the reinsurance (for example, whole life, term, or universal life), and the basis (for example, automatic or facultative), the type (for example, YRT, modified coinsurance, or coinsurance), and the method (for example, first dollar quota share or excess quota share) of the reinsurance coverage to be provided by the reinsurer. For instance, the treaty might state,

> *"Amounts of individual life insurance that have been issued by the ceding company or its subsidiaries to standard and substandard lives on any of the plans of insurance listed in Schedule I shall be automatically coinsured under this agreement with the*

participating reinsurers, as defined in Schedule III, on a 50 percent first dollar quota share basis up to the maximum retention limit specified in Schedule I."

The provisions generally refer interested parties to the schedules for the specific retention limits and acceptance limits on the reinsurance coverage. We discuss these schedules in more detail later in this chapter.

As a general rule, an automatic reinsurance treaty contains more specific and restrictive parameters than a facultative treaty. Policies automatically reinsured *must* be accepted by the assuming company, so the automatic reinsurance treaty specifies what types of policies can be submitted. In contrast, policies reinsured facultatively are individually underwritten and provide the assuming company with an opportunity to accept or decline the risk.

For example, in describing the reinsurance to be provided, an automatic reinsurance treaty might specify certain risks that are excluded from coverage. Most automatic treaties state that if (1) the ceding company intends to retain less than its available retention limit for the insured's age and mortality rate and (2) the ceding company has submitted a case for facultative consideration outside the treaty, then that case cannot be submitted for automatic reinsurance. Further, most automatic treaties state that if the assuming company has declined to issue facultative coverage on a case, the ceding company cannot resubmit that case for automatic coverage. Figure 10-9 describes other situations in which most treaties also exclude automatic coverage.

The treaty typically states that the ceding company may facultatively submit to any reinsurer any of the coverages that do not qualify for automatic reinsurance—perhaps because the age of the insured, face amount, risk classification, financial justification, or some other aspects do not match the specified requirements. In addition, the ceding company may submit policies facultatively because it prefers to have the assuming company's underwriters review the case.

If the reinsurance is to be placed in a pool, the treaty describes the placement by noting the quota shares that will be apportioned to each reinsurance partner. The treaty may also specify that the pool members will automatically accept their prescribed share of the risk whenever coverage is available in the reinsurance pool and when no exclusions apply. This provision protects the ceding company by ensuring that the agreed-upon coverage is available and protects the assuming company from having to accept a greater-than-anticipated share of the cessions.

Schedules of Reinsurance Coverage

Various schedules attached to the treaty provide the specific parameters of the reinsurance coverage agreed to by the parties. A treaty typically

FIGURE 10-9. Some Situations in Which Most Treaties Exclude Automatic Coverage.

- The amount of life insurance previously reinsured and currently applied for and to be reinsured under the treaty exceeds the specified automatic binding limit
- The amount of life insurance in force on a life in all companies plus the amount currently being applied for with all companies exceeds the jumbo limit
- The insurance is being issued using underwriting guidelines that differ from the agreed-upon selection criteria specified in the treaty
- The insurance is being issued in a manner not specified in the treaty—for instance, as a conversion of group insurance or as a policy exchange
- Full first-year commissions have not been paid on the underlying risk
- The substandard mortality rating assigned by the ceding company to the risk exceeds a specified level
- The insurance is being reinsured on a plan not specified in the treaty, for example, joint last-to-die policies
- The life to be reinsured does not meet other criteria acceptable to both parties—for instance, the insured is not a resident of a specified jurisdiction such as the United States or Canada
- The policy is a continuation of coverage of a previously issued policy that has been reinsured with another agreement or that was fully retained by the ceding company

Source: Adapted from Jane Lightcap Brown and Jennifer W. Herrod, *Reinsurance Administration* (Atlanta: LOMA, © 2000), 94. Used with permission; all rights reserved.

includes schedules describing the plans of insurance to be covered, the amounts to be reinsured and the limits on those amounts, and the premium rates. We will discuss the plans of insurance and amounts to be covered below.

Plans of Insurance. A schedule typically lists all of the insurance plans to be covered by the treaty. The schedule also describes any riders, such as waiver of premium for disability benefits (WP) and accidental death benefits (ADB) that will be covered under the treaty. Figure 10-10 shows an example of a schedule for a plan of insurance.

FIGURE 10-10. Schedule Showing Plans of Insurance Covered.

This treaty covers single, joint-first-to-die, and joint-last-to-die individual life insurance, and supplementary benefits and riders issued directly by the ceding company on insureds who are residents of the United States of America or its territories or Canada at the time of issue of the policy.

Source: Excerpted from Jane Lightcap Brown and Jennifer W. Herrod, *Reinsurance Administration* (Atlanta: LOMA, © 2000), 95. Used with permission; all rights reserved.

Amounts of Reinsurance and Related Limits. A provision or a schedule in the reinsurance treaty specifies the method to be used in calculating the net amount at risk and the retention limits of the ceding company. The schedule may specify a retention limit for each risk level and for additional benefits offered by the policies, such as waiver of premium or accidental death benefits. For automatic reinsurance, the ceding company usually reinsures only amounts that exceed the company's stated retention limit for a certain insurance product up to a specified limit. Most treaties also state a ***minimum cession***, which is the smallest amount of risk that an insurer will cede. For facultative reinsurance, the assuming company may or may not require the ceding company to keep its stated retention on the policy. Figure 10-11 shows an example of a retention limits schedule in a treaty.

FIGURE 10-11. Schedule of Retention Limits.

LIMITS OF RETENTION: RST LIFE INSURANCE COMPANY
Whole Life Insurance

Issue Age	Standard–Table 4	Table 5–Table 8	Table 9–Table 16
0–60	$100,000	$50,000	$25,000
61–70	$50,000	$25,000	$25,000
71–80	$25,000	$25,000	$25,000

Waiver of Premium
Same as Whole Life Insurance

Source: Excerpted from Jane Lightcap Brown and Jennifer W. Herrod, *Reinsurance Administration* (Atlanta: LOMA, © 2000), 96. Used with permission; all rights reserved.

If the treaty calls for nonproportional reinsurance plans, a schedule generally specifies the amount the reinsurer will pay based on the number or amount of claims submitted under the coverage.

A schedule in a reinsurance treaty also specifies the reinsurer's binding limits and usually specifies the lower and upper issue ages and the risk level for each type of coverage. For instance, a treaty for term insurance might state that no one under the age of 6 or above the age of 70, and no one with a mortality rate greater than a specified level, will be reinsured under the treaty.

The binding limits schedule also typically specifies the jumbo limit, which we defined earlier as a limit that specifies the maximum dollar amount allowable of total insurance in force and applied for with all insurers on any one life that will be automatically accepted by a reinsurer. Figure 10-12 shows an example of a binding limits schedule.

FIGURE 10-12. Schedule of Binding Limits.

AUTOMATIC ACCEPTANCE LIMITS OF REGENT RE

Life Insurance: Retroceded

Regent Re will automatically accept 50% of the excess on assumed business, subject to the following maximums:

Issue Age	Standard	Substandard 101%–300%	Substandard 301%–500%	Substandard 501%+
0–80	$1,000,000	$1,000,000	$500,000	$500,000

Waiver of Premium Disability Benefits

Provided that the underwriting classification of the life risk does not exceed 200% total mortality, the reinsurer will automatically accept 50% of the excess over the ceding company's retention for an amount up to, but not exceeding, the lesser of (a) the amount corresponding to the life insurance being automatically reinsured and (b) the amount corresponding to $50,000 of annual premium waived. Under no circumstances will the reinsurer automatically accept any waiver of premium disability benefits risk when the face amount of the associated life insurance for the total line of waiver of premium disability benefits in all companies exceeds $10,000,000.

Source: Excerpted from Jane Lightcap Brown and Jennifer W. Herrod, *Reinsurance Administration* (Atlanta: LOMA, © 2000), 96. Used with permission; all rights reserved.

Key Terms and Concepts

reinsurance treaty
proportional reinsurance
yearly renewable term (YRT) reinsurance
net amount at risk (NAR)
coinsurance
coinsurance with funds withheld
modified coinsurance (modco)
excess quota share arrangement
first dollar quota share arrangement
excess of retention arrangement
layering
first excess
second excess
third excess
alphabetic split
nonproportional reinsurance
automatic reinsurance
automatic binding limit
jumbo limit
facultative reinsurance
shopping
facultative-obligatory (fac-ob) reinsurance
Canadian Reinsurance Conference (CRC)
articles
schedules
parties to the agreement provision
entire agreement provision
treaty effective date
reinsurance effective date
recapture
notice of cancellation
minimum cession

Endnotes

1. ACLI, *Life Insurers Fact Book 2000* (Washington, D.C.: American Council of Life Insurers, 2000), 153.
2. Ibid., 150.

CHAPTER 11

Reinsurance Administration

CHAPTER OUTLINE

OBJECTIVES

After reading this chapter, you should be able to

- Describe three different methods of administering reinsurance
- Explain the methods insurers use to exchange information
- List and discuss administrative activities reinsurers perform
- Describe the methods insurers and reinsurers use to handle problems that arise

Reinsurance administration involves the day-to-day details of handling a case from the moment the ceding company seeks reinsurance to the moment the reinsurance is no longer in force. When an insurer and a reinsurer develop a business relationship, the two parties have several mutual obligations and expectations about administration of the reinsured coverages. Each party expects the other to conduct business in an ethical manner, to establish and maintain a clear, accurate exchange of information, and to provide contractually arranged services. In addition, the reinsurer typically assists the insurer in developing new products, in underwriting cases, in assessing and handling claims, in controlling risk, and in providing guidance and advice concerning industry trends. In return, the reinsurer expects the insurer to provide timely, significant information concerning premiums, policy data, and claims.

Because accurate, complete, and timely administration is essential for the effective and efficient operation of both the reinsurer and the ceding company, the reinsurance treaty in each reinsurance relationship provides the guidelines for the way policies are administered. The specific methods of administration vary from treaty to treaty and company to company. We will describe the administration activities that generally take place. Because the details of administration can vary greatly, remember that the procedures that we describe may be somewhat different from the procedures that your company uses in administering reinsurance.

The reinsurance treaty assigns the administrative responsibilities to the ceding company or the assuming company, depending on the needs, wishes, and capabilities of the parties. Remember that the ceding company may be an insurer or a reinsurer, and the assuming company may be a reinsurer or a retrocessionaire.

We'll begin our discussion of reinsurance administration by explaining three methods of administering reinsurance. Next we'll discuss one of the most fundamental aspects of reinsurance—the ongoing and timely exchange of information between insurer and reinsurer—and explain the procedures used for periodic reinsurance audits. Then we'll consider the administrative activities of reinsurance administration. Finally, we'll discuss how reinsurers handle problems that may arise.

Methods of Administering Reinsurance

Ceding companies and assuming companies typically use one of three methods to administer their reinsurance arrangements: individual cession administration, self administration, or bulk administration. We discuss each method below.

Individual Cession Administration

In ***individual cession administration***, the assuming company administers the reinsurance and bills the ceding company for the premiums and other amounts owed for individual lives reinsured. The ceding company provides the assuming company with detailed information about individual policies and informs the assuming company of any changes that affect the reinsurance. The assuming company uses this information to calculate the net amount at risk, premiums, expense allowances, and reserves. The assuming company provides periodic reports to the ceding company outlining the current status of the reinsurance.

Self Administration

Self administration is a method of reinsurance administration in which the ceding company maintains detailed records for each ceded policy and provides periodic reports outlining each risk ceded and premiums due to the assuming company. The assuming company uses the information provided by the ceding company to manage its risk. The assuming company maintains the right to monitor the ceding company's handling of the administration through onsite audits or reviews.

Bulk Administration

In ***bulk administration***, the ceding company administers the reinsurance and periodically submits summarized reports on premiums and on the policies to the assuming company. However, the ceding company does not provide individualized detailed information about risks reinsured until a claim needs to be processed. The assuming company does not manage retention on an individual policy basis; thus the ceding company does not report individual in-force and retention information. However, the assuming company receives information related to individual policies at the time of claim processing.

FAST FACT

In the United States, between 1996 and 1999, reinsurance premiums assumed in the accident and health market rose at an average annual rate of 2%, compared to a slight decline in the life and annuity market for the same time period.[1]

Exchanging Information

From the first queries about coverage to the last exchange of claim and payment data, insurers and reinsurers maintain a continual flow of information. Negotiating treaties and agreements, shopping for facultative coverage, providing underwriting advice and information, checking treaties for details of implementation, calculating the amount of coverage to be ceded or assumed on a particular case or a group of cases, calculating premium and claim amounts due and paid, producing innumerable reports on all sorts of administrative transactions, and checking the quality of every aspect of reinsurance administration—all of these activities demand rapid, accurate information in a form that can be collected, organized, corrected, modified, and communicated to those who need it.

Today, conducting the business of reinsurance without using electronic technology is impossible to imagine. For example, ceding companies and assuming companies typically rely on e-mail, voice mail, fax machines, and computer-based information systems to conduct daily reinsurance transactions. You'll recall from Chapter 1 that two examples of technology currently being used to enhance reinsurance administration include integrated image processing and electronic data interchange (EDI). Insight 11-1 describes many of the issues facing reinsurers regarding the exchange of information via EDI.

Reinsurance Audit

Another way that ceding companies and assuming companies exchange information is through a reinsurance audit. A ***reinsurance audit*** is a formal examination of an insurer's reinsurance records to evaluate whether those records contain accurate details. A reinsurance audit helps ensure that both parties to a reinsurance agreement understand and have complied with the terms of the agreement. A reinsurance audit may focus primarily on underwriting or claim administration. Performing a reinsurance audit benefits both parties by

- Verifying that all policy details and types of reinsurance information are transferred correctly from the ceding company's file to the reinsurer's file

- Ensuring that the insurer and reinsurer have established adequate internal controls of reinsurance information and procedures for paper and electronic administration

- Enabling both parties to discuss and resolve inconsistencies and work flow discrepancies related to reinsurance administration

- Providing evidence for external auditors and regulatory agencies that reinsurance is being properly ceded and administered

The ceding company is expected to perform self-audits. However, self-audits do not replace the need for the reinsurer to perform an

Insight 11-1. Reinsurance EDI Moves to the Web.

Recently the much talked-about eXtensible Markup Language (XML) has moved from an interesting idea to the forefront of business-to-business (B2B) e-commerce solutions XML is often considered the "new" HTML (HyperText Markup Language), which is the most commonly used method of presenting and transferring information via the Web. Even those who are not Web experts are aware that HTML exists, and many recognize it as the cornerstone for most Web processing today.

XML takes HTML a major step forward by providing the ability to add structured data exchanges onto the already powerful presentation capabilities of HTML. Even in the paper-entrenched world of reinsurance, companies have realized that electronic data exchange can speed up processing, eliminate errors, improve customer relations and, most importantly, reduce costs.

Much time and money have been invested to develop data standards for exchanging routine reinsurance transactions among cedents, brokers and reinsurers. EDI standards approved by EDIFACT (the UN standards body) have been available within the global reinsurance industry for several years, and investment in using those standards has been significant.

However, as more companies choose the Internet as their preferred method of B2B electronic communication, they recognize the limitations of the existing EDI standards. Corporate technology infrastructures are changing to support Web-enhanced business processes. E-mail is the norm for external communication with trading partners, and critical business documents are increasingly sent as e-mail attachments. Web sites containing information about all facets of the business down to specific transactions are popping up everywhere. We will continue to see this explosive growth in the use of the Web to create an e-business environment in reinsurance.

Traditional EDI, that is EDI structures and exchanges based on time-tested guidelines that follow the rules of recognized standards bodies, doesn't easily fit into this new Web model. Specialized software solutions and communication capabilities are still needed, which differ from the Internet and Web facilities being deployed today.

It is difficult to combine data from traditional EDI transactions with non-structured data that is exchanged via other means, such as e-mail and Web sites. And, although the various EDI standards bodies help ensure that numerous conflicting standards are not developed for the same business purpose, the inherent delay in getting new requirements incorporated is unacceptable in the rapid-paced Internet world.

The need to exchange structured data, which spawned the development of EDI standards, remains the same. EDI is intended for the computer-to-computer exchange of information with no human intervention. Computers need rules to understand the data they are trying to process. Standardizing those rules allows organizations to avoid developing custom processes for every business partner, and results in easily defined B2B data exchanges and a less costly way of doing business.

The introduction of the Web and all of its new capabilities does not eliminate the need for structured data exchanges. In fact, it actually makes it more critical that organizations consider this need when defining their B2B e-commerce goals to ensure a seamless flow of information directly into their corporate databases.

With the recognition that XML was quickly being accepted as the conduit for B2B activity over the Internet, the JV partners initiated a project in late 1999 to develop XML standards for reinsurance data. As EDIFACT EDI standards were already in place and in use, it was a natural progression to take those standards and to move them into XML. The most important goal, however, was not just to "convert" the standards into an XML format, but to analyze the business data and rules embedded in the EDIFACT structures and quickly create a set of usable XML reinsurance transactions.

XML holds great promise for the future. It is strongly supported by all major computer software vendors and is being embraced by every industry sector on a global basis. XML may turn out to be one of the most important recent Web developments to enable B2B e-commerce. For an industry that is as information-intensive as reinsurance, any method that can deliver an easier way to exchange information electronically is welcome.

The reinsurance XML transactions focus on the most common back-office exchanges: premiums, claims, adjustments and references. These are a natural fit for XML as they are already standardized and much of the data can flow automatically between systems, yet each has components that need to be viewed by people to complete the business processing.

These transactions also often involve additional supporting information that is acquired through other means, including e-mail and Web sites. This is a good fit with the new Web-enhanced infrastructure model that many reinsurance organizations are already implementing.

Source: Excerpted from Lisa Masarek, "Reinsurance EDI Moves to the Web," *National Underwriter*, Life & Health/Financial Services ed. (22 May 2000). Reprinted with permission from *National Underwriter.*

on-site audit. Most reinsurance audits are performed by the reinsurer, who conducts the audit at the site of the ceding company. Prior to the audit, the reinsurer reviews at its offices certain information such as system formats, treaties, premium calculations, face amounts, and expected versus actual results.

The date and duration of a reinsurance audit are sometimes selected several months in advance and are arranged at the convenience of the ceding company. The reinsurer generally sends the insurer a list of objectives for the audit and the types of materials and procedures the audit team will review. In return, the insurer provides the reinsurer with a procedures manual or other document that explains how reinsured coverages are handled. Having written procedures enables the audit team to become familiar with the ceding company's administrative approaches and, therefore, saves time during the audit. Figure 11-1 lists typical questions found on a policy audit questionnaire.

The insurer provides the reinsurer with randomly selected samples of reinsured plans of insurance, in-force policies, and claims. The audit team selects an additional sample to help verify further the accuracy of retention limit and other calculations.

During the visit, the audit team is given reasonable access to the insurer's records, although the insurer usually protects the confidentiality of files by prohibiting the audit team from making copies of certain documents and reports. Generally, a reinsurer's team of auditors recommends enhancements to the ceding company's workflow or systems. The audit team also meets with representatives from the ceding company to present and discuss the results.

When the audit has been completed, the audit team presents its findings to the reinsurer's management. The reinsurer also sends a copy of the audit report to the management of the ceding company. The report contains the audit results as well as recommendations. If required, the audit team or members of the reinsurer's management meet with the management and the reinsurance administration staff of the ceding company to review the results of the audit and to resolve discrepancies. Figure 11-2 lists some of the benefits to the ceding company of an audit by the reinsurer.

Administrative Activities

The business of reinsurance requires many administrative activities, including (1) negotiating and drafting treaties, (2) underwriting cases, (3) paying premiums, (4) modifying policies, (5) paying claims, (6) recapturing coverages, and (7) evaluating in-force reinsurance. We'll discuss these important activities in this section.

FIGURE 11-1. Typical Questions on a Policy Audit Questionnaire.

Information About the Insured and His Policy

- Insured's name
- Reinsurer's policy number
- Ceding company's policy number
- Cession number
- Treaty number
- Insured's date of birth
- Insured's age at time of issue
- Mortality rate
- Policy year date (date the policy became effective)
- Insured's tobacco use class
- Underwriting basis
- Insured's sex

Treaty Compliance

Is the cession within the automatic limit outlined in the treaty or has it been exceeded?

Is the cession within the reinsurer's retention or has it been exceeded?

Has the client kept its full retention?

Is the insured within the age limit set out in the treaty?

Is the insured within the mortality rate set out in the treaty?

Is the policy effective date within the effective date of the treaty?

Are all plans and benefits applied for covered under the treaty?

Premium Verification

- Net amount at risk
- Year that is being audited
- The rate per thousand of in-force per treaty
- The annual premium calculated based on net amount at risk and rates in treaty
- The substandard rate per thousand per investigation
- The commission rate per the treaty
- The premium calculated based on the treaty
- The expected net premium
- The rate per thousand used by the client
- The annual premium calculated by the client
- The substandard rate per thousand calculated by the client
- The substandard premium calculated by the client
- The commission rate per the client
- The commission calculated based on the client
- The actual net premium

Rates and Accuracy

Is the cession administered on the rate set used in the treaty?

Is calculation of the premium the same as the client's?

Has the correct quota share been applied?

When was the premium paid?

Comments and Follow-Up

Is there anything else the auditors need to know about this case to understand it?

Is there anything about this case that needs to be discussed with the ceding company's employees during the audit?

FIGURE 11-2. Benefits of an Audit.

- Early detection of errors through an audit—can prevent the financial strain for an insurer and a reinsurer that would be caused by undetected errors
- Knowledgeable, outside review of ceding company's capabilities
- Resolution of issues between the insurer and the reinsurer before a claim is made
- A benchmark for the ceding company against its peers, who also have been audited by the reinsurer
- Recommendations from the reinsurer that might increase ceding company's efficiency or improve ceding company's systems
- Verification of insurer's own internal audit

Negotiating and Drafting Treaties

In Chapter 10, we discussed the contents of a reinsurance treaty. Negotiating and drafting an automatic or a facultative treaty require that the parties (1) discuss the provisions that each wishes to include and (2) resolve any differences.

When an insurer plans to develop a new product, one of the primary considerations is whether reinsurance is available at an attractive cost that the product's underlying actuarial assumptions can support. Most insurers planning to cede coverage under new products arrange for reinsurance in advance of offering the product on the market. After the insurer's marketing staff and actuaries have determined the new product's premiums, cash values, and reserves, the insurer typically requests bids for reinsurance from several reinsurers. The insurer also specifies the type of administration that will be used for the new product and any other special considerations required for it. Using this information, the reinsurer's actuarial staff calculates an appropriate reinsurance premium.

Underwriting Cases

Before an insurer decides to seek facultative reinsurance on a case, the underwriter may already have performed some underwriting on the case. After the case is submitted to one or more reinsurers for bids, reinsurance underwriters assess the risk and decide whether to offer reinsurance. After the insurer has received the risk assessment and premium information, its underwriters decide whether to accept the bid for reinsurance.

Because the ceding company is not required to submit underwriting evidence to the reinsurer under automatic agreements, the ceding company performs all underwriting for such cases. However, the ceding company might consult with the reinsurance underwriter on cases covered by an automatic agreement. Insight 11-2 explains how some reinsurers are enhancing their relationships by providing underwriting technology.

Insight 11-2. Insurers as Technologists.

For some major carriers, the lines are blurring between offering insurance and providing technology. Insurers like Hartford Life and Lincoln Re are at the forefront of assisted underwriting software, providing their clients or producers with high-tech tools that streamline the underwriting process to give them a competitive edge.

Lincoln Re, Fort Wayne, Ind., has two patented systems, an automated new-business system and one that enables almost instantaneous assessment of mortality risk. Hartford Life says its software can shave weeks off the individual-life application process, making the whole procedure easier for stockbrokers, financial planners and bank investment representatives who are not full-time agents.

By extending this kind of technological helping hand, these companies also are realizing substantial rewards—an outcome that the rest of the industry is duly noting. Lincoln Re, for example, estimates that between 1997 and 2000 one-fourth to one-third of its new reinsurance premiums were driven by the company's ability to help insurers develop new products or modify old products using the Lincoln Mortality System.

When the mortality system was introduced in 1993, "we were far and away the first," said Tracy Choka, second vice president and director of the underwriting research and development team at Lincoln Re. "In the past two to three years, I think our competitors have been trying to deliver the same type of tool." The system is used to price Lincoln Re's own business, as well as help reinsurance clients that want to get into the supercompetitive term insurance market.

Robert Hartwig, chief economist of the Insurance Information Institute, said that this is becoming a very competitive field as insurers and reinsurers develop all sorts of proprietary underwriting software. "It's an inevitable and probably favorable trend," he said of the increasing use of this software in both the life and property/casualty realms. "This can be used to enhance speed and increase production, and to contemplate situations we humans can't always fathom."

However, he cautioned, while no software can replace or supplant the human underwriter, it can free him or her to spend more time on devising ways to provide coverage to previously uninsurable segments of the population.

Source: Excerpted from Barbara Bowers, "Insurers as Technologists," *Best's Review* (April 2001): 115. © A.M. Best Company, Inc.; used with permission of the publisher.

Paying Premiums

The party administering the reinsurance calculates the amount of reinsurance premium due by multiplying the amount reinsured by the reinsurance premium rate as described in the treaty. For instance, if a reinsurer is to cover 80 percent of a $100,000 term life policy (so that the amount reinsured is $80,000) at a rate of $1.30 per thousand, the annual reinsurance premium is $80 \times \$1.30 = \$104$.

After the reinsurance premium on each covered policy has been calculated, the insurer submits the required premium along with a listing of the reinsurer's share in each risk and other information about commission payments and allowances.

Modifying Policies

Policy modifications, such as changing benefits, changing plans, and changing ratings, require the insurer and the reinsurer to cooperate. For all policy changes, both the insurer and the reinsurer have a mutual obligation to maintain reinsurance in force on terms fair to both parties.

Generally, if the ceding company increases the amount at risk, the reinsurer treats the increase as a new reinsurance cession. In such a situation, the reinsurer is not obligated to reinsure the increase unless bound to do so by an existing treaty. In contrast, if the ceding company decreases the amount at risk, the reinsurer decreases the amount of reinsurance in the same proportion. For example, if the amount at risk on a ceded policy decreases 20 percent, the amount of reinsurance coverage also decreases 20 percent.

When a ceding company has to revise a policy from inception, the policy is restructured on a new premium rate basis from the date of issue of the initial policy. Then the reinsurer usually makes an adjustment for the difference in reinsurance premium without interest.

If a policy terminates for any reason, such as the death of the insured, a lapse, or a surrender, reinsurance terminates on the same date the policy terminates. If premiums have been paid on the reinsurance for a period beyond the date of termination, the reinsurer in most cases provides a premium refund. However, some treaties provide that no refund is made on termination in the event of death.

Sometimes a lapsed or canceled policy is reinstated. ***Reinstatement*** is the process by which an insurer puts back into force a life insurance policy that has either been terminated for nonpayment of premiums or been continued as extended term or paid-up coverage. When a policy that was reinsured on a facultative basis is reinstated, the ceding company is obligated to give the reinsurer copies of the application for reinstatement and the underwriting documents. The reinsurer has the right to amend the reinsurance terms on the policy if the risk has changed significantly. For certain limited coverages, the reinsurance treaty specifies that a reinstated policy is automatically reinsured on the date of reinstatement, with notice of reinstatement being mailed to the reinsurer within a reasonable time. If any policy change increases or decreases the reinsurance premium, the reinsurer makes an appropriate modification to the premium amount due.

Handling Claims

An important part of reinsurance administration is handling claims. A ceding company buys reinsurance to receive reimbursement for covered claims when they are due. To ensure that appropriate claims are paid in a timely manner, each reinsurance treaty contains a claim provision. Figure 11-3 summarizes the information contained in a typical reinsurance treaty claim provision.

FIGURE 11-3. Information in a Reinsurance Treaty Claim Provision.

- The ceding company's authority to handle claims, including any limits on that authority
- The procedures the ceding company must follow to be reimbursed for paid claims
- How the ceding company and assuming company will share responsibility for expenses related to claims and adjustments to the benefit amount
- The conditions under which the assuming company will share in responsibility for extra-contractual damages
- The manner in which claims will be reported

The Ceding Company's Authority and Claim Procedures

Because the insurance contract is an agreement between the ceding company and the policyowner, the claim provision typically states that the ceding company has the authority to make decisions on claims and that the reinsurer is bound by the ceding company's decisions. The claim provision requires the ceding company to notify the reinsurer promptly of a claim and to provide the reinsurer with copies of proofs of loss and other claim-related documents as soon as possible after a claim is submitted.

The claim provision typically states that the reinsurer will pay the reinsurance benefits to the ceding company in a lump sum. The treaty typically specifies conditions under which the ceding company is required to obtain a recommendation from the reinsurer before settling an insurance claim. For example, the ceding company might be required to consult with the reinsurer if the

- Claim is resisted by the ceding company
- Claim occurs during the policy's contestable period
- Reinsurer has assumed more than 50 percent of the risk covered by the reinsured policy
- Claim involves an accidental death benefit rider

In addition, the claim provision usually states that the reinsurer must be given the opportunity to review the claim file of any claim that is to be denied or contested or for which unusual claim investigation expenses are expected—for example, a disability income claim that requires a lengthy, detailed series of investigative reports before the insurer can determine whether or not to pay the claim. The ceding company is usually required to consult with the reinsurer before settling such a claim or making a commitment to settle it. The treaty may state that the reinsurer will pay a proportionate share of the cost of the investigation of claims and any interest accrued on the policy proceeds while the investigation was being conducted.

Contest or Denial of a Claim

Typically, the ceding company and the assuming company work together to determine whether to contest or deny a claim. By joining in the contest, the reinsurer becomes responsible for its share of the expenses of the contest and becomes eligible for any reduction in liability as well. On rare occasions, the reinsurer may decide not to participate in the contest or denial of a claim. In this situation, the reinsurer is required by the treaty to pay its proportionate share of the full death benefit due and any expenses incurred to date to the ceding company and is, thereafter, excused from any responsibility for other expenses related to the claim. If the ceding company chooses to contest the claim and is granted a reduction in liability, the reinsurer does not share in this reduction.

The treaty specifies which claim expenses the reinsurer will share when it joins a contest. Some treaties state that the reinsurer will be responsible for claim expenses only up to the amount of risk the reinsurer held on the reinsured policy and that the reinsurer will not be held responsible for any extracontractual damages, such as punitive or compensatory damages charged to the ceding company. Other treaties specify that the reinsurer will share proportionately in any such damages, unless the damages are assessed against the ceding company for an act committed solely by the ceding company.

The claim provision also typically describes the appropriate reinsurance payments for other types of claims, such as those involving waiver of premium. For example, in the case of waiver of premium for disability claims, the treaty generally requires the reinsurer to pay the ceding company its proportionate share of the waived premium annually. The ceding company is required to continue paying the reinsurance premiums.

If an insured commits suicide during the policy's exclusion period, the policy provisions describe the benefit to be paid. Typically, this benefit, known as the limited death benefit, is the amount of the premiums paid minus any indebtedness to the company. The reinsurer refunds the reinsurance premiums or pays its share of the limited death benefit, depending on the reinsurance treaty provision.

Recapturing Coverages

When a ceding company decides to increase its retention limit on certain coverage, the ceding company may also decide to recapture reinsured business whose retention limit is lower than the new, higher limit. The ceding company is not required to recapture in-force business, but may choose to do so to reduce the cost of reinsurance. Many reinsurers require that coverage be maintained in force for a specified period, usually 10 years, although the length of the period varies from one plan of insurance to another.

Under the laws of most jurisdictions, at the time a ceding company raises its retention limit, the insurer must inform a reinsurer of its intention to recapture ceded business if the ceding company intends to do so. If the ceding company fails to notify the reinsurer of its intention to recapture, most jurisdictions provide that the ceding company has thereby forfeited its right to recapture the reinsured coverage. No recapture is provided for facultative reinsurance because the reinsurer would not be able to recover its underwriting expenses until future profits are realized.

Evaluating In-force Reinsurance

An insurer periodically reviews the amount and type of reinsurance in force using electronic data and assesses whether the established form of reinsurance administration is being implemented correctly and cost-effectively. Figure 11-4 provides a summary of the in-force reinsurance elements that insurers evaluate periodically.

Handling Problems

Every business relationship, no matter how well planned and congenial, can experience difficulties. Instead of waiting for problems to develop and then determining how to address them, the parties to a reinsurance agreement anticipate the occasional occurrence of problems by stating the procedures to be used to resolve problems. These problems include errors and omissions made in the administration of the reinsurance treaty, disputes that require arbitration, and the financial insolvency of one of the reinsurance parties.

FIGURE 11-4. In-force Reinsurance Review.

In addition to certifying that the insurer is keeping its full retention limits according to treaty provisions, an in-force reinsurance review also enables the insurer to learn whether

- Cases are being ceded appropriately
- Premiums are being calculated correctly
- Claims are being handled properly and accurately
- Changes in policies are being reported in a timely fashion
- Correct formulas (if any) are properly used in accordance with treaty provisions
- Certain coverages should be recaptured
- Operations should be reconfigured in order to reduce the costs of administration
- All reinsurers are provided the desired level and quality of service

Errors and Omissions

The reinsurance treaty establishes the basis for ceding and assuming business under the agreement. All parties to the agreement intend that activities carried out under the treaty, including the administration of the reinsurance treaty, be handled in a fair and mutually beneficial manner. However, errors or omissions of information can weaken the fair and equitable arrangement between the parties. The errors and omissions clause or provision of a reinsurance treaty sets the treaty apart from other types of legal contracts by providing a possible approach to restore the parties to an equitable status.

The errors and omissions provision states that, if either party to the treaty does not comply with the terms of the agreement through unintentional mistake or clerical error, then both parties will be restored to the position they would have occupied if the unintentional mistake or clerical error had not occurred. The provision requires that if a party cannot be restored to its rightful position, the two parties will make a good faith effort to correct the error in a way that is fair and that upholds the parties' original intent.

In some cases, restoring the parties to a fair position can be extremely difficult, if not impossible. For example, if a ceding company fails to follow its published guidelines for ceding automatic business, as required by the reinsurance treaty, and an omission is discovered at claim time, the reinsurer might assert that it would not have accepted the risk and the ceding company could be left to pay the entire claim.

The errors and omissions provision states that both parties are obligated to do their best to ensure that all errors are discovered and corrected as quickly as possible. Moreover, the errors and omissions provision states that the provision will not cancel any rights or obligations established by the treaty as long as both parties work to handle errors appropriately.

The errors and omissions provision applies only after reinsurance has begun. The errors and omissions provision typically applies only to clerical errors, not to errors that involve business decisions made by one party or the other. However, the provision usually does not cover a situation in which a ceding company chooses not to check its records for additional policies covering the life of a proposed insured. If the ceding company issues a policy and in so doing exceeds its retention limits, the errors and omissions provision will not apply. Such an error is considered to be a management decision and not a clerical error. Other situations in which the errors and omissions provision does not apply include failure to send a facultative cession, failure to send a document that would affect an underwriting decision, and failure to perform full underwriting or other routine requirements as required by the treaty.

If the ceding company fails to cede reinsurance that it is required to cede automatically under the treaty, the errors and omissions provision usually requires the ceding company to (1) notify the reinsurer of the oversight as soon as it is discovered, (2) provide the reinsurer with all relevant information about the cession, and (3) pay all reinsurance premiums due from the date the policy should have been ceded.

Normally, the errors and omissions provision covers policies mistakenly ceded even though they exceed the reinsurer's jumbo or automatic binding limits. If the reinsurer determines that it would have declined the risk or if the reinsurer already has reached its retention limit on that case or if the ceding company does not have a facultative treaty with the reinsurer, the reinsurer has no obligation to accept the risk. In such a situation, however, the reinsurer can choose to accept the risk as a goodwill effort, or the ceding company can try to reinsure the risk facultatively with another reinsurer.

Arbitration

Arbitration is the process of resolving a conflict through the use of impartial industry experts, known as arbitrators, who hear the facts as presented by each side and determine an appropriate outcome for the dispute. The arbitration provision of a reinsurance treaty typically specifies that disputes that cannot be solved through negotiation between the parties to the treaty must be resolved through arbitration rather than litigation (legal proceedings). Arbitration is preferable to litigation for four reasons:

1. Arbitration helps ensure that the intentions of the parties when the treaty was established are taken into consideration.

2. Arbitration is seen as a more appropriate way for the parties to handle disagreements because the specific technical issues involved can be more fairly assessed by insurance industry experts than by civil courts.

3. Arbitration is less costly, faster, easier, and more flexible. The American Arbitration Association of New York City Rules of Arbitration, the rules upon which many treaties base the requirements for the arbitration process, allow for more freedom in the procedures and the types of information accepted as admissible than do courts of law.

4. Unlike litigation, arbitration allows the parties to keep confidential business information from becoming a matter of public record.

The arbitration provision usually specifies that three arbitrators be selected to hear the arguments and to make a decision. The provision typically requires that the arbitrators be current or former officers of life insurance companies and usually stipulates that the officers can have no present or former affiliation with either party or their subsidiaries.

In addition, the arbitration provision typically specifies that within 30 days of the selection of the arbitration panel, the arbitrators must choose a date and location for the proceedings. Some treaties specify in advance the location, typically a neutral location and not the city of the home office of either company.

The arbitration provision also requires the three arbitrators to make their decisions based on their interpretation of the terms and conditions of the treaty and on the customs of the insurance industry. The three-person panel is usually required to submit its written decision to both parties within 60 days of the hearing, unless both parties agree to some other time period. The majority decision is final, and no appeal process is possible. The decision is filed with a court having jurisdiction over the parties to the treaty.

The two parties to the treaty generally share expenses for arbitration.

Insolvency

Although the insolvency of either party to a reinsurance treaty is unlikely, occasionally insolvency—a company's inability to meet its debts or to pay policy benefits when they come due—does occur. To protect the interests of the parties and to protect the insureds who rely on the ceding company's financial strength, the insolvency provision describes the rights and responsibilities of the ceding company and the assuming company in the event that either party becomes insolvent.

Insolvency of the Ceding Company

The insolvency provision typically states that, upon the insolvency of the ceding company, the reinsurer is obligated to pay any amounts due to the ceding company's liquidator immediately upon verification that such amounts are rightfully due. In this context, the term *liquidator* refers to a person assigned to handle the affairs of a company as it goes through insolvency proceedings. The reinsurer must pay its part of the claim in full, even if the ceding company has failed to pay all or a portion of any claim.

In addition, the insolvency provision requires the ceding company's liquidator to give the reinsurer adequate notice of any pending claims for which the reinsurer has assumed risk. The reinsurer has the right to investigate any claims at its own expense and to deny claims on behalf of the ceding company, as it deems necessary.

Insolvency of the Assuming Company

The insolvency provision typically requires an insolvent assuming company to notify the ceding company immediately of its insolvency and to provide the ceding company with any applicable documentation. This provision generally gives the ceding company the right to terminate the reinsurance agreement immediately as a consequence of the insolvency of the assuming company and to recapture all reinsured risk within a specified period of time.

The treaty usually requires that the ceding company must notify the reinsurer in writing of its intent to recapture coverage and to specify an effective date for the recapture, generally the date of the reinsurer's insolvency. The ceding company usually needs to arrange for replacement reinsurance before effecting the recapture. The reinsurer remains responsible for any payments due prior to the date of termination.

Key Terms and Concepts

individual cession administration
self administration
bulk administration
reinsurance audit
reinstatement
arbitration

Endnote

1. ACLI, *Life Insurers Fact Book 2000* (Washington, D.C.: American Council of Life Insurers, 2000), 153.

CHAPTER 12

Scope and Organization of Claim Administration

Chapter Outline

Claim Philosophy and Claim Practices

Organization of Claim Administration
- Claim Analyst
- Claim Supervisor
- Claim Support Staff
- Organizing the Workflow in Claim Administration

Authority Levels for Claim Administration

Activities in Claim Administration

Legal Issues Affecting Claim Administration
- Privacy and Confidentiality
- Claim Fraud

Objectives

After reading this chapter, you should be able to

- Describe typical insurance company claim philosophy and practices
- Discuss the typical organization of a claim administration department
- Explain authority levels in claim administration
- Discuss claim administration activities
- Discuss the legal issues affecting claim administration

You have learned that one of the most important results of fair underwriting is protection of both an insurer and its insureds from excessive risk. Similarly, sensible claim practices help ensure that an insurer and its policyowners are not exposed to the risk that will result if the insurer pays inappropriate claims. Effective claim administration fulfills the insurer's responsibilities to its insureds to (1) pay all valid claims promptly and accurately and (2) deny any claim that is not covered or that is fraudulent.

People handling claims are frequently in contact with the insurer's underwriters to verify information submitted with an application or used to make an underwriting decision. The relationship between claim administration and underwriting is so important that many insurers have focused on establishing close ties between these two company functions. Insight 12-1 outlines some of the approaches insurers have used to foster cooperation between claim administration and underwriting.

Claim handling also involves consultation with the insurer's medical and legal staff and with agents or specialized vendors who can help gather or verify information related to a claim. Statistical information generated by the claim function is used by the insurer's actuaries in setting premium rates for existing and new products, as well as by the insurer's auditors in checking the overall accuracy of underwriting decisions by examining the type, size, and frequency of claims submitted under various products. The insurer's product development staff also uses claim information in developing new products.

In this chapter, we'll give you an introduction to claim administration. We'll first explain the importance of an insurer's claim philosophy in guiding its claim practices. Next, we'll define the job accountabilities of a claim analyst, a claim supervisor, and support staff in claim administration, and we'll describe the workflow methods that are normally used. After discussing the authority levels used in claim administration, we'll examine the basic activities involved in claim administration and review the most important legal issues affecting claim administration.

Claim Philosophy and Claim Practices

An insurer's ***claim philosophy*** is a precise statement of the insurer's principles for conducting claim administration. The claim philosophy, which is usually developed for each company by its senior management, guides the decisions made by claim analysts. The claim philosophies of all insurers are focused on rapid, equitable, and courteous administration of claims.

Insight 12-1. Fostering Cooperation Between Claim Administration and Underwriting.

Having a close relationship between claim administration and underwriting helps an insurer manage risk effectively, enhance the accuracy and quality of both underwriting and claim decisions, and therefore compete successfully in a highly competitive environment. Recognizing the importance of this relationship, insurers have taken steps to foster cooperation between claim administration and underwriting by

- Involving staff from underwriting and claim administration during the development of new insurance products, and using data from both functions to evaluate the probable success of a new product
- Using staff from both functions to review policy documents, including applications and claim forms, to check for potential underwriting and claim problems
- Physically locating claim administration and underwriting near each other to facilitate personal communication and data exchanges
- If physical proximity is not possible, enabling both functions to communicate frequently and to consult on problems relating to the cases each is handling
- Providing cross training so that staff gain a deeper knowledge and better understanding of the work requirements and challenges of both functions

Using the insurer's claim philosophy as a basis, the senior management of claim administration develops ***claim practices***, which are expressed as statements that guide the day-to-day handling of claims. The claim practices of most insurers include the following commitments:

- To handle claims on a timely basis and to notify a claimant if an extended time period is necessary to gather information for a claim decision
- To apply the provisions of policies consistently
- To train claim staff so that they can perform their duties professionally and accurately and can document claim handling appropriately
- To investigate questionable claims
- To obtain high-quality medical and legal advice when needed to make a decision on a claim
- To provide claimants with courteous, prompt, and complete explanations of claims for which benefits are not payable or are limited
- To permit claimants to submit additional supporting information on a denied or limited claim
- To provide satisfactory means for appeal of denied claims

FAST FACT

Life insurance companies in the United States paid $74 billion in health insurance benefits in 1999.[1]

The International Claim Association (ICA) has developed and distributed a Statement of Principles that any insurance company may adapt for use in handling claims. The ICA's Statement of Principles is presented in Figure 12-1.

FIGURE 12-1. The International Claim Association's Statement of Principles.

INTERNATIONAL CLAIM ASSOCIATION
STATEMENT OF PRINCIPLES

The International Claim Association, in recognition of the need to continue public trust and confidence in the insurance industry, reaffirms the following principles:

1. Claimants shall receive prompt acknowledgment of communications with respect to their claims.
2. Claimants are entitled to prompt investigation of all facts, and the fair settlement of their claims after liability has become reasonably clear.
3. Member companies shall not impose unnecessary requirements, nor compel claimants to institute unnecessary litigation in order to recover amounts due.
4. Recognizing the obligation to pay promptly all just claims, there is an equal obligation to protect the insurance-buying public from increased costs due to fraudulent or nonmeritorious claims.
5. Claim personnel shall not misrepresent facts or policy provision.
6. Member companies shall maintain accurate insurance claim records and use due care to maintain appropriate levels of confidentiality with respect to information received and maintained.
7. Claim personnel shall be encouraged and assisted in further developing their expertise and professionalism in the field of claim administration.

Source: International Claim Association. Reprinted with permission.

Organization of Claim Administration

The claim function is organized so that tasks are distributed appropriately and so that work can be accomplished efficiently and effectively. A vice president of claim administration usually manages the work of claim administration. In large companies, several senior managers usually are each assigned to handle a particular type of claim. For instance, some insurers establish managers for life, medical and dental, and disability claims, whereas other insurers establish managers for individual and group claims. Insurers that have sold policies to large groups might assign a manager to oversee the claims for those groups, and some insurers establish teams to handle claims.

The day-to-day operations of claim administration are performed by claim analysts, claim supervisors, and support staff. We'll look first at the job accountabilities of these positions, and then we'll discuss the ways that the workflow in claim administration can be organized.

Claim Analyst

At the heart of claim administration is the claim analyst, who evaluates the merits of submitted claims and makes decisions on them. A claim analyst is responsible for a number of activities. Figure 12-2 summarizes some of the duties of a claim analyst.

Claim analysts generally receive extensive training in contract provisions and medical terminology and develop a solid knowledge of the legal considerations affecting claims.

Many insurers establish groups of claim analysts who work together to resolve questions on difficult claims, much as the members of an underwriting team or committee cooperate to assess unusual cases. Some insurers also establish a group of claim analysts who are authorized to approve routine or uncomplicated claims in much the same manner that the jet underwriting unit approves routine applications for insurance.

Many insurers use electronic systems to evaluate and pay routine claims, particularly for health coverages. These systems can receive electronic information, make claim decisions, authorize payment of benefits, generate checks, and send proceeds to policyowners and beneficiaries. No human intervention is necessary for ordinary cases. Any claim that has unusual features that do not exactly match the parameters established for the electronic system is assigned to a claim analyst.

FIGURE 12-2. Duties of a Claim Analyst.

- Analyzing claims to determine the type of coverage held
- Assessing medical information
- Requesting additional information needed to determine benefits
- Determining the person or entity to pay
- Calculating payable benefits
- Explaining claim denials, payments, and contract provisions to agents, clients, beneficiaries, and health care providers

Claim Supervisor

A claim supervisor oversees the work of several claim analysts and support staff and establishes efficient and effective claim handling procedures. The claim supervisor not only handles many difficult and large-amount claims, but also assigns work to claim analysts according to their experience and knowledge.

The claim supervisor usually decides on the type and amount of training needed by each claim analyst and either provides the training personally or arranges to have it provided. If a state department of insurance has received complaints about claim handling, the claim supervisor usually responds to such complaints. The claim supervisor assists actuaries with claim audits, maintains records of products, and generates periodic production reports that show the type and quality of claim decisions made by claim analysts. Finally, the claim supervisor serves as liaison with the insurer's medical director and legal staff and obtains information that claim analysts need to reach decisions.

Claim Support Staff

When claims arrive, in either paper or electronic form, support staff order information needed for a claim decision, establish files and assign case or file numbers to claims, exchange information with other functional areas of the insurance company, and perform other routine actions designed to facilitate the decision-making process. When a claim is approved, support staff ensure that a check is prepared and sent to the person or entity who is to receive benefits. In some insurance companies, support staff also handle telephone calls and electronic mail from clients and agents, and send letters and claim forms to them.

Organizing the Workflow in Claim Administration

The workflow in claim administration is organized according to the type and amount of claims to be administered. Every insurer establishes its own approaches to moving claims through the decision-making process. Systems similar to those used for underwriting can be used to handle claims. Thus, an insurer might choose to allocate claims according to a case assignment system, a work division system, or a combination of the two systems.

When claims are handled by a case assignment system, they are divided according to the type of claim (for example, dental, medical reimbursement, or disability income), the dollar amount of the claim, the geographic area from which a claim is received, or the group under whose coverage a claim is submitted. The claims received from people insured under large group policies can be assigned to one or several claim analysts who specialize in handling only those claims. As with underwriting, each claim analyst is given sufficient authority to approve claims of a certain type and amount. Generally, the more experience a claim analyst has, the higher the amount of claim that person can approve without having the claim reviewed by a more experienced analyst.

Under a work division system, claim staff might work independently to investigate and make decisions on claims, or they might be organized into work units similar to those used for underwriting, including teams and committees. Complicated claims are usually handled by highly experienced claim analysts and claim supervisors and are referred to the insurer's medical staff and legal staff if necessary.

Some insurers establish branch offices whose primary purpose is to administer claims. One of an insurer's branch offices might handle only claims submitted under one type of coverage, and other branch offices might handle claims submitted under other types of coverage. Alternatively, an insurer might send simple claims for small amounts of coverage to one branch office, where the claims can be handled electronically and benefit payments can be sent quickly to insureds or service providers.

Some insurers hire third-party administrators to handle claims, particularly routine claims. Information systems and electronic data interchange (EDI) can speed the claim administration process by sending information rapidly among an insurer and its reinsurers, agents, clients, and other sources of claim information. Insurers also use outside investigative agencies for claims submitted within the contestable period.

The types of files necessary to support claim administration are similar to those used for underwriting. Whether an insurer uses paper or electronic files, or a combination of both, the claim analyst is responsible for maintaining a complete record of the progress and disposition of every claim. Particularly when a claim analyst reaches a decision to deny a claim, full written documentation to support the denial must be made a part of the claim file. Although some claims are completed within a short time, other claims—for example, those for long-term disability—can continue for months or years. The claim analyst updates such files and ensures that their contents are current.

Authority Levels for Claim Administration

Like underwriters, claim analysts are given increasing amounts of decision-making authority as they gain experience and as they demonstrate enhanced ability and quality of judgment. A person who is new to claim administration usually handles small-amount, routine claims that present few difficulties or unusual circumstances. A more senior claim analyst or a claim supervisor normally reviews the new claim analyst's work. As the claim analyst gains more experience, he has more decision-making authority; handles less routine, more challenging cases that involve higher coverage amounts; and performs his work without the review of a more experienced person. Experienced claim analysts and claim supervisors usually process claims that require extensive investigation or consideration.

Because information systems can handle many types of claims quickly, accurately, and cost-effectively, many insurers use them, especially for health claims that require small payments for routine treatments. Claims that do not fit the parameters specified for electronic handling are assigned to claim analysts for assessment and decisions.

Activities in Claim Administration

Claim administration involves several activities that are essentially the same for most types of coverage. Generally, a person or system handling a claim determines whether or not the information submitted on a claim matches the coverage provided by an in-force policy and, on that basis, makes a decision to approve or deny coverage.

In verifying that an insurance contract was in force when an insured-against event occurred, a claim analyst determines the date when coverage began. If coverage is no longer in force, the claim analyst determines the date when coverage ended.

A claim analyst who receives a claim under group coverage verifies that the loss occurred while the coverage was in force and that the person suffering the loss is covered by the group policy. The analyst also verifies that any employment requirements imposed by the policy have been met, that is, that the employee submitting the claim has been employed for the required length of time and has worked at the required location.

FAST FACT

Payments to beneficiaries of group life insurance policies amounted to $15 billion in the United States in 1999.[2]

Legal Issues Affecting Claim Administration

When an insurer denies a life, health, or disability insurance claim, the result can be a lawsuit brought on behalf of a policyowner or a beneficiary. If an insurer is found to have denied coverage properly, the insurer's legal costs are limited to expenses associated with defending the suit. Those expenses, however, can be considerable, as they include not only attorneys' fees and other legal expenses, but also the time required for the insurer's employees to gather information, consult with attorneys, give depositions, and testify in trials. Although insurers generally hire outside legal counsel to present the defense of a suit in court, the insurers often call on their employees, and sometimes on agents, to help the outside legal counsel.

If an insurer is found to have improperly denied a claim, the insurer bears these same expenses and, sometimes, additional costs. A court can require an insurer that has been found to have improperly denied a claim to pay ***extra-contract damages***, which are money awards that exceed the amount of policy benefits and which are compensatory or punitive. ***Compensatory damages*** are money awards to pay a plaintiff for the damage he has suffered from the insurer's wrongdoing. ***Punitive damages*** are money awards intended to punish an insurer that has acted in a malicious, fraudulent, or oppressive manner toward a plaintiff and, thus, to dissuade others from similar behavior.

Many states have adopted the National Association of Insurance Commissioners' (NAIC's) Unfair Claims Settlement Practices Act, which specifies standards for the investigation and handling of claims. The act defines unfair claim practices and notes that such practices are improper if they are (1) committed flagrantly and in conscious disregard of the act or (2) committed with such frequency as to indicate a general business practice to engage in that type of conduct. Figure 12-3 lists the unfair claim practices defined under the act that pertain to life and health insurance.

To protect itself against improper claim denial, an insurer usually provides in-depth, ongoing training about changes in laws and statutes affecting claim administration for all claim supervisors, analysts, and support staff. Two legal issues with which claim analysts must be especially familiar are (1) privacy and confidentiality and (2) claim fraud.

Privacy and Confidentiality

Insurers take great care to protect themselves, the public, and the insurance industry from fraudulent or mistaken claims. However, they also must take care to follow all laws that govern a person's right to privacy. When they investigate claims, analysts must use only lawful, reasonable, and ethical means to obtain information. Many jurisdictions prohibit conducting an investigation under a false pretext. In addition, claim analysts must also protect the confidentiality of information gathered during a claim investigation.

In 1999, Congress passed the ***Financial Services Modernization Act***, more commonly referred to as the ***Gramm-Leach-Bliley (GLB) Act***, which allows convergence among the traditionally separate components of the financial services industry—financial institutions,

FIGURE 12-3. Unfair Claim Practices Defined Under the NAIC's Unfair Claims Settlement Practices Act.

- Knowingly misrepresenting to claimants and insureds relevant facts of policy provisions relating to coverages at issue
- Failing to acknowledge with reasonable promptness pertinent communications with respect to claims arising under policies
- Failing to adopt reasonable standards for the prompt investigation and settlement of claims arising under policies
- Not attempting in good faith to arrive at prompt, fair, and equitable settlement of submitted claims in which liability has become reasonably clear
- Compelling insureds or beneficiaries to institute suits to recover amounts due under policies by offering substantially less than the amounts ultimately recovered in suits brought by insureds or beneficiaries
- Refusing to pay claims without conducting a reasonable investigation
- Failing to affirm or deny coverage of claims within a reasonable time after having completed investigation related to such claims
- Attempting to settle or settling claims for less than the amount to which a reasonable person would believe the insured or beneficiary was entitled by reference to written or printed advertising material accompanying or made part of an application
- Attempting to settle or settling claims on the basis of an application that was materially altered without notice to, or knowledge or consent of, the insured
- Making claim payments to an insured or a beneficiary without indicating the coverage under which each payment is being made
- Unreasonably delaying the investigation or payment of claims by requiring both a formal proof of loss form and subsequent verification that would result in duplication of information and verification appearing in the formal proof of loss form
- Failing in the case of claim denials or offers of compromise settlement to promptly provide a reasonable, accurate explanation of the basis for such actions
- Failing to provide forms necessary to present claims within 15 calendar days of a request with reasonable explanation regarding their use

Source: Adapted from NAIC, *Unfair Claims Settlement Practices Act*, Section 4, 1997. Reprinted with permission from the National Association of Insurance Commissioners.

securities firms, and insurance companies. In broad terms, the GLB Act describes (1) how the financial services industry will be structured in the future and (2) how the financial services industry will be regulated and supervised. The GLB Act also describes the rights of customers to protect the privacy of personal financial information and the remedies for violations of the Act's privacy provisions. Figure 12-4 summarizes the privacy provisions included under Title V of the GLB.

The GLB Act calls upon regulators in each state to enact laws governing specific financial services entities. The National Association of Insurance Commissioners (NAIC) has responded by proposing a

FIGURE 12-4. Privacy Provisions of the Gramm-Leach-Bliley (GBL) Act.

The privacy provisions included under Title V of the GLB require all financial institutions to

- Disclose their privacy policies regarding the sharing of non-public, personal information with both affiliates and third parties. Such disclosure must take place at the time of establishing a customer relationship and not less than annually as long as the relationship continues.
- Notify customers of any sharing of non-public, personal information with nonaffiliated third parties.
- Provide customers with an opportunity to "opt-out" of sharing non-public, personal information subject to certain limited exceptions.

Source: "Summary of Provisions of the Gramm-Leach-Bliley Financial Services Modernization Act," http://www.senate.gov/~banking/conf/grmleach.htm (4 April 2001).

Privacy of Consumer Financial and Health Information Regulation to govern the activities of health care organizations and insurers. State regulations based on the NAIC model would affect the way health care organizations, insurers, and other users share protected financial and health information.

Claim Fraud

Most people who submit insurance claims are honest. Claimants occasionally make mistakes in providing information on claims, but generally their intent is to submit legitimate claims and to receive only legitimate benefits. Unfortunately, some people try to manipulate the claim system to obtain benefits to which they are not entitled.

Claim fraud is an action by which a person intentionally uses false information in an unfair or unlawful attempt to collect benefits under a policy. Claim fraud can be committed by an insured, a beneficiary, a medical caregiver or provider, an agent, an attorney, an employee of an insurance company, or any other person who is in a position to influence a claim decision or to benefit from illicit claim payments. From false billings and bribes to unnecessary and overpriced prescriptions, the varieties of fraud are limited only by the ingenuity of those who intend to take advantage of insurance companies. Figure 12-5 provides some of the warning signs of a fraudulent claim.

Those who submit fraudulent claims drive up the costs of private health insurance and government health coverage programs, increase

FIGURE 12-5. Warning Signs of a Fraudulent Claim.

The medical information on a series of claim forms is exactly the same.

The claimant and physician information seems to be written in the same handwriting.

The claim form submitted is a photocopy, not an original.

White-outs, typeovers, and erasures suggest that the claim form has been altered.

Medical terms are misspelled or inconsistent with the diagnosis or treatment.

In an alleged emergency, the claimant insisted on seeing his own doctor instead of going to a hospital for treatment.

The claimant exhibits unusual knowledge about medical procedures, insurance coverages, and claim handling.

The agent who submitted the application for the coverage also submitted the applications for other people who submitted questionable claims.

The coverage is in the contestable period.

The coverage was issued within the last six months.

The claimant provides a post office box instead of a street address.

The coverage seems to be excessive for the risk.

Instead of actual medical records, a very general statement of diagnosis and treatment is provided.

The claimant does not sign the statement authorizing the insurer to obtain additional information from medical caregivers, MIB, and others.

The claimant threatens involvement of attorneys or the claim analyst's supervisor if the claim is not paid rapidly, or volunteers to come to the insurance company to collect the proceeds.

The format of medical statements provided by the health care provider is not consistent.

The attending physician's statement contains a rubber stamp of the physician's signature or is a photocopy.

A subjective diagnosis such as stress or fatigue is provided.

Information on the claim form is omitted or differs from information in the insurer's files.

The length of treatment and symptoms for a medical diagnosis appear extreme.

Without a logical reason, the claimant consults medical caregivers who do not practice in the claimant's geographic area.

The claimant provides suspiciously detailed or suspiciously vague information and documentation concerning the claim.

The claimant names the same employer, physician, and attorneys as other claimants who have submitted questionable claims.

Source: Adapted from Jane Lightcap Brown and Jennifer W. Herrod, *Reinsurance Administration* (Atlanta: LOMA, © 2000), 211. Used with permission; all rights reserved.

employers' premiums for workers' compensation coverage, and seriously damage the strength and reputation of insurers. Moreover, fraudulent claims can cause insurers to have inadequate funding to pay claims, to lose present or future business because of customer dissatisfaction, and to reduce their staffs. Every insurer has an obligation to protect itself and its insureds from these and other negative outcomes, including the loss of public trust and support that can seriously damage the industry.

Key Terms and Concepts

claim philosophy
claim practices
extra-contract damages
compensatory damages
punitive damages
Financial Services Modernization Act
Gramm-Leach-Bliley (GLB) Act
claim fraud

Endnotes

1. ACLI, *Life Insurers Fact Book 2000* (Washington, D.C.: American Council of Life Insurers, 2000), 98.
2. Ibid., 95.

CHAPTER 13

Administering Life Insurance Claims

Chapter Outline

Handling Life Policy Claims
- Determining Whether a Loss Has Occurred
- Determining Whether a Loss Is Covered
- Gathering Additional Information and Notifying Claimants

Handling Supplemental Life Insurance Coverage
- Waiver of Premium for Disability
- Accidental Death Benefit
- Family Benefit

Calculating Policy Benefit Amounts
- Amount of Death Benefits
- Amount of Additions
- Amount of Deductions
- Adjustments for Misstatements of Age

Paying Benefits Appropriately
- No Named Beneficiary
- Death of the Beneficiary
- Disqualification of the Beneficiary
- Disappearance of the Beneficiary
- Change in Beneficiary
- Assigned Policy Proceeds
- Payment to Attorneys or Tax Collectors
- Unusual Claims
- Settlement Option Administration

Objectives

After reading this chapter, you should be able to

- Explain the importance of a claimant's statement, an authorization to release information, and a death certificate in handling a life insurance claim
- Discuss the claim considerations for handling a death claim involving an insured's disappearance
- Describe the claim considerations for handling a death claim involving suicide
- Discuss the claim handling considerations for coverage that is supplemented by a waiver of premium for disability, an accidental death benefit rider, or family benefit coverage
- Describe how insurers calculate benefits
- Explain how insurers ensure that they pay benefits appropriately

A person filing a claim for life insurance benefits can be a beneficiary of a policy, a person handling the deceased person's estate, or a person representing the interests of minor children or other people needing special assistance. A claim analyst is responsible for ensuring that every claim is paid appropriately. Failure to pay claims accurately can subject the insurer to financial or legal complications and can hinder the insurer's ability to compete effectively.

The steps involved in handling life insurance claims include (1) verifying whether a covered loss has occurred, (2) determining whether supplemental benefits are payable, (3) calculating the amount of policy benefits payable, and (4) ensuring that the benefits are paid to an appropriate person and in an appropriate manner. In this chapter, we'll explain the general procedures involved in handling each of these steps. We'll also discuss some of the special considerations involved in handling life insurance claims accurately and equitably.

Handling Life Policy Claims

After receiving notice of a claim, a claim analyst verifies that the loss has occurred and that the loss is covered under a policy.

Determining Whether a Loss Has Occurred

A beneficiary or an agent usually notifies an insurer of an insured's death by submitting a claimant's statement. A ***claimant's statement***, also called a *claim form,* is a document in which a claimant provides information about the deceased insured, including the date, place, and cause and circumstances of death. The claimant's statement also typically provides

- The names of all physicians or other practitioners who were consulted for any condition related to the deceased insured's cause of death or who were consulted in regard to the deceased insured's health within the past five years

- Information about all of the deceased insured's hospital confinements within the past five years

- The signature of the claimant, an authorized representative, or next of kin on an ***authorization to release information***, a section of the claimant's statement that permits an insurer to obtain claim-specific information from medical caregivers and institutions, government agencies, other insurers, consumer reporting agencies, and other sources

Figure 13-1 shows a typical claimant's statement for life insurance.

FIGURE 13-1. Typical Claimant's Statement for Life Insurance.

Full Name of Deceased	Number	Contract Number(s)

Home Address	City/State/Zip	Home Phone Number ( )
Name of Last Employer	Last Occupation	Date Last Worked
Business Street Address	City/State/Zip	Business Telephone Number ( )
Please indicate desired method of settlement	Was policy assigned?	Are any bankruptcy proceedings now pending against Deceased or any claimants?

CHILDREN OF DECEASED WHO ARE NOW LIVING :		CHILDREN OF DECEASED WHO HAVE DIED:		
Name and Address	Date of Birth	Name	Date of Birth	Date of Death

Date of Death	Cause and Circumstance of Death
Place of Death	

LIST ALL PHYSICIANS OR OTHER PRACTITIONERS CONSULTED FOR ANY CONDITION RELATED TO THE CAUSE OF DEATH

Name	City/State	Dates Consulted

LIST OTHER PHYSICIANS OR PRACTITIONERS CONSULTED IN THE PAST FIVE (5) YEARS

Name	City/State	Reason for Consultation

LIST ALL HOSPITAL CONFINEMENTS IN THE PAST FIVE (5) YEARS

Name	City/State	Reason Confined

CONTINUED ON REVERSE SIDE

Figure 13-1. Typical Claimant's Statement for Life Insurance (continued).

CONTINUED FROM REVERSE SIDE

NAME OF DECEASED: ______________________________

AUTHORIZATION TO RELEASE INFORMATION

Upon presentation of the original or a reproduction of this authorization, I authorize any medical professional, hospital or other medical-care institution, insurance support organization, pharmacy, governmental agency, insurance company, employer, benefit plan administrator, accountant, or financial advisor to provide ABC LIFE INSURANCE COMPANY or any investigative service or other agent acting on its behalf, or an agent, attorney, consumer reporting agency or independent administrator acting on its behalf, information concerning employment, finances or insurance, advice, care or treatment provided the deceased person named above, including information relating to mental illness, use of drugs, use of alcohol, HIV (AIDS virus) and/or sexually transmitted diseases.

NOTICE	Under applicable state law, any person who knowingly files a claim containing false or misleading information, or who conceals information with intent to defraud or mislead an insurance company or other person, may be guilty of a felony or subject to other criminal and/or civil penalties.
NEW YORK RESIDENTS ONLY	Any person who knowingly and with intent to defraud any insurance company or other person files A Statement of Claim containing any materially false information, or conceals for the purpose of misleading, information concerning any fact material thereto, commits a fraudulent insurance act, which is a crime, and shall also be subject to a civil penalty not to exceed five thousand dollars and the stated value of the claim for each such violation.
SIGNATURE OF CLAIMANT	I represent the information on the front of this form is true and complete and I understand that such information will be used by ABC LIFE INSURANCE COMPANY for the purpose of evaluating a claim for insurance benefits.

____

Signature of Claimant, Authorized Representative, or Next of Kin   Date   Age   Social Security Number

____

Claimant's Address   Street   City   State   Zip Code   Phone Number

____

Signature of Estate Representative (if not Claimant)   Date
(Please enclose a certified copy of Letters of Administration)

For claims assistance, please call ABC Life Insurance Company.

MAIL TO: ATTN: LIFE CO. BENEFITS

A claim analyst occasionally has difficulty obtaining a claimant's statement. A beneficiary or the next of kin of a deceased insured may be unwilling to sign the statement and to authorize collection of information about the insured. Usually the claim analyst tries to persuade the people closest to the insured to cooperate. In extreme situations in which no one cooperates with the investigation, the claim analyst may obtain a court order specifying what information can be obtained and the sources that can be used in gathering it.

Even when a claim analyst obtains a completed claimant's statement, the analyst can have difficulty obtaining detailed information from some sources. Concerns about patient privacy and confidentiality cause some medical caregivers to refuse to give insurers copies of a patient's entire medical file or to edit the medical records before releasing the information to the insurer. In some situations, attorneys or claimants try to control the information by requesting that all information is sent to them before it is sent to the insurer. The claim analyst then challenges the request to maintain the objectivity of information sources.

After receiving the claimant's statement, the claim analyst collects proof of loss to verify that the insured-against loss has occurred. A typical proof of loss is a death certificate. A ***death certificate*** is a document that attests to the death of a person and that bears the signature—and sometimes the seal—of an official authorized to issue such a certificate. Because of concerns about protecting the privacy of individuals and of ensuring the confidentiality of sensitive information, death certificates in some jurisdictions list only "natural causes" rather than specifying the cause of death as being from a particular disease. Most insurers in the United States accept an official death certificate, either an original or a certified copy, as proof of loss. Most Canadian insurers accept an official death certificate, an APS, a coroner's certificate of death, or a hospital's certificate of death as proof of the death of an insured.

In some circumstances, an insurer requires additional evidence such as newspaper clippings or an autopsy report. Certain jurisdictions have held that an insurer must accept as proof of death a document that attests to the death of an insured and that is signed by a person with knowledge of the insured's death. In such circumstances, the insurer generally obtains copies of official death records, if any are available, to corroborate information in the unofficial document.

If the age of a deceased is in question—for example, if the age on the death certificate is different from the age in the policy records or on the application—the claim analyst usually asks for a birth certificate or other acceptable proof of age. If an insured has died outside North America, or if an insured has disappeared and death can only be presumed, the claim analyst follows different courses of action.

Death Outside North America

Claim analysts sometimes have difficulty establishing that a loss has occurred when the insured dies outside North America. Because formalities and procedures for registration of death in other countries are not always as rigorous as those in the United States and Canada, situations in which the insured dies abroad increase the likelihood of fraud. Therefore, additional investigation and care are usually required to verify the validity of the claim. If documents offered as proof of death are in a language other than English, the claim analyst must have a qualified person translate the documents.

Disappearance of the Insured

Occasionally an insured person's death must be presumed because the person has disappeared. If a claim involves a death resulting from a specific peril that can account for an insured's disappearance, and if no other suspicious circumstances exist, the claim analyst generally approves the claim. For example, suppose a Boy Scout leader takes a group of Scouts on a hike in the mountains. A sudden thunderstorm causes flooding, and the Scouts see their leader swept away in a torrent. His body is not recovered. In such a situation, if the body were not found after a reasonable period and if no evidence of foul play were found, the claim analyst would more than likely approve the claim.

If an insured has disappeared without either a specific peril or definite proof of death, the claimant cannot provide proof of death in support of the life insurance claim. Without such proof the insurer is unable to pay the policy benefits without further investigation. However, if an insured has been continually absent from his home for a specified period, seven years in most jurisdictions, an insurer or a claimant can apply to a court for an order presuming death. If the court evaluates the evidence and is satisfied that the insured is more than likely deceased, the court issues a ***presumptive death certificate***, which is a court-issued document stating that a person is presumed to be dead. Figure 13-2 lists the four elements that the court considers before issuing a presumptive death certificate.

However, if opposing evidence is submitted showing that the insured may still be alive, the case is usually referred to a jury for a decision. When a claim analyst receives a presumptive death certificate, any proceeds due on a death claim are processed according to the date of death shown on the court order.

If through investigation the claim analyst locates an insured person who does not want to have her whereabouts revealed, the claim analyst respects the insured's wishes. The claim analyst can, however, justify nonpayment of insurance benefits only by obtaining a signed, dated,

FIGURE 13-2. Considerations for Issuing a Presumptive Death Certificate.

1. Whether the insured has been missing from his home or usual residence for seven years
2. Whether the insured's absence has been continuous and whether any factors such as large debts, marital problems, or criminal indictments exist that would give cause for the disappearance
3. Whether the insured can be located by diligent search and inquiry
4. Whether the people most likely to hear from the insured have not heard from him

and notarized statement from the insured attesting to identifying information such as date of birth, place of birth, and the names of such people as the insured's parents, spouse, and children.

Reappearance of the Insured

Suppose an insured has been declared dead by a court and the insurer has paid the policy proceeds in full. If the insured person later reappears, the insurer usually has the right to recover the money because it was paid under a mistake of fact. If the insurer paid less than the full amount of benefits in a compromise settlement, however, the insurer generally cannot recover the benefits because courts will not disturb a compromise settlement.

Determining Whether a Loss Is Covered

In deciding whether the insurer is liable to pay benefits for a loss, the claim analyst first determines the status of the policy and verifies the insured's identity. Then the analyst examines all policy exclusions, including those for aviation, avocations, and suicide. If a proposed insured's death has occurred during underwriting and before the policy has been delivered, the analyst determines whether the insurer is liable for paying benefits.

Aviation Exclusion

Recall from Chapter 5 that aviation exclusion riders are typically used in cases in which the aviation hazard (1) is too great for any coverage, (2) cannot be measured, or (3) the policyowner does not want to pay a higher premium for the policy. If a policy contains an aviation exclusion and the insured dies while engaged in the excluded activity, benefits are limited to the sum of premiums paid or the cash surrender value, whichever is greater.

Avocation Exclusion

An avocation exclusion typically covers activities, such as skydiving, auto racing, and rock climbing, that are considered dangerous. An avocation exclusion usually provides that, if an insured dies from participation in a specified avocation, no death benefits—or, if the policy so states, only limited death benefits—will be payable.

Suicide Exclusion

If an insured person dies as a result of verified suicide, the claim analyst checks the policy to determine the period during which a death by suicide is ineligible for coverage under the policy. Most jurisdictions provide for a two-year suicide exclusion period. Generally, this period begins in the United States on the date of original policy issue. If the original policy lapses and is reinstated, in most jurisdictions the period still is considered to have begun on the date when the original policy was issued. In Canada, although the suicide exclusion period begins on the date of policy issue, if a policy has been reinstated, this period begins again on the date the policy is reinstated. The length of the new suicide exclusion period is the same as the length of the original period.

> **FAST FACT**
>
> In 1997, 1.3% of deaths in the United States were due to suicide.[1]

If the claim analyst determines that an insured died by suicide within the exclusion period, the insurer returns only the premiums paid and does not pay policy benefits. Returning the premiums paid is considered to be payment of the limited benefit agreed upon when the application for insurance was submitted and when the insurer accepted the risk. Returning the premiums is not considered to be a refund, and the insurer is not considered to have rescinded the coverage. By invoking the suicide exclusion, the insurer is not contesting the policy nor attempting to rescind it, but instead is affirming the validity of the contract by applying the limited-benefit-for-death-by-suicide provision in the contract. During the investigation of a death by suicide, the claim analyst is governed by the statutes of the jurisdiction in which the coverage was issued.

In establishing that a person committed suicide, an investigator must establish the existence of and show a direct relationship among (1) the deceased's intention to commit suicide, (2) the deceased's self-destructive action, and (3) the death resulting from that action. If an insurer denies a claim for basic death benefits under a life insurance policy based on the suicide exclusion and is sued, most jurisdictions require that the insurer bear the burden of showing that the insured committed suicide. In a case in which the facts indicate that an insured committed suicide, but no definite proof of suicide is discovered, courts generally have held that the death is not a result of suicide. Concerning benefits for accidental death, however, most jurisdictions require that the claimant or beneficiary bear the burden of showing that the cause of death was not suicide, but was the result of an accident.

Death of the Proposed Insured During Underwriting

When a proposed insured dies after his application has been submitted but before underwriting has been completed and the policy issued, claim administration and underwriting must work together closely to ensure that an equitable decision is made concerning payment of policy benefits. Information in the application and the circumstances of the death help determine whether the insurer is liable to pay policy proceeds.

Most individual life insurance applications and premium receipts contain a ***change in health statement*** that requires a proposed insured to notify the insurer in writing if her health or any material information in the application changes before the policy is delivered. Some insurers require the agent and the policyowner to sign a change in health statement at the time the policy is delivered. The change in health statement helps protect an insurer against antiselection that might result if an insured's health changes significantly during underwriting, and particularly if the insured dies during that period from such a health change. A typical change in health statement is shown in Figure 13-3.

To deny policy benefits because of a change in the proposed insured's health during the time of underwriting, most jurisdictions require the insurer to show that (1) the change in health directly affected the degree of risk for the case, (2) the proposed insured knew of the change in health, and (3) no ambiguity exists in the change in health statement. If a proposed insured dies as the result of a sudden event such as an accident or an acute condition about which the proposed insured had no prior knowledge, benefits are payable under the policy if a temporary

FIGURE 13-3. Typical Change in Health Statement.

I understand that no policy based on this application will be effective unless all of my statements and answers in the application continue to be true as of the date I receive the policy. I understand that if my health changes or any of my answers or statements change prior to delivery of the policy, I must so inform the insurer in writing.

insurance agreement was issued and may be payable if a conditional premium receipt was issued.

Although suicide is excluded during the suicide exclusion period by a statement in the life insurance contract, during underwriting, no contract has yet been issued. To determine what action to take if a proposed insured commits suicide during underwriting, most insurers rely on the language of the premium receipt, which should state clearly that coverage under the receipt will be effective subject to the limitations contained in the policy applied for—and such a policy would contain the suicide exclusion provision.

Gathering Additional Information and Notifying Claimants

After determining that a loss has occurred and that the loss is covered, the claim analyst next gathers whatever additional information is needed to make a decision on the claim for life insurance benefits. Particularly if the policy is still contestable, the claim analyst gathers such information as medical records, motor vehicle reports, and criminal court records and may also order an investigative consumer report.

During the course of investigating the claim, the claim analyst informs the claimant of progress by sending status letters. If the claim analyst discovers information that indicates misrepresentation or fraud, the analyst explains the effect of misrepresentation or fraud on the claim decision and cites the sources of information on which the decision was based. If the claim is denied, the analyst sends the claimant a denial letter explaining that if the claimant can provide additional information that might refute the information on which the denial was based, the insurer will consider such information in reexamining the claim.

Handling Supplemental Life Insurance Coverage

As we explained in Chapter 6, the insurance protection provided by most life insurance policies can be expanded by supplemental benefit riders, including those for waiver of premium for disability, accidental death benefit, and family benefit coverage. If such supplemental riders are involved in a claim, the claim analyst determines whether additional benefits are due under the policy.

Waiver of Premium for Disability

If a person becomes totally disabled and is insured under a life insurance policy that includes a waiver of premium for disability (WP) rider, the insurer waives payment of all premiums that become due during the period of disability. If an insured claims benefits under a WP rider, the claim analyst first verifies that the claimant has satisfied the waiting period, if any is required, and then verifies that the claimant is in fact totally disabled according to the definition in the rider. To make this determination, the claim analyst typically uses such tools as the claim form, the disability information form, the claimant's medical records, including the Attending Physician's Statement, the claimant's financial records, and the claimant's job description and statements from the claimant's employer. If a claimant in the United States has been awarded Social Security disability benefits, the claim analyst obtains a copy of the Social Security Award letter from the insured.

The disability information form submitted by the claimant contains such information as

- The initial date of disability
- The claimant's occupation
- Additional sources, if any, of disability income, including names and addresses of providers of such benefits

Initial review of a disability claim is especially important if the disability appears to be one that will continue for a year or longer. The experience of most insurers indicates that disabilities lasting one year or more are likely to continue past two years. Therefore, gathering information on a potentially long-term claim is essential to ensure that the claim is valid.

If the claim analyst finds that the claimant has also filed a claim for disability income coverage or a waiver of premium request with another insurer, the claim analyst usually sends a letter of inquiry to the other insurer to verify the claim-related information. Sometimes the other insurer will have information that will enable the claim analyst to make a rapid judgment on the claim. In addition, the claim analyst verifies that if the life insurance policy contained waivers of coverage for participation in certain activities, such as specified dangerous avocations, the disability did not result from such participation.

Most insurers review each active waiver of premium case at least annually to determine whether the claimant is still disabled and eligible to receive the benefits of the waiver of premium rider, and to certify that the total of claims paid has not exceeded the maximum benefit payable, if the coverage has such a limit. Claims for disabilities that the insurer's experience has shown are usually short-term may be reviewed more frequently, usually every three to six months. Generally, a claim analyst telephones the claimant at home or at work to ask about the claimant's medical condition and to check the type of work, if any, that the claimant is able to perform. If a claimant does not supply proof of continued disability, most insurers notify the claimant that she is being removed from waiver status and that she will be responsible for paying future life insurance premiums if she wants the coverage to remain in force.

Waiver of premium claimants who have received benefits for two years are generally classified in one of two ways:

1. Claimants who show little possibility of eventual rehabilitation
2. Claimants who may be expected to improve or for whom new medical treatments may promise partial or complete recovery

The claim analyst usually verifies the continuing status of a claimant in the first group by obtaining a statement annually from the claimant's medical caregiver. For a claimant in the second group, the claim analyst typically continues to update the case annually, gathering information to demonstrate the claimant's current condition and ability to work and pay life insurance premiums.

When a claim analyst handles a waiver of premium claim submitted under group coverage, the claim analyst checks two additional items. First, the analyst determines whether the claimant has satisfied the group policy's actively-at-work provision and the employee class definition, if any. If the claim analyst finds that the employee's disability began before the original effective date of the group coverage, the analyst usually does not approve waiver of premium benefits. Second, the claim analyst determines that the claimant satisfies the policy's definition of full-time employee, if the coverage is only for such employees. To make such a determination, the claim analyst examines payroll records and the employee's enrollment card.

Accidental Death Benefit

The purpose of the accidental death benefit (ADB) rider is to provide an additional death benefit above the face amount of the policy if the insured's death occurs as the result of an accident. An insurer may charge an extra premium for ADB coverage issued to people who have hazardous occupations or may decline to issue the ADB rider.

Some policies contain accidental death benefit provisions with certain limitations related to the insured's age, the time span during which death occurred, and the proximate cause of death. For instance, an accidental death benefit provision may specify that benefits will be paid only until age 70. A beneficiary of an insured who dies at age 71 cannot, therefore, expect accidental death benefits to be paid under the policy. Most insurers specify 90 days as the maximum time span allowed between an injury and a death to qualify the death as accidental, although some policies allow longer periods. Some cases can present conflicting information about the ***proximate cause*** of a death—that is, the event that directly caused a death or the event that led to an unbroken chain of events resulting in death. For instance, an insured might have suffered a heart attack or a stroke—a natural event—that resulted in a fatal vehicle accident or other mishap. In such a case, the claim analyst examines the autopsy report and medical records to ascertain the immediate cause of death. If the death resulted from the natural event, no accidental death benefits would be payable. If the death resulted from the mishap, accidental death benefits would probably be payable.

FAST FACT

In 1997, 4.2% of deaths in the United States resulted from accidents and motor vehicle accidents.[2]

Family Benefit

An insured with individual life insurance coverage may add a family benefit rider to insure the lives of a spouse and children. Such a rider usually provides coverage in a lesser amount on the spouse and each child than on the primary insured. After a policy with such a rider is issued, children who are born or adopted into the family, or who become part of the family by marriage, are usually covered when they reach the age of at least 15 days (or whatever minimum age the rider specifies). A family benefit rider usually covers a child born in or out of wedlock, but this type of rider generally does not cover foster children.

When a life insurance claim is submitted under a family benefit rider, the claim analyst verifies that the deceased is either a spouse or a natural child, adopted child, or stepchild of the primary insured. The documents that the claim analyst uses for such verification include a marriage certificate, a birth certificate, or an adoption certificate.

Calculating Policy Benefit Amounts

In figuring the amount of life insurance benefits to be paid to a claimant, the claim analyst determines three amounts: (1) the amount of the basic death benefit, (2) the amount of any additions to that figure, and (3) the amount of any deductions from that figure. The claim analyst checks many details of the coverage, including information about policy dividends, policy loans, policy premiums, additional coverage and accidental death benefits, and various kinds of interest.

The analyst may also adjust the amount of policy benefits for misstatements of age.

Amount of Death Benefits

The amount of the death benefit due upon the death of the insured is based on the face amount of the policy. The claim analyst begins, therefore, by determining the amount of the basic death benefit payable. Usually the basic death benefit is the face amount of the policy. However, if the policy application contained a misstatement of age, the policy's face amount will be adjusted to account for the misstatement, as we'll discuss later in this chapter.

FAST FACT

In Canada in 1999, death benefits under life insurance policies accounted for over $3.3 billion, including $22 million of additional benefits paid for accidental deaths as provided for in some life insurance policies.[3]

Amount of Additions

The claim analyst next determines any amounts that should be added to the amount of basic death benefits. See Figure 13-4 for a list of the amounts that can be added to basic death benefits.

We'll provide an example of how additions to a death benefit are calculated in the next section.

FIGURE 13-4. Amounts Added to Basic Death Benefits.

- Paid-up additional insurance
- Accidental death benefits
- Excess premiums paid in advance
- Policy dividends not yet paid
- Policy dividends left with the insurer to earn interest
- Interest on delayed claims payment
- Loan interest paid in advance

Amount of Deductions

The claim analyst might also deduct certain amounts from the basic death benefit, including

- Premiums due but unpaid during the grace period
- Loans against the policy
- Unpaid interest on any policy loans

If the insured died during the grace period and had neglected to pay the premium due by the end of that period, the amount of premiums due would be subtracted from the death benefit. Further, if the policyowner had taken out a loan against the policy, the amount of the loan and any interest on that loan would be deducted from the amount of the death benefit. Insight 13-1 provides an example that illustrates additions to and deductions from a death benefit.

Insight 13-1. Calculating Additions to and Deductions from Death Benefit.

Suppose that Malcolm Wright purchased a life insurance policy in the amount of $200,000 plus a $150,000 accidental death benefit rider. The policy bore no dividends. Later, Malcolm chose to buy $60,000 of additional coverage. At the time of Malcolm's death, which resulted from an accident, he (1) had paid $500 in advance premiums and (2) had an outstanding policy loan of $22,000 plus $1,500 of interest on that loan. The claim analyst would calculate the total benefit payable under this policy as follows:

Face value of policy	$200,000
+ ADB rider	+ 150,000
+ Additional coverage	+ 60,000
+ Premium paid in advance	+ 500
– Unpaid policy loan	– 22,000
– Unpaid interest on policy loan	– 1,500
Total death benefit payable	**$387,000**

Adjustments for Misstatements of Age

As you have learned, the premium for most individual life insurance policies is affected by the age of the insured. Similarly, life insurance premiums for small-group coverage may require individual premiums that are affected by the age of each insured person. In either situation, when a life insurance claim is submitted, the claim analyst verifies the age of the deceased insured to be certain that the premiums paid have accurately reflected the amount of risk borne by the insurer. If the claim analyst determines that the age of the insured was misstated on the application for insurance, and if a different age on the application would have resulted in a different premium being charged, then the analyst adjusts the amount of death benefits appropriately. Such an adjustment is permitted throughout the life of the policy and is not affected by the incontestability clause.

Generally, an adjustment for misstatement of age results in a death benefit amount equal to the death benefit that the premium paid would have purchased at the correct age, according to the insurer's published premium rates at the time of policy issue. Insight 13-2 provides an example that illustrates how an insurer would calculate the death benefit if an insured's age were misstated.

Insight 13-2. Calculating the Death Benefit with a Misstatement of Age.

Suppose that Genevieve Montague mistakenly stated her age as 34 when she purchased $150,000 of whole life insurance. She was charged an annual premium of $1.42 per thousand, or $213 ($1.42 × 150).

At the time of her death, the claim analyst discovered a discrepancy between Genevieve's age as stated on the application and her age at time of death—in fact, the insured was 43 years old when she applied for coverage. According to the insurer's published premium rates at the time of policy issue, the paid premium of $213 a year would have purchased $136,000 of whole life insurance. Therefore, the amount of death benefit due is $136,000, plus and minus any additions or deductions.

If Genevieve's age had been lower than 34 at the time of application, the amount of coverage that the premium purchased would have been more than $150,000; in that situation, the claim analyst would adjust the amount of the death benefit upward accordingly.

The burden of showing that an insured was *older*—at the time of the application—than the age stated on the application rests with the insurer. The burden of showing that an insured was *younger*—at the time of the application—than the age stated on the application or than the age calculated by the insurer rests with the claimant. Proof of an insured's age can be established by various documents, including

- A copy of the insured's birth certificate or birth record
- A certificate of baptism, bar or bat mitzvah, or other religious ceremony that establishes the insured's age at the time of the ceremony
- A record of birth written in a family Bible

In addition to checking age information on the claim form and using the sources we have mentioned, the claim analyst also attempts to verify an insured's correct age by noting such elements as

- The ages of the insured's children
- The date when the insured retired
- Records of government- or employer-paid retirement benefits

Besides increasing or decreasing the death benefits payable, an adjustment for age sometimes causes an insured to be ineligible to receive certain benefits. If the accidental death benefit, for instance, is payable only until an insured reaches a specified age, usually 65 or 70, then an insured whose age at death exceeds the limit will probably not be eligible for the accidental death benefit.

Paying Benefits Appropriately

The claim analyst must determine the right person or entity to receive the death benefits and the correct manner in which the benefits are to be paid. Usually the beneficiary—a spouse, a child or children, an estate, a trust, a charity, or almost any other entity—is clearly named on the insurance application. However, a number of circumstances can complicate the claim analyst's responsibility to ensure that the benefits are paid to the correct person. These circumstances include situations in which no named beneficiary exists; the named beneficiary has died, been disqualified, or disappeared; a change in beneficiary has occurred; policy proceeds have been assigned; payment is made to attorneys or tax collectors; or unusual circumstances exist that require special handling of policy proceeds. After we examine these complicating circumstances involving determination of the right payee, we'll briefly discuss the administration of settlement options used for paying policy benefits.

No Named Beneficiary

If a policy does not name a beneficiary, the claim analyst usually designates the benefits as payable to the estate of the deceased insured. According to the laws of some jurisdictions, however, in such a situation the policy proceeds are payable to a designated class of beneficiaries who become eligible when no beneficiary has been named or when no named beneficiary survives the insured.

Death of the Beneficiary

If the beneficiary named in an insurance policy has predeceased the insured, the claim analyst checks the application and other information in the case file to determine whether an alternate beneficiary was named. Such a beneficiary, called a ***contingent beneficiary*** or *secondary beneficiary,* is the person or entity named to receive life insurance benefits if the primary beneficiary has died before the insured. If no contingent beneficiary was named, the proceeds are paid to the policyowner or the policyowner's estate.

Disqualification of the Beneficiary

A beneficiary who is deliberately responsible for the death of an insured is legally disqualified from receiving policy proceeds. If an insurer can show that the beneficiary applied for insurance on the life of the insured with the intent of profiting from the insured's death, then the insurer is required to return only the amount of premiums paid with interest. If, however, the policy was applied for in good faith, but the designated beneficiary is judged to have been deliberately responsible for the insured's death, then the insurer must pay the policy proceeds, but not to that designated beneficiary.

The insurer usually delays payment of the proceeds until the investigation into the insured's death is complete. If the investigation continues for a long period, the insurer generally deposits the amount of policy proceeds with a court for disbursement after a legal decision has been reached concerning the beneficiary's guilt or innocence. In some situations, the insurer is allowed to pay the proceeds to a contingent beneficiary or to the insured's estate instead of paying the proceeds to a beneficiary if that beneficiary has been convicted of murdering the insured. A verdict of "not guilty" in a criminal action is separate from the verdict in a civil suit, so that a beneficiary found not guilty in a criminal case can be denied policy proceeds if he is held in a civil trial to have wrongfully caused the insured's death.

Disappearance of the Beneficiary

If a named beneficiary has disappeared and cannot be located within a reasonable period, the insurer generally follows the laws and statutes prevailing in the state or province in which the beneficiary's last address is located. Most states have adopted variations of the NAIC Uniform Disposition of Unclaimed Property Act, which requires an insurer to hold the proceeds for a specified period—typically five to seven years—and then deposit with the state all proceeds that cannot be paid to a missing beneficiary. The state holds the money in trust for such a beneficiary, who may petition the state for the property. In all the Canadian provinces except Quebec, an insurer deposits unpayable proceeds with a court, which then determines the proper payee. In Quebec, three years after proceeds become payable, insurers are required by law to deposit proceeds payable to untraceable beneficiaries with the ***public curator***, a person authorized to handle the affairs of missing people, among others.

Change in Beneficiary

When an insured has changed the beneficiary of a policy, the claim analyst verifies that the change was accurately made and that the new beneficiary is eligible to receive the policy proceeds. Almost every beneficiary is a ***revocable beneficiary***—that is, a beneficiary whose right to policy proceeds can be canceled or reduced by the policyowner at any time before the insured's death. At the time the insured dies, the insurer will pay the policy proceeds to the beneficiary named in the policy. If a policyowner has named an ***irrevocable beneficiary***—that is, a beneficiary whose right to policy proceeds cannot be canceled by a policyowner unless that beneficiary consents to the cancellation—then the insurer must pay the benefits to that irrevocable beneficiary. Only when an irrevocable beneficiary dies or signs a release can the policyowner name another beneficiary.

In Canada, before July 1, 1962, a spouse, child, parent, or grandchild named in any life insurance policy issued before July 1, 1962, was considered a ***preferred beneficiary***, and the policyowner could not change the beneficiary to anyone outside this group of family members and could neither obtain a policy loan nor surrender nor assign the policy benefits without the written consent of the preferred beneficiary. The rights of a preferred beneficiary continue until that beneficiary dies, is divorced from the spouse-insured, or signs a release. Policies issued in Canada after July 1, 1962, do not have to follow the legal concept of preferred beneficiaries. However, a claim analyst must follow the earlier law for claims arising from any policies issued before July 1, 1962.

In both the United States and Canada, if the claim analyst determines that the person who made the beneficiary change was mentally incompetent, then the change is legally ineffective, and the original beneficiary receives the policy proceeds. If a former beneficiary wishes to challenge a change of beneficiary, the burden is upon the former beneficiary to prove the incompetence of the policyowner to make the change. The claim analyst is not legally bound, however, to question the competence of every policyowner who changes a beneficiary. If an insurer pays the policy proceeds to a new beneficiary and then discovers later that the beneficiary change was made by an incompetent policyowner, the insurer is usually not bound by law to pay the proceeds a second time to the original beneficiary.

FAST FACT

During 1999, life insurers in the United States paid $41 billion to beneficiaries of policyowners who died.[4]

Assigned Policy Proceeds

Some or all of the rights to receive the proceeds of a life insurance policy can be transferred to another person or entity, such as a business or a trust, by means of an ***assignment***. An ***absolute assignment*** is an irrevocable transfer of all the rights of a life insurance policy from one party to another. A ***collateral assignment*** is a transfer of some ownership rights from one party to another, usually for a temporary period. For example, insurance policies are often assigned as collateral for the balance due on a loan, and, after the loan is paid, all rights under the policy return to the policyowner. The claim analyst generally checks to see that no outstanding absolute or collateral assignment exists.

Payment to Attorneys or Tax Collectors

If an attorney notifies a claim analyst that he represents a claimant, the analyst usually sends the proceeds to the attorney for subsequent payment to the claimant. Some insurers prefer to make checks for such payments payable to the claimant, and others make the checks payable jointly to the claimant and the attorney.

If an insured owes taxes, a tax collector cannot legally collect policy proceeds to satisfy the tax debt. A tax collector can, however, lay claim to the cash value of a life insurance policy as payment for unpaid federal income taxes. A claim analyst may need to consult with the insurer's legal department to determine appropriate treatment for complex tax collection issues.

Unusual Claims

A claim analyst occasionally encounters a claim that has unusual characteristics or that requires special handling. Such unusual claims may involve adverse claimants, community-property laws, divorce, simultaneous deaths, or accelerated death benefits.

Adverse Claimants

When a claim analyst receives conflicting claims from two or more claimants, the analyst (1) consults with the insurer's legal department and (2) conducts a thorough claim investigation according to the insurer's established procedures for handling adverse claimants. During the investigation, the analyst notifies the adverse claimants of the conflicting claims and provides each claimant with complete information about the facts of the case, including details about the beneficiary designations, policy provisions, assignments, and any other relevant information.

If the claimants can reach a resolution between themselves, the claim analyst must obtain written notice of their decision and pay the policy proceeds in accordance with that decision. If the claimants cannot reach such a resolution, however, the insurer typically initiates an ***interpleader***, a claim settlement method by which an insurer pays the proceeds to a court, advises the court that the insurer cannot determine the correct party to whom the proceeds should be distributed, and asks the court to decide the proper recipient or recipients. The insurer uses an interpleader only when it acknowledges that it is liable for paying benefits, not when it is contesting a claim. Particularly when a claimant sues the insurer for the proceeds, most insurers immediately respond with interpleader in order to have an appropriate decision made by the court.

Community-Property Laws

If a policyowner lives in a state governed by community-property laws, the claim analyst must consider those laws in determining the correct beneficiary. ***Community-property laws*** provide that a spouse is entitled to receive an equal share of earned income and an equal share of property acquired by the other spouse during a marriage. When a person dies in a state governed by community-property laws, the spouse is entitled to at least half of all community property. When a person applies for and is issued an insurance policy on her life during marriage and pays the premium with community property funds, the policy is considered to be community property. The policy proceeds are also community property if the beneficiary is the estate of the insured or someone other than the spouse. If the beneficiary is the policyowner's spouse, the proceeds are usually considered the spouse's separate property.

If a policyowner-insured who is a resident of a community-property state dies and leaves all life insurance proceeds to the spouse, the claim analyst has no problem in determining the beneficiary. But suppose that a deceased policyowner-insured who had been living in a community-property state selected someone other than the spouse to receive life insurance benefits.

Community-property states have passed ***exculpatory statutes***, which are laws that permit an insurer to pay life insurance proceeds according to the terms of a policy without fear of double liability. If the insurer has received prior written notice of a conflicting claim, the insurer must respond to that notice. Otherwise, the insurer is legally liable to pay the policy proceeds to the named beneficiary, regardless of other conditions. To prevent possible conflict resulting from appearing to ignore or avoid a spouse's legal property right, however, insurers generally obtain a release from a surviving spouse before paying policy proceeds above a certain amount—usually $10,000—to anyone other than the spouse.

Divorce

When a claim analyst handles a life insurance claim on the life of a divorced spouse who did not change the beneficiary designation from her former spouse, under the laws of most jurisdictions, the analyst pays the proceeds to the former spouse. However, some states have divorce statutes that automatically remove a former spouse as beneficiary unless the former spouse is renamed as beneficiary after the divorce or in the divorce decree. If a divorce decree specifies that a policyowner-insured must continue to pay premiums on life insurance and names the divorced spouse as beneficiary, no problem exists if the policyowner-insured complies with the decree requirements.

However, sometimes the policyowner-insured continues to pay premiums, but names someone other than the former spouse as beneficiary. In such a situation, if the claim analyst has received no notice of a new beneficiary and pays the policy proceeds to the former spouse as beneficiary, the insurer is not liable to pay benefits a second time if the new beneficiary submits a claim.

Simultaneous Deaths

In some situations, an insured and the primary beneficiary die simultaneously. If the claim analyst cannot determine with certainty the order of death, insurers generally apply laws designed to handle this problem. State simultaneous death acts in the United States are patterned on the Uniform Simultaneous Death Act drafted by the National Conference of Commissioners on Uniform State Laws; in all Canadian provinces except Quebec, it is the Uniform Life Insurance Act; and in Quebec, it is the Quebec Insurance Act.

According to these laws, when both the insured and the primary beneficiary die at the same time and the order of their deaths cannot be determined, the insurer is to presume that the insured survived the beneficiary—that is, the beneficiary died first. Paying the policy proceeds under this presumption may require payment to the insured's estate or to another named beneficiary. To cover situations in which a beneficiary survives an insured by a brief time, some policies use a ***survivorship clause***, also called a *common disaster clause* or *time clause,* which provides payment of proceeds to the beneficiary if the beneficiary lives longer than the insured for at least a specified period such as 10 days or 30 days.

Accelerated Death Benefits

Some insurers offer life insurance policyowners who are also the insureds the option of taking an accelerated death benefit. You'll recall from our discussion in Chapter 7 that an accelerated death benefit is a portion of a policy's benefits paid during life to a terminally ill policyowner-insured who has a remaining life expectancy of less than a specified period, usually ranging between six months and two years. When the policyowner-insured dies, the amount of the death benefit payable under the policy to the named beneficiary is reduced by the amount of the accelerated death benefit that was paid out to the policyowner-insured. Each insurer that offers an accelerated death benefit option designs its own requirements and benefit payout percentages, but the usual range is between 60 and 80 percent of the basic life benefit.

In administering claims for the accelerated death benefit, most insurers are concerned with establishing eligibility, accurately handling irrevocable beneficiaries and absolute assignments, and avoiding fraud. Determining a policyowner-insured's eligibility for the accelerated death benefit requires that the policyowner-insured meet the insurer's definition of terminal illness and of life expectancy. If a policyowner-insured has named an irrevocable beneficiary or has made an absolute assignment of policy proceeds, the claim analyst must obtain a signed acknowledgment of payment of an accelerated death benefit from the people affected. Because only a portion of the death benefit is accelerated, the policy continues to provide some degree of protection for beneficiaries and assignees. If a policyowner-insured wants to receive accelerated death benefits during a policy's contestable period, the claim analyst helps to prevent fraud by verifying every element of the claim and the policyowner-insured's medical condition before approving the payment of benefits.

Settlement Option Administration

A life insurance policy provides certain options for the way the proceeds are paid to the beneficiary upon the death of the insured. The most common of these options include paying the benefits in a lump sum, paying the benefits in installments during a fixed or lifetime period, and paying the benefits in fixed amounts. Some policies allow a beneficiary to leave the proceeds with the insurance company to earn interest for a certain period before the principal is disbursed.

If the insured or the beneficiary chooses payment of a lump sum, the claim analyst requests a check to be made payable to the beneficiary and sees that the payment is sent to the beneficiary or to a bank or other financial institution. If policy proceeds are to be paid in installments during a fixed or lifetime period or for fixed amounts, the claim analyst sends the beneficiary an ***installment certificate*** that specifies the amount of each benefit payment and/or the period during which benefit payments will be made. The installment certificate also specifies whether a beneficiary is permitted to withdraw all or part of the proceeds during the payment period.

If policy proceeds are being left with the insurer to earn interest, the claim analyst usually sends the beneficiary a ***certificate of indebtedness***, which specifies a guaranteed minimum interest rate that the insurer will pay on the proceeds and the frequency with which the insurer will make interest payments to a beneficiary. Like an installment certificate, the certificate of indebtedness also specifies whether the beneficiary can withdraw all or part of the proceeds.

Key Terms and Concepts

claimant's statement
authorization to release information
death certificate
presumptive death certificate
change in health statement
proximate cause
contingent beneficiary
public curator
revocable beneficiary
irrevocable beneficiary
preferred beneficiary
assignment
absolute assignment
collateral assignment
interpleader
community-property laws
exculpatory statutes
survivorship clause
installment certificate
certificate of indebtedness

Endnotes

1. ACLI, *Life Insurers Fact Book 2000* (Washington, D.C.: American Council of Life Insurers, 2000), 195.
2. Ibid.
3. CLHIA, *Canadian Life and Health Insurance Facts* (Toronto: Canadian Life and Health Insurance Association, 2000), 15.
4. ACLI, 95.

CHAPTER 14

Administering Medical Expense and Long-Term Care Insurance Claims

Chapter Outline

Administering Medical Expense Insurance Claims
- Determining Whether a Medical Expense Has Occurred
- Determining Whether a Medical Expense Is Covered
- Calculating Policy Benefit Amounts
- Paying Benefits Appropriately

Administering Long-Term Care Insurance Claims
- Long-Term Care Benefits
- Determining Whether a Long-Term Care Expense Has Occurred
- Determining Whether a Long-Term Care Expense Is Covered
- Paying Long-Term Care Benefits Appropriately
- Group Long-Term Care Coverage

Objectives

After reading this chapter, you should be able to

- Describe the methods insurers use to determine whether a medical expense has occurred
- Discuss the procedures insurers use to determine whether a medical expense is covered by a policy
- Explain the methods insurers use to calculate medical expense benefits
- Describe the methods insurers use to pay medical expense benefits appropriately
- Describe the procedures used to determine whether a long-term care insurance loss has occurred
- Describe the benefit triggers for long-term care policies
- Describe the typical exclusions and limitations found in long-term care policies
- Describe the methods insurers use to pay long-term care benefits appropriately
- Explain the differences between individual and group long-term care coverage

Although a life insurance policy generally produces only one claim for each insured, medical expense policies can produce dozens of claims during the lifetime of an insured. Furthermore, claim analysts might receive hundreds of medical expense and long-term care claims in a single day. Each claim must be handled promptly, accurately, and completely, in accordance with the insurer's claim philosophy, its other business practices, and legal requirements.

In this chapter, we'll discuss medical expense and long-term care insurance claim administration. First, we'll describe the methods insurers use to administer medical expense insurance claims. Then, we'll explain the procedures insurers use to administer long-term care insurance claims.

Administering Medical Expense Insurance Claims

Claim analysts who handle medical expense claims need much of the same kind of technical knowledge that underwriters need, because claim analysts assess the validity and accuracy of technical information about diseases and physical and mental conditions. In the first chapter of this textbook, we explained the importance of information systems in enhancing the activities involved in insurance administration.

Most insurers have implemented sophisticated medical expense claims handling systems that not only verify information about the coverage and the insured, but also calculate benefit amounts, produce checks or transfer funds electronically to pay benefits, and generate printed explanations of benefits so that each policyowner receives specific information about the amount of benefits paid for each claim. In most insurance companies, only claims requiring special examination are handled individually by a claim analyst. Whether a computer or a person evaluates a claim, the same steps are generally involved. In our discussion of medical expense claim administration, we will review those steps in some detail and will refer always to a claim analyst, although for many coverages the administration process is often implemented by an information system. Insight 14-1 describes the effects that Health Insurance Portability and Accountability Act (HIPAA) regulations are having on insurers' processing and exchanging information, including claims.

Generally, medical expense policies include a provision requiring that a claim be submitted within a specified period—usually 30 to 90 days—from the date the loss was incurred. Because claim analysts need

Insight 14-1. Ready or Not, HIPAA Is Here.

As the deadline approaches, health insurers should be planning to comply with proposed standards for the electronic exchange of health information. One of the major provisions of the Health Insurance Portability and Accountability Act is "administrative simplification." This provision seeks to establish standards and requirements to enable the electronic exchange of some health information. The electronic exchange of information is expected to improve the efficiency and effectiveness of the health care system, according to HIPAA.

The estimated costs to implement the proposal and the savings it will bring are staggering:

- Implementation costs range from $5.3 billion to $17.3 billion.
- Estimated annual savings range from $8.9 billion to $20.5 billion.

Roughly speaking, companies can estimate that costs will be between two and four times what they spent preparing for 2000. Maybe HIPAA should be called HIPPO!

Health care providers and health plans that conduct business electronically must use many different formats for electronic transactions. About 400 formats exist for health care claims. With a national standard for electronic claims and other transactions, health care providers will be able to submit the same transaction to any health plan in the United States, and the health plan must accept it. Health plans will be able to send standard electronic transactions, such as remittance advices and referral authorizations, to health care providers. These national standards will make electronic data interchange a viable and preferable alternative to paper processing for providers and health plans alike.

The final rules for HIPAA's Standards for Electronic Transactions and code sets have been released. The compliance date for all but small health plans is no later than 24 months after the effective date of this final rule. Small health plans have an extended compliance date of no later than 36 months after the effective date. It is suggested that health plans give providers up to one year from the effective date to make the necessary changes to their systems.

According to the new HIPAA rules, transactions may not be rejected because the health plan's system does not recognize valid standard codes. Also, a health plan cannot require other organizations to use their local codes. If standard codes are not sufficient to process a benefit, for instance, procedures are in place to apply for a new code.

To determine how the standard transaction sets and codes affect your organization, check out the following exceptions and distinctions:

- The employer may choose to send the enrollment and disenrollment transaction electronically in either standard or nonstandard format.
- The Eligibility/Benefit Response must be used between a health care provider and a health plan or between two health plans. If the inquiry is from a third-party administrator to another business associate of a health plan, the standard transaction is not required.
- The standard transaction format for claims or encounter information does not have to be used if a managed care company is reporting to a state Medicaid agency for payment for the care delivered. But the health plan premium payment transaction between the state Medicaid agency and the managed care organization must be in the standard transaction format.
- The standard transactions are not needed when a health care provider is electronically sending information to a health care clearinghouse it has contracted with to bill health plans. But the health care clearinghouse must send the standard transactions to the health plans.
- Companies engaged in workers' compensation programs, property/casualty programs or disability insurance programs are not required to use the standard transactions.
- A health plan cannot require a health care provider to provide more data than is required on the standard transactions, and a health care plan cannot reject a standard transaction set fully completed by a health care provider.

Under the statute, failure to comply with standards may result in monetary penalties of up to $100 per violation.

Many companies already are engaged in planning or implementing their HIPAA Gap Analysis. They have leveraged their experience with solving the Y2K computer glitch and appointed the person who led that effort to do the same for the HIPAA project. Others have assigned a senior officer to head the effort because of the complexity of HIPAA for their companies, and most hospitals have assigned their compliance officer to handle the change HIPAA will bring. Those who have not begun planning should begin now.

Source: Excerpted from Jeri Ostling, "Ready or Not, HIPAA Is Here," *Best's Review* (December 2000): 132.

to gather additional information for certain claims, insurers prefer to receive claims promptly so that such information gathering can take place as soon as possible after the loss has occurred, while records are readily available. Whether a claim is submitted by paper or by electronic transmission, most insurers offering group health coverage use a uniform claim form or electronic format developed under the guidance of the Health Insurance Association of America (HIAA) in the United States or the Canadian Life and Health Insurance Association (CLHIA) in Canada. Submitting claim information in a uniform manner enables people submitting claims to provide complete, accurate information and enables claim analysts to examine claims rapidly and precisely.

In certain respects, handling medical expense claims is similar to handling any other kind of claim. The claim analyst is responsible for verifying that the reported loss occurred and that both the insured and the loss are covered by the policy. If benefits are due, the claim analyst is also responsible for seeing that they are paid appropriately. In the next section, we'll discuss these and other details of administering medical expense claims.

Determining Whether a Medical Expense Has Occurred

Medical expense claims are usually submitted either (1) manually on paper claim forms completed by insured people and their health care providers or (2) electronically by health care providers and their staffs who communicate directly with insurers. In determining whether a loss has occurred, the claim analyst typically interprets the diagnostic and treatment codes included in paper or electronic submissions.

Diagnostic and Treatment Codes

To help health care providers and insurers communicate, special codes have been developed to describe specific medical diagnoses and treatments. ***Diagnostic and treatment codes*** are numbers and words that represent specific medical diagnoses and treatments. These codes include (1) a number that identifies each diagnosis or treatment and (2) a brief, specific description of each diagnosis or treatment. Diagnostic and treatment codes enable anyone familiar with the coding system to tell immediately what information is being reported.

One of the most commonly used codes for medical *diagnoses* is the ***International Classification of Diseases and Related Health Problems***, which is generally referred to as the ICD and to which claim analysts refer by its most current edition—for example, the 10th edition is called ICD-10. One of the most commonly used codes for medical *treatments* is the ***Physicians' Current Procedural Terminology***, generally referred to as CPT. Figure 14-1 shows some of the codes commonly used to identify diagnoses and treatments associated with appendicitis.

In examining diagnostic and treatment codes reported on claims, the claim analyst first determines whether the codes are accurate and complete. Suppose that a claim analyst received a claim for an appendectomy with the diagnosis coded 540 (acute appendicitis with peritonitis, including rupture of the appendix) and the treatment coded 44960 (appendectomy for ruptured appendix with abscess or generalized peritonitis). Because the diagnosis code and the treatment code appear to be consistent, the claim analyst would note no problem with that portion of the claim.

But suppose instead that the diagnosis was coded 540.9 (acute appendicitis without mention of peritonitis) and the treatment was coded 44960 (appendectomy for ruptured appendix with abscess or generalized peritonitis). In such a situation, because the codes appear to be inconsistent, the claim analyst would check with the health care providers and the insured to verify the diagnosis and the treatment and to clarify the apparently conflicting information. Using the codes, the claim analyst can determine whether each treatment fits the requirements of ***medical necessity***—that is, a criterion requiring that the prescribed medical procedure is one that (1) is considered effective and that is normally used for the specified illness or injury and (2) does not

FIGURE 14-1. Codes Commonly Used for Diagnoses and Treatments of Appendicitis.

Diagnosis Code	Diagnosis
540	Acute appendicitis with peritonitis, including rupture of appendix
540.1	Acute appendicitis with peritoneal abscess
540.9	Acute appendicitis without mention of peritonitis
542	Other appendicitis, including chronic or recurrent attacks

Treatment Code	Treatment
44900	Incision and drainage of appendiceal abscess
44955	Appendectomy performed at time of another major procedure
44960	Appendectomy for ruptured appendix with abscess or generalized peritonitis

exceed in scope, duration, or intensity the level of care needed to provide safe, adequate, and appropriate diagnosis or treatment.

Generally, an inconsistent diagnostic or treatment code indicates a simple human error that can be corrected by communicating directly with the health care provider. For example, most insurers do not pay benefits for both an office visit and an emergency room visit for the same injury or illness on the same day. Similarly, most insurers do not pay separate benefits for both a surgical procedure and preoperative and postoperative office visits related to that procedure. When a claim analyst notices that a health care provider has reported overlapping codes—say, for both a surgical procedure and a postoperative checkup—the analyst notifies the health care provider and, unless unusual circumstances apply, does not approve benefits for postoperative visits because they are generally included in the surgical procedure benefits.

Medical Expense Claim Form

The medical expense claim form provides basic information from both the insured and the health care provider. The information provided by the insured generally includes

- The name, address, sex, and date of birth of the patient—that is, the person incurring the loss
- The relationship of the patient to the insured (dependent or self)
- The nature of the illness or injury on which the claim is based
- The name, address, sex, and date of birth of the primary insured
- Authorization from the patient (or, if the patient is a minor, from the insured) for all physicians, hospitals, health care providers, pharmacists, or other agencies and organizations to release information concerning the patient's records

A completed claim form also indicates whether the patient is covered by other insurance, whether the illness or injury resulted from the patient's occupation, and whether the claim is the result of an accident. If the claim is related to an occupational illness or injury, medical expenses typically would be covered by workers' compensation, not by individual or group medical expense insurance. If the claim is the result of an accident, the claim form indicates whether the claimant expects to receive or has received payment for medical expenses from another source as the result of a lawsuit or settlement. Space is provided for additional information about these responses.

The claim form information provided by the health care provider generally includes

- The name, address, and Tax Identification Number of the health care provider
- The name of the patient
- The nature of the illness or injury, including appropriate diagnostic codes
- The type of services rendered, including appropriate treatment codes
- The dates on which services were delivered
- The locations at which services were delivered
- The charges for those services

If the patient or the health care provider submits bills for drugs and medicines along with the claim form, each bill usually shows

- The name of the person for whom medication was prescribed
- The date(s) of purchase and the charge for each prescription
- Each prescription number, the nature of each medication, and the drug identification number (DIN)
- The name and address of the pharmacy

Itemized Receipt

A health care provider typically provides each patient with an itemized receipt that gives detailed information about diagnosis and treatment. The information on such a receipt usually includes the name of the health care provider, a specific diagnosis, the expenses involved in diagnosis and treatment, and the date on which those expenses were incurred. As proof of claim, most insurers require original itemized receipts, not photocopies. Itemized receipts may be given by any health care provider, ranging from a physician or paramedic to a laboratory, a hospital, or an outpatient clinic.

Most itemized receipts include diagnostic or treatment codes and, therefore, can be interpreted accurately and rapidly. If, however, such a receipt contains only a written description of diagnosis or treatment, the claim analyst usually communicates with the health care provider to clarify the information. Figure 14-2 illustrates a portion of a typical receipt from a physician specializing in obstetrics and gynecology.

FIGURE 14-2. Portion of a Typical Medical Receipt.

Date of Service ____________ Name ____________

Address ____________

Social Security No. ____________ DOB ____________

Procedures		Laboratory		Diagnosis	
57500	Cervical Biopsy	82465	Cholesterol	789	Abdominal Pain
58100	Endometrial Biopsy	82565	Creatinine	795.0	Abnormal Pap
57511	Cryotherapy	82728	Ferratine	285.8	Anemia
59000	Amniocentesis	82947	Glucose	250	Diabetes
59050	Fetal Monitoring	86317	Hepatitis C	617.9	Endometriosis
58990	Hysteroscopy	86996	OB Profile	620.2	Ovarian Cyst

Remarks ____________

Provider Signature ____________

Determining Whether a Medical Expense Is Covered

To determine whether a medical expense is covered by a policy, a claim analyst verifies that the policy covers both the claimant and the medical expense. The claim analyst also verifies that the premiums have been paid and that the coverage is in force. This verification is especially important if a claimant has been covered under a group policy and has converted her group coverage to individual coverage.

If the claimant is the primary insured, the claim analyst usually has little difficulty determining whether the person is covered for the stated loss. However, for family insurance or group insurance, the claim analyst determines whether the claimant is a qualified dependent of the primary insured. Generally, dependents include not only the spouse, but also unmarried dependent children—natural, adopted, and stepchildren—who are under age 19 (or, if a full-time student, under age 23 to 25, depending on plan provisions) and who are chiefly dependent upon the insured for support and maintenance.

FAST FACT

In 1999, 15.5% of people in the United States were not covered by health insurance.[1]

The claim analyst also checks the policy to be sure that the loss reported on the claim is covered under the policy and has not been excluded by a rider. Some insurers have entered all policy provisions into a database so that claim analysts can quickly check details of coverage. Because many individual and group medical expense policies have been custom-designed and contain various kinds and levels of coverages and exclusions, the claim analyst usually refers to a file copy of the policy contract to ensure that the claim assessment of the losses is accurate.

Exclusions and Limitations

Policy exclusions and limitations specify as exactly as possible the conditions that a policy will and will not cover. These exclusions and limitations can cover a wide range, and they differ from one policy to another. The most common types of medical exclusions and limitations include the following:

- *Those defining the health care provider*. Some policies specify that covered medical care must be delivered by a licensed dentist or a resident physician or an intern—but not a nurse or nurse's aide—who is employed by or officially associated with a specific kind of medical facility.

- *Those defining the medical facility.* Most policies state that coverage extends only to certain types and levels of facilities. For example, a policy might not cover certain treatments and procedures delivered in a patient's home, in a health care provider's office, or in an outpatient clinic.

- *Those defining the type of medical procedure*. Many policies limit or exclude benefits for corrective treatments (such as orthopedic shoes, eyeglasses, and hearing aids), preventive treatments (such as vaccinations, inoculations, and weight reduction programs), and some diagnostic treatments (such as sight and hearing examinations, certain X-rays, heart scans, coronary artery disease risk assessment programs, and any diagnostic treatment when no injury or illness exists).

- *Those defining the type of medical condition*. Most policies define the type of medical conditions for which treatment is covered. For example, a typical definition of "sickness" is any sickness or disease that first makes itself known after the policy is in force and while the policy is in force. Similarly, an "injury" is typically defined as an accidental bodily injury that results in loss independently of sickness and other causes.

- *Those defining the fees charged by the health care provider and the medical facility*. Most policies set limits on the amount of coverage provided for certain medical procedures, for the maximum benefits allowed for one period of illness or for a single injury, and for the number of medical procedures allowed within a stated period of time. These limits are established according to the usual and customary fees for such treatments within the applicable geographic area. In addition, all policies specify the charges that will be covered by the policy. Figure 14-3 illustrates a typical list of charges covered by a medical insurance policy.

FIGURE 14-3. Typical List of Charges Covered by Medical Insurance Policy.

- Hospital charges for the average semiprivate room and board during necessary hospital confinement
- Confinement in an intensive care unit or cardiac care unit of a hospital
- Hospital charges for services and supplies
- Treatment by a physician or surgeon
- Anesthesia and its administration
- X-ray and laboratory examinations
- Services of a radiologist for diagnosis or treatment
- Services of a professional physical or speech therapist acting under the direction of a physician
- Professional ambulance service for emergency transportation to the nearest hospital
- Services and supplies furnished by an ambulatory surgical facility
- Medical supplies such as blood and blood plasma, surgical dressings, casts, splints, crutches, oxygen, and approved drugs
- Specified expenses for care provided by a hospice or licensed home health care agency

Besides the limitations and exclusions we've just noted, some policies contain other prohibitions to coverage. All health insurance policies prohibit payment for unnecessary care or treatment. In addition, many health policies also exclude coverage for the following kinds of expenses:

- Routine health care and checkups
- Routine physical examinations
- Cosmetic surgery unless needed to repair damage suffered in an accident covered under the policy, for reconstructive surgery, or for restoration to normal bodily function
- Self-donated blood and blood replacement

- Custodial care
- Any work-related illness or injury that is covered by workers' compensation insurance
- Intentionally self-inflicted wounds or illness, or wounds suffered in an assault on another person or in an attempt to commit a crime

Some health insurance policies require an insured to obtain a ***preadmission certification***, sometimes called *precertification*, which is a statement from the insurer approving nonemergency, inpatient hospital treatment. Preadmission certification is usually required for surgical, maternity, substance abuse, and mental health hospital admissions. Emergency medical care generally does not require preadmission certification.

To provide preadmission certification, an insurer requires the claimant's attending physician to demonstrate a genuine medical need for prescribed care prior to the time that care is to be delivered. Information required from the physician includes (1) the diagnosis or reason for hospital confinement, (2) signs and symptoms indicating a need for such care, (3) the proposed treatment or surgical procedure, and (4) the expected number of days of confinement. Most insurers require a physician to provide this information at least two days before the hospital admission; many insurers allow the information to be transmitted to the insurer electronically or by telephone. If an insured must stay in the hospital longer than the period approved through preadmission certification, the claim analyst usually obtains medical information from the physician to determine the medical necessity of the extended stay before approving payment for the extended period.

If the claim analyst determines that an insured has been treated as an inpatient in a hospital and has not obtained preadmission certification, the analyst invokes whatever provision the policy makes for such an omission. In most situations, the insured is responsible for paying (1) an additional deductible above the usual deductible that applies to an overnight hospital stay and (2) an additional percentage of the room and board charges. If an insured was denied preadmission certification, but still received the hospital treatment and submitted a claim for that treatment, the claim analyst invokes the policy provision for such action, which usually requires the insured to pay a larger amount of the total cost of the hospital stay or, under some contracts, to pay the full cost of the stay.

Other Policy Provisions

In addition to checking the exclusions and limitations contained in a policy, the claim analyst verifies whether the policy contains other provisions that permit the insurer to pay for services not generally covered by the basic policy. For example, a policy that offers extended care coverage might permit a claimant to receive benefits to pay for skilled nursing care—from a registered nurse or a licensed practical nurse—working in an outpatient clinic or in the patient's home. Rather than assume that a claim is covered, the claim analyst is responsible for checking a policy in detail, for paying full benefits for all covered treatments, and for denying benefits for all claims not covered by the policy provisions.

The claim analyst also verifies whether a policy contains a ***subrogation clause***, which gives the insurer a contractual right to recover payments made to an insured for medical care if that insured receives payment for damages through a legal action. Recall that a medical claim form asks a claimant to state whether she expects to receive or has received payment for medical expenses as the result of a lawsuit or settlement. If a claimant is reimbursed for medical expenses as the result of such a legal action, the insurer is eligible to recover whatever amount it has paid in medical benefits.

For example, suppose an insured is involved in an automobile accident, and the insurer pays $15,000 for medical costs resulting from the accident. The insured later sues the person who caused the accident and is awarded $45,000 by the court. If the insured's policy contains a subrogation clause, the insurer can recover up to $15,000 to offset the medical expenses incurred.

Calculating Policy Benefit Amounts

After a claim analyst assesses a claim and determines that it should be paid, the next step is to determine the amount of benefits to be paid under the policy. Insurers generally use one of several approaches to determine the amount of payable benefits. We discuss the most common of these approaches in the rest of this section.

Diagnostic Related Groups

In an attempt to reduce some of the costs of unnecessary medical care, the Medicare system in the United States introduced diagnostic related groups as a method of paying claims, and some insurers have adopted this method. ***Diagnostic related groups (DRGs)*** is a payment method under which an insurer will pay hospital charges not according to the number and types of services delivered, but according to the diagnosis for a patient. If a hospital delivers care for a certain diagnosis at a lower cost, the hospital keeps the full amount allowed for treatment of a patient having that diagnosis. If a hospital spends more in treating such a patient than is reimbursed, however, the hospital loses money on the transaction.

Under a DRG system, a patient's diagnosis is translated to a DRG, and the insurer reimburses hospitals, but not other health care providers, for that DRG according to a payment schedule. If a patient's diagnosis cannot be classified under a DRG, the insurer handles the patient's case individually to determine how much to pay for each medical service. Certain kinds of hospitals—those specializing in care for cancer, psychiatric disorders, long-term care, and children's diseases, and those providing rehabilitation services—are exempt from the requirements established for DRGs.

In handling a claim based on DRGs, the claim analyst ensures that the hospital has provided a DRG that accurately describes the patient's condition and that the treatment provided is consistent with that DRG. The claim analyst also verifies that the patient was not discharged too early from the hospital as part of a cost-containment effort. For some conditions, premature discharge may result in later medical complications for which the insurer may be liable.

Schedule of Benefits

For claim purposes, a ***schedule of benefits*** is a listing of medical treatments and the maximum benefit amounts an insurer will pay for each treatment. Using a schedule of benefits enables a claim analyst to determine the amount of policy benefits due. This schedule is not to be confused with the schedule of benefits used in group insurance to specify the amount of coverage provided for each class of insureds, a topic we discussed in Chapter 8. Figure 14-4 illustrates a portion of a typical schedule of benefits.

Maximum Limit

Another approach to calculating policy benefits is a ***maximum limit*** approach, which involves payment of a specified amount of total benefits for claims arising from a single injury or incident, or one

FIGURE 14-4. Portion of a Typical Schedule of Benefits.

PROCEDURE	BENEFIT AMOUNT
Hysterectomy	$1,650 per procedure
Cesarean section	$1,370 per procedure
Appendectomy	$1,025 per procedure
Tonsillectomy	$ 380 per procedure

period of sickness. A maximum limit approach might also establish the maximum number of days of coverage for specific services—for instance, the number of days of hospital admission or of treatment in a rehabilitation center. Many health insurance policies also contain a ***lifetime maximum benefit***, which is the maximum amount that the policy will pay for all eligible medical expenses an individual incurs while insured under the policy.

Reasonable and Customary Limits

By establishing ***reasonable and customary limits***, an insurer specifies that the amount paid for a claim must conform to the amount most frequently charged for each medical procedure in a given geographical area. An insurer can obtain information about reasonable and customary amounts from such sources as the Health Insurance Association of America (HIAA). Alternatively, large insurers generally develop enough historical information to determine what rates are reasonable and customary in the areas in which their insureds receive medical treatment.

Under a policy that uses reasonable and customary limits, an insured might submit a claim for $500 for a specific treatment. If the reasonable and customary charge for that treatment in the insured's geographical area is $450, the insurer will most likely limit the benefit to $450. On the other hand, if the reasonable and customary charge for that treatment in the insured's geographical area is $600, the insurer will consider the charge of $500 as acceptable for the treatment. In addition to geographical area, reasonable and customary charges for a given procedure take into account the training and experience of the physicians in the area. If the insurer typically pays for the specified procedure at 80 percent of the total charge, in the first case the insurer would pay a benefit of $360 (0.80 × $450) and in the second case would pay a benefit of $400 (0.80 × $500).

Paying Benefits Appropriately

After examining a claim and determining the extent of the insurer's liability for it, the claim analyst decides whether the amount of benefits should be reduced as a result of deductibles, applicable exclusions or limitations, or coordination of benefits with other insurers or with other providers. After making such determinations, the claim analyst submits the claim to be paid.

Deductibles

The claim analyst first reduces the amount of covered expenses by any applicable deductible. Some basic or hospital-surgical medical plans have no deductibles, so that the insurer pays the first dollar of medical costs up to any specified dollar or percentage limit. In such a situation, the claim analyst does not subtract any deductible amount from the benefits due.

Comprehensive medical plans, by contrast, usually require an ***initial deductible***, which is an amount an insured must pay before an insurer pays any medical expenses. After the initial deductible is paid, the insurer pays the remaining amount, usually up to a specified dollar or percentage limit. If a policy contains a provision for ***coinsurance***—which is the percentage of all eligible medical expenses, in excess of the deductible, incurred as a result of sickness or injury and which the insured is required to pay—the claim analyst calculates the amount of coinsurance and deducts that amount from the benefit amount.

For example, suppose that a policy has an annual $500 deductible, pays 80 percent of covered medical expenses above the initial deductible, and requires that the remaining 20 percent of the amount in excess of the deductible is to be paid as coinsurance. If an insured has incurred $5,000 of covered medical expenses, payments are made as follows:

The insured pays
$1,400 = $500 initial deductible plus $900 coinsurance
($5,000 – $500 = $4,500; $4,500 × 0.20 = $900)

The insurer pays $3,600 in benefits
($5,000 – $500 = $4,500; $4,500 × 0.80 = $3,600)

Coordination of Benefits

The claim analyst determines whether the insured is covered under any other insurance plan that is paying benefits for the expenses claimed. Many people are eligible for coverage under more than one group medical expense plan—for example, spouses who both work typically are eligible for coverage under their own employer's group policy and under their spouse's group policy. Therefore, group medical expense plans usually include a ***coordination of benefits (COB) provision***, which prevents duplicate benefit payments for the same expense by more than one insurer or by a government program. If an insured is covered by more than one policy, the claim analyst checks the policy's COB provision to determine the insurer's responsibility for paying benefits.

Some individual health insurance policies contain an ***overinsurance provision***, which specifies that, under certain circumstances, policy benefits will be reduced if the insured has more insurance than needed to cover medical expenses.

Payment of Benefits

After calculating the amount of benefits due to a claimant, the claim analyst requests that payment be sent to the appropriate recipient. In many situations, the claimant has signed an ***assignment of benefits***, which is a statement on the claim form that directs an insurer to pay benefits directly to a health care provider rather than to an insured. A typical assignment of benefits statement says simply, "I authorize payment of medical benefits to the undersigned physician or supplier for service(s) described." If an insured has not signed an assignment of benefits statement, the claim analyst usually sends the benefit payment directly to the insured. After making a decision on each claim, the claim analyst sends the claimant an ***explanation of benefits (EOB)***, which is a detailed statement showing each treatment or medication submitted as part of a claim, the insurer's decision concerning payment of each charge, any amount that is considered as a deductible or a copayment, an explanation of any charge for which part or all of the charge will not be paid, and the total amount sent to the health care provider.

Administering Long-Term Care Insurance Claims

With the increase in life expectancy predicted to occur in the coming decades will come an increase in the number of people who may require long-term care. Because the costs of long-term care can quickly deplete savings, many people are turning to LTC insurance to provide for that care. Recall from Chapter 7 that long-term care (LTC) coverage pays for medical or other health-related services required in a person's home or in a nursing facility. People who have exhausted their savings and who do not have private LTC policies frequently rely on federal health programs such as Medicaid.

However, the cost to federal programs, including Medicaid, is such that in 1996 the U.S. Congress passed the Health Insurance Portability and Accountability Act (HIPAA), providing tax breaks to encourage citizens to buy private LTC policies. HIPAA also established qualified LTC plans. A ***qualified LTC plan*** is a plan that provides all the features HIPAA requires and consequently is eligible for favorable tax treatment under federal law. Upon passage of the law, all other LTC plans consequently became nonqualified plans not eligible for this favorable tax treatment.

Today, most LTC plans offered by insurers meet HIPPA's requirements and, therefore, are considered to be qualified plans. Qualified versus nonqualified status does not affect how LTC claims are administered. For both types of plans, the claim analyst relies on the definitions in the policy to determine whether a covered loss has occurred and, when applicable, to calculate and pay the benefit amount.

> **FAST FACT**
>
> For long-term care facilities, the average length of stay for all stays of 90 days or longer is 2.5 years.[2]

LTC policies provide a variety of benefit types and amounts. Therefore, claim analysts for LTC products rely on the definitions in the policies to help them make claim decisions. In addition to communicating with insureds and physicians, LTC claim analysts frequently communicate with nursing home staff or home health care providers. In this section, we'll describe the LTC benefits typically provided and the way in which claims for such benefits are administered. Insight 14-2 describes how insurers use care coordination to provide appropriate LTC benefits.

Long-Term Care Benefits

LTC policies generally provide coverage for nursing home care; home health care; adult day care; and alternate care, including hospice care and assisted living facility care. We discuss each of these types of benefits below.

A ***nursing home*** is a custodial facility that provides basic nonmedical and medical care as necessary to patients. Today, most LTC policies that insurers issue also include a benefit for long-term care provided in the insured's home. ***Home health care*** can include skilled or nonskilled nursing care, physical therapy, and home health assistance provided by a state-licensed and/or Medicare-certified home health agency.

Adult day care is care provided to adults in a group setting during hours when primary caregivers are working. Candidates for adult day care are not bedridden and typically live at home under the care of an adult child or other relative who is not able to care for the patient during normal working hours.

Policies that provide ***alternate care benefits*** cover nonconventional services developed cooperatively by a physician and an insurer to substitute for more expensive nursing home care. Alternate care can include special medical care and treatments, such as visits by a mobile dialysis unit so that the insured can receive kidney dialysis treatments at home, or medically necessary modification of an insured's home, such as installation of a wheelchair ramp and modification of doorway, encouraging mobility and allowing the insured to remain at home.

In addition, alternate care benefits usually cover expenses at different sites of care, such as hospices and assisted living facilities. A ***hospice*** is a facility that specializes in the treatment of terminally ill people, typically providing the services of doctors and nurses to care for a patient and provide pain relief 24 hours a day. Typically, the cost of care in a

Insight 14-2. Coordinating Care Can Control Claims.

Most long-term-care policyholders hope they won't ever have to live in a nursing home. Most insurers feel the same way, but to keep it from happening to their clients, they need to take more initiative in managing claims.

"We are strong proponents of a mandatory approach to care coordination," said Barbara Prescott, senior vice president of claims management at AUL Reinsurance Management Services, a subsidiary of American United Life Insurance Co. in Indianapolis. "What that allows us to do is have early intervention at the time of the first claims notice, so we are sure that we take the most appropriate course of action."

Care coordination aims to delay costly institutionalization and support informal caregivers, such as family members, who provide 85% of long-term care in the United States today, Prescott said. It also seeks to manage the insured's illness, preserve function and prevent deterioration. Home- and community-based care is more effective and more cost effective, but it has to be managed up front, she said.

AUL believes that using an independent, licensed and objective third party is the best way to assess an insured's needs, determine a course of action and coordinate the plan. The coordinator's first step is to visit the insured at home. "You really have to take a holistic approach on an individual basis," Prescott said. "That's why the initial evaluation is so important. You're not sitting back as an insurer and reading a statement from the insured's doctor, who might have a self-interest in prompting utilization. A care coordinator will balance that. A coordinator cannot also be a provider."

A lot of states are not in line with AUL's thinking, because they associate it with the case-management element of managed care, the part that employs a primary-care physician, Prescott said. "But care coordination is proactive, because it takes the wishes of family into consideration," she said. "Very seldom will a physician get involved. Physicians really aren't in a position to evaluate, because they don't see patients in their homes."

This year, AUL has started a pilot program that introduces disease-management components to its care coordination. The idea is to identify certain chronic conditions that could lead to further disabilities. For example, AUL's coordinator might schedule a bone-density test and take steps to prevent the insured from falling and fracturing an arm or leg. Or the coordinator might compile a full listing of an insured's prescribed drugs and share that information with a doctor or pharmacist. "We know that the elderly can be overmedicated and that there can be adverse drug interactions," she said, and sometimes the insured's doctor isn't aware of all medications he or she is taking.

Sometimes, the reason for disability can be an acute medical condition that might be covered under a medical policy, not simply a chronic lack of ability to perform an activity of daily living. Some individual insurers, including John Hancock Financial Services and Aegon, are trying to identify those situations as well, Prescott said.

"Best practices are still evolving," she said. "You'll see more clinicians in the process. How these clinicians are used is another story. Some are involved in the decision making on claims, but I'm of the school that the business side of the house is making the benefit decisions. The clinician is there to provide for continuous quality improvement and appropriateness of plan recommendation. Once a claim is approved, it's vital you monitor it appropriately and intervene at the appropriate points."

Source: Excerpted from Ron Panko, "Coordinating Care Can Control Claims," *Best's Review* (March 2001): 86.

hospice is much lower than the cost of care in a hospital or nursing home. An ***assisted living facility*** is a residential facility designed to meet long-term care needs by providing accommodations, board, and access to medical services. Assisted living facilities usually offer individual accommodations for residents, allowing more privacy for residents than do nursing homes and enabling elderly couples to stay together.

Determining Whether a Long-Term Care Expense Has Occurred

When an insured or a member of an insured's family requests LTC benefits, the claim analyst sends a claim form to the insured. The LTC insurance claim form has three parts: (1) a general information section to be completed by the insured or her guardian, if applicable; (2) an attending physician's statement; and (3) a nursing services report.

The claim analyst uses the information on the claim form to verify the insured's loss. If the claim analyst requires additional information, he requests the information from the appropriate party. The claim analyst may also speak directly with the insured and/or the insured's family, the physician, and the nursing staff to understand the circumstances of the insured's case. After verifying the loss, the claim analyst verifies policy coverage of the loss.

Determining Whether a Long-Term Care Expense Is Covered

The claim analyst determines that the insured's LTC policy covers the claim by verifying that the insured meets the conditions stated in the policy. For qualified plans, the conditions are prescribed by HIPAA. State regulations, particularly those based on the NAIC Long-Term Care Model Act and the NAIC Long-Term Care Insurance Model Regulation, limit the conditions that insurers can include in LTC policies. These regulations are designed to protect the public and to promote the availability of long-term care coverage and flexibility in product design. State laws based on the NAIC model acts mandate many of the policy provisions that we will discuss in the following sections.

Benefit Triggers

An LTC policy usually specifies that benefits are payable when any one of three benefit triggers occurs:

1. Inability of the insured to perform a certain number of the activities of daily living (ADLs) without assistance
2. Cognitive impairment, or mental incapacity, of the insured
3. A doctor's certification that long-term care is medically necessary for the insured

We discuss each of these triggers below.

Inability to Perform Activities of Daily Living (ADLs). Recall from Chapter 7 that activities of daily living include eating, bathing, dressing, transferring (getting in and out of bed), and toileting.

LTC policies typically specify that the insurer will pay benefits if the insured cannot perform listed ADLs—usually two or three—without assistance for a certain period of time, typically 90 days. The claim analyst relies on a doctor or another health care professional to verify that an insured person is unable to perform an ADL.

Cognitive Impairment. You'll recall from our discussion in Chapter 7 that a cognitive impairment is a reduction in a person's ability to think, reason, or remember. To assess cognitive impairment, specialists use several tests to measure mental functions. Cognitive impairment severe enough to require regular supervision or assistance to protect the insured and others around the insured triggers LTC benefits. Alzheimer's disease and severe senility are examples of cognitive impairments covered under most LTC policies. Many policies treat cognitive impairment as a benefit trigger even if the insured can perform all of the ADLs without assistance.

Medical Necessity. A third benefit trigger in LTC policies is a doctor's certification that it is medically necessary for the insured to have long-term care as part of medical treatment. For example, suppose that several weeks ago Lorna Sweet fell down the steps to her home and fractured her arm and several ribs. Although she no longer requires hospitalization, her physician has determined that a stay in a skilled nursing facility is essential to Ms. Sweet's recovery and rehabilitation. Because medical necessity is a benefit trigger in Ms. Sweet's policy, she is eligible to receive LTC benefits. If an insured needs long-term care but is not sick or injured, then the benefit trigger must be something other than a doctor's certification of medical necessity.

After the claim analyst determines that a relevant benefit trigger has occurred, the analyst next checks the exclusions and limitations in the policy to make sure that the insured meets the other conditions required for benefits.

Exclusions and Limitations

Most LTC policies specify certain exclusions and limitations. Figure 14-5 lists a number of the situations and conditions for which insurers typically will not pay benefits. Most LTC policies issued in the United States also exclude care that is provided outside the United States because such care is difficult to monitor. In addition, LTC policies usually exclude care that is provided free, such as through a veteran's hospital. If a claim analyst determines that one of these exclusions applies to the insured, the analyst sends a letter to the insured explaining why the insurer is denying benefits.

To some extent, every LTC policy excludes from coverage conditions that existed prior to the LTC policy's effective date. In addition, many LTC policies have an ***elimination period***, which is the number of days

FIGURE 14-5. LTC Policy Exclusions and Limitations.

Benefits are not paid for

- ✗ Injury sustained during war
- ✗ Alcohol or drug dependency (although some policies will cover long-term care for drug dependency if the addiction is to prescription drugs)
- ✗ Self-inflicted injury
- ✗ Injury incurred during the commission of a felony
- ✗ Mental illness and nervous disorders that cannot be traced to an organic cause (most states prevent insurers from excluding Alzheimer's disease)

after long-term care begins that a person insured under an LTC policy must wait before benefit payments begin. Most insurers allow an applicant to choose the elimination period for their LTC policy and offer elimination periods of between 0 and 100 days or longer. The longer the elimination period, the lower the policy premium, assuming all other factors are equal.

Almost all LTC policies issued today are guaranteed renewable for life, meaning that the policy cannot be canceled and the benefits provided cannot be changed as long as the policyowner pays the premiums on time. The insurer can, however, change the premium charged for a guaranteed renewable policy if the change is for an entire class of insureds. Most LTC policies issued today also contain a ***waiver of premium provision*** that allows an insured to stop paying premiums at a specified point while the insured person is receiving long-term care and the insurer is making benefit payments under the policy.

If the claim analyst determines that the age listed on the application is incorrect, he reviews the misstatement of age provision to determine the appropriate action. Recall from Chapter 13 that most misstatement of age provisions state that policy benefits will be adjusted to the level that the premiums would have bought based on the insured's correct age.

Paying Long-Term Care Benefits Appropriately

After the claim analyst has determined that the insured is entitled to an LTC benefit, the analyst determines the amount of the benefit and sends the payment to the insured, or to the insured's treatment provider if an assignment of benefits has been made. LTC policy benefits are usually stated as a daily benefit amount, which is the amount the insurer will pay for each day of an insured's long-term care. For example, a policy might state that a benefit of $150 per day will be payable when the insured meets the conditions specified in the policy.

Certain types of additional benefits describe the benefit amount in different ways. For example, the benefit amount for home health care and for adult day care is typically 50 percent of the policy's daily benefit amount. The maximum benefit payable may also be smaller for such benefits. For example, assume that Jamal Ahmad has an LTC policy that provides a benefit amount of $150 per day and a maximum benefit amount of $300,000. Mr. Ahmad's home health care benefit, however, specifies that the maximum daily amount is $75 per day, and the maximum benefit amount for this type of care is $150,000.

Payment of some benefits, such as alternate care benefits, reduces the maximum benefit amount payable under the LTC policy. For example, if the maximum benefit amount for an LTC policy is $200,000 and the insured receives $40,000 in alternate care benefits, the remaining maximum benefit amount for long-term care will be $160,000.

Claim analysts generally use the indemnity benefit method or the reimbursement method to determine the daily benefit amount. In the ***indemnity benefit method***, the insurer pays a specified benefit amount regardless of the actual expenses incurred for the care of the insured. For example, if Sarah Linden's LTC policy pays $140 per day and her nursing home costs $100 per day, Ms. Linden will receive $140—that is $40 more than the actual nursing home cost. If the nursing home costs $150 per day, Ms. Linden will receive a benefit amount—$140—that is, $10 less than the actual cost.

Newer LTC policies generally use the ***reimbursement method***, in which the insured receives reimbursement for approved long-term care expenses up to a maximum limit specified in the policy. Under the reimbursement method, the insured never receives a benefit amount higher than the actual charges for the care. Using our example with Ms. Linden, if Ms. Linden's policy specified that LTC expenses would be reimbursed up to a maximum limit of $140 per day, then Ms. Linden would receive a benefit amount of $100 per day if the nursing home cost was $100 per day and a benefit amount of $140 per day if the nursing home cost was $150 per day.

The claim analyst reviews the policy provisions and determines the exact benefit amount to be paid. As the claim analyst administers the claim over time, he carefully monitors the insured's condition and treatment to make sure that the insured still qualifies for benefits. Depending on the status of the insured and the policy provisions, the benefit amount may change over time.

Inflation Protection

Insurers typically offer inflation protection riders that compensate for future inflation of long-term care costs. The ***inflation protection rider*** either automatically increases the benefit amount by a specified percentage each year or allows the insured to opt for a higher daily benefit at specified intervals during the lifetime of a policy, without having to show evidence of insurability. When a policy has an inflation rider, the claim analyst calculates the benefit amount using the formula specified in the rider.

Legal Issues

Claims for LTC benefits sometimes involve an insured who has a family member or friend handling his finances and claim submission. In such a situation, the claim analyst identifies the person who has legal authority to act for the insured and obtains the appropriate authorization to release medical records. In addition, the claim analyst obtains a valid assignment of benefits from the person who has legal authority to act for the insured if benefits are to be paid directly to a treatment provider. If benefits are not assigned, the insurer typically continues to pay benefits directly to the insured, but mails the payment to the person who is acting for the insured.

Group Long-Term Care Coverage

Generally, group LTC policies and individual LTC policies specify the same benefit triggers. In addition, the claim administration process for both types of coverage is basically the same.

Insurers marketing employer-provided group LTC coverage frequently offer benefits to not only the employee, but also to her spouse, the employee's parents, and the spouse's parents. Employers recognize the lost productivity associated with organizing and managing the care of a family member requiring long-term care services, and, thus, insurers have designed products to assist employees in providing this care. In addition, the eligible age for group LTC coverage is typically 18, much lower than the age required for individual policies.

Owners of group LTC policies—usually employers—generally pay 100 percent of the LTC premium, which is typically 30 to 40 percent lower than the premium for individual coverage. However, home health care benefits and adult day care benefits are usually optional features rather than standard features. The benefit amount for such optional features is typically 50 percent of the maximum daily rate for nursing home care. The elimination period in group policies is typically mandatory and often longer than in individual policies.

Group Provisions Not Found in Individual Policies

Group LTC policies typically feature two provisions not found in individual policies. The ***portability provision*** is a provision that permits a group member who leaves the group to take her coverage with her and continue to pay premiums. A claim analyst administering a group claim makes sure that an insured who has left a group has elected to use the portability feature and has paid all premiums due before approving benefits.

If the group LTC policy does not offer the portability feature, the policy typically offers a ***conversion provision***, which allows the insured group member leaving the group to change from the group coverage to an individual policy offered by the same insurer. The individual policy benefits are generally not as generous as the group plan benefits. If a claim analyst receives a claim for an insured who has left the group, the analyst determines whether an individual policy now covers the insured and, if so, administers the claim according to the provisions of the individual policy.

Key Terms

diagnostic and treatment codes
International Classification of Diseases and Related Health Problems (ICD)
Physicians' Current Procedural Terminology (CPT)
medical necessity
preadmission certification
subrogation clause
Diagnostic Related Groups (DRGs)
schedule of benefits
maximum limit
lifetime maximum benefit
reasonable and customary limits
initial deductible
coinsurance
coordination of benefits (COB) provision
overinsurance provision
assignment of benefits
explanation of benefits (EOB)
qualified LTC plan
nursing home
home health care
adult day care
alternate care benefits
hospice
assisted living facility
elimination period
waiver of premium provision
indemnity benefit method
reimbursement method
inflation protection rider
portability provision
conversion provision

Endnotes

1. Conning & Company, *Insurance Trends: First Quarter, 2001* (Hartford: Conning & Company, 2001), 184.
2. James M. Glickman, "A Long-Term Commitment," *Best's Review* (October 2000): 138.

CHAPTER 15

Administering Disability Income and Critical Illness Insurance Claims

Chapter Outline

Objectives

After reading this chapter, you should be able to

- Describe the general provisions of disability income contracts
- Discuss supplementary benefits under disability income coverage
- List the information sources insurers use to handle disability income claims
- Describe the methods insurers use to administer rehabilitation
- Explain the procedures for terminating disability income coverage
- Discuss the methods insurers use to settle disability income claims
- Describe how insure process critical illness coverage claims

When a person insured under disability income (DI) insurance is unable to work because of a disabling injury or illness, the insurer generally compensates that person for a portion of the income she lost because of the disability. This form of coverage may be long-term or short-term and may provide a variety of benefits depending on the specific policy provisions. Disability income insurance usually does not provide medical expense coverage.

Under critical illness (CI) coverage, a lump sum benefit is paid to the insured regardless of expenses incurred as a result of the illness, the insured's ability to work, or the loss of income. The insured can use the benefit in any way.

In Chapter 7 we discussed the underwriting principles used in assessing applicants for DI and CI coverage. For DI coverage, you'll recall that the underwriter checks both primary and secondary income sources in determining the amount of DI coverage for which an applicant is eligible. Because DI benefits are not intended to replace all of an insured's regular earnings when he is disabled, the benefit amount is usually figured as a percentage (normally between 60 and 75 percent) of regular income provided in a series of monthly payments. Some policies specify that the insurer will pay a flat income benefit if the insured becomes disabled. Generally, the DI insurance benefits are provided in a series of monthly payments.

On the other hand, underwriting for critical illness (CI) coverage focuses on the potential of future incidence of a particular impairment or group of impairments. The number of impairments covered can range from a minimum of three or four to thirty or more.

In this chapter, we'll begin by explaining the basic and supplementary provisions of DI contracts with which claim analysts must be familiar. Next we'll examine the information sources that claim analysts use for examining disability claims. Then we'll discuss administration of DI claims. Last, we'll consider how claim analysts handle CI claims.

General Provisions of Disability Income Contracts

Handling DI claims requires the claim analyst to be very familiar with the definitions and provisions of the insurance product. The general provisions of DI insurance contracts cover the definitions of injury and

FAST FACT

In the United States, premiums for individual disability insurance in force grew at an average annual rate of 11% between 1997 and 1999.[1]

sickness, contestability, elimination period, benefit period, disability, benefit amount, renewability, and exceptions and limitations. In this section, we'll explain the actions that the claim analyst typically takes for these policy provisions.

Injury and Sickness

Every DI policy defines injury and sickness as each will be covered under the contract. Generally, an ***injury*** is defined as an accidental harm resulting from an unforeseen external force (1) causing trauma to a person's body and (2) occurring while the DI policy is in force. In addition, an injury is normally defined as a condition resulting independently of sickness. Usually a ***sickness*** is an illness or a disease that (1) includes pregnancy unless it is specifically excluded under the contract and (2) begins while a person is insured under the policy. A claim analyst uses the claim form and medical record to ensure that a claimant's condition meets the policy's definition of injury or sickness.

Contestability

Most short-term and long-term DI policies provide for a specified contestable period. Any material misstatement or material misrepresentation that an insured made in the application for insurance is grounds for rescission of the policy. Recall from Chapter 3 that rescission is a legal action by which an insurer seeks to void a policy. For any claim in which a material misstatement or a material misrepresentation appears to be evident, the claim analyst determines whether the contestable period is still in effect.

Elimination Period

Some DI policies specify an ***elimination period***, which is the amount of time between the time that a covered disability begins and the time that an insured is eligible to receive benefits. The purpose of an elimination period in DI insurance is to eliminate the expense of administering small amounts of benefits for injuries or illnesses that last only a brief time. The claim analyst verifies that any required elimination period has been satisfied before approving DI benefits.

Benefit Period

The ***benefit period*** of a DI policy is the length of time during which DI benefits will be paid, typically lasting from less than a year to age 65 or

70. Some long-term DI contracts specify that DI coverage will be offered until the insured's normal retirement age; other contracts provide for lifetime DI benefits.

Definition of Disability

In order to be eligible to receive benefits under a DI contract, an insured must meet the contract's definition of disability. The claim analyst ascertains whether an insured has met the policy's definition of a particular level of disability, which may vary from one policy to another. The levels of disability covered under disability contracts typically include total disability, presumptive total disability, residual disability, partial disability, and recurring disability.

Total Disability

The most commonly used definition of ***total disability*** in both short-term and long-term DI contracts includes the complete and continuous inability of an insured at the beginning of his disability to perform the essential duties of his regular occupation. The total disability definition for long-term disability usually specifies that after an insured has been disabled for a specified period, usually two to five years, the person is considered totally disabled only if the disability prevents him from fulfilling the requirements of *any occupation* for which he is reasonably fitted by education, training, or experience. Insurers typically distinguish between an "own occupation" disability—one that prevents an insured from performing the essential duties of his regular occupation —and an "any occupation" disability—one that prevents an insured from performing the essential duties of any occupation for which he is reasonably fitted.

Presumptive Total Disability

Some DI policies specify that if an insured suffers a presumptive total disability, that insured is eligible to receive DI benefits. A ***presumptive total disability*** is a condition that automatically causes an insured to be considered totally disabled. Such a loss is usually severe, such as total and permanent blindness, loss of speech or hearing in both ears, or loss of two limbs. For a presumptive total disability, the elimination period is usually waived. If an insured with a presumptive total disability is able to return to work, even in his own occupation, most insurers do not reduce the amount of DI benefits nor cease payment of benefits. The benefit period for presumptive total disability usually lasts until the end of the policy's maximum benefit period.

Residual Disability

Under most DI contracts, an insured is considered to have suffered a ***residual disability*** (also known as a *partial disability*) if he is not totally disabled, but is still unable to function as before the sickness or injury, and therefore suffers a reduction in income of at least the percentage—typically 20 percent to 25 percent—specified in the DI plan. Some insurers, in addition to the reduced income requirement, also specify that meeting the definition of residual disability requires that an insured need ongoing medical care and/or be unable to work for the length of time needed to perform his usual occupational duties.

Many insurers require that an insured satisfy an elimination period before becoming eligible for benefits for a residual disability. An insured usually must be disabled between 30 and 90 days before she becomes eligible for residual DI benefits.

Recurring Disability

Sometimes an insured experiences a period of total or residual disability, recovers from the disability, and is able to return to work. The condition that originally caused the disability may recur, with the result that the insured is once again totally or residually disabled. A ***recurring disability*** is one that is the result of the same cause as for an original disability and that reappears after (1) the original period of disability and (2) an intervening period of recovery.

Most DI policies provide that if such a disability (1) recurs within six months from the date the previous disability ended and (2) results from the original sickness or injury, then the insurer will consider the new disability period as a continuation of the original disability period. If more than six months has elapsed since the end of the previous disability and if the new disability results from the original sickness or injury, most insurers consider the new disability *not* to be a continuation of the previous disability and, therefore, establish new elimination and benefit periods. Benefits for recurring disability help the insured because the elimination period is waived. However, the length of the benefit period remains unchanged.

Benefit Amount

As we have noted, DI coverage is intended to replace some, but not all, of an insured's earnings. The amount of benefits is usually set during underwriting. If an insured's salary has increased significantly since the time of underwriting the coverage, or if an insured has developed significant other sources of income—for instance, from investments or a second job—the benefit amount remains as agreed in the contract for total disability.

Renewability

In handling individual disability policy claims, a claim analyst reviews a policy's specifications for renewability to determine whether the insured is, in fact, still covered by the policy. Generally, renewability is an essential feature of a DI policy because it determines whether an insurer continues to be responsible for the risk over a period of time. Four types of renewability provisions are those for noncancelable, guaranteed renewable, conditionally renewable, and optionally renewable coverage.

Noncancelable

The most liberal form of renewability for DI coverage is ***noncancelable***, which means that, until the insured reaches a specified age (usually age 65), the insurer will not cancel the coverage, increase the premiums, or change the policy provisions as long as the premiums are paid. A claim analyst evaluating a noncancelable DI policy has only to verify that the premiums are paid to date on the coverage.

Guaranteed Renewable

Guaranteed renewable DI coverage offers the same continued coverage as noncancelable coverage *except* that the insurer can increase the premiums, not for an individual insured, but for all the policyowners within a defined class of insureds. Classes may be defined by age group, sex, policy type, occupation, or other specific criteria. In verifying that a guaranteed renewable policy is still in force, the claim analyst checks whether the premiums are paid to date and whether any increase in premium that has been communicated to the insured has been reflected in recent premium payments.

Conditionally Renewable

A DI policy that is ***conditionally renewable*** sets criteria that the insured must meet to renew the coverage. The most frequently established criterion is continued employment or ongoing membership in a professional or other organization. Verifying coverage under a conditionally renewable DI policy requires the claim analyst to check that the insured continues to meet the criteria established for that coverage. A refusal to renew a conditionally renewable DI policy cannot be based on the health of the insured.

Optionally Renewable

Optionally renewable DI coverage enables an insurer to change premium rates at any time and to cancel the coverage with sufficient notice to an insured.

Exceptions

If a disability is named in a policy as one for which no coverage is offered, then claims for such a disability will not be paid. Most DI policies specify that DI benefits will not be paid for injuries or sickness that result from an act of declared or undeclared war, as well as suicide or attempted suicide, whether an insured is sane or insane.

Some DI policies provide that on the first day that an insured enters full-time active duty in any branch of the armed forces of any country, DI coverage is suspended until full-time active duty is completed. Generally, full-time active duty does not include active duty training that lasts for two months or less.

Supplementary Benefits Under Disability Income Coverage

The supplementary benefits included under many DI policies are waiver of premium for disability, a cost of living increase benefit, a rehabilitation benefit, a transplant donor benefit, and future increase options.

Waiver of Premium for Disability

Unlike a waiver of premium for disability rider in a life insurance policy, a waiver of premium rider in a DI policy automatically becomes effective as soon as monthly DI benefits become payable. You'll recall that a waiver of premium for disability rider for a life insurance policy provides that after an insured has been disabled for a specified period—usually 60 to 90 days—premiums for the life insurance policy will be waived for as long as the insured is disabled. If the insured has paid any premiums during the specified period, those premiums are refunded. The claim analyst is responsible for ensuring that premium refunds are correctly and promptly made. In the case of a waiver of premium for disability rider for a DI policy, the "specified period" generally refers to the elimination period or another period cited in the policy.

Cost of Living Increase

After an insured has received total disability benefits for a specified, uninterrupted period—usually 12 consecutive months—a ***cost of living increase benefit*** provides an increase in the monthly disability benefit. This increase is typically a percentage of the monthly benefit amount. The assumption underlying a cost of living increase benefit is that an employed person would probably continue to receive periodic salary increases. If a policy contains a cost of living increase provision and the insured continues to be disabled, the claim analyst authorizes an increase in the benefit amount according to the terms of the provision.

Rehabilitation Benefit

During any period when an insured is receiving total or partial disability benefits, the ***rehabilitation benefit*** provides that an insurer will reimburse the insured for the expenses associated with participation in a rehabilitation program. The definition of a rehabilitation program is specified in the DI policy and typically requires that any such program must be operated by a federal, state, or provincial government or must be offered by a licensed hospital, vocational school, business school, or accredited college. Rehabilitation may include physical, educational, or vocational assistance. Some insurers offer rehabilitation reimbursements to some insureds even if the DI policy does not contain this type of provision, particularly if the insured seems to be motivated to work and if rehabilitation will cost less than projected DI benefits.

Most insurers require an insured who requests such rehabilitation benefits to consult with the insurer and reach agreement on the type and extent of rehabilitation services that will be reimbursed. In addition, most policies set a dollar limit on the total amount of rehabilitation benefits or on the type of rehabilitation services that will be reimbursed. The dollar limit is usually a multiple, such as 10 or 12, of the policy's maximum monthly disability benefit. For example, if a DI policy paid a maximum monthly disability benefit of $1,000 and the rehabilitation limit was 12 times the maximum monthly disability benefit, the total amount that the policy would pay for rehabilitation services would not exceed $12,000.

Transplant Donor Benefit

A ***transplant donor benefit*** specifies that if an insured undergoes surgery to donate a part of his body to another person, the insurer will treat that surgery as a sickness and will pay benefits for it. If the surgery results in total disability, benefits will be paid under the policy. Most insurers limit the transplant donor benefit by requiring that a transplant surgery occur at least 12 months after the policy's effective date. Among other facts, the claim analyst verifies that the required time period has passed since the policy date.

Future Increase Option

Some insurers allow insureds to exercise a ***future increase option*** to buy additional DI protection without providing evidence of insurability. The waiting period and the maximum benefit period for each increase are usually the same as for the original policy. The premium for each increase is figured using the rates in effect at the insured's attained age at the time the increase is purchased. If any extra premiums or riders are attached to the original policy because of an impairment stated on the policy application, they also apply to future increases. After an insured exercises a future increase option, the insurer generally requires proof that the insured's earnings meet the insurer's financial underwriting requirements so that the insured does not attempt to purchase coverage that she cannot afford and that might provide an incentive to avoid work.

Information Sources for Disability Income Claims

Evaluation of a DI claim involves not only establishing the presence of a disability, but also determining the future ability of the insured to perform the duties of her current job or of another job. In addition, the evaluation may focus on planned rehabilitation for the insured so that she will be able to return as soon as possible to work at her own occupation or at another occupation.

In handling claims under DI coverage, the claim analyst typically uses two basic sources of information: the claim form and the attending physician's statement (APS). Additional medical, financial, personal, and employment information may be requested if necessary. The claim analyst uses financial documents, including income tax documents, if he needs financial information for a claim.

Disability Income Claim Form

When a disability claim analyst receives notice of a claim, the analyst immediately sends the insured a claim form for filing proof of loss. Most insurers require that the insured submit the claim form within a specified time, usually 30 to 90 days, after the onset of disability, but most insurers also permit an insured to submit a claim form after this time, particularly if the nature of the disability prevented the insured from submitting the claim in a more timely manner.

Claim forms for both short-term (also called *weekly income*) claims and long-term claims ask for essentially the same kinds of information, but a claim for long-term DI benefits typically requires considerably more information than does a claim for short-term DI benefits. Both short-term and long-term disability claim forms contain a section that the insured completes and a section that the attending physician completes. If either type of claim is submitted under group coverage, the claim form also contains a section that the employer completes. Each insurer determines what information it needs to make a claim decision as accurately and efficiently as possible. Figure 15-1 provides an example of a claim form for short-term DI claims.

Using information on the claim form, the claim analyst assesses the type of illness or injury and the cause of the disability. The cause of disability is especially important for two reasons. First, the insurer's liability for coverage depends on whether the cause fits the policy's definitions. Some policies, as we have noted, provide different elimination periods depending on whether a disability results from an illness or an accident. If an insured has submitted a disability claim under coverage that specifies a one-week elimination period for disability resulting from an illness, but no elimination period for disability resulting from an accident, the date on which payments begin depends on the nature of the cause. The claim analyst verifies the cause to ensure that benefits are appropriately paid, neither sooner nor later than provided in the policy.

Second, coverage depends on whether the cause of disability is a risk excluded from the policy. Most disability policies exclude such causes of disability as attempted suicide, self-inflicted injuries, and occupationally related disabilities or sicknesses that are covered under a government program such as workers' compensation, which we'll define later in this chapter. Some disability policies exclude or provide only limited coverage for disabilities resulting from mental or nervous conditions or from participation in specified dangerous avocations.

APS and Medical Information

The APS is critical for DI claim analysis because it provides detailed information about the nature and cause of the disability, along with supporting evidence that includes the physician's diagnosis, the results of laboratory and other tests, the types of treatment and medication recommended, and the places and dates of treatment. By reviewing the APS, the claim analyst can usually determine a great deal about the nature and extent of the disability and the probable prognosis.

FIGURE 15-1. Short-Term Disability Income Claim Form Under Group Coverage.

PART I—Employee:

Your Employer's Name | Group Number

Your Name	Ctf. No./Social Security No.	Birth Date Mo. Day Yr.	Sex ❒ M ❒ F

Your Home Address (Street Address, City, State, Zip)

This Claim is For ❒ Illness ❒ Accident	Illness/Injury Is Work Related ❒ Yes ❒ No

Nature of Illness or Injury

IF ACCIDENT	Date Accident Occurred	Time ❒ AM ❒ PM	Place
	Details of Accident		

I hereby authorize ______________ and/or ______________
(insert your primary doctor's name) (insert the name of your hospital)

to release to ABC Life Insurance Company or its representative any and all information with respect to myself that may have bearing on the benefits payable under this plan. I certify that the above information in support of this claim is true and correct. A copy of this authorization shall be considered as effective and valid as the original. This authorization shall be valid for 60 days.

Date ______________ Signature of Insured ______________

PART II—Employer's Certification: Please include a copy of the job description with this form.

Name of Employee

Group Number	Certificate Number	Employment Date	Insurance Eff. Date	Insurance Class

I certify that the Employee is ❒ a full-time active employee working a minimum of 30 hours per week or ❒ on disability leave.

If employment has been terminated, give date: ______________
Is illness due to occupational causes? ______________
Date absence began: ______________ Date returned to work: ______________
Amount of earnings: Weekly $ ______________ Monthly $ ______________
If premium for Weekly Income is contributory, give percent of employee's contribution _____%

Name of Employer	Mailing Address

Date ______________ Signed by ______________
Representative of Employer

Figure 15-1. Short-Term Disability Income Claim Form Under Group Coverage (continued).

PART III—Attending Physician's Statement:

Patient's Name   Date of Birth

Diagnosis and concurrent conditions:

PHYSICAL IMPAIRMENT (*as defined in Federal Dictionary of Occupational Titles)

- ❒ Class 1 — No limitation of functional capacity; capable of heavy work* No restrictions (0–10%)
- ❒ Class 2 — Medium manual activity* (15–30%)
- ❒ Class 3 — Slight limitation of functional capacity; capable of light work* (35–55%)
- ❒ Class 4 — Moderate limitation of functional capacity; capable of clerical/administrative (sedentary*) (60–70%)
- ❒ Class 5 — Severe limitation of functional capacity; incapable of minimal (sedentary*) activity (75–100%)
- ❒ Remarks

MENTAL/NERVOUS IMPAIRMENT (if applicable)

(a) Please define "stress" as it applies to this claimant.

(b) What stress and problems in interpersonal relations has claimant had on job?

- ❒ Class 1 — Patient is able to function under stress and engage in interpersonal relations (no limitations).
- ❒ Class 2 — Patient is able to function in most stress situations and engage in most interpersonal relations (slight limitations).
- ❒ Class 3 — Patient is able to engage in only limited stress situations or engage in only limited interpersonal relations (moderate limitations).
- ❒ Class 4 — Patient is unable to engage in stress situations or engage in interpersonal relations (marked limitations).
- ❒ Class 5 — Patient has significant loss of psychological, physiological, personal and social adjustment (severe limitations)
- ❒ Remarks

Do you believe the patient is competent to endorse checks and direct the use of the proceeds thereof? ❒ Yes ❒ No

Is condition due to injury or sickness arising out of patient's employment? ❒ Yes ❒ No

Date symptoms first appeared or accident happened: ____________

If patient was referred by other physician, give name: ____________

Address of other physician: ____________

Date patient first consulted you for this condition: ____________

Is patient still under your care for this condition? ❒ Yes ❒ No

Patient was continuously totally disabled (unable to work) from ______ through ______

Patient was partially disabled from ______ through ______

If still disabled, date patient should be able to return to work: ____________

Physician's Name (Type or Print)	Degree	SS# or ID#	Telephone ( )

Mailing Address

Date	Signature of Attending Physician

Some physicians are reluctant to state that an insured is in fact disabled, usually because a physician may not know the details of an insured's occupation and is, therefore, not in a position to judge the presence of disability. Most physicians will, however, provide sufficient information for the claim analyst to determine whether the insured is disabled under the terms of the policy. Because a claim for disability is not as easily verified as a claim for death or a claim for medical reimbursement, the claim analyst who handles disability claims needs special training in evaluating the nature and extent of physical and mental impairments and in determining to what extent such impairments hamper the performance of specific job duties.

To encourage a physician to help determine the presence and extent of a disability, a claim analyst sometimes sends the physician information about the policy provisions relating to disability and a copy of the insured's job description from the employer. Using this information, the physician can help the claim analyst determine whether the insured is disabled under the terms of the policy and whether the insured is capable of performing some or all of the specified job duties. If a physician cannot or will not verify a claimed disability, the claim analyst usually requires the insured to undergo an examination by an independent medical professional named and paid by the insurance company. The claim analyst also may consult the insurer's medical director, who can provide insight into medical diagnoses and treatments and can advise the claim analyst during the investigation of a DI claim. None of these professionals—the attending physician, the independent medical professional, or the medical director—makes a final decision on a claim. After consultation with these experts, the claim analyst is responsible for making that decision.

To obtain further medical information about a claimant, the claim analyst can consult MIB and the Disability Insurance Records System (DIRS), which is managed by MIB and which provides insurers with information designed to alert them to the presence of overinsurance—particularly other coverage applied for or in force. This information is especially important for individual DI policies during the contestable period.

Financial Information

The claim analyst is responsible for obtaining the correct financial documents to verify the income loss to a disabled insured and to examine those documents closely so as to determine the appropriate amount of benefits. If an insured has suffered a disability, the claim analyst requires financial documents to verify the amount of financial loss suffered. Generally, a W-2 form or 1099 form in the United States or a T4 form in Canada, as well as other tax forms that identify income from other sources, is sufficient to establish the level of the insured's previous income.

If a disabled insured is the sole proprietor of a business, the claim analyst usually obtains federal income tax returns for the business, along with a profit and loss statement, to verify the level of income that the insured derived from the business. If a disabled insured is a partner in a business, a copy of the partnership tax return usually provides enough information for the claim analyst to establish the income level of the insured. Other forms of businesses such as regular corporations and "S" corporations—in which income and expenses are reported as though the corporation were a partnership—require that other financial documents be submitted in support of a DI claim.

Personal Information

For some DI claims, the disability may continue for an unusually long time although the insured appears to be only moderately ill or injured. The claim analyst may need to gather personal information on an insured to determine whether the disability is responsible for the insured's slow recovery or whether other factors are playing a part. The claim analyst has access to the same kinds of investigatory techniques that an underwriter has, including personal interviews with the insured. Although inspection reports are not widely used for investigations of DI claims, the analyst does have access to such resources. The usual information developed by an inspection report focuses on the degree of an insured's disability, the presence of overinsurance, and verification of information on income and employment. Moreover, claim analysts sometimes consult with the insurer's legal staff or with accountants inside or outside the insurance company to verify the details of financial records, particularly for large-amount claims under business disability coverages. Surveillance is sometimes used to discover whether an insured is working at an undisclosed occupation or is engaging in other activities that are inconsistent with the disability.

Employer Information

If a claim analyst determines that he needs further information concerning the insured's employment, he usually asks the employer for the necessary information. The type of information usually requested includes details about an insured's job duties, compensation, and place and hours of work. Figure 15-2 illustrates a sample job analysis form for a long-term DI claim. The claim analyst may also need to determine whether the employer anticipates continuing to employ the insured if the insured is able to return to work. If the insured can work

FIGURE 15-2. Job Analysis Form for Long-term Disability.

To be completed by the employee's supervisor

This claim is for (Employee's Name)

Employee's Social Security Number	Date of Disability (Month, Day, Year)

A. General information about the employee's job

Job Title	Minimum education or training required

Does the employee perform supervisory functions?

❒ Yes ❒ No If yes, how many people are supervised? ______________ Describe job duties.

Check the items below that relate to the employee's job. Use these definitions for the frequency of occurrence:
Occasionally means the person does the activity up to 33% of the time.
Frequently means the person does the activity 34% to 66% of the time.
Continuously means the person does the activity 67% to 100% of the time.

	OCCASIONALLY	FREQUENTLY	CONTINUOUSLY
Relate to others	❒	❒	❒
Written and verbal communication	❒	❒	❒
Reasoning, math and language	❒	❒	❒
Makes independent judgments	❒	❒	❒

Which of the following describe the employee's working environment? Check all that apply.

❒ Unprotected heights ❒ Changes in temperature or humidity ❒ Exposure to dust, fumes, and gases
❒ Being near moving machinery ❒ Driving automotive equipment ❒ Other hazards

Is the employee required to travel? ❒ Yes ❒ No If yes, complete the following information:

How does the employee travel? (Automobile, plane, train, etc.)	Where does the employee travel?	What percent of the time does the employee travel?

B. Information about the physical aspects of the employee's job

Check the items below that relate to the employee's job and complete the information requested. Use these definitions for the frequency of occurrence:
Occasionally means the person does the activity up to 33% of the time.
Frequently means the person does the activity 34% to 66% of the time.
Continuously means the person does the activity 67% to 100% of the time.

ACTIVITY	FREQUENCY OF OCCURRENCE				
	OCCASIONALLY	FREQUENTLY	CONTINUOUSLY	Describe Activity	Weight
❒ Standing	❒	❒	❒		
❒ Walking	❒	❒	❒		
❒ Sitting	❒	❒	❒		
❒ Balancing	❒	❒	❒		
❒ Stooping	❒	❒	❒		
❒ Kneeling	❒	❒	❒		
❒ Crouching	❒	❒	❒		
❒ Crawling	❒	❒	❒		
❒ Reaching/working overhead	❒	❒	❒		
❒ Climbing:	❒	❒	❒		
❒ Stairs	❒	❒	❒		
Number of stairs: ______					
❒ Ladders					
Height of ladder _____					
❒ Pulling	❒	❒	❒	________________	_____ lbs.
❒ Lifting/Carrying	❒	❒	❒	________________	_____ lbs.
❒ Pushing				________________	_____ lbs.

Figure 15-2. Job Analysis Form for Long-term Disability (continued).

Can the job be performed by alternating sitting and standing?
❐ Yes ❐ No

Does the job require using the feet to operate foot controls?
❐ Yes ❐ No If yes, on what type of equipment?

How important is good vision in the job?

What are the major tasks requiring use of one or both hands?	One Hand	Both Hands
______	❐	❐
______	❐	❐
______	❐	❐

C. Information about the job as it relates to the disability

Can the job be modified to accommodate the disability either temporarily or permanently?
❐ Yes ❐ No If yes, explain

Is it possible to offer the employee assistance in doing the job (through use of technology or personal assistance, for example)?
❐ Yes ❐ No If yes, explain

D. Attachments and Signature (Attach a copy of the employee's job description)

Name of person completing this form

X ______

Signature Title Date

Telephone Fax

only under certain conditions, such as reduced hours or revised responsibilities, the claim analyst attempts to learn whether the employer is willing to accommodate those needs.

Administering Disability Income Claims

After examining the information submitted on a DI claim, the claim analyst orders whatever additional information is needed. As soon as all necessary information has been collected, the claim analyst makes a decision on the claim and notifies the claimant of that decision.

If the decision is to deny the claim, the claim analyst sends a letter to the claimant, explaining the basis for the denial. If the decision is to pay the claim, in whole or in part, the claim analyst sends a letter to the claimant and specifies the benefits to which the claimant is entitled. A copy of the letter is usually sent to the agent who originally sold the DI policy.

As part of information gathering before making a claim decision, the claim analyst verifies whether the claimant is also covered by another form of disability coverage. An important goal of the claim analyst is to ensure that a claimant does not receive a disproportionate amount of compensation from various sources of disability insurance. Generally, all DI plans, whether public programs or private coverage, provide that a claimant may not receive a total of more than 60 to 80 percent of pre-disability earnings. The purpose of such a limitation is not to reduce the costs of claims, but rather to motivate disabled people to return to work if recovery is possible.

In the United States, two pieces of legislation affect the handling of DI claims. One is the Family Medical Leave Act (FMLA), which states that an employer must allow an employee to take unpaid leave if the employee's own serious health condition makes job performance impossible. Generally, a serious health condition in this context is one that will require (1) absence from the workplace for more than three calendar days and (2) continuing treatment from a health care provider. The FMLA also mandates unpaid leave for childbirth and certain chronic conditions such as diabetes and asthma even though treatment at any time might last less than three calendar days.

Another piece of legislation that affects the handling of DI claims is the Americans with Disabilities Act (ADA), which provides that if an employee suffers a disability, the employer must make certain accommodations to enable the employee to continue employment. For example, if a disabled employee must work from a wheelchair, the employer is obligated to make certain changes in the employee's workstation to accommodate the wheelchair. If an employee has developed an ongoing disease such as diabetes, the employer is obligated by the ADA to make allowances in the employee's work schedule so that the employee can make periodic insulin level checks and eat if necessary. The claim analyst, aided by the insurer's legal staff, verifies that an employee who wishes to return to work is accommodated under the provisions of the ADA. When an employee suffers a disability that is likely to be long-term, but that is not so serious that the employee could not work at some occupation, the claim analyst oversees the case and sometimes helps the employer determine whether accommodations can be made that will permit the employee to return to work on a full- or part-time basis.

Coordinating Other Disability Income Benefits

In addition to DI benefits under a contract of insurance, an insured may be eligible for DI coverage provided by a number of other sources. In the United States, ***workers' compensation*** is government-mandated insurance that provides benefits to covered employees and their dependents if the employee suffers a job-related injury, disease, or death. Workers' compensation is administered by each state, and its benefits vary considerably from one state to another. Social Security Disability Income (SSDI) in the United States and social insurance under the Canada Pension Plan (CPP) and the Quebec Pension Plan (QPP) in Canada (as well as through the Unemployment Insurance Programme) provide DI benefits when a worker is so severely impaired physically or mentally that he cannot perform any substantial work and is not expected to recover within 12 months. A person must be disabled for at least five months before becoming eligible to submit a claim for disability benefits through such government-sponsored insurance programs. These programs also encourage workers to return to work by providing benefits for a nine-month trial work period (during which the worker tries to return to work) and an additional three-month grace period. In addition, some states in the United States provide residents with DI payments for disabilities that are not work-related, and some employers in the United States and Canada include DI benefits under their group life insurance coverage.

The claim analyst notifies an insured who is covered by more than one type of disability coverage of any applicable ***offset***, which is a federal tax provision that allows an insurer to use the benefits paid under one type of insurance coverage to reduce the benefits paid for another type of coverage. The purposes of an offset are (1) to ensure that a disabled person does not receive an excessive total amount of benefits and (2) to encourage the disabled person to return to work. The types of coverage usually resulting in offsets to DI coverage include Social Security in the United States and social insurance in Canada, as well as workers' compensation, employer sick leave benefits, and other DI coverage (for instance, an insured who becomes covered by a group DI policy at work may also be covered by an individual DI policy he purchased earlier). Some DI policies further specify that the amount of DI or retirement benefits paid to an insured's spouse or children may also be considered in calculating the offset to DI benefits.

> **FAST FACT**
>
> Musculoskeletal disorders affect about 1 million workers and cost the United States $45 to $54 billion in compensation expenses, lost wages, and decreased productivity each year.[2]

When a claim analyst determines that a claimant is eligible for DI coverage under Social Security, the analyst sends the claimant a notice that the offset will be used in determining the amount of benefits that the insurer will pay. Some insurers provide a claimant with several options, usually (1) to reduce the amount of monthly DI benefits from the insurer by the amount of DI benefit paid by Social Security or another source or (2) to pay the monthly benefit with no reduction until the claimant has time to apply for Social Security DI benefits. When the Social Security DI benefits begin, the claimant is then obligated to notify the insurer that such payments have begun and to repay the excess amount he has received from the insurer. Figure 15-3 shows a typical statement of long-term DI payment options.

FIGURE 15-3. Statement of Long-Term Disability Payment Options.

LONG-TERM DISABILITY PAYMENT OPTIONS

Insurer____________________ (Herein referred to as "we" and "us")

Policy No.__________ Claim No. __________ Date of Disability ____________________

Issued to ____________________ Address ____________________

Claimant ____________________ Address ____________________

The policy under which you are covered provides that Long-Term Disability benefits will be reduced by the amount of Social Security benefits that **you and your spouse and family** are eligible to receive. The policy also provides that if you do not apply for Social Security benefits, the policy benefits will be reduced by the amount of Social Security benefits **you and your spouse and family** would be eligible to receive if application had been made.

We understand that the Social Security Administration has not yet made a decision concerning your benefits. Until the Social Security Administration makes a decision, your Long-Term Disability benefits can be handled in one of two ways:

❒ 1. We can estimate the amount of Social Security benefits **you and your spouse and family** will receive and reduce your monthly policy benefit by this amount. If Social Security benefits are estimated, the monthly policy benefit will be adjusted when we receive proof of the amount awarded by Social Security or that Social Security benefits have been denied and the denial is not being appealed. If your Social Security application is denied and the denial is not being appealed, the amount estimated will be returned to you in a lump sum.

❒ 2. We can pay you a monthly benefit with no reduction for estimated Social Security benefits until Social Security makes a decision. This may result in an overpayment by us. You must supply us with a copy of the Social Security decision and repay any overpayment. In addition, if Social Security makes an award, we will reduce your monthly policy benefit by the amount of Social Security benefits **you and your spouse and family** receive according to the policy provisions. If you want to elect this option but have not yet applied for Social Security benefits, you must agree to apply for them immediately. If you do not apply for Social Security benefits, we will use approach #1.

Please tell us which approach you want to use by checking box #1 or box #2 and signing this form. If you make no selection, we will use approach #1. If you have any questions, please contact us.

(Insured)	(Witness)
(Address)	(Address)
(Date)	(Date)

Managing Benefits for Mental Illness and Substance Abuse

Because disabilities resulting from mental illness and substance abuse are often more difficult to specify and define than are disabilities resulting from physical sickness and injury, insurers manage such claims carefully. Particularly for difficult-to-define conditions such as depression or anxiety, the claim analyst has to make decisions based on more subjective data than that which usually accompanies a physical injury or illness claim.

Generally the most effective way to manage benefits for mental illness and substance abuse is to define in the policy the conditions that are covered, the level of coverage for each, and any other requirements for payment of benefits. The responsibility of the claim analyst is to verify that an insured who has applied for such benefits has complied with the policy requirements and definitions.

In handling a claim for mental illness, the claim analyst often performs a work site assessment to determine the claimant's usual job duties. The assessment is the first step in deciding the extent to which the claimant is prevented by mental illness from performing his job functions. During a ***work site assessment***, a claim analyst or an investigator interviews an employer and reviews the actual job duties and the claimant's level of success in performing those duties. The claim analyst or investigator also obtains a specific job description for the claimant, learns the criteria by which the claimant's performance is evaluated, and determines whether such factors as downsizing or legal difficulties have affected the claimant's job. If a claimant is self-employed, the analyst or investigator obtains as much detail as possible about the claimant's work by using client appointment records, contracts, financial documents, and interviews with clients.

Managing Benefits for Continuing Claims

An insured may be disabled for a considerable period of time, during which the claim analyst remains informed about the insured's condition and his ability to return to some form of employment. Most insurers require a disabled insured to submit proof of continuation of the DI claim, usually at monthly intervals. An exception is made for insureds who are clearly totally disabled and whose medical prognosis indicates little chance of recovery to near-normal functioning. For such insureds, most insurers require only semiannual or annual proof that an insured continues to be disabled and, therefore, eligible for benefits.

The length of time a person is disabled for a specified injury or illness can vary widely. Most insurers develop information based on their experience and on published medical information about the typical disability period for injuries and illnesses, and use that information in evaluating claims. Claim analysts use that information as a guide in assessing a claim. Such information might indicate, for example, that a fracture of the femur (thigh bone) near the hip can be expected to cause a disability ranging on average from 8 to 12 months, whereas a person who undergoes a hip replacement is typically considered disabled for 4 to 5 months.

Sometimes insurers base the expected length of disability on the type of work that an insured performs. For instance, if an insured who usually performs a job requiring sedentary activity undergoes surgical repair for a foot abnormality, the expected length of disability may range from three to four weeks. By contrast, a person whose work requires light to medium physical activity may be expected to be disabled during recovery from the surgery for a period ranging from four to six weeks.

The claim analyst does not consider this information to be absolute, however. Some insureds who suffer specified illnesses or injuries may be able to return to work within a shorter time than the periods specified, whereas other insureds may require extensive treatment or physical therapy and may not be able to return to work for periods longer than those stated.

Estimating the length of time an insured will be disabled is one of a claim analyst's most important duties, but this task is difficult because the duration of a disability can vary depending on several factors. An insured's previous medical condition can affect the length of disability: a person who was quite healthy prior to an illness or injury may recover more rapidly than a person who was not in good health before becoming disabled. Other factors that can affect the length of a disability include the insured's age, the severity of the disability, the presence of complications and other physical and mental conditions, and the type of treatment available for the disability. In addition to these factors, an insured may or may not be motivated to return to work, may have a greater or lesser economic need to return to work, or may not be able to find work suitable for his present physical and mental condition.

Most proofs of a continuing DI claim are brief, consisting of a statement of continuing disability that is completed by the insured or by someone familiar with the insured's condition. Few insurers require a new APS each month, although if a disability appears to be short-term, the claim analyst may need APS information to determine that the disability is in fact continuing.

Requiring proof of a continuing DI claim is not intended to harass disabled people, but is intended to help an insurer disburse claim funds in a responsible manner. If an insured continues to be unable to perform job duties according to the terms of the DI policy, the insurer continues to pay benefits according to the contract's provisions. However, an insurer that paid unjustified benefits for disability or any other cause could put itself and other insureds in financial jeopardy. As we have mentioned previously, one of an insurer's principal accountabilities is to pay all legitimate claims and to deny all others. Obtaining proof that a claim continues to be legitimate exemplifies an insurer's responsible business conduct.

If an insured recovers from a disability and is no longer eligible to receive DI benefits, the insured—or, for group coverages, sometimes the employer—sends the insurer a notice of recovery from disability. After receiving such a notice, the claim analyst stops payment of DI benefits. Figure 15-4 shows a typical notice of recovery from disability.

FIGURE 15-4. Notice of Recovery from Disability.

NOTICE OF RECOVERY FROM DISABILITY

(This form to be sent to the Insurance Company by the Employer as soon as possible after the Employee recovers)

THIS IS TO INFORM YOU THAT ______________________________
(Name of Employee)

insured under Group Policy No. ______________________ Certificate No. ____________________

returned to work on ______________________ 20_____, having recovered from his recent disability

on ______________________ 20_____.
(Last Day of Actual Total Disability)

____
Employer

Date ______________________ 20_____.

By ______________________________

Form 1113 Rev. 1-00

Administering Contestable Claims

Recall that most DI policies provide for a two-year contestable period for material misstatements or material misrepresentations in the application for insurance. In addition, group DI contracts generally provide that, to be covered under the contract, a group member must meet certain requirements. For example, a person who wishes to enroll in a group plan after the usual date for such enrollment or who wishes to obtain an amount of insurance higher than the usual amount offered must submit evidence of insurability. If that evidence includes deliberately false information, the coverage can be voided, and no benefits will be due if a claim was filed.

Further, a person who claims to be insured under a group contract is sometimes shown to be ineligible for the group coverage. For instance, if a group contract requires that all eligible insureds must work at least

36 hours per week, a claimant who works only 30 hours per week is not eligible in many jurisdictions for benefits under the group contract.

Administering Questionable Claims

Some DI claims raise questions that must be answered before the claim analyst can make a decision to pay or deny them. A claim analyst investigates most questionable claims, but insurers sometimes turn over complex or highly unusual claims to an outside investigative agency. For most questionable claims, additional information from the insured, the policyholder, health care providers, and independent medical examiners enables the claim analyst to reach a decision.

The most common circumstances in which claims may be considered questionable and may require additional investigation include late notice of claim, occupational injuries, termination of employment, problematic diagnosis, problematic prognosis, and infrequent medical attention.

Late Notice of Claim

If notice of a claim is not submitted within a reasonable period of time after a disability is alleged to have begun, the notice is considered late. Because most genuinely disabled insureds need money to replace lost income and, therefore, tend to file DI claims promptly, a late notice of claim may indicate a suspicious claim. The claim analyst determines whether an investigative report is needed of the claimant's activities during the period of alleged total disability. After a claimant has returned to work, a medical examination is of no value in determining the degree of disability during the period when the claimant was not at work.

Occupational Injuries

If an injury that occurred in the work environment has produced disability, a government-sponsored insurance program such as workers' compensation may be liable for paying disability benefits. The claim analyst conducts a thorough investigation to see whether the claimant is eligible for other coverage.

Termination of Employment

If a claimant's employment has been terminated for any reason—including voluntary resignation or retirement, discharge, and temporary layoff—the claim analyst typically investigates to determine the cause of termination. Because an employee who has been terminated from work usually seeks employment elsewhere or applies for unemployment compensation, the claim analyst checks whether the claimant is able to work or has filed a claim for DI benefits from another source.

Problematic Diagnosis

The diagnosis offered for a claimant's disability is sometimes nonspecific or vague. In either case, the claim analyst undertakes an investigation to determine the exact diagnosis.

If an attending physician reports symptoms rather than a diagnosis, the claim analyst probes to determine the exact diagnosis. For instance, a medical report stating that a patient is experiencing nausea, dizziness, enlarged lymph nodes, tremors, seizures, or backache is not sufficient to present a clear picture of a claimant's physical condition. These symptoms could be caused by any number of conditions.

A diagnosis that is so vague that it reveals little about a claimant's true medical or psychological condition is incomplete for claim purposes. Such a diagnosis provides no details on which the claim analyst can base a reasonable assessment of the claim. For example, a diagnosis may state only that a claimant suffers from anemia, arthritis, anxiety, pneumonia, hepatitis, or stroke with no accompanying details or explanations. Any of these conditions could be of minor or major concern, depending on their extent. Given such a vague diagnosis, the claim analyst typically interviews or requests further written information from the physician in order to discover precisely what condition has caused the claimant's disability.

Problematic Prognosis

An ambiguous or unreasonably extended prognosis usually requires careful investigation to determine the extent of a disability. Occasionally a physician indicates only that a claimant's prognosis is "unknown," "indefinite," or "uncertain" and refuses to state a date by which the claimant can be expected to return to work. Certain medical conditions do defy accurate estimates of continuing disability. However, for other conditions—particularly those for which the prognosis seems inconsistent with the cause of disability—the claim analyst persists in trying to learn from the physician a reasonable estimate of recovery time.

Sometimes an attending physician repeatedly extends the period of time during which a claimant will be disabled. If the physician offers only an indefinite prognosis or changes the previous estimate of the date of return to work and if the nature of the disability does not appear to warrant such an extended prognosis, the claim analyst generally attempts to elicit from the physician specific information about the disability and the specific work activities in which the claimant can reasonably be expected to take part.

Infrequent Medical Attention

When a claimant appears to need medical attention only infrequently, the claim analyst is alerted to the possibility that the reported disability should be investigated. An independent medical examination and an activities check of the claimant are usually used to determine whether the apparently infrequent medical attention is all that is warranted.

Administering Rehabilitation

In addition to examining and making decisions on DI claims and monitoring the progress of claimants, some claim analysts administer rehabilitation programs for eligible insureds. ***Rehabilitation*** is the process of helping a disabled person return to work, either at her own occupation or at another occupation if she is unable to perform the duties of her own occupation. Rehabilitation may include medical treatment, vocational training, job placement, and any other activities that help a disabled insured return to gainful employment.

Rehabilitation can provide a valuable service to an insured by enabling him to reenter the work force. Rehabilitation also benefits an insurer by saving a significant amount in claim costs. Because rehabilitation is so important to both insureds and insurers, many insurance companies have established specialized teams of highly trained rehabilitation specialists who assist claim analysts in handling all such cases.

An insurer's rehabilitation team typically handles cases of many kinds, including musculoskeletal injuries, blindness, hearing impairments, cardiovascular and respiratory problems, substance abuse, and depression and other mental or nervous conditions. So much progress has been made in the development of special equipment such as voice-activated computers, specially designed work areas, and supplementary equipment that many people who would have been unemployable in the past can now return to work, sometimes in their original occupations with appropriate modifications to accommodate their disabilities. The provisions of the ADA, as we have mentioned, require employers to make reasonable accommodations so that disabled people can return to the workplace. Vendors specializing in rehabilitation can help an insurer manage many rehabilitation activities including evaluating the skills of disabled people, providing career counseling, performing job market surveys, and designing and building the devices needed to enable disabled people to return to work.

Rather than allow a considerable length of time to pass before beginning rehabilitation efforts, most insurers approach disabled insureds early in the period of disability to assess the prospects of an insured's being able to return to work. Generally, the longer a claimant receives disability payments, the more difficult it is for that person to take the steps necessary to prepare herself for active participation in the workplace and the less likely the person is to be motivated to return to work. Insight 15-1 discusses how early intervention programs can help disabled employees return to work.

To gather information about an insured's training, education, and experience, the claim analyst typically asks the insured to complete a brief questionnaire, which the claim analyst can use to guide planning for the insured's rehabilitation. Figure 15-5 illustrates such a rehabilitation information questionnaire.

As we have mentioned, many DI policies include a rehabilitation provision specifying that the insurer will pay for the costs of rehabilitation training. Further, many DI policies provide that a disabled insured who wishes to return to work will be granted a trial period, usually of one year, during which benefits will continue to be paid, typically in an amount that is reduced by some percentage according to the amount the insured is able to earn during that period. For example, if an insured is able to earn $2,000 per month during the trial year, his monthly DI benefits might be reduced by 50 percent of those earnings, or $1,000. If, during or following such a trial work period, the disabled employee decides that he is not yet able to return to work, the full long-term DI benefits will resume.

Terminating Disability Income Benefits

DI benefits terminate in several circumstances: when a policy's maximum benefit period is reached, when a claimant is no longer disabled under the terms of the policy, and, for group coverage, when an employee or a group is no longer eligible for coverage.

End of Maximum Benefit Period

When an insurer has paid benefits to the end of the maximum benefit period, the claimant is no longer eligible to receive DI payments. An insured who has received benefits under the "own occupation" definition of disability may reach the time limit of benefits paid under this requirement and may then be eligible for benefits paid under the "any occupation" definition. If the policy provides for payment of benefits only if an insured cannot work at his own occupation, then all benefits terminate at the end of the maximum benefit period.

Insight 15-1. Early Intervention = Substantial Savings.

All too often the importance of early intervention in managing an employer's overall disability costs is overlooked. However, once an employee has been out of work due to illness or injury for 12 weeks or more, chances of the person returning to work are 50/50 at best.

That's why, when evaluating disability program options, producers should recommend disability products that include early intervention programs with demonstrated favorable results. Consider: A recent study shows formal early intervention programs can return employees to work 20% sooner and save employers a significant amount on disability-related costs. Just released by Sun Life Financial, the study tracks outcomes of nearly 1,000 short-term disability (STD) claims between 1997 and 1999. (You can see the results at www.sunlife-usa.com.) To help clients evaluate early intervention programs, brokers should raise these questions:

1. Is a formal early intervention program already in place?

A formal program is one that routinely screens STD claims for rehabilitation potential according to predetermined guidelines. It also has a dedicated staff whose main goal is to identify and work with rehabilitation candidates. Having such a program is important because if return to work efforts don't begin during the STD stage, by the time the claim transfers to long-term disability (LTD) status, it may be too late to impact recovery. Early intervention also dramatically reduces the length of a disability claim and can help more claimants—47% more—return to work during the STD stage. And, the process not only reduces duration of claims but also reduces the number of STD claims that become LTD claims.

2. What makes for a strong early intervention program?

The best programs focus on the needs of individual claimants on a case-by-case basis. They use objective criteria to identify claims where the disability duration could be excessive if not properly managed, or, to identify claims requiring assistance in coordinating an early or modified return to work.

3. Who evaluates disability claims?

Case managers should be from vocational rehabilitation or medical staff, preferably those who have professional credentials such as the CRC (Certified Rehabilitation Counselor). They should work on a case-by-case basis, making adaptations to meet individual claimant needs. To expedite recovery and return to work, they should foster communication between employer, employee, physician and disability carrier.

4. Is the carrier demonstrably committed to early intervention?

Tell-tale signs of commitment include: The carrier fully integrates vocational rehabilitation resources into its early intervention program; it uses early intervention as the catalyst in its overall disability management practice; and it tracks and analyzes its own claims data (so it can quantify if the program is working).

5. What happens if, despite early intervention efforts, the claim becomes an LTD claim?

Check to be sure the same case manager stays with the claimant for the duration of the claim, even if the claim does transfer to LTD status. If the program doesn't do that, the claim may transfer to another rehabilitation specialist unfamiliar with the case—and that could seriously jeopardize chances of the employee returning to work. Also, check to be sure the carrier fully integrates its STD and LTD claims processes—systems and procedures. This will minimize any disruption in benefit payment and return-to-work efforts.

In sum, early intervention is the first line of defense in controlling STD/LTD costs. Without it, employers risk higher absenteeism, higher staffing costs, and lower productivity. In today's tight labor market, those are hits no employer can afford to take.

Source: Excerpted from Ken Arruda, "Early Intervention = Substantial Savings," *National Underwriter*, Life & Health/Financial Services ed. (5 March 2001): 29. Reprinted with permission from *National Underwriter*.

FIGURE 15-5. Rehabilitation Information Questionnaire.

Name ______________________ Policy Number ______________________

We are currently interested in receiving your response to the following questions so that we may continue to evaluate your claim and to understand your circumstances and needs. Please complete these questions and return the questionnaire to us in the enclosed postage-paid envelope.

1. Educational Background

Circle highest grade completed 1 2 3 4 5 6 7 8 9 10 11 12

Did you attend college? _____Yes _____No

Major field of study ______________________

Degree(s) received ______________________

Were you in the armed forces? _____ Yes _____No

Branch of service ______________________

Highest rank ______________________

Specialty ______________________

Please list any additional education or training you have had (carpentry, auto repair, sales, etc.).

2. Work Experience

Please list chronologically all the jobs you have had.

Dates Type of Work Physica Requirements Supervisory Experience, if any

____

____

____

3. How do you spend your time during the day? ______________________

____

4. How do you feel about returning to work? ______________________

____

5. If work was available that met your abilities and limitations, would you be interested in exploring the possibility of doing it? Please explain. ______________________

____

6. Do you have a special interest in specific occupations or work activities? Please explain. __________

____

7. Have you made efforts to explore work-related possibilities? Please explain. ______________

____

Please feel free to make any additional comments on the reverse side of this questionnaire. We appreciate your cooperation.

______________________________ ______________________
Signed Date

End of Disability

A claim analyst can terminate DI benefits to a claimant at any time that the analyst concludes that the claimant is no longer disabled according to the policy requirements. Making such a decision requires the analyst to gather sufficient information to be certain that the claimant is no longer eligible for benefits.

End of Employee or Group Eligibility

Termination of DI coverage under group insurance typically results when

- An employee is no longer a member of an eligible class covered under a group policy
- The employee's class is no longer eligible for coverage under the policy
- The employee is no longer employed by the organization that is the policyholder for the group coverage
- The group policy lapses because of nonpayment of premium
- The group policy is canceled or not renewed

Most group policies contain a provision that if the policyholder—that is, the employer—fails to pay any premium within the grace period, the policy terminates at midnight on the last day of the grace period. A policyholder who does not wish to renew a group policy or who wishes to cancel the policy can do so, usually by giving advance written notice to the insurer. Similarly, an insurer that does not wish to renew a policy can usually do so by giving written notice to the policyholder on any premium due date, at least 31 days in advance if

1. the number of employees insured is less than 10 or
2. fewer than 100 percent of the employees eligible for a noncontributory plan are insured under it or
3. fewer than 75 percent of the employees eligible for a contributory plan are insured under it or
4. the policyholder fails to furnish information that the insurer may reasonably require.

Settling Disability Income Claims

Instead of paying claims throughout a benefit period, sometimes insurers offer a claimant a ***claim settlement***, which is a lump-sum payment of money from the insurer to the claimant in exchange for the claimant's agreement to release the insurer from further responsibility for coverage under the policy. In effect, a claim settlement cancels the coverage under the DI policy. When an insured accepts the terms of a settlement offer, the insured usually signs a full, final, and complete release of all liability.

Most insurers present the offer of claim settlement in writing to the insured. Such an approach has the advantages of (1) indicating that the offer is freely made and that the insured is free to accept or reject the offer and (2) verifying that the insurer has given full consideration to the financial needs, vocational opportunities, and other factors of the insured's case. Typically a settlement offer is made as negotiable, meaning that the claimant can make a counteroffer if the terms of the insurer's offer are not satisfactory. If the claimant rejects the settlement offer, the insurer has a continuing contractual obligation to pay DI benefits according to the provisions of the policy. A claim settlement can be offered whether a claim is disputed or undisputed.

Disputed Claims

Some claim settlements result from a disputed claim in which the insurer and the claimant cannot agree on all the terms of the claim. For instance, suppose a claimant reports that a disability is the result of an injury or illness, but that information developed during the course of claim investigation indicates strongly that the disability resulted from a preexisting condition excluded by a policy provision. If the insurer cannot gather sufficient proof to support its contention that the disability is not covered under the policy, the insurer may offer to settle the claim by paying the insured a lump sum instead of paying a series of DI benefits. The advantages to an insurer of settling a disputed claim are that the insurer saves the costs of litigating the claim and of committing its staff resources to the conflict over a lengthy period.

Some claim disputes are resolved through mediation. ***Mediation*** is a conflict resolution method in which an impartial third party facilitates negotiations between the parties in an effort to create a mutually agreeable resolution to the dispute. During such mediation, the claim analyst may be asked to provide specific information gathered during the investigation of a claim. In general, this information includes

- The reason for the dispute
- The provisions of the policy
- Medical information, including the results of independent medical examinations
- Other information gathered by investigators

Undisputed Claims

Other claim settlements result from the insurer's attempt to provide a greater amount of benefits to a claimant early in the claim, rather than paying DI benefits over a period of time. Such an approach is appropriate when a claimant for DI insurance needs a large sum of money to pay for unusual rehabilitation, to obtain education or training appropriate to another vocation, to purchase a business that can be managed even with the disability, or to invest the lump sum so as to realize a steady stream of income well into the future, beyond the time period during which DI benefits would be paid. Particularly when a DI insurance policy covers only the insured's "own occupation," the insured may want to receive benefits in a lump sum in order to have funds to begin another career.

Offering a lump-sum settlement is to the insurer's advantage because the costs of administering the DI claim over a period of time are eliminated. The lump-sum settlement is advantageous to the claimant, as well, because the lump sum can be used to arrange a suitable lifestyle that accommodates the disability. Providing a settlement for a claimant may result in a unique, innovative solution to the claimant's special needs. While disabled, few people could expect to obtain such an amount of capital with which to restructure their lives.

In offering a lump-sum settlement, an insurer typically advises the claimant to seek professional advice on the legal and tax implications, accounting, and investment issues related to the settlement. In no case does the insurer provide such advice to a claimant because to do so would risk a possible charge of conflict of interest. Further, the insurer typically considers what approach—lump-sum payment or series of benefit payments—is in the best interest of the claimant. The degree to which the claimant is financially dependent on a monthly benefit and the ability of the claimant to use a lump-sum payout to provide for his own well-being are issues that the insurer weighs in reaching a decision about a settlement.

Handling Critical Illness Coverage Claims

The most important task for the claim analyst who administers critical illness (CI) coverage claims is to determine whether the insured's condition meets the requirements of the illness as it is described in the policy or rider. Using the physician's statement and medical office records, along with hospital records and lab reports submitted with the claim form, the claim analyst determines whether the insured's condition matches the definition in the policy. The claim analyst also determines whether any exclusions or limitations apply.

As is true of DI claims, CI claims involve benefit payments to an insured. In addition, a physician's statement is required for both DI and CI claims. However, the DI claim involves investigation into whether the medical condition has caused restrictions in the insured's ability to perform occupational duties, while the CI claim involves investigation into the diagnosis of a covered condition.

Administering CI claims is similar to administering life insurance claims because the benefit is typically paid out in one lump sum. Any investigation of either type of claim must be done thoroughly at the time of claim submission because after the benefit payment has been made, the claim analyst has no opportunity to conduct a more detailed investigation. Unlike life insurance claims, in which little analysis is usually required to determine that death has occurred, critical illness claims typically require analysis to determine whether the insured's condition satisfies the condition defined in the contract.

Key Terms and Concepts

injury
sickness
elimination period
benefit period
total disability
presumptive total disability
residual disability
recurring disability
noncancelable
guaranteed renewable
conditionally renewable
optionally renewable
cost of living increase benefit
rehabilitation benefit
transplant donor benefit
future increase option
workers' compensation
offset
work site assessment
rehabilitation
claim settlement
mediation

Endnotes

1. ACLI, *Life Insurers Fact Book 2000* (Washington, D.C.: American Council of Life Insurers, 2000), 55.
2. "Study on Musculoskeletal Disorders Complicates Employer Risk Factors," *Best's Review* (March 2001): 78.

CHAPTER 16 Scope and Organization of Customer Service

CHAPTER OUTLINE

Benefits of Providing Effective Customer Service

Organization of Customer Service

Providing Service to Customers
- Service for Policyowners, Insureds, and Beneficiaries
- Service for Agents
- Handling Complaints

Customer Service and Conservation
- Conservation and Policyowners
- Conservation and Agents

Qualities of Effective Customer Service

Delivering Effective Customer Service
- Determining Strategies for Effective Customer Service
- Automating and Simplifying Customer Service Delivery
- Documenting Customer Service Guidelines and Procedures
- Ensuring Excellent Communication

Evaluating Customer Service
- Evaluating the Speed of Customer Service
- Evaluating the Quality of Customer Service

OBJECTIVES

After reading this chapter, you should be able to

- Discuss the benefits to insurers of providing effective customer service
- Describe the typical ways that insurers organize customer service departments
- Discuss customer service provided to policyowners, insureds and beneficiaries
- Discuss customer service provided to agents
- Explain how customer service helps conservation
- List the qualities of effective customer service
- Describe the delivery of effective customer service
- Discuss the methods insurers use to evaluate customer service

To this point in your study of insurance administration functions, you've seen the importance of underwriting, reinsurance handling, and claim administration. You've also seen the many ways in which underwriting, reinsurance handling, and claim administration cooperate with one another, with other functional areas of the insurer, and with agents and insurance regulators to treat insured people and groups equitably. Now we'll turn our attention to another insurance administration function, customer service. Because effective service to clients is a cornerstone of successful organizations, customer service is an essential insurance administration function.

As we mentioned in Chapter 1, customer service refers to the broad range of activities, consistent with contractual provisions, that help keep customers satisfied so that they will continue doing business with an insurer and speak positively about the insurer to other potential customers. Some companies use different terms to refer to customer service, for example, *policyowner service* or *client service*. For purposes of this textbook, in the next two chapters, we will use customer service to refer to all the service activities performed for agents and for the people or parties who own insurance policies. Although agents have a different relationship to an insurer than do the other people served by customer service, most insurers provide service to agents as a part of customer service.

In our discussion of customer service, we will refer to customer service as both (1) the functional unit that performs specified activities and (2) the activities performed by customer service staff. Customer service staff members typically are known as *customer service representatives (CSRs)*. To simplify the discussion, we will use the terms *customer service department* and *customer service representatives (CSRs)* to refer to the organizational unit and the employees who provide services to policyowners, insureds, beneficiaries, agents, and other customers. Where necessary, we will explain how individual and group customer service differs.

During the often lengthy period when an insurer and a policyowner are linked by the provisions of an insurance contract, various customers—purchasers, insureds, beneficiaries, and others—can have many questions that require prompt attention if the policyowner and/or insured are to be satisfied with the insurer's service and products. In addition, the policyowner might require certain changes to be made in the contract—name, address, coverage type and amount, or beneficiary. In addition to making these changes, the insurer continues to collect premiums and also might make loans, pay dividends, and provide information.

Customer service is the part of insurance administration that helps maintain important contractual and business connections between the insurer and its customers. Customer service also enhances the insurer's reputation for taking good care of its customers and thereby assists agents in making further sales. Finally, customer service helps an insurer to compile information for reports to insurance regulatory organizations and to preserve its existing business.

In this chapter, we will begin by explaining the benefits of providing good customer service and the numerous ways of organizing a customer service department. After outlining the types of service that insurers deliver to various types of customers and insurance regulatory organizations, we will examine the relationship between customer service and policy conservation. In subsequent sections of the chapter, we'll discuss the qualities and ways of delivering and evaluating effective customer service. In the next chapter, we'll look at some of the details of delivering customer service for various kinds of insurance coverage.

Benefits of Providing Effective Customer Service

An insurer that establishes and maintains superior customer service enhances business in a number of ways:

- *Building long-term customer loyalty*. Customers who are satisfied with an insurer's service are more likely to renew and increase their current coverage and to buy new products. They may also recommend the insurer to friends and family members. In addition, an insurer with a reputation for effective customer service increases its ability to attract new customers and to recruit and retain its sales force.

- *Improving profitability.* Retaining business and agents can greatly increase an insurer's profit margin, because it is less costly to keep an existing customer than to gain new customers. Avoiding the time and resources required to replace customers and agents lost due to poor service allows the insurer to direct those resources into building its business.

- *Differentiating an insurer from its competitors*. Coverage from various insurance companies can seem about the same to many potential purchasers. An insurer can distinguish itself from others by offering customer service that fulfills customers' needs as rapidly, completely, and courteously as possible.

- *Enhancing the insurer's work environment*. Working for an organization that prides itself on delivering good service makes employees feel proud and helps motivate them to excel at their jobs. In contrast, poor customer service can cause employees' morale to drop as they cope with the stressful effects of dealing with unhappy or angry customers.

Organization of Customer Service

Like underwriting and claims, customer service departments can be organized in various ways according to the types of business an insurer does and according to the preferences and operating approaches of each insurer's management. Some insurers establish one department or area to deal with every kind of service to its customers. Other insurers divide customer service activities by product, by distribution system, by client, or by type of service requested.

In organizing customer service activities by product, an insurer usually trains specific employees to respond to the questions concerning one or two products—for example, an individual disability income product or a group life insurance product. An employee who understands all the details of a product, especially a complex one, is able to provide top quality service to customers.

Some companies organize customer service activities based on how the products are sold or distributed to customers. For example, one customer service group provides service for products sold by mail, and a different customer service group provides service for products sold by agents.

Another way to organize customer service activities is according to clients served. For instance, some employees handle inquiries only from agents, while other employees respond to requests from large group clients. Particularly when an insurer provides coverage for a very large group, assigning certain employees to handle the service for that group can prove efficient. The employees learn the needs and typical requests of the group and can develop response systems that provide rapid, accurate customer service.

Yet another way of organizing customer service is to assign employees to different types of requests for service. Using this organizational mode, an insurer would assign certain employees to make address or beneficiary changes, others to work with policy loans, and so on. In dividing customer service activities by function, insurers typically establish such divisions as policy administration, premium billing, coverage transfers from other insurers, conservation, loans, cancellations and surrenders, and agent service.

Providing Service to Customers

An insurer's customer service representatives (CSRs) provide essential contacts with policyowners, insureds, beneficiaries, and agents. Our discussion will focus on the general principles of customer service, not on all the details that a CSR has to master.

In this section, we'll outline the general types of customer service delivered to policyowners, insureds, and beneficiaries, and we will discuss these services in more detail in the next chapter. After explaining the types of customer service provided to agents, we'll explain how customer service handles complaints to comply with insurance regulatory organizations.

Service for Policyowners, Insureds, and Beneficiaries

Most customer service provided to policyowners, insureds, and beneficiaries involves providing information and processing changes to policies. Specifically, customer service activities for policyowners, insureds, and beneficiaries generally include

- Changing the owner and/or the beneficiary of a policy
- Changing addresses
- Changing coverage or adding riders
- Determining cash values, loans, and dividends
- Changing policy features such as how dividends are used and nonforfeiture options
- Sending premium due notices and handling premium payments
- Changing billing arrangements and methods of payment
- Answering questions on coverage amounts, policy provisions, and billings
- Providing information about claims submission, status, or settlement
- Processing policy disbursement requests such as loans, partial withdrawals, surrenders and cancellations
- Changing fund allocations for variable life insurance policies

Service for Agents

Providing reliable and effective service attracts and retains successful agents to sell an insurer's products. Agents want an insurer to provide high-quality service to policyowners because selling an insurer's products is easier if the insurer has a reputation for providing superior customer service.

To help agents solicit and sell business, CSRs provide insurance product information and help agents understand how to submit information about proposed insureds—for instance, to know which forms to complete and what additional information to submit with an application. In these ways, customer service helps agents submit complete application information and, therefore, increases the probability that underwriters can promptly evaluate the application.

Agents also need information to service their existing customers. Many policyowners consider the agent to be their link to the insurance company and, therefore, communicate directly with the agent when they have questions or problems. Answering customer questions promptly is vital to a continuing relationship between the policyowner, the agent, and the insurer. The agent typically bears the burden of a policyowner's irritation if the insurer makes errors in transactions, is unresponsive to requests for information, or otherwise fails to meet policyowner expectations. CSRs provide information and service to help agents provide top-quality service directly to policyowners. CSRs can refer customers to their agents for needs-based selling if a product is not meeting customer needs or when customers want a personal visit. Establishing and maintaining a productive relationship between customer service and agents is important to the agents' effectiveness and the insurer's competitive position.

Some CSRs also calculate and pay commissions to agents. If an insurer enables agents, at a policyowner's request, to make certain contractually permitted changes to policies and to submit the changes to the insurer, CSRs usually oversee and maintain records of the changes.

Handling Complaints

Handling complaints takes priority over many other customer service tasks. An insurer's customer service function must comply with requirements of local insurance regulators by maintaining accurate, complete, and current records of oral or written complaints for annual submission to insurance regulatory organizations. State and provincial departments of insurance generally reconcile insurers' annual reports of complaints with records of complaints submitted directly to those departments. In jurisdictions that have established standards of promptness in handling complaints, state and provincial departments of insurance determine how quickly each insurer has responded to filed complaints and what, if any, actions the insurer took to resolve problems involving response times.

To organize complaint records, an insurer generally establishes categories that describe typical complaints. Then CSRs assign each complaint to the category that most accurately describes it. For example, an insurer might establish the following categories for complaints related to claims: claim procedures, delays, unsatisfactory settlements or settlement offers, and denial of claim. Any claim-related complaint that does not fit adequately into one of these categories would be placed in a "miscellaneous" category. In explaining the handling of each complaint, the insurer usually specifies that for each complaint (1) a satisfactory explanation was given to the person who submitted the complaint, (2) corrective action was taken, or (3) no corrective action was deemed necessary.

Insurers gather information on complaints not only to satisfy regulatory requirements, but also as a management tool to find weaknesses in the ways they are doing business. An increase in one type of complaint generally indicates a need to examine the causes and circumstances of the complaints and to take whatever remedial action is appropriate. Complaints that could have legal implications are usually referred to the insurer's legal staff. Such complaints might involve customer demands for reinstatement beyond the period allowed, allegations that instructions to the insurer or its agents were not followed, or allegations that the insurer's employees or agents behaved in an incompetent, negligent, or dishonest manner.

Customer Service and Conservation

Another important customer service function is to preserve the insurer's existing business. ***Conservation*** is the process of ensuring that the insurer retains issued policies on its books for as long as possible. Many insurers consider conserving existing business to be as important as selling new policies. Conservation efforts are essential because a policyowner can cancel his policy coverage at any time, either by letting the policy lapse or by surrendering the policy.

FAST FACT

In 1999, the voluntary termination rate for individual life insurance policies in the United States was 5.8%.[1]

Because an insurer incurs many expenses in underwriting and issuing a policy, the insurer generally cannot offset its initial costs unless a policy remains in force for at least several years. A policy begins to provide returns to the insurer only after those initial costs have been recovered. Therefore, insurers make every effort to provide top-quality service to every customer to retain business. Ideally, an insurer would like to conserve every policy sold. In reality, this goal is difficult, but providing excellent customer service is one way that an insurer conserves business. An insurer's conservation efforts typically focus on policyowners and agents.

Conservation and Policyowners

A strong relationship between an insurer and its policyowners is one of the best ways to conserve business. Answering questions, making requested changes, and providing other types of services enable the insurer to enhance its relationship with its policyowners. By monitoring all customer complaints, an insurer can often identify and help policyowners who appear concerned about their coverage or who indicate dissatisfaction with the insurance company. Figure 16-1 lists ways that customer service representatives help conserve policies.

CSRs might also contact policyowners who have not paid premiums in a timely manner to indicate the insurer's interest in continuing the business relationship and to seek ways to satisfy the policyowners' needs. Some insurers provide rewards to CSRs who prevent policies from lapsing or being surrendered by discussing the coverage with the policyowner, trying to determine the reason for the lapse or surrender, and taking appropriate steps to encourage the policyowner to keep the policy in force.

In most insurance companies, CSRs who handle lapses and surrender requests are trained to offer contractual options such as reduced paid-up insurance or policy loans either by phone or by letter that may persuade policyowners to leave the coverage on the insurer's books. If a policy has been in force for a specified period of time—usually at least six months—and has lapsed, some insurers offer an extended

FIGURE 16-1. The Ways Customer Service Representatives Help to Conserve Policies.

- CSRs help customer understand coverage
- CSRs help customer understand the policy's flexible options as appropriate
- CSRs offer other products to better meet customer's needs either through home office or agent
- CSRs who are courteous and professional encourage customers to return to the company for other insurance needs

reinstatement period—typically 60 to 90 days—from the due date of the premium without requiring evidence of insurability.

Insurers also conserve business by informing policyowners of upcoming changes in premiums or coverage. For policies that require higher premiums at certain ages, a CSR usually informs each policyowner of the change and asks whether the policyowner is interested in discussing other coverage options with an agent. If a certain type of coverage terminates on a specific birthday of the insured—for instance, the 60th or 70th—most insurers send policyowners a letter stating that the coverage will terminate on that date and asking whether they would like to have an agent explain how to continue coverage with the insurer. Because customers can feel resentful if the only time they hear from an insurer is on the occasion of such a change, however, many insurers maintain frequent contact with customers throughout the length of the business relationship. Some insurers mail an annual summary of benefits statement that explains all existing coverages and the benefits paid during the previous year. Another way that insurers stay in touch with customers is to ask about their satisfaction with the insurer's service, a topic we will discuss later in this chapter.

Simplifying the payment of premiums is another approach insurers use to conserve business. Coverage whose premiums are paid on a monthly basis by check is the most likely to lapse and to experience problems with late payments. Therefore, many insurers allow insureds to pay premiums through ***electronic funds transfer (EFT)***, an automatic premium payment approach whereby a policyowner authorizes his financial institution to withdraw funds from an account to pay each renewal premium. In some cases, insurers accept credit cards for premium payments. Some insurers also pay benefits—particularly small amounts, such as those paid for certain health claims—by EFT.

Insurers also acknowledge that customers' needs change and that insurance coverage may no longer be needed. Surveying customers about the reasons for the termination of their coverage can help insurers determine if they need to make changes to their products or their procedures to improve policy conservation. Every insurer hopes that, if the customer does terminate his coverage, he will purchase other products from the insurer in the future, if the insurer provided good customer service in the past.

As you can tell, insurers have devised a number of ways to conserve business. Figure 16-2 lists several approaches to conservation, including ones we've discussed and others.

Conservation of Orphan Policyowners

An ***orphan policyowner*** is a policyowner whose original agent is no longer available to provide service. The agent may have moved from the

FIGURE 16-2. Approaches to Conserving Business.

- Giving agents access to information about payments that policyowners make to flexible-premium policies so that agents can take action if payments decline or fall below the required level
- Providing annual reports containing projections of values on flexible-premium policies to ensure products are meeting policyowners' current and future needs
- Providing multiple reminders of premiums due
- Sending notices of late premiums to both policyowners and agents
- Conferring with policyowners who make maximum loan requests to ensure that policy values are adequate to keep coverage in force
- Advising policyowners who request a policy surrender about alternatives, such as a policy loan
- Offering insureds who leave a group plan options for continuing their coverage on an individual basis
- Offering a toll-free number and a Web site or email address for policyowners to contact the insurer
- Surveying policyowners about their satisfaction with agents and products to identify problems and devise solutions
- Providing extensive and ongoing training to CSRs
- Testing the effectiveness of notices, letters, and other policyowner communication to determine the most effective and efficient approaches
- Tracking the relationship between conservation and persistency, and publicizing the results to staff and management

area, stopped marketing the insurer's products, retired, or died, or the policyowner may have moved to another geographic area that his original agent does not serve. Without regular communication from the agent, a policyowner could be likely to cancel or surrender the policy and purchase coverage from another insurer whose agent can provide ongoing service.

To help conserve the business of orphan policyowners, most insurers attempt to contact such people and recommend an agent who is in the same geographic area. Alternatively, an insurer might contact a nearby agent directly and ask the agent to contact the orphan policyowner. Insurers generally offer some financial incentive to agents to encourage them to "adopt" orphan policyowners and provide them with effective service. Some insurers have established a program to communicate regularly with every policyowner so that even if a policyowner becomes an orphan, she will still feel that she has strong ties to the insurer and can obtain answers to questions and solutions to problems.

Some insurers have established electronic tracking of agent activities to identify agents who are no longer active and may have left orphan policyowners. The sooner an insurer can identify an orphan policyowner, the more likely the insurer can conserve that person's business. In addition, some insurers establish a sales desk in the home office to work with orphan policyowners by phone or by mail to fulfill policyowner needs for additional insurance products.

Conservation Through Superior Claim Service

Customers who purchase insurance generally interact with an insurer or its agents when the coverage is sold and when a claim is submitted. For health insurance, a customer may interact with the insurance company many times. When customers are dissatisfied with claim service, they are likely to feel frustrated. Therefore, customer service employees in insurance companies that want to provide top-quality service usually communicate regularly with employees in claims to encourage rapid, accessible, customer-focused, and simplified claim handling. Customers want their claims processed as rapidly as possible; they want easy ways to get in touch with the insurer to submit a claim; and they want personal treatment and clear explanations while their claims are being handled. Insurers whose claim handling satisfies these customer desires enhance their relationship with customers.

Conservation Through Customer Feedback

Conservation of business requires clear communication, so most insurers communicate regularly with customers to demonstrate the insurers' interest in meeting customer needs. In addition, most insurers evaluate customers' needs through telephone surveys and printed questionnaires. Some insurers have established online feedback systems to gather information about customers' needs, preferences, and knowledge of insurance products and services. In designing an online feedback system, an insurer must take into consideration the need to preserve customers' privacy and confidentiality. Transmitting contract numbers, personal identification numbers, and other confidential information may inhibit customers' willingness to use such a system, so most insurers do not require that kind of information from customers who complete an online survey.

Some insurers' online feedback systems permit customers to respond freely about any topic. Typically, such a system invites customers to send an email, using a statement similar to the following:

> We welcome your questions and invite you to ask our experts questions about life and health insurance—24 hours a day, 7 days a week. We also welcome your thoughts about the way we have treated you as a customer and how we might serve you better. Please write your questions and comments in the space below, and then click on "SEND" to e-mail your response to us. We will immediately acknowledge receipt of your response, and we'll provide you with a prompt answer.

Other online feedback systems provide surveys to which customers can give responses. Figure 16-3 illustrates an online feedback survey system from one insurer's Web site.

FIGURE 16-3. Excerpts from an Insurer's Online Feedback Survey System.

LUTHERAN BROTHERHOOD *Potluck*

•*Home* •*Members* •*Congregations* •*Communities* •*Institutions* •*About Us* •*Potluck*

FREE LUTHERAN BROTHERHOOD WALL CALENDAR

Need a wall calendar? We'll send you one—free!
But please, could you answer a few questions first?

1. How often do you visit www.luthbro.com?

❍ Daily ❍ Weekly ❍ Monthly ❍ Rarely

2. What's the main reason for your visit to www.luthbro.com today?

❍ Look up daily price information for mutual funds and/or annuities
❍ Read the latest news about Lutheran Brotherhood
❍ Contact my district representative
❍ Learn about products and services from Lutheran Brotherhood
❍ Follow-up on a topic I heard about or read about elsewhere
❍ Other: [ ]

3. What is the most important function or content you would like to see added to www.luthbro.com?

❍ Access to all of your account information
❍ More detailed information about products and services
❍ Downloadable forms (which ones): [ ]

Thanks for responding to our survey. Now, let us know where to send your free calendar!

First Name: [ ] MI: [ ]
Last Name: [ ]
Address 1: [ ]
Address 2: [ ]
City: [ ] State: [select-- ▼]
Zip: [ ]
E-mail: [ ]

I am Lutheran
❍ Yes ❍ No (You can still request a calendar)

I would like to receive more information about Lutheran Brotherhood products, services and offers.

❍ Yes ❍ No (I can still request a calendar)

[Click here to request your calendar!]

Source: Lutheran Brotherhood, "Free Lutheran Brotherhood Wall Calendar," *Potluck*, http:www.luthbro.com/potluck/calendar_request/index.htm (2 February 2001). Used with permission.

Conservation and Agents

Most insurers have found that the principal cause of lapse or transfer of business is lack of agent involvement with policyowners. By educating agents about the need to match coverage to the specific needs of proposed insureds and by providing prompt, accurate responses to agents' questions, the insurer demonstrates its support of agents' sales and retention efforts and encourages the submission of high-quality business. Insurance companies often encourage agents to contact their customers at least once a year to review customers' needs and to maintain relationships.

Some insurers also structure their commissions to reward agents whose business remains in force for an extended period. For instance, an insurer might pay an agent a ***persistency bonus***, a sum of money that represents an increase in the agent's commission when a policy continues in force beyond an initial period, usually five years. Some insurers also require that a memo from the agent explaining the reason for the request accompanies every surrender form and that the policyowner making the request be contacted by telephone by a CSR.

Some unethical agents attempt to generate commission income by replacing policies they have originally sold with new policies underwritten by a different insurer. To help prevent such replacements, insurers who receive notice of surrenders and lapses not only contact the agent, but also send a letter to the policyowner with information comparing the coverage and the premiums of the previous policy and the new policy. Insurers sometimes penalize agents whose conservation percentage is low by excluding the agent from promotional competitions or by reducing the amount of commission paid to the agent on other policies.

In attempting to conserve business, insurers also train agents in providing on-going, top-quality customer service. In addition, insurers try to recruit agents who are concerned with selling only coverage that is appropriate for customers' needs; provide those agents with information about the insurer's underwriting principles and requirements; and maintain records of the persistency of each agent's business.

Qualities of Effective Customer Service

Effective customer service is prompt, courteous, complete, accurate, and confidential. An insurer that delivers customer service with these qualities enhances its strength and competitive position, and keeps its policyowners, insureds, and other customers satisfied.

Prompt customer service strengthens the organization. By contrast, delays can result in frustrated customers, reductions in new business, lapses and surrenders of coverage, and even legal actions against the insurer. A policyowner who has to wait an unreasonable period of time to obtain a policy loan or to receive information about submitting a claim may well be irritated. To enhance the promptness of response to customers, many insurers have established increased hours of service.

Courteous CSRs strengthen the bond between an insurer and its customers. Considering the feelings of customers and making every effort to handle transactions politely and professionally can make transactions a pleasant experience for everyone involved.

Providing complete service is sometimes a challenge, especially when requests for service cover a variety of transactions or when transactions are complicated or unusual. Attending to the details of each transaction helps ensure that all parts of a transaction are completed and that the customer will be fully satisfied. Providing complete service saves time for customers, agents, and CSRs, and reduces the insurer's expense in unnecessary follow-up correspondence and customer contacts.

Providing accurate information is critical because giving a customer the wrong data can result in an inappropriate and potentially damaging decision. If, for instance, a CSR incorrectly tells an agent that a certain policyowner has changed the beneficiary of a policy, the agent could later offend the policyowner or the beneficiary by mentioning the wrong person as the beneficiary or otherwise proceeding as though another beneficiary had been named. Especially when a service transaction involves money, accuracy is important in avoiding inconvenience to customers and embarrassment for the insurer. Most insurers enhance accuracy by creating checklists, worksheets, and procedures manuals that guide CSRs through the steps of transactions, particularly those that are complex or have various options. In addition, insurers provide either manual or electronic logs by which CSRs can record every customer transaction processed. Certain transactions also may be audited by a senior processor or CSR.

Confidentiality is essential in customer service as in all other aspects of insurance administration. A contract of insurance between an insurer and a policyowner requires that the insurer protect the customer's privacy. The CSR must remember, for example, that usually only the policyowner and the insurer are parties to the insurance contract. No beneficiary or other person is a party to the contract. Therefore, no one except the policyowner has the right to receive information from the insurer about the status of a policy—whether the policy is in force, whether its premiums have been paid to date, whether a policy loan has been requested, or who the beneficiary is. Governmental privacy regulations also determine what type of policy information can be released and to whom that information can be released. Insurers generally establish specific guidelines indicating what information can be released to which people so that CSRs do not make errors that can damage the confidential bond between insurer and policyowner.

Delivering Effective Customer Service

Every insurer wants to deliver service so that all customers are satisfied. Determining specific strategies for providing service, automating and simplifying service delivery procedures, ensuring that service guidelines and procedures are appropriately documented and accessible, and establishing excellent telephone communication are some of the approaches insurers use to deliver effective customer service.

Determining Strategies for Effective Customer Service

Insurers implement various customer service strategies according to the types of coverage involved and the type, frequency, and complexity of the service transactions required. Each insurer adopts strategies that reflect its attitude toward customer service and serve as a guide for employees in their interactions with customers.

Customer service strategies generally focus on all types of customer interactions, including written and spoken communications and face-to-face meetings. As an illustration of such strategies, Figure 16-4 shows the customer service strategies formulated by one health insurer.

FIGURE 16-4. Customer Service Strategies of One Health Insurer.

- ✔ We will treat all customers, internal and external, as individuals with value.
- ✔ We will approach every customer contact from the customer's point of view.
- ✔ We will treat each customer contact as an opportunity to build a relationship, not just to process a transaction.
- ✔ We will ensure that our customers receive accurate and timely responses.
- ✔ We will ensure that each customer service employee has the technical and thought-process skills to consider all possible implications before taking appropriate action.
- ✔ We will continually seek to improve our written communication by using personalized letters and by acknowledging important events in the lives of our customers.
- ✔ We will continually seek to improve our spoken communication by returning all telephone calls within 30 minutes of receipt and by asking permission before placing any customer on hold, informing the customer first of the anticipated hold time.
- ✔ We will continually seek ways and implement technologies to make it easier for customers to do business with us.

Source: USAA Life Insurance Company. Adapted with permission.

Automating and Simplifying Customer Service Delivery

Replacing traditional paper documents with electronic documents available online enables many insurers to provide faster, more accurate customer service. Many insurers allow customers to download forms or perform transactions online. For example, variable life insurance policyowners can check variable unit prices at an insurer's Web site. In addition, policyowners can download forms from a Web site. Finally, many insurers' Web sites encourage customers to contact the customer service center by email. Insight 16-1 explains how one insurer is using the Internet to provide customer service.

Streamlining routine changes into one or two steps or only one document also helps CSRs deliver rapid service. Efficiency translates into increased productivity in customer service as in other areas of the insurance business.

Documenting Customer Service Guidelines and Procedures

To ensure consistency and accuracy in the service provided to all customers, insurers document the guidelines and procedures that CSRs are to use. Insurers use many means of documenting such guidelines

Insight 16-1. Life Company Expands Online Service Functions.

The customer service section of Northwestern Mutual Life's Web site is called the Customer Service Connection. It has two major sections, one on life and disability insurance and one on annuities and IRAs. The life and disability insurance section has six parts, under the following headings:

- Name, address, and policy changes
- Paying your premiums
- Disability claim—if you have become disabled
- Death claim—if the insured person has died
- Receiving life insurance and annuity/IRA proceeds
- Making the most of your policy

One attractive feature of this list is that it allows people who want to file claims to avoid reading a lot of detail about issues that are extraneous to claim filing. Someone who goes to the death claim section sees the following headings:

- How do I submit a life insurance claim?
- Once the claim is approved, how will payment be made to the beneficiary(ies)?
- Receiving life insurance and annuity/IRA proceeds

Someone who wants to submit a claim is instructed to open a form called "report of insured's death form." That form requests the insured's name, date of birth, policy number, cause of death, exact date of death, address, place of death, other policies owned by the insured, the filer's name, relationship to the insured, and daytime phone number. The filer can then submit the form online. The site allows the filer to view a completed sample report of death form. Then the site describes alternative ways payments can be made to beneficiaries.

Source: Adapted from Jean C. Gora, "Life Companies Expand Online Service Functions," *Resource* (April 1999): 47. Used with permission.

and procedures, including manuals kept on each employee's desk and electronic systems that provide each CSR with information on how to handle practically any customer service situation that can arise.

Some insurers also use software programs to help employees track individual files. With such programs, an employee can record every customer interaction and thereby develop a complete history of each transaction. Although such detailed information is not necessary and usually is not collected for routine transactions, it can be invaluable in handling lengthy or complex transactions on which more than one CSR has worked or that have to be transferred temporarily to a manager for consideration and advice.

One of the most important ways of ensuring consistent service is to inform every employee promptly about changes in guidelines and procedures. If an insurer uses an electronic procedures manual, such changes can be highlighted or presented in a bright color to capture employees' attention. If an insurer uses a printed manual, employees are typically required to update their manuals regularly and follow the most recent procedures and guidelines. Most insurance companies assign one employee or one team, depending on the size of the department, to be responsible for updating documentation and communicating the changes to all the staff.

Ensuring Excellent Communication

Although other technologies have become increasingly important in maintaining communication between an insurer and its customers, the telephone continues to provide an essential link. In remaining aware of customers' needs and in gathering information to fulfill them, CSRs use telephones extensively.

At some insurance companies, a customer service unit known as a ***call center*** handles questions and requests when customers contact the insurer by telephone, typically using a toll-free number. At some other companies, a customer service unit known as a ***customer contact center*** handles questions and requests when customers contact the insurer by any method—for example, by telephone, fax, or e-mail. Policyowners frequently want answers to their questions at times other than normal business hours. Call centers and customer contact centers are responding to this need by expanding their service hours.

Call centers and customer contact centers typically provide computer reference screens that CSRs can refer to for answers to customers' questions. Some CSRs who work in the center respond only to general customer questions, directing specific inquiries to more experienced CSRs. Other centers may have more experienced CSRs available to handle even the most complex customer service questions. In some insurers' customer contact centers, lengthy, unique, or complex questions are transferred to a special team that handles such questions.

Because some of the people who contact an insurer's office are upset or angry, CSRs are taught skills to help handle such contacts. In particular, CSRs are taught (1) to empathize with customers, allowing them to vent their feelings, and (2) to understand that customers are not angry with CSRs in particular, but at the situations about which they are contacting the insurer. By repeating and summarizing the customer's concerns, the CSR can validate those concerns and help the customer understand that the employee is eager to help. Rather than indulge in blaming, denying fault, or making excuses, the CSR asks questions to help control the dialogue and to obtain information needed to resolve problems.

In being trained to communicate effectively with customers, CSRs are taught to avoid using technical terms used by insurance industry employees, but instead to use everyday language and to keep their responses simple and specific. Rather than saying, "Your EOB just arrived, and co-payments and deductibles are being accounted for so that our comm center can cut a check," a CSR might be trained to say, "We now have everything we need to handle your claim, and we'll mail your check this afternoon."

Providing customer service by telephone over a long period can lead to employee frustration and burnout. Therefore, most insurers allow telephone service representatives to rotate off this service for certain hours each day or to work in other customer service areas for weeks or months before returning to telephone duties. Insurers also involve telephone service representatives in new product design to help prevent some of the problems that might later arise when the product is serviced.

Evaluating Customer Service

Because customer service is important to an insurer's success, most insurers examine both the speed and the quality of their service transactions. Although evaluating the *speed* of customer service delivered is easier than evaluating its *quality*, both measurements of customer service are essential in tracking customer satisfaction.

Evaluating the Speed of Customer Service

Insurers typically determine whether they are delivering rapid customer service by establishing benchmarks for various aspects of customer service and then comparing their actual performance to the benchmarks. A ***benchmark*** for a specific process is a performance standard that has been achieved by a recognized leader in that process and represents the company's goal for its own performance of the process.

Insurers typically establish benchmarks for various elements associated with customer service, including the average speed of answering telephone communications, the rate at which callers abandon a call because it has not been promptly answered, and the length of time required to complete various transactions such as completing loan and dividend withdrawals or responding to a policyowner's or an agent's request for information. Establishing turnaround times for accomplishing specific customer service activities is the most common method insurance companies use to assess the quantity and speed of service delivered.

An insurer may review the amount of time required to fulfill a typical customer request—for example, a policy loan—and may decide that three days or two days or one day is the standard by which all such requests should be fulfilled. Thereafter, the insurer maintains records of the length of time for CSRs to "turn around" or fulfill each policy loan request and calculates the average time required to fulfill a typical request. If an insurer discovers that its turnaround times vary significantly from the standards set, management investigates the cause of the variance and, if necessary, takes steps to help employees more closely adhere to the standard. These steps may involve hiring additional staff, additional training, system enhancements, or temporarily assigning other staff to customer service and enhancing certain systems, such as tracking systems and procedures information systems.

Usually, measures of turnaround time include (1) the day that a request is received and (2) the day the request is fulfilled. If mail is involved, a mailing date is used as a measure of turnaround time. Typical turnaround times vary from one insurer to another. Generally, however, fulfilling a policy loan request takes between one to three days; a beneficiary change, three to five days; a policy replacement, one to three days; and a cash surrender, three to five days. Some insurers specify that their stated standards do not reflect the best possible or even optimal service, but serve as a measure of the minimum acceptable average level of performance.

Counting the number of customer service transactions and comparing that count to established standards is accomplished manually or electronically. Generally, the transactions count is completed weekly and is examined by management to assess trends, to identify problems, and to inform CSRs of how well they are fulfilling their accountabilities. The number and complexity of transactions accomplished are expected to increase as a CSR gains experience. Because accuracy is critical in customer service, the number of transactions is not as important as the quality of those transactions. However, insurers make use of the information on number of transactions in their staffing considerations.

Evaluating the Quality of Customer Service

Most insurers establish various systems to track the quality of customer service. For example, randomly selected customers may receive mail surveys or telephone inquiries, asking the customers' views on the type of customer service they have received and inquiring about their level of satisfaction with it. Customers may be asked to comment on such elements as the following concerning spoken and written customer service:

- Friendliness and professionalism of customer service staff
- Easily understood communication
- Timeliness of service
- Accuracy in completing a request
- Overall level of service

Insurers also establish focus groups, composed of customers, to discuss customer service elements and to suggest specific ways insurers can improve their customer service. In addition, many insurers carefully assess customers' complaints to determine the cause of the problems, possible methods of avoiding the causes of complaints, and ways of improving the insurer's ability to respond to complaints effectively.

As we mentioned earlier, many insurers have established telephone or online feedback systems that enable a customer to provide an assessment of customer service directly to the insurer. A customer who is uncomfortable using such technology is given the option to speak directly with a CSR.

To track the quality of service delivered by individual employees, many insurers require managers, senior staff, or trainers to monitor a percentage of each employee's transactions. A manager or trainer might examine files of completed cases and those in progress and might listen to live or taped telephone calls between customers and the employees. Figure 16-5 illustrates a portion of a checklist used to evaluate the quality of telephone conversations between CSRs and customers.

Generally, a manager looks especially carefully at cases that are returned to a CSR for additional work as the result of an error in the initial transaction. Sometimes the manager makes follow-up telephone calls to customers to ask how well their cases were handled and to solicit suggestions for improving the service. Insurers also use peer review, by which employees monitor and evaluate one another's service delivery. Peer review requires careful training so that the assessments will be consistent.

FIGURE 16-5. Checklist Used to Evaluate the Quality of Phone Conversations.

- ✔ Identify self and offer assistance
- ✔ Determine the reason for the call by listening carefully
- ✔ Express help/regret/acknowledgment appropriately
- ✔ Request and verify caller information
- ✔ Use caller's name and sir or ma'am as appropriate
- ✔ Accept appropriate responsibility for actions taken or not taken
- ✔ Provide accurate, complete information in an organized fashion
- ✔ Inform caller of any risks involved
- ✔ Summarize action to be taken and verify customer's understanding, giving an expected timeline where appropriate
- ✔ Offer additional assistance
- ✔ Offer alternative solutions to problems
- ✔ Avoid insurance jargon
- ✔ Use appropriate presentation: pace, inflection, enunciation, courtesy, personalization
- ✔ Use "please" and "thank you"
- ✔ Use a proper approach to placing a customer on hold or transferring customer to another department
- ✔ Avoid short or curt answers
- ✔ Remain calm and avoid becoming defensive
- ✔ End call by saying "Thank you for calling" and "Have a nice day"
- ✔ Accurately record the call

Finally, insurers use questionnaires, focus groups, and other means of enabling CSRs to give feedback concerning their jobs and to recommend ways of improving the work accomplished in customer service. On the basis of employee feedback, insurers typically revise procedures, organizational methods, and standards when such revisions seem likely to increase the speed and to improve the quality of customer service.

Key Terms and Concepts

conservation
electronic funds transfer (EFT)
orphan policyowner
persistency bonus
call center
customer contact center
benchmark

Endnote

1. ACLI, *Life Insurers Fact Book 2000* (Washington, D.C.: American Council of Life Insurers, 2000), 22.

CHAPTER 17

Customer Service Practices

Chapter Outline

Objectives

After reading this chapter, you should be able to

- Discuss how customer service departments provide information and answer questions
- Describe the process for making changes to a policy
- Discuss how customer service departments handle financial transactions for customers
- Describe the relationship between customer service and underwriting

In the last chapter, we reviewed general customer service principles and practices. In this chapter, we'll discuss the specific ways that an insurer's customer service staff handle various types of insurance service transactions.

Because customer service staff need to handle each request accurately, courteously, and promptly, they receive extensive and ongoing training in the many details of responding well to policyowner requests and in the provisions of various policy contracts. Further, insurers provide agents and policyowners with forms to request various types of customer service transactions. Although some insurers use a separate form for each type of transaction, most insurers have developed multipurpose forms for similar types of transactions and thereby reduce the complexity of fulfilling policyowner needs. For example, an insurer might group together on one form the requests for changes of ownership, beneficiary, name, address, and assignment. Another form may group requests for cash surrender, policy loans, allotment of dividends, and reinstatement. Each insurer designs its own service request form and may include all available customer services or only selected ones. Some insurers develop separate forms for specific services; we will examine some of these types of forms later in this chapter. In addition to requests submitted on such forms, CSRs also accept requests submitted by telephone, fax, and through an insurer's Web site.

Providing Information and Answering Questions

CSRs are responsible for responding to many requests for information and complaints about various aspects of coverage and service. Customer service training is intensive and complex so that staff have the information they need to fulfill policyowners' needs. A complete list of the types of questions fielded by an insurer's customer service staff would fill many pages, but the most frequently encountered policyowner questions relate to

- Changing the owner's name or the beneficiary
- Changing an address
- Changing coverage or adding/deleting riders
- Type and amount of coverage and policy features
- Determining cash value and administering loans and dividends

- Billing questions
- Handling premium payments
- Fulfilling other policyowner needs, including obtaining duplicate policies and surrendering, converting, reinstating, or terminating a policy
- Handling returned mail

In the following discussion, we will first distinguish between the types of information generally requested for individual and for group insurance. In discussing other types of customer service activities, we will not distinguish between these types of coverage unless such a distinction is necessary because many of the customer service activities apply equally to individual and group insurance.

Information for Individual Insurance

Individual policyowners often have questions about their coverage and need assistance in submitting claims and other administrative details. An insurer's customer service staff provide valuable information to policyowners, which may increase customer satisfaction and also help conserve coverage.

From the time a policy is sold until the relationship between the individual policyowner and the insurer comes to an end, a policyowner can have questions about almost anything related to the coverage. When a child is born, a marriage dissolves, a spouse dies, a medical caregiver moves or retires, an insured suffers a debilitating illness or injury, or other life changes occur, a policyowner might need information. Successful insurers train CSRs to know the answers to the most commonly asked questions and to be familiar with information sources necessary to locate the answers to uncommon questions. An experienced CSR can be invaluable in tracking down information requested by a policyowner.

Information for Group Insurance

You have learned that *installation* is the series of activities involved in issuing a master contract and its individual certificates to an insured group. Customer service plays a part in ensuring that a group policy is installed correctly and completely. The role of customer service in group installation generally involves providing information and answering questions about the plan's eligibility requirements, benefits, and provisions, as well as the portion of the premium, if any, that each employee must pay.

The employer or group that sponsors group insurance coverage typically informs the group insureds about the policy purchase. The insurer provides sample letters, brochures, enrollment forms, and other information that can be distributed to the group insureds. Customer service might help prepare these materials.

While a self-administered group policy is in force, a representative of the insurance company provides customer service by answering questions and assisting the group in administering the coverage effectively. This representative maintains close contact with the insurer's claim staff to identify and help resolve any problems. For instance, if an insured group member is having difficulty in providing information required to process a claim, the insurer's representative may advise the employee or the group plan administrator about the required information and ways to obtain it. To provide adequate assistance to group members, the insurer's representative must be well informed about the coverage, the claim administration process, and the general administration of group products.

FAST FACT

Group purchases are a fast-growing segment of life insurance sales in the United States, climbing 31% in 1999 to $967 billion, a $227 billion rise over 1998.[1]

In addition to providing information as requested, the insurer's representative also enhances communication by making periodic calls on each insured group. During these calls, the representative checks the activities of the group plan administrator in administering the plan, informs the administrator of changes in laws and insurance practices that affect the group plan, and provides guidance if the plan administration fails to meet the insurer's standards. The representative also helps conserve the business by discussing the group's evolving needs for coverage and suggesting changes to the coverage. By evaluating the group's claim history, the representative helps prepare the group for the next year's rates, which often depend on the level of claims made by the group during the preceding year. The representative also presents the administrator and other group officials with rating information based on employee census information, incurred claims, and other information relating to the group's experience. If necessary, the representative recommends changes to the coverage, including increased or decreased deductibles, changes to coinsurance requirements, or changes to contractual provisions.

Changing the Owner's Name or the Beneficiary

The name of the policyowner or beneficiary may need to be changed for several reasons. Sometimes a name has been misspelled, and correction is needed to satisfy an owner or a beneficiary. More commonly, a name change results from marriage, divorce, adoption, or a court order. Most insurers require a policyowner to complete and sign a form requesting the name change, and many insurers also require a copy of a marriage license, divorce decree, or other documentation verifying the name change. When a name change is requested because of naturalization of citizenship, many insurers require as proof a notarized sworn ***affidavit***, which is a written statement made before an official who is authorized to administer oaths. After a name change has been made, a CSR sends the policyowner verification of the change. Figure 17-1 illustrates a name change form used by some insurance companies to indicate a name change of an insured, a policyowner, or a beneficiary. Note that this form would be used for beneficiary name changes, not to change the beneficiary of the policy; however, some companies may include several transactions on one form versus having separate forms for each request.

CSRs must be familiar with the numerous and often complex ways in which beneficiaries may be designated. Many different people and entities can be named as the beneficiary of a life insurance policy. These include the spouse and children of an insured person, other people who may be unrelated to the insured, trustees under trust agreements or wills, the estate of the insured, and others. Moreover, a policyowner can specify contingent, concurrent, or irrevocable beneficiaries, and can further specify distribution of proceeds per stirpes or per capita. These beneficiary designation terms are defined in Figure 17-2.

Many insurers establish guidelines for submitting beneficiary changes. The guidelines are designed to prevent mistakes in recording

FIGURE 17-1. Name Change Form.

❒ Insured ❒ Owner ❒ Beneficiary

From ______________________ Former Signature ______________________
First, Middle, Last

To ______________________ Present Signature ______________________
First, Middle, Last

Reason for name change: ❒ Marriage ❒ Divorce ❒ Correction
❒ Other (attach certified copy of court order)

FIGURE 17-2. Beneficiary Designation Terms.

- *Contingent beneficiary.* The person or entity designated to receive life insurance policy proceeds if the primary beneficiary should die before the person whose life is insured. Also called secondary beneficiary and successor beneficiary.
- *Concurrent beneficiaries.* The designation of more than one person or entity to share, if living in payment of the proceeds on the death of the insured. The shares will be distributed equally, unless otherwise provided.
- *Irrevocable beneficiary.* The designation of a beneficiary that cannot be revoked or changed without the written consent of such beneficiary.
- *Per stirpes.* A method of dividing policy benefits among the living members of a class of beneficiaries (such as children or grandchildren of an insured person) and the descendants of deceased members of that class. Children of a deceased member share their deceased parent's or other relative's portion of the benefit equally as representatives of the deceased person. For example, a policyowner-insured who has three children—Abraham, Benjamin, and Carol—might provide that each child would receive one-third of the policy proceeds, per stirpes. If Benjamin died before the insured died, then at the insured's death Abraham and Carol would each receive one-third of the proceeds, and the heirs of Benjamin would receive equal shares of the remaining one-third of the proceeds. If Benjamin died without heirs, however, Abraham and Carol would each inherit one-half of the policy proceeds. Many insurers prohibit the use of some classes, such as "nieces and nephews of the insured" or "children of the insured's brother," in per stirpes beneficiary designations because such classes are not specific in naming the persons who are to be included in the division of the proceeds.
- *Per capita.* A method of dividing policy benefits among beneficiaries without regard for different degrees of relationship. Each beneficiary receives an equal portion of the proceeds. For example, a policyowner-insured who has three children—Abraham, Benjamin, and Carol—might provide that each child would receive one-third of the policy proceeds, per capita. If Benjamin died before the insured died, then at the insured's death Abraham and Carol would each receive one-half of the proceeds, whether or not Benjamin had heirs.

a policyowner's beneficiary designation and to avoid delays in the event of a claim. Among the most common guidelines are the following:

- The full name—given name and surname—of the beneficiary is required; initials are not acceptable. For example, "John and Louise Jones" is acceptable, but "Mr. and Mrs. John Jones" is not acceptable.
- The relationship of the beneficiary to the policyowner must be specified.
- Dates of birth for minors must be provided.

- Use of the words "or," "either/or," "and/or" makes the designation unacceptable because the intent is not clear.

- Names that are scratched out or marked over, or that contain correction fluid marks, are not acceptable.

- Information about the beneficiary that would allow the insurer to locate him at the time of a claim should be provided. Such information includes social identification or Social Security number, address, or date of birth.

- Dollar amounts cannot be specified for any or all beneficiaries. Fractions (such as one-fourth or two-thirds) and percentages (such as 30 percent or 70 percent) can be used to specify unequal shares.

- The enrollment card or beneficiary form must be signed and dated by the policyowner.

- If a trust is designated, the exact date, legal name of the trust, and the trustee's name must be provided. Because some trust documents are difficult to interpret, some insurers attach a disclaimer noting that the insurer is not obligated to inquire into the terms of the trust agreement and will not be liable after the policy proceeds have been paid.

Changing the name of an owner or a beneficiary requires that the insurer modify many different insurance records. The master policy file, the billing file, the agent's file, and other documents should all be in accord with one another. Generally, an insurer's computer-based information system automatically changes a name in all locations when it is changed in any location. Therefore, if a policyowner, for example, requests a change in her name, that change will be reflected throughout the insurer's records. If the insured later files a claim under the coverage, her name will already be updated in the insurer's claim files so that the claim can be handled quickly and efficiently. A copy of the face page of the policy or an endorsement to the policy is usually sent to the policyowner to verify that the insurer has made the requested change.

Changes of beneficiary cannot be made by telephone, but the request for a change form can be submitted by phone. CSRs mail a change of beneficiary form which, when returned, is compared to the policyowner's signature on file. If the original beneficiary was designated irrevocably, that person is also required to sign the request for a change of beneficiary before the change can be made.

Assigning Policy Ownership

As we noted in Chapter 13, assignment of a life insurance policy is a transfer of some or all of the rights to receive the proceeds of a life insurance policy. The insurance company is not a party to the assignment, which involves only the ***assignor***—the person or entity that transfers ownership rights—and the ***assignee***—the person or entity that receives ownership rights. Ownership of some or all of the rights to a policy is most often transferred when a policyowner wishes to use the cash value of a life insurance policy as collateral for a loan or when a divorce results in one party's assumption of full ownership of an insurance policy. As you learned in Chapter 13, irrevocable transfer of all the rights of a life insurance policy is known as absolute assignment, whereas the transfer of some rights of policy ownership is known as collateral assignment. Figure 17-3 illustrates an absolute assignment form.

FIGURE 17-3. Absolute Assignment Form.

Absolute Assignment

Policy # ______________________ Life of ______________________

The undersigned hereby assigns and transfers without any exception, limitation, or reservation whatsoever to

[Name and address of each assignee]

all (his, her, its, their) assignable benefits, interest, property, and rights in the policy described above.

The nature and effect of this assignment shall be as indicated in the following expressions of intent and purpose, namely

- This assignment is ❐ for a valuable consideration. ❐ without a valuable consideration.
- If two or more assignees are named above, their interests under this assignment shall be as indicated in the line before which an "X" is inserted below.
  - ❐ Joint owners with right of survivorship between them
  - ❐ Common owners with no right of survivorship between them
  - ❐ Life interest, use, and enjoyment in ______________________
    [Name of life owner]

with absolute control and power of disposition in such assignee during his or her lifetime; remainder interest in other assignee(s). If there are two or more assignees entitled to receive remainder interests, such interests shall be of the nature indicated in the line before which an "X" is inserted below:

  - ❐ Joint owners with right of survivorship between them
  - ❐ Common owners with no right of survivorship between them

- This assignment cancels and rescinds any reversionary provision in favor of the assignor or his estate, whether contained in the policy or in any writing or provision pertaining to the policy.
- This assignment does not affect or change the beneficiary designation or settlement presently contained in the policy assigned. Proceeds payable on death will be paid in accordance with such designation or settlement unless same be hereafter changed by the assignee(s), when the right to make such change exists under the policy.

In an absolute assignment, the assignee, in effect, becomes the owner and the beneficiary of the policy, and the assignor may no longer change the beneficiary or exercise the conversion privilege. At death, only the assignee can choose a method of settlement because the assignee now has all these rights. In a collateral assignment, the rights assigned revert to the assignor when specified requirements—such as repayment of a loan—have been satisfied. When such requirements have been fulfilled, the assignee notifies the insurer that the assigned rights of ownership are being returned to the assignor.

Because the insurer is not a party to the assignment, the insurer rarely asks the reason for the assignment. The role of CSRs in an assignment is to record the change of ownership so that rights of ownership are granted to the proper party and so that, in the event of a claim, benefits can be disbursed to the appropriate party.

Before recording an assignment, CSRs check whether the policy has an irrevocable beneficiary. If so, that beneficiary must sign the request for assignment. If the irrevocable beneficiary refuses to sign the request, no assignment can be made. The insurer also reviews the policy provisions to determine whether any problems exist that would interfere with an assignment.

Changing an Address

One of the most common changes requested is a change of address for an individual policyowner; a request for a change of address for a group of insureds occurs less often. An insurer needs to send premium notices, checks, and correspondence to the correct addresses for all policyowners.

When an insurer's customer service department receives an address change request by telephone, the caller is usually required to provide her Social Security or social insurance number, current address, and other identifying information to verify authorization to make the change. Like changing a policyowner's or beneficiary's name, changing an address requires that all of an insurer's records reflect the change. At some companies, after the CSR makes the changes, he mails a verifying letter to the policyowner.

Changing Coverage or Adding Riders

Policyowners often want to increase or decrease the amount of coverage provided by a policy, to add or delete people from coverage, or to modify the coverage by adding or deleting riders. Perhaps a policyowner has been promoted and earns a higher income, so he wants to increase the amount of his disability income coverage. Or perhaps a family has added one or more children or other dependents and needs to increase the amount of life insurance on the wage earners. Changes to group insurance coverage are typically frequent as employees join and leave an organization. When a business is purchased and several formerly key employees are laid off, the key person coverage on those employees needs to be removed. In response to these and other types of requests, customer service handles the ongoing changes in insurance coverage.

Increasing the amount of coverage can be accomplished by

- Increasing the dollar amount of insurance or the period during which benefits will be paid
- Reducing the deductible amount or the elimination period
- Adding a new type of benefit not offered under the existing coverage

Because increasing the amount of coverage may increase the risk for the insurer, granting a policyowner an increase in coverage often requires additional underwriting.

Decreasing the amount of coverage can be accomplished by

- Reducing the dollar amount of insurance or the period during which benefits will be paid
- Increasing the deductible amount or the elimination period
- Removing one or more benefits offered by the existing coverage

Decreasing the amount of coverage generally does not require additional underwriting because such a reduction does not increase the insurer's risk. Therefore, CSRs can usually approve a decrease in coverage on receipt of a signed request from a policyowner.

Previously we discussed riders and their uses in revising the amount and type of coverage provided under various types of insurance. Among the many benefits that can be added by riders are guaranteed insurability, accidental death benefit, and waiver of premium for disability. We noted that in applications for new coverage, the decision whether to approve a rider is usually left to underwriting. When a policyowner makes a request for such a revision of coverage, the CSR first evaluates if the product allows for the requested change and, if so, sends the customer the appropriate forms to sign. A policyowner requests changes of coverage by submitting a special form to the insurer. Figure 17-4 illustrates part of a typical form used to request a change of coverage.

FIGURE 17-4. Portion of a Typical Change of Coverage Request Form.

For Contract/Policy Number________________________

Add Optional Benefits:

- ❒ **Disability Waiver of Premium:** If you suffer an accident that results in a covered disability, this option guarantees that your premium will be paid for you while you are disabled.
- ❒ **Waiver of Monthly Deduction:** If you suffer an accident or illness that results in a covered disability, this option guarantees that your cost of insurance will be paid for you while you are disabled.
- ❒ **Accidental Death Benefit (ADB) of $** ____________________. If you die as the result of a covered accident, this option will pay your beneficiary an *additional* amount above the face amount you have selected for the policy.

Increase Coverage:

- ❒ Increase coverage to $ ____________________
- ❒ Increase Accidental Death Benefit to $ ____________________

Rate Review:

- ❒ Change from Tobacco User to Non-Tobacco User
- ❒ Medical/Avocation Rate Review

Removing or canceling a rider requires no underwriting action because the risk to the insurer is decreased when the coverage is changed. Instead, the CSR calculates the new premium, submits a new premium bill to the policyowner, and, if necessary, sends a premium refund to the policyowner.

Determining Cash Value and Administering Loans and Dividends

The ***cash value*** of an individual life insurance policy is the amount of money, before adjustment for factors such as policy loans or late premiums, that a policyowner will receive if the policyowner (1) requests a policy loan, (2) allows the policy to lapse, or (3) cancels the coverage and surrenders the policy to the insurer. Cash value is a feature of most types of permanent life insurance such as whole life and universal life.

Many insurers accept telephone requests from policyowners for disbursements including dividend payments, surrenders, or loans of amounts lower than a specified maximum amount. Key personal information about the policyowner is requested to verify that the caller is the policyowner. Allowing policyowners to perform monetary transactions by phone enhances the service provided to customers.

Policy loans made on individual life insurance coverage are actually cash advances issued to policyowners. The policyowner repays the policy loan with interest. If the loan is not fully repaid, the amount of the outstanding policy loan, plus interest, is deducted from the amount of death benefits paid under the policy at the time of a claim. Figure 17-5 illustrates a sample request for a policy loan.

FIGURE 17-5. Sample Request for Policy Loan.

Policy Loan Request

❒ Maximum Loan Value OR ❒ For loan of $ ________________

- The policy is hereby assigned to the insurer as security for the said loan and interest under the terms of this agreement.
- Interest will be due and payable on the loan in arrears or in advance as stated in the policy. The rate of interest will be stated in the policy.
- If the loan and interest thereon together with all other indebtedness under the policy at any time exceeds the policy's cash value, all liability of the insurer under the policy will terminate, subject to any right of reinstatement provided in the policy.
- Any provision of the policy requiring endorsement by the insurer for a loan is hereby waived.
- The undersigned hereby certify that they are of the age of majority.

When a CSR receives a request for a policy loan, she examines the policy record to ensure that the request has been made by an eligible person and that, if the policy has been assigned or has an irrevocable beneficiary, the necessary signatures of the assignee or beneficiary (or a spouse in a community property jurisdiction) are correctly provided. By comparing the signatures on the loan form to the signatures on the insurer's records, the CSR verifies that the person or people requesting the loan are entitled to do so. If the signatures do not match, the CSR typically sends a letter with a loan form to the insured and instructs the insured to return the form with a notarized signature. Although the policy loan does not have to be repaid, most insurers offer policyowners a choice of one of the following loan repayment plans:

- *Dividend plan.* The insurer applies available dividends plus future dividends against the loan amount.

- *Coupon plan*. The insurer supplies the policyowner with coupons to return with periodic payments against the loan amount.
- *Automatic deduction plan*. The policyowner authorizes the insurer to automatically deduct a set amount from the policyowner's bank account each month until the loan is repaid.
- *Lump sum plan*. The policyowner submits a check or money order for the entire loan plus the loan interest due.
- *Partial loan repayment plan*. The policyowner submits a check or money order for a partial loan payment.

After calculating the cash value of the policy and verifying that it is adequate to fulfill the requested loan, the CSR then issues a check in that amount. If the cash value is inadequate to fulfill the requested loan, most insurers issue a check for the greatest amount available and notify the policyowner of the reason for not granting the full amount requested.

FAST FACT

In the United States, life insurer loans to policyowners against the cash value of their life insurance policies amounted to $99 billion by the end of 1999.[2]

Most insurers offer policyowners the option of obtaining an automatic premium loan to cover unpaid premiums. An ***automatic premium loan (APL) provision*** in a policy allows an insurer to pay overdue premiums on a policy by establishing a loan against the policy's cash value. In most jurisdictions, such an option is available only if the policyowner requests it. If a policyowner who has chosen an APL option fails to pay a premium on a timely basis, the insurer automatically grants a loan if the policy's loan value is sufficient to cover the amount of premium plus interest. A policyowner's use of the automatic premium loan option can signal a potential lapse or surrender of the policy. The CSR, therefore, attempts to conserve the business by notifying the policyowner and the agent that the loan has taken effect.

A ***policy dividend*** is a payment made by an insurer to a policyowner and can be paid on both individual and group insurance coverage. On individual coverage, a policy dividend is a refund of excess premium paid to the owner of an individual participating life insurance policy. Generally, a policy dividend on individual coverage reflects the insurer's decision to reduce the cost of the coverage by returning to the policyowner a portion of the premium already paid. A person who owns a participating life insurance policy elects a dividend option at the time of policy application. The policyowner is usually free to change the selected option at any time while the policy is in force. The available options usually include

- Receiving cash payment of dividends on a periodic basis, usually quarterly or annually

- Applying dividends to pay some or all of the premiums on the policy
- Applying dividends to pay some or all of the loan on the policy, if any
- Allowing dividends to accumulate at interest, adding to the policy's cash value
- Using dividends to buy additional insurance

On group coverage, a policy dividend is the portion of a group insurance premium that the insurer returns to a group policyholder whose claim experience is better than what was predicted when the premium was calculated.

The customer service department is responsible for computing the amount of policy dividends available at any given time and for making appropriate changes to the insurer's records when a policyowner changes the dividend option. If the policyowner chooses to receive cash payment of dividends or to withdraw some or all of the dividends that have been left to accumulate with interest, the CSR calculates the amount of dividends and makes appropriate disbursements to the policyowner. Although dividend earnings are not taxable in the United States, any interest earned on accumulations is taxable. Typically, automated systems in customer service calculate any amount of taxes due.

If a policyowner chooses to apply existing dividends to buy additional insurance, the CSR verifies that the additional coverage is allowable without further evidence of insurability. Elements the insurer generally considers include the amount of insurance already in force, the amount of coverage that dividends would purchase, and the applicant's risk classification. If additional evidence of insurability is necessary, the CSR usually notifies both the policyowner and the insurer's underwriters of the required evidence.

Handling Variable Insurance Products

Variable life insurance is a form of whole life insurance under which the death benefit and the cash value of the policy change according to the investment performance of funds that are kept separate from an insurer's other investments. Most variable life insurance products permit a policyowner to choose from several separate funds and to change the selection at least annually and sometimes more often.

Therefore, in addition to processing requests for policy loans, surrenders, and changes in name, address, beneficiaries, and premium mode, CSRs also help policyowners of variable life products (1) reallocate money from one investment fund to another and (2) designate the allocation of future premium payments. In the first instance, a policyowner moves currently invested money from one type of investment to another—for example, from a money market or bond account to a growth and income stock account. In the second instance, a policyowner specifies the investments into which future premiums will be placed. Most insurers allow policyowners to make reallocation choices by telephone or in writing, although some insurers require written notification of the policyowner's desire to reallocate funds. Depending on the jurisdiction, CSRs who assist policyowners with variable life products may be required to obtain special licenses. An increasing number of insurers offer policyowners the option of making changes in fund allocation through the insurers' Web sites.

Handling Premium Payments

In some insurance companies, customer service sends premium due notices and handles premium payments. Many insurers use automated systems to generate these notices. In order to continue a policy in force, a policyowner must send premium payments to the insurer according to an established schedule, which may be monthly, quarterly, semiannually, or annually. Customer service sends notices to policyowners to remind them of premiums due and maintains records of premiums due and paid.

If a policyowner is late in paying a premium, most insurance companies send the policyowner a ***policy grace notice*** (also called a *lapse notice*), which is a written notification that the policy's grace period is about to expire. The ***grace period*** is a specified period after a renewal premium is due and unpaid during which a policy, including all riders, remains in force. If a premium is paid during the grace period, the premium is considered to have been paid on time. The policy grace notice is mailed to a policyowner as a reminder that the premium is due within the grace period. Figure 17-6 shows one version of wording used in a policy grace notice.

Some policyowners choose to increase or decrease the frequency of premium payments. For example, a policyowner who has previously paid monthly premiums for health insurance may decide to change to a semiannual or annual premium payment mode because the premium charged for less frequent payments is usually somewhat lower than for more frequent payments. Insurers sometimes do not permit changes in premium payment frequency because of complications resulting from due dates that are inconsistent with a policy's anniversary. If a policy

FIGURE 17-6. Sample Policy Grace Notice.

There is no longer sufficient surrender value in your policy to prevent termination or lapse of the policy. Accordingly, your policy has entered a grace period and will lapse if sufficient premium to continue your policy is not received before the end of the grace period.

In order to continue your coverage in force, you must pay the minimum premium, which is $__________________. This premium must be received on or before the grace period expiration date, which is ______________________.

We appreciate your business and hope that you will remit your premium promptly.

has a waiver of premium provision and the premiums are currently being waived, an insurer generally does not allow a change to a more frequent premium payment mode. Generally, when a policyowner submits a request for a change of premium payment frequency, a CSR can approve the change if the request meets the insurer's premium payment requirements.

If insurance coverage provides for a change of premium at the time an insured reaches a specified age, customer service sends the policyowner a premium bill or a notice that reflects the new premium. In addition, customer service notifies the staff responsible for paying agents' commissions to modify the premium-based commission amount due, if any, to an agent. Customer service also handles various other age-related changes to certain coverages. For example, a health insurance policy might specify that an insured can continue to be covered if the insured is still employed past a certain age. Similarly, some types of coverage terminate when an insured reaches a specified age, and other types of coverage provide that an insured becomes eligible for alternative coverage at a stated age. For these and other types of changes, CSRs are responsible for notifying policyowners of coverage changes and premium rates and arranging premium payment according to policy provisions.

To conserve business, most insurers either have CSRs send agents a list of policyowners whose premium payments have become 20 to 90 days overdue or send agents a copy of the payment notice. Agents thus have an opportunity to contact policyowners who have not paid their premiums in a timely manner and to encourage them to retain the coverage or to modify it so that the coverage and the premium amount more nearly match their current needs.

Fulfilling Other Customer Needs

In addition to the functions already discussed, customer service fulfills other policyowner needs, including obtaining a duplicate copy of a policy and surrendering, converting, reinstating, or terminating a policy.

Obtaining a Duplicate Policy

A policyowner or other person may need to obtain a duplicate copy of a policy when the original policy has been lost or destroyed, or is otherwise unavailable. Most insurers require a written statement that the policy has been lost or destroyed, signed by the policyowner. A duplicate copy of a policy is stamped to indicate that it is a duplicate, and the insurer's file contains a record of the duplicate issuance. Figure 17-7 illustrates a typical lost policy request form.

Before issuing a duplicate copy of a policy, the CSR helps to avoid potential legal problems by verifying that the duplicate copy is needed and that the original copy is gone. If a problem arises in verifying the loss of the original policy, the CSR usually issues a certificate of insurance rather than a duplicate policy. The ***certificate of insurance***, also

FIGURE 17-7. Typical Lost Policy Request Form.

For Contract/Policy Number ______________________

I request a:
- ❐ Certification of my policy (no charge)
- ❐ Duplicate policy ($30 fee enclosed to cover expenses)

My policy was:
- ❐ Lost
- ❐ Destroyed
- ❐ Other ______________________

Send the above to: ❐ Policyowner ❐ Agent ______________________

The undersigned hereby represents that the above numbered policy was lost or destroyed. This policy is not now assigned, nor has it been otherwise transferred or encumbered in any manner. No person, firm, or corporation has or claims the right to possession of this policy.

I agree that should the original policy be found or in any way come into my possession, I will return the duplicate policy to the insurer.

Signature ______________________ Date ______________________

known as a *certificate of coverage,* verifies that coverage exists, but does not contain all the details of provisions and riders that the original policy may have contained.

Surrendering a Policy

A policyowner might decide to surrender a policy by requesting that coverage cease and that the insurer send the policyowner the cash value of the policy. When a CSR receives such a request, he first makes certain that the person who submitted the request is legally entitled to surrender the policy. If a policyowner has assigned some or all of the rights to the policy, then the policyowner is not allowed to surrender it without the assignee's authorization. Figure 17-8 illustrates a typical cash surrender request form.

Before administering a request to surrender a policy, the CSR usually attempts to conserve the business by contacting the policyowner to ask whether an alternative action might fulfill the policyowner's needs. For instance, the CSR might suggest that the policyowner use accumulated policy dividends to pay premiums or request a policy loan for the same purpose, or reduce the amount of coverage if the original amount is no longer needed.

Processing the request for policy surrender requires a CSR to calculate the cash value and to deduct the amount of any outstanding loans. Some insurers also require the policyowner to submit the policy to the insurer before the surrender is completed and the cash value is disbursed to the policyowner. Usually, the signature of the policyowner is required to surrender the contract.

FIGURE 17-8. Typical Cash Surrender Request Form.

Return your policy OR complete a Lost Policy Request Form.

I request payment of the cash surrender value in exchange for surrender of the attached policy.

Effective Date: ____________________

Apply proceeds to Policy #____________________ (if applicable)

Reason for surrender (check all that apply):

❒ Changing insurance needs ❒ Affordability

❒ Replacing with new insurance from another insurer

❒ ____________________

Converting a Policy

A ***conversion privilege*** is a policy provision that permits a policyowner to convert group insurance coverage to coverage under an individual insurance policy or, in certain prescribed situations, to change coverage from one type of policy to another—for instance, to change from an individual term insurance policy to an individual whole life insurance policy. An employee who ceases employment through retirement or termination may be eligible to continue certain types of group coverage by exercising the conversion privilege if one is included in the group contract. Generally a policyowner who exercises the conversion privilege is not required to submit evidence of insurability, particularly if the increase in risk to the insurer is only slight.

A CSR does check several items, however, in handling a request for policy conversion. First, the CSR makes sure that the conversion occurs during the conversion period if one is specified in the policy contract. In addition, most insurers require that the first premium payment for the new, or converted, policy be remitted when the conversion request is made. After verifying that the correct premium has been submitted, the CSR prepares a new policy and updates the policyowner's records to reflect the converted coverage.

Reinstating a Policy

As we have mentioned, reinstatement is the process by which an insurer puts back in force a policy that lapsed because of nonpayment of renewal premiums. Reinstatement provides advantages for both the insurer and the insured. The insurer is able to keep business on its books without incurring the high first-year expenses normally associated with acquiring new business. The insured continues to have insurance protection that might no longer be offered to new applicants or for which the insured might not be able to qualify because of advanced age or impairments developed since the original coverage was issued. In addition, a reinstated policy usually maintains the original, usually lower premium and typically can be reinstated with more liberal underwriting standards than would apply to an application for new coverage. Figure 17-9 shows a typical application for reinstatement of coverage.

When a policyowner applies for reinstatement of a lapsed policy, the CSR determines whether the policy contains a ***reinstatement provision***, which is a provision that describes the conditions a policyowner must meet for an insurer to reinstate a policy within a specified time after lapse. The right to reinstate a policy is generally not available if the policyowner has surrendered the policy for its cash value; the reinstatement provision does not obligate the insurer to reinstate the policy.

FIGURE 17-9. Typical Application for Reinstatement of Coverage.

Policy # ____

Insured ____

Name of Employer________________________________

Application for Reinstatement of Policy Described Above

1. Your present occupation: ____
2. Have you for any reason received medical attention or advice since the date you became covered by the policy in question? If so, give the nature of the illness, date, and name of the physician:

   ____

   ____

   ____
3. Do you declare that you are of sound constitution and temperate habits, and that you are now in good health? ____________________
4. Are you now, have you in the past, or do you intend to engage in any form of aviation? _______
5. Name and address of family physician:

   ____

   ____

I hereby certify that the above declarations are complete and true, and I agree that no reinstatement shall take effect until this application is approved by the insurer at its home office.

Date ____________________ Signature ____________________

Most insurers require applicants for reinstatement to pay back premiums. Some insurers, however, allow policies that meet certain strict criteria to be reinstated without payment of back premiums in order to encourage reinstatement of policies that may have lapsed because of temporary financial hardship, as explained in Figure 17-10.

Most reinstatement requests also require the applicant to complete a medical questionnaire. If there have been no significant changes in the applicant's health since the original policy was issued, the CSR reinstates the policy without further investigation. However, if evidence

FIGURE 17-10. Reinstatement by Redating.

Some insurance companies attempt to conserve canceled business, especially that of smaller amount policies, by permitting lapsed policies to be reinstated without requiring the payment of back premiums. Policies that have lapsed, but that meet certain criteria, can be reinstated by advancing the policy date and the paid-to date (the date to which premiums were paid up) by the number of months that the policy has been lapsed. No back premiums are collected.

A policy reinstated in this manner generally must meet the following criteria:

- The policy must be less than two years old and have no cash value.
- It must have been lapsed for more than 60 days, but not more than six months beyond the paid-to date.
- The face amount plus any supplementary term coverage cannot exceed a specified amount, usually $20,000 to $30,000.
- Redating can occur only once during the life of the policy.

shows the possibility of significant change, the CSR usually directs the underwriting staff to ask for additional evidence of insurability or to review the application. After reviewing this evidence, the underwriter can recommend one of three actions:

1. Grant reinstatement as requested
2. Decline reinstatement if the risk has increased so much that the underwriter cannot justify allowing the person to remain in the original risk class
3. Offer to reissue the policy at a higher premium charge

FAST FACT

In Canada in 1999, about $9 out of every $10 made in payments by life and health insurance companies went to living policyowners, for a total of $31.4 billion in payments.[3]

CSRs can approve routine reinstatements that have adequate documentation of unchanged health conditions and that meet height/weight requirements. More complex applications for reinstatement involving deteriorated health or high amounts of coverage are usually referred to underwriting.

Terminating a Policy

If a policyowner does not renew a policy contract, or if premiums have not been paid on a policy and the policyowner does not respond to a series of premium due notices, then the policy is terminated in accordance with the insurer's established procedures. A CSR sends a letter or notice to the policyowner stating that the coverage has been terminated. Most insurers also instruct CSRs to notify agents when coverage has been terminated so that the agents can determine the cause for the termination.

Handling Returned Mail

Many areas of an insurance company designate staff to handle mail that has been returned. Claims and underwriting, to name two, are careful to investigate returned mail and to send it to its intended recipients, if possible. Customer service is also concerned with handling returned mail because of the need to communicate with the customer, to conserve business, to operate in a cost-effective manner, and to ensure that requested changes, loans, and other transactions are completed promptly and accurately.

For most insurers, the first step in attempting to resend mail to its intended recipients involves checking whether a more current address has been received. An insurer's information system may contain updated address information. If, after checking the system, a CSR discovers that no current address has been entered, a code is put into the system to show that mail was returned and that no further mail should be sent to that address.

Many insurance companies subscribe to a national database that allows CSRs to search for a more current address by entering a recipient's name, Social Security or social identification number, date of birth, and last known address. Insurers usually pay only for successful searches—that is, searches that result in identification of a usable address.

For mail related to variable insurance and other regulated products, CSRs usually intensify the search by calling directory assistance in the city of the last known address and attempting to seek a new address. In many instances, CSRs call an agent to inquire about the location of the addressee.

At the completion of a search, if a CSR has been unable to find a viable address, another code is usually entered into the information system to indicate that the insurer not only received returned mail, but also could not locate a mailing address. Having made a good faith attempt to find the addressee, the CSR files the undelivered mail and hopes that the client will later contact the insurer.

The Relationship of Customer Service and Underwriting

We have already mentioned several circumstances in which CSRs consult with underwriters when additional evidence of insurability is required. In addition, several types of policy changes may involve underwriting.

A policyowner's financial situation, insurability status, or insurance needs can make it necessary or desirable for the policyowner to request a change in the terms of a policy contract after it has been in force for some time. The policyowner might want to (1) change the policy to a different type of insurance, (2) obtain a rate reduction, (3) add benefits to the original policy, or (4) increase the amount of coverage. A policyowner who wants to make such changes in policy terms must complete a policy change application, specifying the requested changes.

The underwriter's primary concern, as you have learned, is to evaluate the risk represented by a proposed insured or a policyowner who wants to make a change in coverage. In considering requested policy changes, the underwriter considers (1) whether a proposed change increases a policy's net amount at risk and (2) whether the insured's original insurability status has changed. CSRs and underwriters work closely to ensure that each requested change is promptly evaluated and that those involved—principally the policyowner and, sometimes, the agent—are kept informed of progress on the case.

Change in Type of Insurance

For a policyowner who wants to make a change in the type of insurance, the underwriter considers several factors, among them the reason for the requested change. A policyowner might want to change the insurance program into a higher-premium plan with a greater investment in the policy. This type of change usually poses no problem for the underwriter because the insurer's net amount at risk will decrease more rapidly under the higher-premium plan than under the original plan. An underwriting problem may result, however, if the waiver of premium benefit is included in the contract because the higher premium for the new plan will increase the amount at risk for the waiver of premium benefit. Thus, a premium increase above a certain dollar amount may require additional evidence of insurability.

When a policyowner requests a change to a lower-premium plan, generally no significant increase or only a moderate increase in the insurer's net amount at risk occurs. Underwriting for such a request can be more liberal than the original underwriting because the first-year acquisition costs, such as the agent's commission, have already been paid. In many insurance companies, therefore, policy changes and conversions involving only moderate increases in the amount at risk are approved by customer service without referral to an underwriter *if* all of the following are true:

1. The insured has no history of impairment or rating.
2. The height and weight of the insured are within current standard limits.
3. All answers on the health declaration of the policy change form are acceptable.

Figure 17-11 shows a sample health declaration section of a policy change request form.

FIGURE 17-11. Sample Health Declaration Section.

Amendment of Application
and
Certification of Health Status

The application for Contract/Policy Number ____________________ is hereby amended as follows:

Except as explained in number 3 below, it is represented and certified that since the date of the original application and the date of the medical examination,

1. The answers to the questions on the original application and on the medical examination form remain true and complete as of today and that there has been no change in the health of the proposed insured that would call for or warrant a change in the answers provided.
2. The proposed insured has not consulted or been examined or treated by a physician or other physical or mental health advisor.
3. (State details for any exceptions to 1 and 2 above.)

____

____

____

It is agreed that the omission of any written exception in the space immediately above shall have the same force and effect as if the word "None" were written in that space.

It is further understood and agreed that if approved by the insurer, this Amendment of Application will become part of the policy and that the policy is issued in reliance upon the truthfulness of the representation contained hereon.

Signed this ______________ day of ____________________, ____________

____________________	____________________
Witness	Proposed Insured
____________________	____________________
Agent	Signature of Applicant if other than Proposed Insured

Rate Reduction

Another type of requested change is reduction or removal of a previously assigned rating or extra premium. Most rate reductions are made in situations in which an insured has received a substandard rating.

In general, a rate reduction is considered either (1) if the insured was originally rated incorrectly or (2) if the reason for the rating is no longer present—for instance, when a disease or condition is either cured or brought under an acceptable degree of improvement or control. An insured person who was rated for being overweight and who later loses the excess weight will more than likely receive a rate reduction if other medical factors remain the same. An underwriter, whose expertise is necessary to evaluate all pertinent medical indicators, typically makes such a decision.

Many insurance companies advise new policyowners that they can request reconsideration for an extra premium rating at certain times, usually on the first or second policy anniversary date. When customer service receives such a request, it is typically forwarded to underwriting for evaluation.

Unlike conversion, rate reduction is not a contractual right. A request for a rate reduction usually requires the insured to submit an application that is similar to the original application, but not as detailed. Such a request also requires evidence of insurability to demonstrate that the insured's case warrants a reduction in the current substandard rating. The costs of any medical reports, tests, or exams are usually paid for by the insured. CSRs are generally responsible for providing the necessary forms to the insured and for answering questions about the procedure followed in considering such a request.

Additional Benefits

After a policy is issued, a policyowner may want to add benefits, as we have already mentioned. Such requests are usually handled in a routine manner by customer service, but, in some cases, underwriting may require evidence of insurability in order to reappraise the risk. Each insurer establishes its own procedures to define those benefits and levels of coverage that do and do not require the involvement of underwriting.

Key Terms and Concepts

affidavit
assignor
assignee
cash value
automatic premium loan (APL) provision
policy dividend
variable life insurance
policy grace notice
grace period
certificate of insurance
conversion privilege
reinstatement provision

Endnotes

1. ACLI, *Life Insurers Fact Book 2000* (Washington, D.C.: American Council of Life Insurers, 2000), 16.
2. Ibid., 129.
3. CLHIA, *Canadian Life and Health Insurance Facts* (Toronto: Canadian Life and Health Insurance Association, 2000), 17.

Glossary

1035 exchange. A transaction in which the cash surrender value of a replaced insurance policy is used as the initial premium for a new policy. [6]

20 percent rule. A method of determining the amount of coverage a proposed insured can purchase, which stipulates that a maximum of 20 percent of the applicant's gross earned income can be used to buy life insurance. [5]

absolute assignment. An irrevocable transfer of all the rights of a life insurance policy from one party to another. [13]

accelerated death benefit. A portion of a policy's benefits paid during life to a terminally ill insured who has a remaining life expectancy of less than a specified period, usually ranging between six months and two years. [7]

accidental death benefit (ADB). A life insurance policy rider that provides an additional death benefit above the face amount of a policy if an insured's death occurs as the result of an accident. [6]

accounting. The process of collecting, analyzing, and reporting financial data. [1]

accredited reinsurer. A reinsurance company that is not licensed in the ceding company's jurisdiction, but (1) meets specified financial and reporting requirements of that jurisdiction and (2) holds a license in and is domiciled in at least one other jurisdiction. [9]

activities of daily living (ADLs). A number of different activities that a person performs every day, including eating, bathing, dressing, getting out of bed, and toileting. [7]

actuarial. An insurer's staff members who use mathematical principles to predict the rates of illness, injury, disability, and death among insureds. [1]

ADB. *See* **accidental death benefit.**

ADLs. *See* **activities of daily living.**

admitted reinsurer. *See* **authorized reinsurer.**

adult day care. Care provided to adults in a group setting during hours when primary caregivers are working. [14]

affidavit. A written statement made before an official who is authorized to administer oaths. [17]

agent. Any person or entity that sells insurance. [1]

agent's statement. A section of an insurance application reserved for the agent's comments about the applicant or the proposed insured. Some agents provide such information in a letter addressed to the insurer. [2]

allowance. A reinsurer's proportionate share of the agent commissions, underwriting costs, administration costs, policy issue costs, and other expenses that an insurer incurs in acquiring a policy. [9]

alphabetic split. A method used to divide risk among reinsurers in which risks are divided among a group of reinsurers by assigning part of the alphabet to each reinsurer and then sending that reinsurer all cases whose insureds' surnames begin with the assigned alphabet letters. Also known as an *alpha split*. [10]

alpha split. *See* **alphabetic split.**

alternate care benefits. Long-term care policy benefits for nonconventional services developed cooperatively by a physician and an insurer to substitute for more expensive nursing home care. [14]

Alzheimer's disease. A type of cognitive impairment, which causes deterioration of a person's intellectual and cognitive functions. Also called *primary degenerative dementia*. [7]

annual premium. The amount that a group policyholder will be charged for the total amount of coverage requested. [8]

antiselection. The tendency of people who suspect or know they are more likely than average to experience loss to apply for or renew insurance to a greater extent than are people who lack such knowledge of probable loss. [2]

APL. *See* **automatic premium loan provision.**

APS. *See* **attending physician's statement.**

arbitration. The process of resolving a conflict through the use of impartial industry experts, known as arbitrators, who hear the facts as presented by each side and determine an appropriate outcome for the dispute. [11]

articles. The standard provisions that make up the body of a reinsurance treaty. [10]

assignee. A person or entity that receives ownership rights. [17]

assignment. A transfer of some or all of the rights to receive the proceeds of a life insurance policy to another person or entity, such as a business or a trust. [13]

assignment of benefits. A statement on a medical expense claim form that directs an insurer to pay benefits directly to a health care provider rather than to an insured. [14]

assignor. A person or entity that transfers ownership rights. [17]

assisted living facility. A residential facility designed to meet long-term care needs by providing accommodations, board, and access to medical services. [14]

assuming company. An insurer that sells reinsurance, so called because it is assuming risk from a direct writing company. [9]

assumption reinsurance. A type of reinsurance that involves the total and permanent transfer of risk from one company to another when a reinsurer purchases a block of inforce insurance, creating contractual relationships with all insureds and assuming responsibility for policy administration and all liabilities. [9]

attending physician. A physician who has provided medical care for a proposed insured. [4]

attending physician's statement (APS). A report by a physician who has treated, or who is currently treating, the proposed insured. [4]

authorization to release information. A section of a claimant's statement that permits an insurer to obtain claim-specific information from medical caregivers and institutions, government agencies, other insurers, consumer reporting agencies, and other sources. [13]

authorized reinsurer. A reinsurance company that is licensed or otherwise recognized by the insurance department in the jurisdiction of the ceding company. Also known as an *admitted reinsurer*. [9]

automatic binding limit. Under automatic reinsurance, the maximum dollar amount of risk on a life the reinsurer will accept without making its own underwriting assessment of the risk. [10]

automatic premium loan (APL) provision. A provision in a life insurance policy that allows an insurer to pay overdue premiums on a policy by establishing a loan against the policy's cash value. [17]

automatic reinsurance. A type of reinsurance under which the ceding company agrees to cede and the assuming company agrees to accept specified types of cases on the underwriting judgment of the ceding company alone, up to a specified amount. [10]

backward number sequence test. A type of cognitive screen, which examines the ability of a proposed insured to recall a series of numbers and name them in reverse sequence. [7]

benchmark. A performance standard that has been achieved by a recognized leader in a specific process and represents the company's goal for its own performance of the process. [16]

benefit period. The length of time during which disability income benefits will be paid, typically lasting from less than a year to age 65 or 70. [15]

benefit transmittal. A document that provides details concerning the insurance benefits being requested for each employee class, the effective date of coverage, how premium billing and claims will be administered, and other information concerning the type of plan being requested for a group. [8]

benefit unit. A specific amount of coverage, for example, the benefit unit for term life insurance, which is usually $1,000 [8]

binding premium receipt. *See* **temporary insurance agreement.**

blended rating. The process of using both manual and experience rating to calculate premiums by assigning a credibility factor to the group's experience and including that factor in the premium calculations. [8]

block of business. *See* **block of policies.**

block of policies. A group of policies issued to insureds who are in the same risk classification. Also known as a *block of business*. [2]

build. The shape or form of a person's body, including the relationship among height, weight, and distribution of the weight. [4]

build chart. A chart that is based on established studies and indicates average weights for various heights for each sex, along with the mortality debits associated with increases in weight. [4]

bulk administration. A method of reinsurance administration in which the ceding company administers the reinsurance and periodically submits summarized reports on premiums and on the policies to the assuming company, but does not provide individualized detailed information about risks reinsured until a claim needs to be processed. [11]

business financial supplement. A specialized questionnaire used in underwriting business insurance that requests information about the type of business, the current financial condition of the business, and the purpose for which the insurance is being requested [6]

business insurance. A type of insurance that provides coverage for the insurance needs of a business organization rather than those of an individual. [6]

call center. A customer service unit that handles questions when customers contact insurers by telephone, typically using a toll-free number. [16]

Canada Health Act. In Canada, legislation that requires that each Canadian province provide its residents with health care coverage for hospital and medical services. [3]

Canada Pension Plan. In Canada, a federal insurance plan that provides disability income benefits and survivor benefits (life insurance) to Canadian employees, including those who are self-employed. [3]

Canadian Reinsurance Conference (CRC). A meeting held each year by Canadian ceding companies and reinsurance companies to discuss current life and health insurance and reinsurance issues. [10]

capacity. The highest dollar amount of coverage that an insurance company is financially able to accept on a specified risk. [9]

captive reinsurer. A reinsurance company that is formed and controlled by an insurance company or another type of insurance marketer for the purpose of providing reinsurance to that insurer or marketer. [9]

case assignment system. A method used to organize underwriting work that enables an underwriter to specialize in certain types of cases. [2]

cash value. For an individual life insurance policy, the amount of money, before adjustment for factors such as policy loans or late premiums, that a policyowner will receive if the policyowner (1) requests a policy loan, (2) allows the policy to lapse, or (3) cancels the coverage and surrenders the policy to the insurer. [17]

ceding company. An insurer that buys reinsurance. [9]

certificate of coverage. *See* **certificate of insurance.**

certificate of indebtedness. A document that specifies a guaranteed minimum interest rate that the insurer will pay on insurance policy proceeds and the frequency with which the insurer will make interest payments to a beneficiary. [13]

certificate of insurance. A document that verifies that insurance coverage exists, but which does not contain all the details of provisions and riders that an original policy may have contained. Also known as a *certificate of coverage*. [17]

cession. A term that describes both the unit of insurance that an insurance company cedes to a reinsurer and the document used to record the transfer of risk from a ceding company to an assuming company. [9]

change in health statement. A statement contained in most individual life insurance applications and premium receipts that requires a proposed insured to notify the insurer in writing if her health or any material information in the application changes before the policy is delivered. [13]

churning. An unethical activity by which an agent induces a policyowner to cash in a policy and buy another, even though the replacement is not in the policyowner's best interest. [6]

CI. *See* **critical illness insurance.**

claim administration. The insurance administration function that assesses each claim made and decides whether or not the claim is justified. [1]

claim form. *See* **claimant's statement.**

claim fraud. An action by which a person intentionally uses false information in an unfair or unlawful attempt to collect benefits under a policy. [12]

claim philosophy. A precise statement of an insurer's principles for conducting claim administration, which is usually developed for each company by its senior management and guides the decisions made by claim analysts. [12]

claim practices. Statements that guide the day-to-day handling of claims developed by the senior management of claim administration using the insurer's claim philosophy as a basis. [12]

claim settlement. A lump-sum payment of money from the insurer to the claimant in exchange for the claimant's agreement to release the insurer from further responsibility for coverage under the policy. [15]

claimant's statement. A document in which a claimant provides information about the deceased insured, including the date, place, and cause and circumstances of death. Also known as a *claim form*. [13]

COB. *See* **coordination of benefits provision.**

cognitive impairment. A reduction in a person's ability to think, reason, or remember. [7]

cognitive screen. A test designed to determine a person's powers of recollection or short-term memory recall. [7]

coinsurance. In reinsurance, a type of proportional reinsurance in which an insurer and a reinsurer share the obligations of a policy, including paying the death benefit and the nonforfeiture values, and establishing the reserves. [10] In medical insurance coverage, The percentage of all eligible medical expenses, in excess of the deductible, incurred as a result of sickness or injury that the insured is required to pay. [14]

coinsurance with funds withheld. A type of proportional reinsurance in which the ceding company retains funds that are due to the reinsurer, usually in an amount equal to the reserve required by law. [10]

collateral assignment. A transfer of some ownership rights from one party to another, usually for a temporary period. [13]

committee underwriting. A method used to organize underwriting work in which a committee of highly qualified people from inside and outside the underwriting function is called together for case assessment. [2]

common disaster clause. *See* **survivorship clause.**

community-property laws. In the United States, state laws, which provide that a spouse is entitled to receive an equal share of earned income and an equal share of property acquired by the other spouse during a marriage. [13]

compensatory damages. Money awards to pay a plaintiff for the damage he has suffered from an insurer's wrongdoing. [12]

compliance. The insurance company function responsible for ensuring that an insurer and its agents follow all applicable state, provincial, and federal insurance requirements and regulations. [1]

conditional premium receipt. A type of premium receipt that makes the applied-for insurance coverage effective from the date of the application, provided that the underwriter ultimately finds the proposed insured to be an insurable risk. [3]

conditionally renewable. A type of disability income policy that sets criteria that the insured must meet to renew the coverage, such as continued employment or ongoing membership in a professional or other organization. [15]

conditions. *See* **schedules**.

conservation. The process of ensuring that an insurer retains issued policies on its books for as long as possible. [16]

consumer report. A communication from a consumer reporting agency that contains information relating to a person's creditworthiness, credit standing, or credit capacity, as well as information about the person's general reputation or personal characteristics. [3]

consumer reporting agency. A person or an organization that regularly prepares consumer reports and furnishes them, either for profit or on a cooperative, nonprofit basis, to other people or organizations. [3]

contingent beneficiary. The person or entity named to receive life insurance benefits if the primary beneficiary has died before the insured. Also known as the *secondary beneficiary*. [13]

contributory plan. Group insurance for which the insureds pay some part of the premium for their insurance coverage and may choose whether to participate in the group insurance plan. [8]

conversion provision. A group long-term care insurance policy provision that allows the insured group member leaving the group to change from the group coverage to an individual policy offered by the same insurer. [14]

conversion privilege. An insurance policy provision that permits a policyowner to convert group insurance coverage to coverage under an individual insurance policy or, in certain prescribed situations, to change coverage from one type of policy to another. [17]

coordination of benefits (COB) provision. A provision in group medical expense plans, which prevents duplicate benefit payments for the same expense by more than one insurer or by a government program. [14]

correspondent. A person in a policyholder's organization who serves as liaison with the insurer. [8]

cost basis. For an insurance policy, the total net premiums paid, *plus* accumulated dividends and *minus* certain specified costs. [6]

cost of living increase benefit. A disability income policy provision that provides for an increase in the monthly disability benefit, typically a percentage of the monthly benefit amount. [15]

CPT. *See* **Physicians' Current Procedural Terminology.**

CRC. *See* **Canadian Reinsurance Conference.**

credibility factor. A percentage that represents the degree to which an underwriter has estimated that the available underwriting information accurately shows the risk represented by a group. [8]

creditor insurance. Insurance coverage that is designed to alleviate the economic loss suffered by a creditor when one of its borrowers dies before the debt is repaid. [6]

credits. A proposed insured's medical, personal, and financial characteristics that have a favorable effect on mortality are assigned "minus" values (such as –25) that lower the number indicating an applicant's predicted percent of standard mortality. [4]

critical diagnosis insurance. *See* **critical illness insurance.**

critical illness (CI) insurance. A type of individual health insurance, which pays a lump sum benefit when the insured is diagnosed with a specified illness. Also known as *critical diagnosis insurance*. [7]

current assets. The items that a company presently has or owns, that can be easily converted to cash, including short-term investments, and cash and cash equivalents. [6]

current liabilities. All the debt that is due and payable within the next accounting period, typically one year, including salaries payable and interest payable. [6]

customer contact center. A customer service unit that handles questions and requests when customers contact an insurer by any method—for example, by telephone, fax, or e-mail. [16]

customer service. The broad range of activities, consistent with contractual provisions, that help keep customers satisfied so they will continue doing business with an insurer and speak positively about the insurer to other potential customers. [1]

death certificate. A document that attests to the death of a person and that bears the signature —and sometimes the seal—of an official authorized to issue such a certificate. [13]

debits. A proposed insured's medical, personal, and financial characteristics that have an unfavorable effect on mortality are assigned "plus" values (such as +25) that increase the number indicating an applicant's predicted percentage of standard mortality. [4]

declined class. Proposed insureds whose impairments and anticipated extra mortality are so great that the insurer cannot provide coverage at an affordable cost for them or who have recent medical events such that mortality cannot be accurately predicted. [2]

delayed word recall (DWR). A type of cognitive screen, which examines the ability of a proposed insured to remember several common words. [7]

dementia. A general term used for mental deterioration that is characterized by loss of certain intellectual abilities such as memory, judgment, and abstract thinking, of such a degree as to interfere with social functioning. [7]

dependent. A spouse or an unmarried child—including an adopted child, stepchild, or foster child—who is under age 19 or to age 25 if disabled or a full-time student, and who relies on an insured person for support and maintenance. [8]

DI. *See* **disability income insurance.**

diagnostic and treatment codes. Numbers and words that represent specific medical diagnoses and treatments. [14]

Diagnostic Related Groups (DRGs). A payment method under which an insurer will pay hospital charges not according to the number and types of services delivered, but according to the diagnosis for a patient. [14]

direct response product. An insurance product sold to consumers by an insurer without the help of an agent, usually through direct mail, advertising in print and other media, telephone solicitation, or the Internet. [6]

direct writing company. An insurer that sells coverage to consumers. [9]

disability income (DI) insurance. A type of individual health insurance that helps replace income lost as a result of sickness or injury. [7]

DRGs. *See* **Diagnostic Related Groups.**

DWR. *See* **delayed word recall.**

EDI. *See* **electronic data interchange.**

EFT. *See* **electronic funds transfer.**

electronic data interchange (EDI). A computer-to-computer information exchange that uses a more uniform format than is used for much remote computing. EDI is neither company-specific nor company-owned, but is a public standard for electronic movement of data. [1]

electronic funds transfer (EFT). An automatic premium payment approach whereby a policyowner authorizes his financial institution to withdraw funds from an account to pay each renewal premium. [16]

elimination period. For long-term care insurance, the number of days after long-term care begins that a person insured under a long-term care policy must wait before benefit payments begin. For disability income coverage, the amount of time between the time that a covered disability begins and the time that an insured is eligible to receive benefits. [14, 15]

employee census. A document that lists demographic information about a proposed group as a unit and about individual people within the proposed group. [8]

employee class. A group of employees categorized by position, earnings, or rank. [8]

Employee Retirement Income Security Act of 1974 (ERISA). In the United States, a federal law that establishes (1) the rights of participants in pension plans, (2) standards for investing pension plan assets, and (3) requirements for disclosing plan provisions and funding. [3]

employment standards legislation. In Canada, legislation that mandates certain employment standards relating to such issues as minimum wage rates, overtime pay, and maximum hours of work. [3]

enrollment application. *See* **enrollment card.**

enrollment card. A form completed by each eligible employee for a group insurance plan that provides the employee's personal data, and includes a statement that the employee signs to indicate that he understands the coverage offered and agrees to have his portion of the premium deducted from his salary. Also known as an *enrollment application*. [8]

entire agreement provision. A reinsurance treaty provision covering the scope of the agreement that states that the treaty and any amendments represent the whole agreement between the parties, which have no further agreement than that stated in the treaty. [10]

EOB. *See* **explanation of benefits.**

ERISA. *See* **Employee Retirement Income Security Act of 1974.**

estate settlement. The process of paying debts after a person's death. [5]

examining physician. A physician who performs an examination of a proposed insured at the request of the insurance company. [4]

excess of retention arrangement. A method of ceding proportional reinsurance in which an insurer cedes specified amounts of coverage that exceed its retention limit. [10]

excess quota share arrangement. A method of ceding proportional reinsurance in which the ceding company keeps its full retention limit and cedes the remaining risk to two or more assuming companies on a percentage basis. [10]

exclusion rider. An amendment that limits a policy's benefits by excluding from coverage certain types of risk, such as death benefits for a death resulting from an aviation accident or disability income benefits for a specified, usually preexisting, condition. [2]

exculpatory statutes. In the United States, state laws that permit an insurer to pay life insurance proceeds according to the terms of a policy without fear of double liability. [13]

exhibits. *See* **schedules.**

expected claim experience. The dollar amount of claims that an insurer estimates that a group will submit. [8]

experience rating. The process of using a group's claim experience to calculate premium rates. [8]

experience refund. A return of a portion of a group insurance premium to a group policyholder whose claim experience is better than had been expected when the premium was calculated. [8]

expert system. A sophisticated computer application that manipulates information based on established facts and an insurer's experience data to suggest solutions to problems. [1]

explanation of benefits (EOB). A detailed statement showing each treatment or medication submitted as part of a claim, an insurer's decision concerning payment of each charge, any amount that is considered as a deductible or a copayment, an explanation of any charge for which part or all of the charge will not be paid, and the total amount sent to a health care provider. [14]

extra-contract damages. Money awards to a plaintiff that exceed the amount of insurance policy benefits and which are compensatory or punitive. [12]

extra-percentage table. The extra mortality for each substandard group expressed as a percentage added to standard mortality as has been shown by the insurer's actual mortality experience. [4]

face-to-face assessment. A meeting between a proposed insured and an interviewer who represents the insurance company and who is usually employed by a vendor to observe an applicant's physical and mental condition. [7]

fac-ob. *See* **facultative-obligatory reinsurance.**

factor table. A chart that shows the maximum amount of insurance, expressed in multiples of a person's salary or total income, that an insurer will typically approve in each of several age ranges. [5]

facultative reinsurance. A type of reinsurance that allows a ceding company to choose whether to ask a reinsurer to consider coverage on a risk, the reinsurer to choose whether it wishes to participate in the risk, and the ceding company to choose whether to accept the reinsurer's offer on the risk, if an offer is made. [10]

facultative-obligatory (fac-ob) reinsurance. A type of reinsurance that is based on an agreement that (1) allows a ceding company to choose whether to submit cases to a reinsurer and (2) requires the reinsurer to accept the cases based on the ceding company's underwriting, up to an amount defined in the agreement, if the reinsurer has available capacity. [10]

Fair Credit Reporting Act (FCRA). In the United States a federal regulation that helps ensure that credit reporting agencies act fairly, impartially, and with respect for the consumer's right to privacy when preparing reports on individuals. [3]

family benefit. A life insurance policy rider that insures the lives of an insured's spouse and children. [6]

family income. From a life insurance perspective, funds needed to replace the ordinary living expenses formerly paid by the income of a deceased person whose wages or other income supplied the needs of a family. [5]

FCRA. *See* **Fair Credit Reporting Act.**

field underwriting. The process of screening applicants who have requested coverage and gathering initial information about a proposed insured. [2]

field underwriting manual. A document developed by an insurance company for agents to use when making initial assessments of proposed insureds. [4]

Financial Services Modernization Act. An act passed by the U.S. Congress in 1999, which allows convergence among the traditionally separate components of the financial services industry—banks, securities firms, and insurance companies. More commonly referred to as the *Gramm-Leach-Bliley (GLB) Act.* [12]

financial status. A person's current income expressed in terms of amount, sources, and permanency, and by the person's net worth. [5]

financial worksheet. A document that enables an underwriter to organize financial information and to develop a clear picture of a person's financial situation. [5]

first dollar quota share arrangement. A method of ceding proportional reinsurance in which the ceding company cedes a certain percentage of the entire risk to the assuming company or companies despite the presence of a retention limit—that is, the ceding company cedes coverage from the first dollar. [10]

first excess. When layering is used, the amount in excess of an insurer's retention limit up to a specified amount that is used to divide reinsurance coverage among multiple reinsurers. [10]

first-to-die policy. A type of multi-life insurance policy that provides that proceeds will be paid when the first of two or more insured people dies. [6]

flat extra premium method. An approach to charging for substandard risks which provides that, for every $1,000 of insurance, a specified extra dollar amount will be added to the standard premium. [4]

flat rating. A rating method used for impairments that present an accident hazard but no additional health hazard. [7]

fraud. An intentional misrepresentation that typically is considered to be far more serious than an unintentional misrepresentation. [3]

fronting. A procedure by which an insurer that is not licensed in a jurisdiction arranges to have another insurer issue requested coverage and then cede the coverage to the unlicensed insurer. [9]

future increase option. A disability income policy option that allows the insured to buy additional disability income protection without providing evidence of insurability. [15]

geriatrics. The branch of medicine dealing with the diseases and conditions of aging. [7]

GI. *See* **guaranteed insurability.**

GLB. *See* **Gramm-Leach-Bliley Act.**

grace period. A specified period after a renewal premium is due and unpaid during which a policy, including all riders, remains in force. [17]

Gramm-Leach-Bliley (GLB) Act. An act passed by the U.S. Congress in 1999, which allows convergence among the traditionally separate components of the financial services industry—banks, securities firms, and insurance companies. Also known as the *Financial Services Modernization Act.* [12]

guaranteed insurability (GI). A life insurance policy rider that gives a policyowner the right to buy additional insurance up to a specified amount at a specified premium rate and at specified times without providing new evidence of insurability. [6]

guaranteed renewable. A type of disability income coverage that offers the same continued coverage as noncancelable coverage *except* that the insurer can increase the premiums, not for an individual insured, but for all the policyowners within a defined class of insureds. [15]

guaranteed-issue product. An insurance product designed so that each applicant who meets certain conditions established by the insurer is automatically issued a policy. [6]

history statement. An attending physician's statement concerning a specific health condition that a proposed insured has admitted having. [4]

home health care. Skilled or nonskilled nursing care, physical therapy, and home health assistance provided by a state-licensed and/or Medicare-certified home health agency. [14]

hospice. A facility that specializes in the treatment of terminally ill people, typically providing the services of doctors and nurses to care for a patient and provide pain relief 24 hours a day. [14]

human resources. The insurance company function that monitors the availability of qualified workers; recruits and screens applicants; helps select qualified employees; plans and presents appropriate orientation, training, and development for each employee; and administers employee benefit programs. [1]

IADLs. *See* **instrumental activities of daily living.**

ICD. *See* **International Classification of Diseases and Related Health Problems.**

illustration of net cost. An explanation of rates that typically covers two or more years, and shows possible future ratings and premiums, provided a group's claim experience remains within the parameters assumed for an insurance product. [8]

impairment. Any aspect of a person's health, family history, occupation, activities, or lifestyle that could increase that person's expected mortality or morbidity risk. [2]

impairment guide. A list of common impairments and the probable underwriting decision for each that insurers provide to help agents gather complete information for health insurance applications. [7]

impairment rider. For health insurance, a policy attachment that excludes from coverage (1) a loss arising from a specified disease or physical impairment or (2) a specific body part. Also known as an *impairment waiver* or an *exclusion rider*. [7]

impairment waiver. *See* **impairment rider.**

income replacement table. A chart that shows the amount of monthly net income earned by a proposed insured with a specified annual net earned income, as well as the total monthly DI benefit that person could obtain. [7]

indemnity benefit method. A method used to determine the daily benefit amount under a long-term care policy under which the insurer pays a specified benefit amount regardless of the actual expenses incurred for the care of the insured. [14]

indemnity benefits. Medical expense benefits stated as a maximum dollar amount that is payable for each covered service. [8]

indemnity reinsurance. A type of reinsurance in which an insurer transfers part or all of the risk for a policy to a reinsurer, which indemnifies the insurer for losses incurred. [9]

individual cession administration. A method of reinsurance administration in which the assuming company administers the reinsurance and bills the ceding company for the individual lives reinsured. The ceding company provides the assuming company with detailed information about individual policies and informs the assuming company of any changes that affect the reinsurance. [11]

industry experience. Collected data about insurance claim experience generated by intercompany and industry-wide studies. [2]

inflation protection rider. A long-term care policy rider that either automatically increases the benefit amount by a specified percentage each year, or allows the insured to opt for a higher daily benefit at specified intervals during the lifetime of a policy, without having to show evidence of insurability. [14]

information systems. The insurance company function that facilitates the collection, manipulation, and distribution of data and information, enabling employees who need the resulting information to get it. [1]

initial deductible. An amount an insured must pay before an insurer pays any medical expenses. [14]

injury. For purposes of a disability income policy, an accidental harm resulting from an unforeseen external force (1) causing trauma to a person's body and (2) occurring while a disability insurance policy is in force and is a condition resulting independently of sickness. [15]

inspection report. A type of investigative consumer report that is developed by a consumer reporting agency and that contains information about a proposed insured's personal life, activities, occupation, and financial status. [5]

installment certificate. A document that specifies the amount of each benefit payment and/or the period during which benefit payments will be made, if insurance policy proceeds are to be paid in installments during a fixed or lifetime period or for fixed amounts. [13]

instrumental activities of daily living (IADLs). A number of activities considered less essential than activities of daily living, including, managing one's own finances, cooking and doing laundry, and shopping for food and clothing. [7]

insurable interest. The condition in which a person or an entity would suffer a genuine economic loss if the event insured against were to occur. [5]

Insurance Act. In Canada, a general statute that contains most of a province's insurance laws and that regulates the conduct of insurers and agents within the province. [3]

insurance administration. The activities associated with assessing risk and issuing policies, obtaining reinsurance, handling claims, and providing customer service. [1]

integrated image processing. A computer-based method of capturing, indexing, storing, retrieving, and distributing documents in electronic form. [1]

interim insurance law. An interpretation of conditional premium receipts that generally holds that, if the agent has accepted payment, the proposed insured is covered until the insurer notifies the proposed insured that coverage has been terminated and returns the premium. [3]

International Classification of Diseases and Related Health Problems (ICD). One of the most commonly used codes for medical diagnoses, generally referred to as the ICD. [14]

interpleader. A claim settlement method by which an insurer pays the proceeds to a court, advises the court that the insurer cannot determine the correct party to whom the proceeds should be distributed, and asks the court to decide the proper recipient or recipients. [13]

investigative consumer report. A type of consumer report that includes information gathered during interviews with people such as friends, neighbors, business associates, and others who are associated with or who have knowledge of the consumer. [3]

irrevocable beneficiary. A beneficiary whose right to policy proceeds cannot be cancelled by a policyowner unless that beneficiary consents to the cancellation. [13]

jet unit underwriting. A method used to organize underwriting work that establishes a group of two to four employees who screen applications that meet specific criteria and who approve certain types of applications for immediate policy issue. [2]

joint-and-last-survivor policy. The most common type of multi-life product, a life insurance contract that provides coverage on two or more lives. [6]

jumbo limit. The maximum allowable dollar amount of total insurance in force and applied for with all insurers on any one life. [10]

juvenile insurance policy. A life insurance policy purchased by an adult to cover the life of a child. [6]

key person. A person whose absence would cause a serious loss to a business. [6]

key-person insurance. Life insurance coverage that protects a business from the losses that occur when a key person dies. [6]

lapse notice. *See* **policy grace notice.**

layering. A method of dividing reinsurance coverage among multiple reinsurers by allowing one reinsurer or a pool of reinsurers to cover all cases in excess of an insurer's retention limit up to a specified amount. [10]

legal. The members of an insurer's staff who help an insurer follow the laws and regulations affecting the insurer's relationships with customers, prospective customers, employees, agents, other insurers, vendors, and government agencies. [1]

lifetime maximum benefit. The maximum amount that a policy will pay for all eligible medical expenses an individual incurs while insured under a policy. [14]

liquidity. The ease with which a company can convert its assets into cash for an approximation of their true value. [6]

long-term care (LTC) insurance. A type of individual health insurance that pays for medical or other health-related services required in a person's home or in a nursing facility. [7]

LTC field underwriting manual. A guidebook provided to agents by an insurer that lists several medical conditions associated with aging and provides general underwriting criteria for those conditions. [7]

LTC. *See* **long-term care insurance.**

managed care. A method of integrating both the financing and delivery of health care within a system that seeks to control the cost, accessibility, and quality of care. [8]

manual rating. Establishing premium rates for broad classes of groups, especially for those with no credible claims experience. [8]

marketing. The way an insurer identifies its customers, defines and develops the products that its customers want, and sells and distributes products to customers. [1]

master application. A document that contains the specific provisions of a requested plan of insurance being applied for and is signed by an authorized officer of a proposed policyholder. [8]

master contract. A legal document certifying the relationship between an insurer and a group policyholder. [8]

material misrepresentation. A misstatement made by an applicant for insurance that is relevant to the insurer's acceptance of a risk. [3]

maximum limit. A payment method which involves payment of a specified amount of total benefits for claims arising from a single injury or incident, or one period of sickness. [14]

mediation. A conflict resolution method in which an impartial third party facilitates negotiations between the parties in an effort to create a mutually agreeable resolution to the dispute. [15]

medical expense insurance. A type of individual health insurance that pays benefits for treatment of sickness or injury. [7]

Medical Information Bureau. *See* **MIB, Inc.**

medical necessity. A criterion requiring that the prescribed medical procedure is one that (1) is considered effective and that is normally used for the specified illness or injury and (2) does not exceed in scope, duration, or intensity the level of care needed to provide safe, adequate, and appropriate diagnosis or treatment. [14]

medical report. A type of Part II application that is designed to be completed by both the proposed insured and an examining physician who records the proposed insured's answers to health history questions. [4]

MIB, Inc. A nonprofit organization established to provide information to insurers about impairments that applicants have admitted to or that other insurers have detected in connection with previous applications for insurance. Formerly known as *Medical Information Bureau.* [4]

minimum cession. A statement in a reinsurance treaty describing the smallest amount of risk that an insurer will cede. [10]

misrepresentation. The presence of false or misleading statements on an application for insurance. [3]

modco. *See* **modified coinsurance.**

modified coinsurance (modco). A type of proportional reinsurance in which the ceding company maintains the entire reserve for each policy. [10]

moral hazard. A characteristic that exists when the reputation, financial position, or mental state of an applicant or a proposed insured indicates that the person is likely to cause a loss intentionally or is likely not to limit a loss after it has occurred. [5]

morbidity. The relative incidence of sickness and injury occurring among a given group of people. [2]

mortality. The relative incidence of death occurring among a given group of people. [2]

motor vehicle record (MVR). A record usually available from consumer reporting agencies and, in most jurisdictions, from public records that contains information about a person's driving history, including information about traffic violations and arrests and convictions for driving-related incidents. [5]

MVR. *See* **motor vehicle record.**

NAIC Model Privacy Act. A model law that establishes standards for the collection, use, and disclosure of information gathered in connection with insurance transactions by insurance institutions, agents, and insurance-support organizations. [3]

NAIC Reinsurance Intermediary Model Act. In the United States, a model law that regulates the activities of reinsurance intermediaries and of ceding and assuming companies that use reinsurance intermediaries' services. [9]

NAR. *See* **net amount at risk.**

net amount at risk (NAR). For a life insurance policy, the policy's death benefit minus the policy's cash value, or reserve. [10]

net worth. The difference between the person's assets and liabilities. [5]

new business. The general term used to describe all the activities required to market insurance, submit applications for insurance, investigate and evaluate the risks associated with those applications, and issue and deliver insurance policies. [1]

noncancelable. The most liberal form of renewability for disability income coverage, which stipulates that, until the insured reaches a specified age (usually age 65), the insurer will not cancel the coverage, increase the premiums, or change the policy provisions as long as the premiums are paid. [15]

noncontributory plan. Group insurance for which the group policyholder pays the entire premium, the insureds pay no part of the premium for their coverage. and coverage is automatic for all eligible members of the group. [8]

nonmedical basis. The amount of insurance for which a person can apply without being required to undergo a medical examination. [2]

nonmedical limits. The total amounts of insurance that an insurer will issue to an applicant without requiring a paramedical or medical examination. [4]

nonmedical supplement. A type of Part II application that contains health history questions that an agent asks of a proposed insured as a substitute for a physical examination. [4]

nonproportional reinsurance. A type of reinsurance that provides coverage on a segment of the ceding company's business, rather than covering individual lives for specific amounts. [10]

notice of cancellation. A method for terminating a reinsurance treaty by sending the other party a written statement to that effect. [10]

not taken. *See* **undeliverable**.

numerical rating system. A method of assigning numbers to individual proposed insureds according to the degree of risk they present to the insurer. [4]

nursing home. A custodial facility that provides basic nonmedical and medical care as necessary to patients. [14]

occupational rating classes. A method used by insurers to group occupations according to the relative degree of risk they present for DI coverage. [7]

offset. In the United States, a federal tax provision that allows an insurer to use the benefits paid under one type of insurance coverage to reduce the benefits paid for another type of coverage (1) to ensure that a disabled person does not receive an excessive total amount of benefits and (2) to encourage the disabled person to return to work. [15]

optionally renewable. A type of disability income coverage that enables an insurer to change premium rates at any time and to cancel the coverage with sufficient notice to an insured. [15]

orphan policyowner. A policyowner whose original agent is no longer available to provide service. [16]

overinsurance. An amount of applied-for insurance that is excessive in relation to the potential loss for which coverage is being purchased. [4]

overinsurance provision. A provision in individual health insurance policies, which specifies that, under certain circumstances, policy benefits will be reduced if an insured has more insurance than needed to cover medical expenses. [14]

paramedical report. A type of Part II application that contains (1) the proposed insured's answers to the same medical history questions that are included in the nonmedical supplement and the medical report and (2) the results of a partial physical examination of the proposed insured conducted by a paramedical examiner. [4]

Part I. The section of a life insurance application that identifies the proposed insured (and the policyowner, if different from the proposed insured), specifies the amount and type of coverage requested, and provides basic insurability information. [4]

Part II. The section of a life insurance application that consists of medical information regarding the proposed insured. [4]

partial disability. *See* **residual disability.**

parties to the agreement provision. A reinsurance treaty provision covering the scope of the agreement that states that the reinsurance agreement exists solely between the ceding company and the assuming company. [10]

partnership insurance. Insurance coverage that provides cash with which surviving partners can purchase the business interest of a deceased partner from that partner's heirs. [6]

percentage-of-income rule. A method for determining the amount of coverage a proposed insured can purchase, which stipulates the amount of money an applicant can afford to spend on insurance according to the applicant's income. [5]

permanent flat extra premium. An approach to charging for substandard risks for cases in which a nonmedical risk is expected to remain constant throughout the life of the policy. [4]

persistency. How well a policy or group of policies remains, or persists, in force. [5]

persistency bonus. A sum of money that represents an increase in the agent's commission when a policy continues in force beyond an initial period, usually five years. [16]

personal history interview (PHI). A conversation with the proposed insured during which an underwriter clarifies information and gathers additional information needed for underwriting. [2]

personal insurance. Insurance purchased by individuals for income replacement, family needs and expenses, and payment of estate taxes. [5]

PHI. *See* **personal history interview.**

Physicians' Current Procedural Terminology. One of the most commonly used codes for medical treatments, generally referred to as CPT. [14]

physiological age. The relative age or youthfulness of a person's vital organs and their functioning. [7]

policy dividend. A payment made by an insurer to a policyowner for either individual or group insurance coverage. [17]

policy grace notice. A written notification that the policy's grace period is about to expire. Also known as a *lapse notice*. [17]

policy issue. The insurance company function that involves preparing the insurance contract and facilitating the delivery of the policy to the customer. [1]

policy issue systems. Automated systems that insurance companies use to produce policy documents, prepare an insurance contract, and facilitate the delivery of a policy to a customer, usually by the agent who sold the policy. [1]

policyowner service. A specific type of customer service that includes all the service activities performed for people or groups who own or hold insurance policies. [1]

pooling. The practice of considering a number of small groups as one large group for risk assessment purposes. [8]

portability provision. A provision found in group long-term care policies that permits a group member who leaves the group to take her coverage with her and continue to pay premiums. [14]

post-notice. A notice that must be sent to an applicant if an underwriter denies an application or rates a policy based wholly or partially on information contained in a report from a consumer reporting agency.

preadmission certification. A statement from an insurer approving nonemergency, inpatient hospital treatment. Also known as *precertification*. [14]

precertification. *See* **preadmission certification.**

preferred beneficiary. In Canada, before July 1, 1962, a spouse, child, parent, or grandchild named in any life insurance policy issued before July 1, 1962, whose written consent was required for the policyowner to change the beneficiary to anyone outside this group of family members, to obtain a policy loan, to surrender a policy, or to assign a policy. [13]

preferred class. Proposed insureds whose anticipated mortality is significantly lower than average and who represent the least degree of risk. [2]

premium rate. The amount an insurer charges for a specified amount of coverage. [8]

premium receipt. A written acknowledgment that an insurer has received the initial premium submitted with an application for insurance. [3]

premium-paying customers. The insureds and policyowners of an insurance company. [1]

pre-notice. A notice sent by an insurer conducting a consumer investigation to disclose clearly and adequately to an applicant that an investigative consumer report may be made. [3]

presumptive death certificate. A court-issued document stating that a person is presumed to be dead. [13]

presumptive total disability. A condition that automatically causes an insured to be considered totally disabled, such as total and permanent blindness, loss of speech or hearing in both ears, or loss of two limbs. [15]

pretext interview. An information-gathering interview conducted by a person misrepresenting himself as someone other than who he really is. [3]

primary degenerative dementia. *See* **Alzheimer's disease.**

professional reinsurer. An insurance company whose sole or primary line of business is selling reinsurance to direct writers. [9]

professional retrocessionaire. An insurance company whose primary business is providing reinsurance to reinsurers. [9]

profitability. The productivity of a company's assets and its return on investment. [6]

proportional reinsurance. A type of reinsurance coverage for which the ceding company and the assuming company agree to share premiums and claims according to a specified amount or a specified percentage of coverage. [10]

proposal for insurance. A document that provides a number of specifications for the insurance coverage approved by an insurer for a proposed group. [8]

prospect. The organization that an agent is soliciting to become the policyholder for a proposed group. [8]

proximate cause. The event that directly caused a death, or the event that led to an unbroken chain of events resulting in death. [13]

public curator. In Quebec, a person authorized to handle the affairs of missing people, among others. [13]

punitive damages. Money awards intended to punish an insurer that has acted in a malicious, fraudulent, or oppressive manner toward a plaintiff, and thus to dissuade others from similar behavior. [12]

qualified LTC plan. A long-term care plan that provides all the features HIPAA requires and consequently is eligible for favorable tax treatment under federal law. [14]

Quebec Civil Code. In Canada, a regulation that governs all life and health insurance contracts in Quebec and specifies what provisions must be included in insurance contracts. [3]

Quebec Pension Plan. In Canada, a provincial plan that provides disability income benefits and survivor benefits (life insurance) to employees in Quebec. [3]

quota share. The portion of risk assumed by each reinsurer in a reinsurance pool. [9]

rate transmittal. A document that specifies the agent's proposed rates for each type of insurance coverage for each class of employees in a group insurance plan. [8]

rated policy. A policy issued to a person considered to have a greater-than-average risk of loss. [7]

rating. Approving a higher-than-average risk by charging a higher-than-usual premium rate for the coverage applied for or by limiting the amount or type of coverage to be provided. [2]

rating schedule. A table developed by an insurer that shows the conversion of total rating debits to a rating percentage. [7]

reasonable and customary limits. An insurer's specification that the amount paid for a claim must conform to the amount most frequently charged for each medical procedure in a given geographical area. [14]

recapture. A reinsurance treaty provision covering the scope of the agreement that describes the process by which a ceding company takes back some or all ceded business from a reinsurer. [10]

reciprocity. An arrangement in which certain insurers and reinsurers agree to cede business to each other and assume risk from each other. [9]

recurring disability. A type of disability that is the result of the same cause as for an original disability and that reappears after (1) the original period of disability and (2) an intervening period of recovery. [15]

rehabilitation. The process of helping a disabled person return to work, either at her own occupation or at another occupation if she is unable to perform the duties of her own occupation. [15]

rehabilitation benefit. A disability income policy benefit that provides that an insurer will reimburse the insured for the expenses associated with participation in a rehabilitation program. [15]

reimbursement method. A method used to determine the daily benefit amount under a long-term care policy under which the insured receives reimbursement for approved long-term care expenses up to a maximum limit specified in the policy. [14]

reinstatement. The process by which an insurer puts back into force a life insurance policy that has either been terminated for nonpayment of premiums or been continued as extended term or paid-up coverage. [11]

reinstatement provision. An insurance policy provision that describes the conditions a policyowner must meet for an insurer to reinstate a policy within a specified time after lapse. [17]

reinsurance. A form of insurance that enables an insurer to be reimbursed for covered losses claimed under insurance policies the insurer has issued. [1]

reinsurance account executive. *See* **reinsurance marketing officer**.

reinsurance audit. A formal examination of an insurer's reinsurance records to evaluate whether those records contain accurate details and that ensures that both parties to a reinsurance agreement understand and have complied with the terms of the agreement. [11]

reinsurance broker. *See* **reinsurance intermediary.**

reinsurance company. An insurer that sells reinsurance coverage. [9]

reinsurance effective date. A reinsurance treaty provision covering the scope of the agreement that states the date on which the reinsurance coverage for a specific risk takes effect. [10]

reinsurance intermediary. A third party who helps ceding companies find appropriate coverage for risks they want to reinsure and, for large-amount and unusual cases, to arrange for sufficient reinsurance from multiple reinsurers if no single reinsurance company will accept the entire risk. Also known as a *reinsurance broker*. [9]

reinsurance marketing officer. An employee who sells reinsurance and coordinates the marketing process for a reinsurer. Also known as a *reinsurance account executive*. [9]

reinsurance pool. An arrangement where an insurer cedes risk and a group of reinsurers assumes the risk. [9]

reinsurance treaty. A formal written agreement to establish a reinsurance arrangement, negotiated and signed by an insurer and a reinsurer. [10]

remote computing. An electronic technology that allows users to (1) input and send information to a computer from a distant site and (2) gain access to the programs and information on a distant computer. [1]

renewal underwriting. For group insurance plans, a type of underwriting in which the underwriter reviews all the risk assessment factors considered when the group was originally underwritten and all changes in the group and its coverage between the previous underwriting and the current time. [8]

replacement. Surrendering an insurance policy or part of the coverage of an insurance policy in order to buy another policy [3]

Request for Proposal (RFP). A document that provides detailed information about the requested coverage and requests a bid from an insurer for providing that coverage. [8]

rescission. A legal action by which the insurer seeks to void a policy or have it declared void. [3]

reserve credit. The accounting entry used to record the reduction of reserves, due to the use of reinsurance, by the ceding company in its Annual Statement or Annual Return. [9]

reserves. Accounts that an insurer maintains for meeting future business obligations, including paying claims. [9]

residual disability. A condition in which the insured is not totally disabled, but is still unable to function as before the sickness or injury, and therefore suffers a reduction in income of at least the percentage—typically 20 percent to 25 percent—specified in the disability income plan. Also known as a *partial disability*. [15]

retention limit. The maximum amount of coverage per life that the insurer will carry at its own risk. [9]

retrocession. A term that describes both the unit of insurance that a reinsurance company cedes to a retrocessionaire and the document used to record the transfer of risk from a reinsurer to a retrocessionaire. [9]

retrocessionaire. A reinsurer that accepts risks from—and sells reinsurance to—another reinsurer. [9]

revocable beneficiary. A beneficiary whose right to policy proceeds can be cancelled or reduced by the policyowner at any time before the insured's death. [13]

RFP. *See* **Request for Proposal.**

risk assessment. A process that involves determining the degree of risk represented by each proposed insured person or group according to a range of criteria established when the insurance product was designed and priced. [2]

risk class. A group of insureds who represent a similar level of risk to an insurance company. [2]

schedule of benefits. Under a group insurance plan, a table that specifies the amount of coverage provided for each class of insureds. [8] For claim purposes, a listing of medical treatments and the maximum benefit amounts an insurer will pay for each treatment. [14]

schedules. The provisions of a reinsurance treaty that cover the more variable elements such as the plans covered, retention limits, binding limits, and premium rates and allowances. Also known as *exhibits* or *conditions*. [10]

second excess. When layering is used, a specified amount of the remaining coverage above the first excess that is ceded by the insurer to a second assuming company (or to a second group of assuming companies). [10]

secondary beneficiary. *See* **contingent beneficiary.**

second-to-die policy. A type of multi-life insurance policy that provides that proceeds will be paid when the second of two or more insured people dies. Also known as a *survivorship policy*. [6]

self administration. A method of reinsurance administration in which the ceding company maintains detailed records for each ceded policy and provides periodic reports outlining each risk ceded and premiums due to the assuming company. [11]

self-funded group insurance plan. *See* **self-insured group insurance plan.**

self-insured group insurance plan. A group insurance plan in which the group sponsor, not an insurance company, is financially responsible for paying claims made by group insureds. Also known as a *self-funded group insurance plan*. [8]

service requirement. The length of time—usually three to six months—that a person must be employed for before being covered under a group insurance plan. [8]

shopping. A procedure that involves submitting cases to several reinsurers to obtain competitive quotes for reinsurance. [10]

sickness. For purposes of a disability income policy, an illness or a disease that (1) includes pregnancy unless it is specifically excluded under a disability income contract and (2) begins while a person is insured under a disability income policy. [15]

sole proprietorship insurance. Insurance that provides coverage on the life of the sole proprietor of a business—and can be used to pay the salary of hiring someone to run the business if the sole proprietor dies—*or* provides funds for a trusted employee or other person to buy a business at the death of the owner. [6]

solvency. A company's ability to pay its debts on time. [6]

special risk. *See* **substandard class.**

specialized medical questionnaire. A document that requests detailed information on a specific illness or condition. [4]

speculation. The purchasing of insurance with the expectation of making a profit on the proceeds. [5]

split elimination period. For a health insurance policy, an increased waiting period for any claims related to an existing impairment, while the usual waiting period is applied to other claims. [7]

split-dollar plan. A type of business insurance that covers the life of an employee and is paid for jointly by the employer and the employee. [6]

standard class. Proposed insureds whose anticipated mortality is average, that is higher than the mortality predicted for people in the preferred class, but lower than the mortality predicted for people in the substandard class. [2]

stock redemption insurance. *See* **stock repurchase insurance.**

stock repurchase insurance. Life insurance that provides the money to pay for a stock purchase. Also known as *stock redemption insurance.* [6]

subrogation clause. An insurance policy provision that gives the insurer the contractual right to recover payments made to an insured for medical care if that insured receives payment for damages through a legal action. [14]

substandard class. Proposed insureds whose anticipated mortality is higher than average, but who are still considered to be insurable. Also known as *special risk*. [2]

supplemental coverage. An amount of coverage that adds to the amount of coverage specified in a basic insurance policy. [6]

supplementary notice. A notice that is sent by an insurer conducting a consumer investigation within five days of a consumer's request for information respecting the nature and scope of the investigation specified in the pre-notice. [3]

surplus. The net amount of money earned from an insurer's operations and left to accumulate. [9]

surplus strain. A decrease in surplus caused by the high initial costs of new policies and the reserve requirements for those policies. [9]

survivorship clause. A life insurance policy clause, which provides payment of proceeds to the beneficiary if the beneficiary lives longer than the insured for at least a specified period such as 10 days or 30 days. Also known as a *common disaster clause* or a *time clause*. [13]

survivorship policy. *See* **second-to-die policy.**

table of underwriting requirements. A table that specifies the kinds of information the underwriter considers in assessing the insurability of a proposed insured. [2]

table rating method. An approach used by insurers to adjust premium rates to compensate for extra mortality that involves charging for substandard risks by dividing those risks into broad groups according to their numerical ratings. [4]

team underwriting. A method used to organize underwriting work in which underwriters are divided into small groups, usually including one or more senior underwriters who handle large-amount or complex cases, and one or more lower-level underwriters who handle simpler cases. [2]

temporary flat extra premium. An approach to charging for substandard risks that involve impairments for which the extra mortality risk is expected to decrease and eventually disappear over a limited time period. [4]

temporary insurance agreement (TIA). A premium receipt that provides insurance coverage of a specified amount for a specified time, usually for the time required to underwrite the case. Also known as a *binding premium receipt*. [3]

third excess. When layering is used, a specified amount of the coverage that remains after the first and second excesses have been ceded that is ceded by the insurer to a third company or group of companies. [10]

third-party applicant. A person who applies for coverage on the life of another person. [5]

TIA. *See* **temporary insurance agreement.**

time clause. *See* **survivorship clause.**

total disability. The complete and continuous inability of an insured at the beginning of his disability to perform the essential duties of his regular occupation. [15]

transplant donor benefit. A disability income policy benefit that specifies that if an insured undergoes surgery to donate a part of his body to another person, the insurer will treat that surgery as a sickness and will pay benefits for it. [15]

treaty effective date. A reinsurance treaty provision covering the scope of the agreement that states that the agreement takes effect on an agreed-upon date. [10]

twisting. The illegal practice of misleading a policyowner about replacement or providing an incomplete comparison of the two policies to the disadvantage of the policyowner. [6]

undeliverable. A term used to describe a policy that a buyer chooses not to accept when an agent attempts to deliver it. Also known as *not taken*. [2]

underwriting. The process of (1) assessing and classifying the degree of risk represented by a proposed insured or a group of insureds with respect to a specific insurance product and (2) making a decision to accept or decline the risk. [1]

underwriting guidelines. General standards that specify the parameters within which an applicant may be assigned to one of the risk classes established for each insurance product. [2]

underwriting manual. A paper or electronic guide to underwriting action that includes the information an insurer uses to assign relative values to life insurance risks and typically provides descriptive information on impairments. [4].

underwriting objective. *See* **underwriting philosophy.**

underwriting philosophy. A philosophy that guides an insurer's risk selection and classification procedures. Also known as *underwriting objective*. [2]

underwriting worksheet. A document that contains records of telephone calls, letters and other communications, documentation of requests for reinsurance, lists of reports and other information requested, and other notations that will explain clearly the manner in which the underwriter has handled the case beginning with the submission of the application to the insurer. [3]

Uniform Accident and Sickness Insurance Act. In the common-law jurisdictions of Canada, legislation that governs both group and individual health insurance contracts. [3]

Uniform Life Insurance Act. In the common-law jurisdictions of Canada, legislation that governs both group and individual life insurance contracts. [3]

variable life insurance. A form of whole life insurance under which the death benefit and the cash value of the policy change according to the investment performance of funds that are kept separate from an insurer's other investments. [17]

waiting period. For a health insurance policy, the period of time that must pass before benefits are payable to an insured. [7]

waiver of premium for disability. A life insurance policy rider that provides that, in the event an insured is totally disabled as defined in the rider, the insurer will waive the payment of all premiums that become due during the period of disability. [6]

waiver of premium for payor benefit. A waiver included in some juvenile policies that provides that an insurer will waive payment of the policy's premiums if the adult policyowner becomes disabled or dies prior to the insured child's attainment of a specified age, usually 21. [6]

waiver of premium provision. A long-term care policy provision that allows an insured to stop paying premiums at a specified point while an insured person is receiving long-term care and an insurer is making benefit payments under the policy. [14]

work division system. A method used to organize underwriting work that divides cases according to the person or group that underwrites them. [2]

work site assessment. An activity performed by a claim analyst or an investigator who interviews an employer and reviews the actual job duties and the claimant's level of success in performing those duties to determine the extent to which the claimant is prevented by illness from performing his job functions. [15]

worker's compensation. In the United States, a government-mandated insurance that provides benefits to covered employees and their dependents if the employee suffers a job-related injury, disease, or death. [15]

yearly renewable term (YRT) reinsurance. A type of proportional reinsurance in which a ceding company buys an amount of insurance coverage that is equal to the net amount at risk on the reinsured portion of the policy for a one-year term premium rate. [10]

YRT. *See* **yearly renewable term insurance.**

Index

Numbers in *italics* refer to figures.

A

D

E

F

G

H

M

N

O

P

Q

R

S

T

U

V

W

X–Z